Shojo Beat Manga

# Millennium Snow

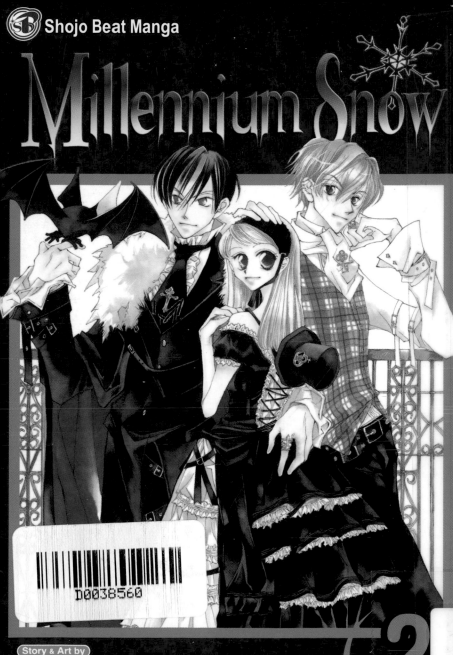

2

Story & Art by
**Bisco Hatori**

Shojo Beat

# Millennium Snow

Vol. 2    Story & Art by **Bisco Hatori**

# Table of Contents

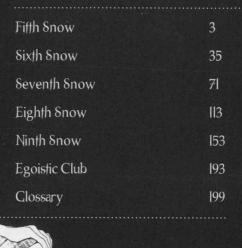

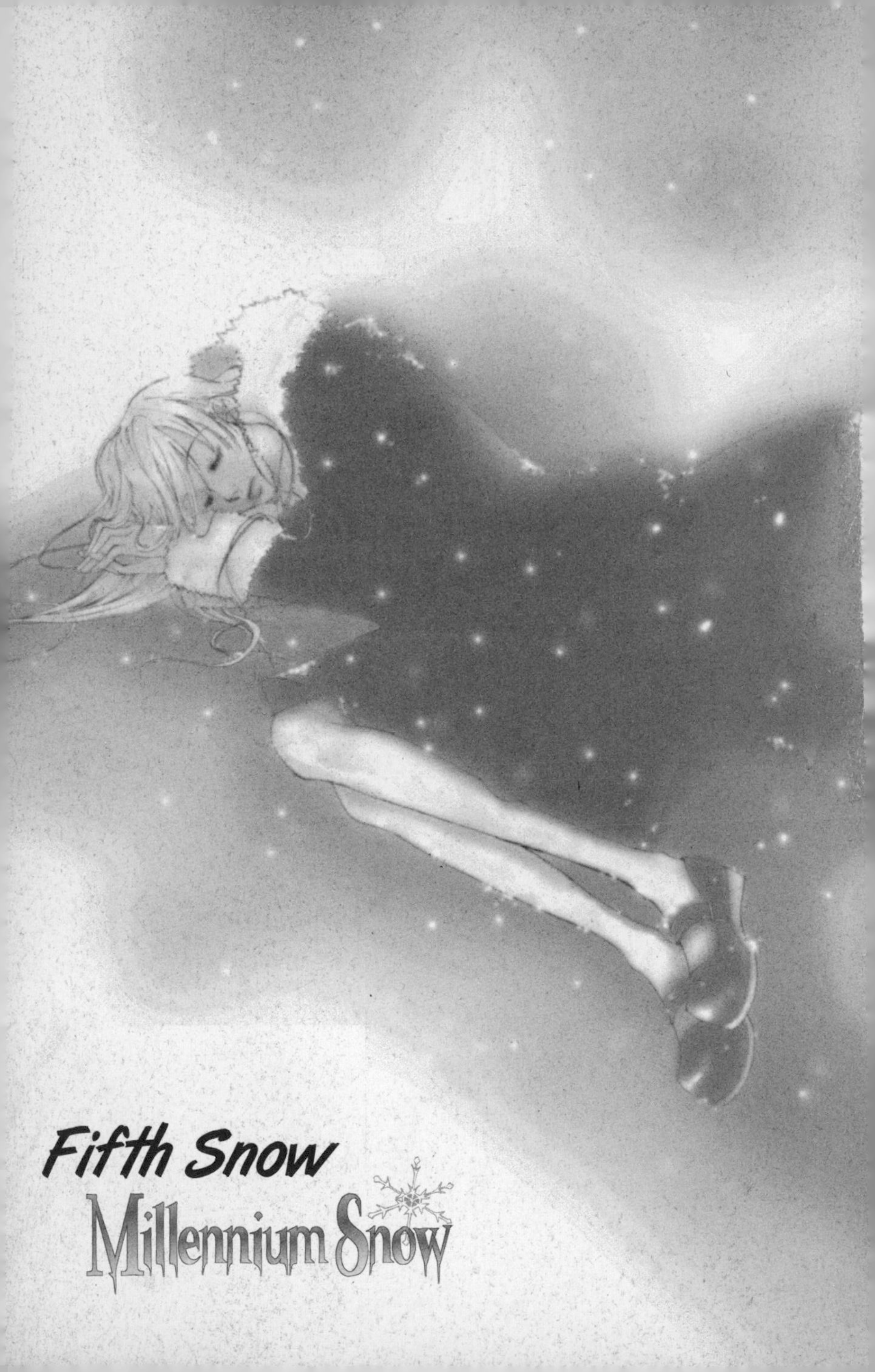
Fifth Snow
Millennium Snow

The Night Before Departure

Some ponder in their own way.
Hmm... Which ones should I take?
Boots are good for snow, but inside the hotel...
※ She ended up taking both.
Some travel light.
I only need one pair of jeans...
...and I can wash every-thing some-how...
Satsuki, take some dried plums with you!
Some are unfit for travel.
Master!! You can't stuff in any more!!
FWOP
FWOP
I need this shirt and these shoes for that jacket, and two coats, of course. And how about these shoes and...

※ Yamimaru went stuffed in a handbag.

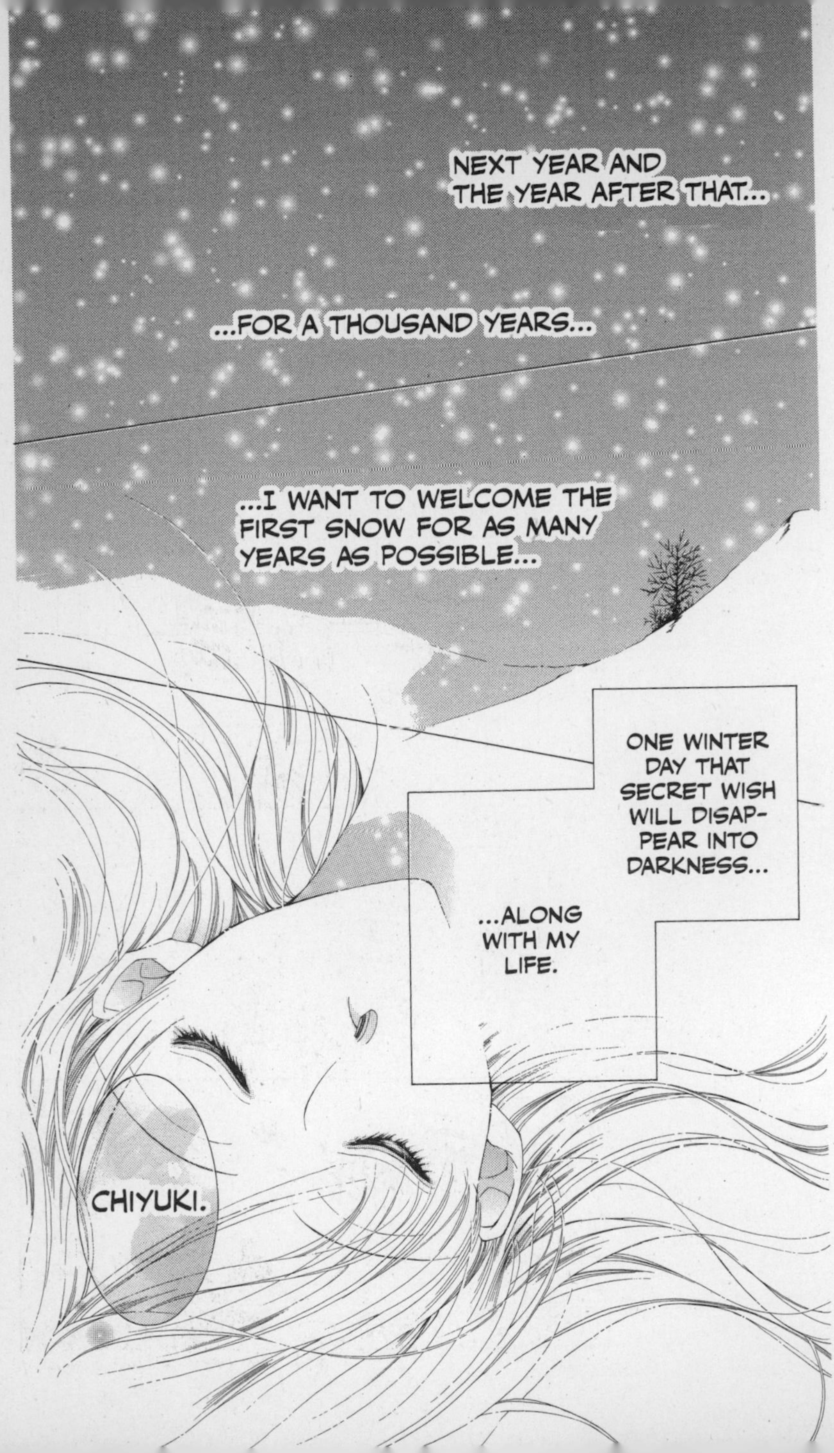
NEXT YEAR AND THE YEAR AFTER THAT...
...FOR A THOUSAND YEARS...
...I WANT TO WELCOME THE FIRST SNOW FOR AS MANY YEARS AS POSSIBLE...
ONE WINTER DAY THAT SECRET WISH WILL DISAP-PEAR INTO DARKNESS...
...ALONG WITH MY LIFE.
CHIYUKI.

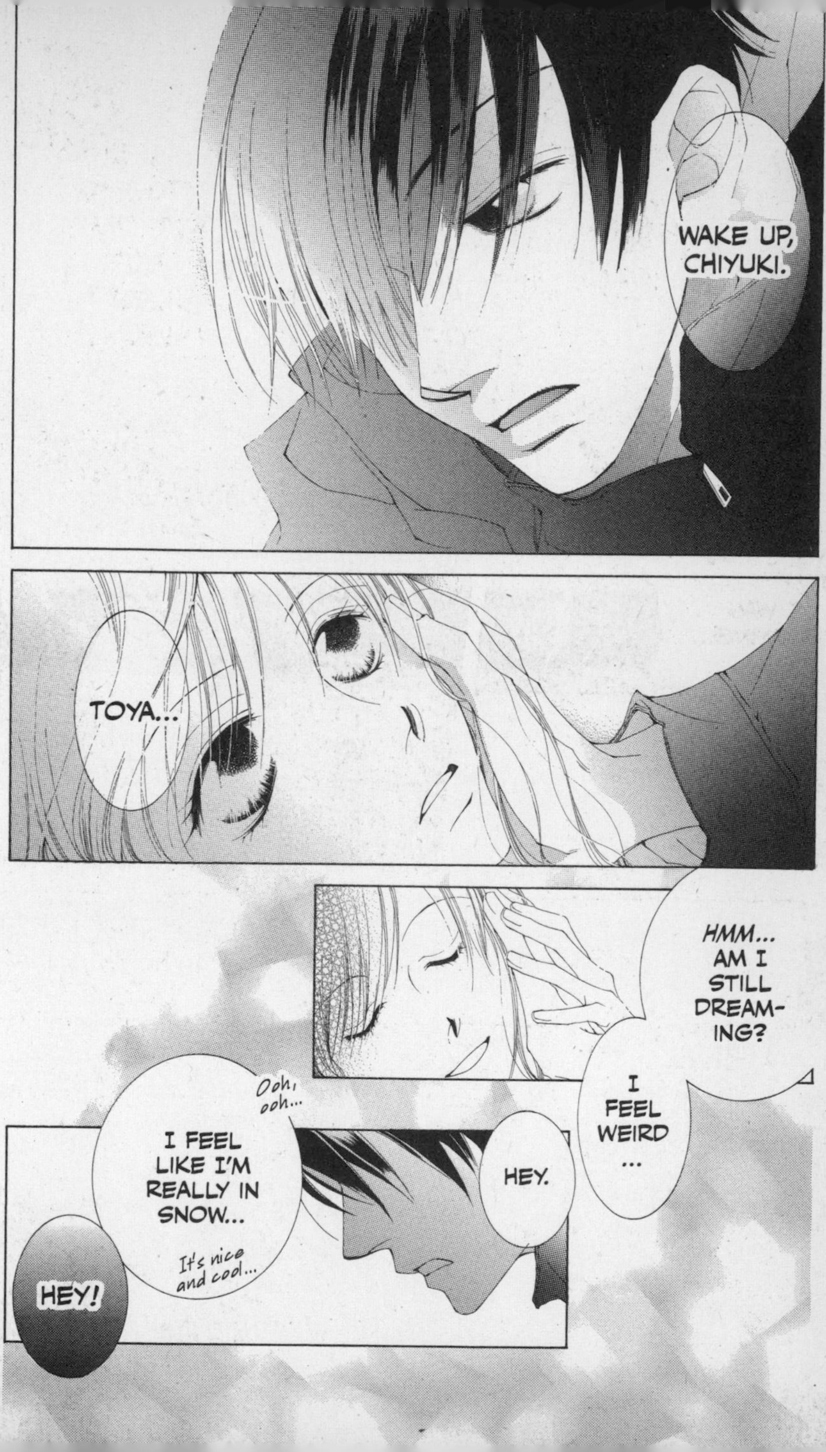
WAKE UP, CHIYUKI.
TOYA...
HMM... AM I STILL DREAMING?
I FEEL WEIRD ...
HEY.
I FEEL LIKE I'M REALLY IN SNOW...
Ooh, ooh...
It's nice and cool...
HEY!

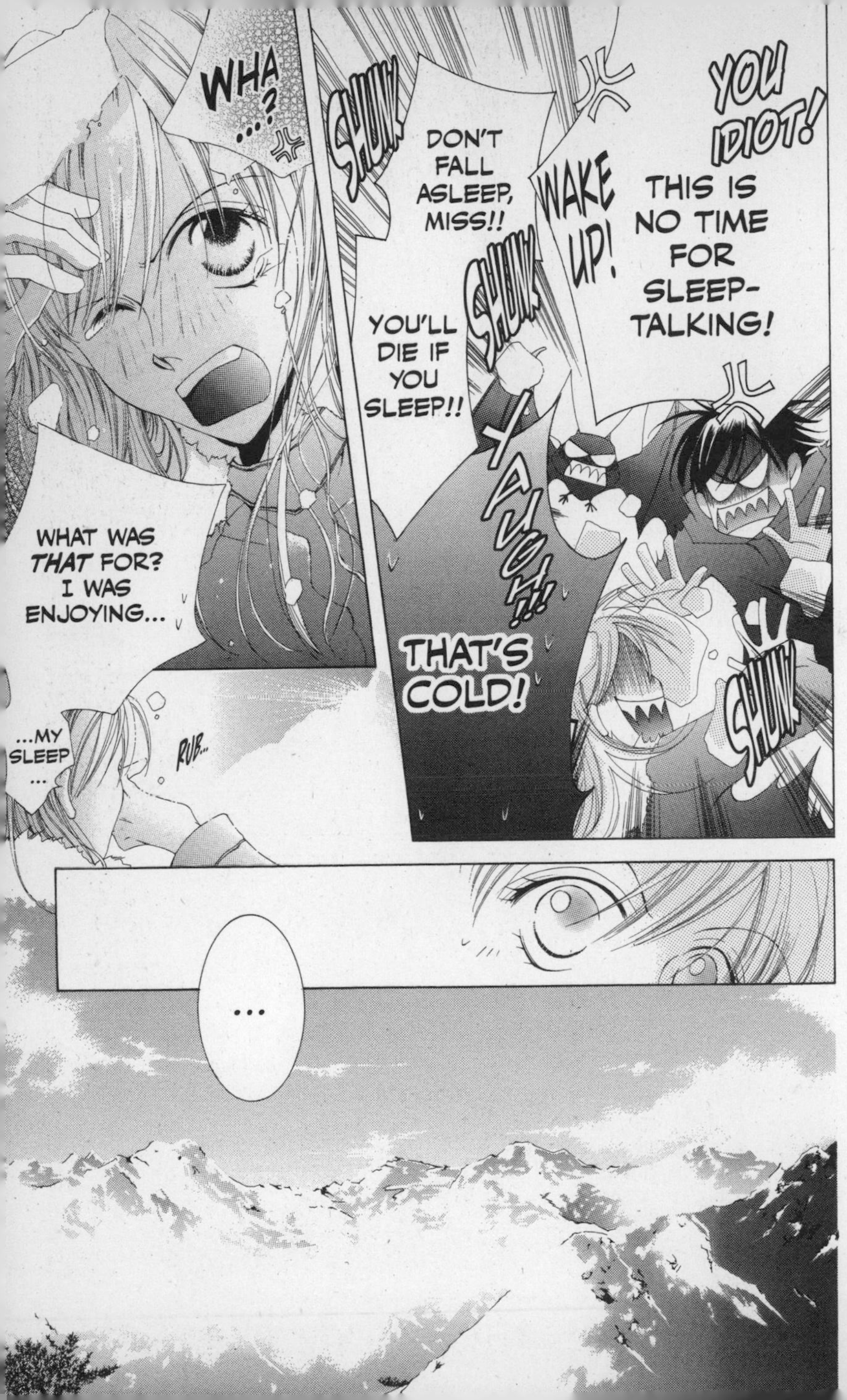
YOU IDIOT!
THIS IS NO TIME FOR SLEEP-TALKING!
WAKE UP!
SHUNK
DON'T FALL ASLEEP, MISS!!
SHUNK
YOU'LL DIE IF YOU SLEEP!!
YAUGH!!!
THAT'S COLD!
SHUNK
WHA ...?
WHAT WAS *THAT* FOR? I WAS ENJOYING...
...MY SLEEP ...
RUB...
...

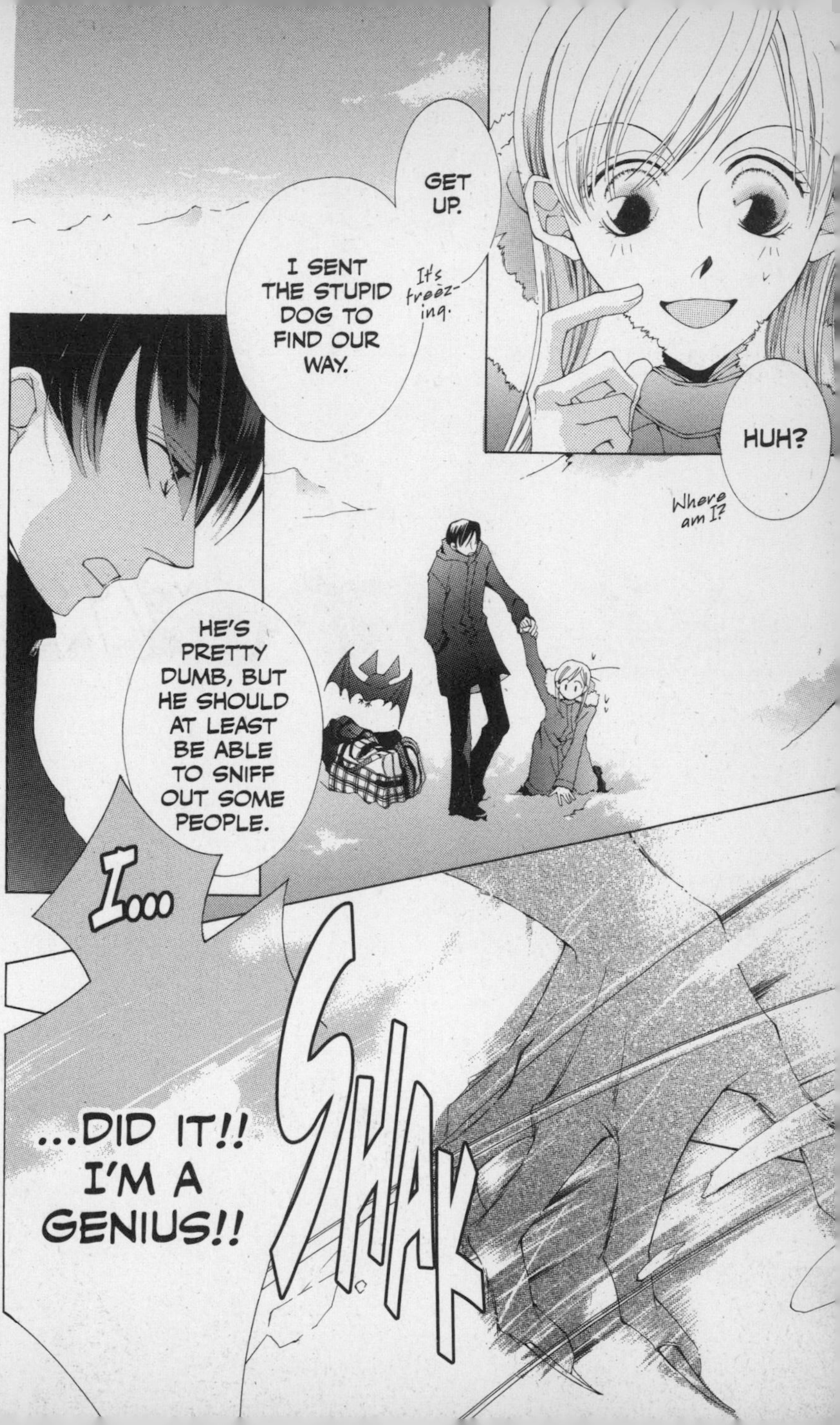
HUH?
Where am I?
GET UP.
It's freezing.
I SENT THE STUPID DOG TO FIND OUR WAY.
HE'S PRETTY DUMB, BUT HE SHOULD AT LEAST BE ABLE TO SNIFF OUT SOME PEOPLE.
I...
SHAK
...DID IT!! I'M A GENIUS!!

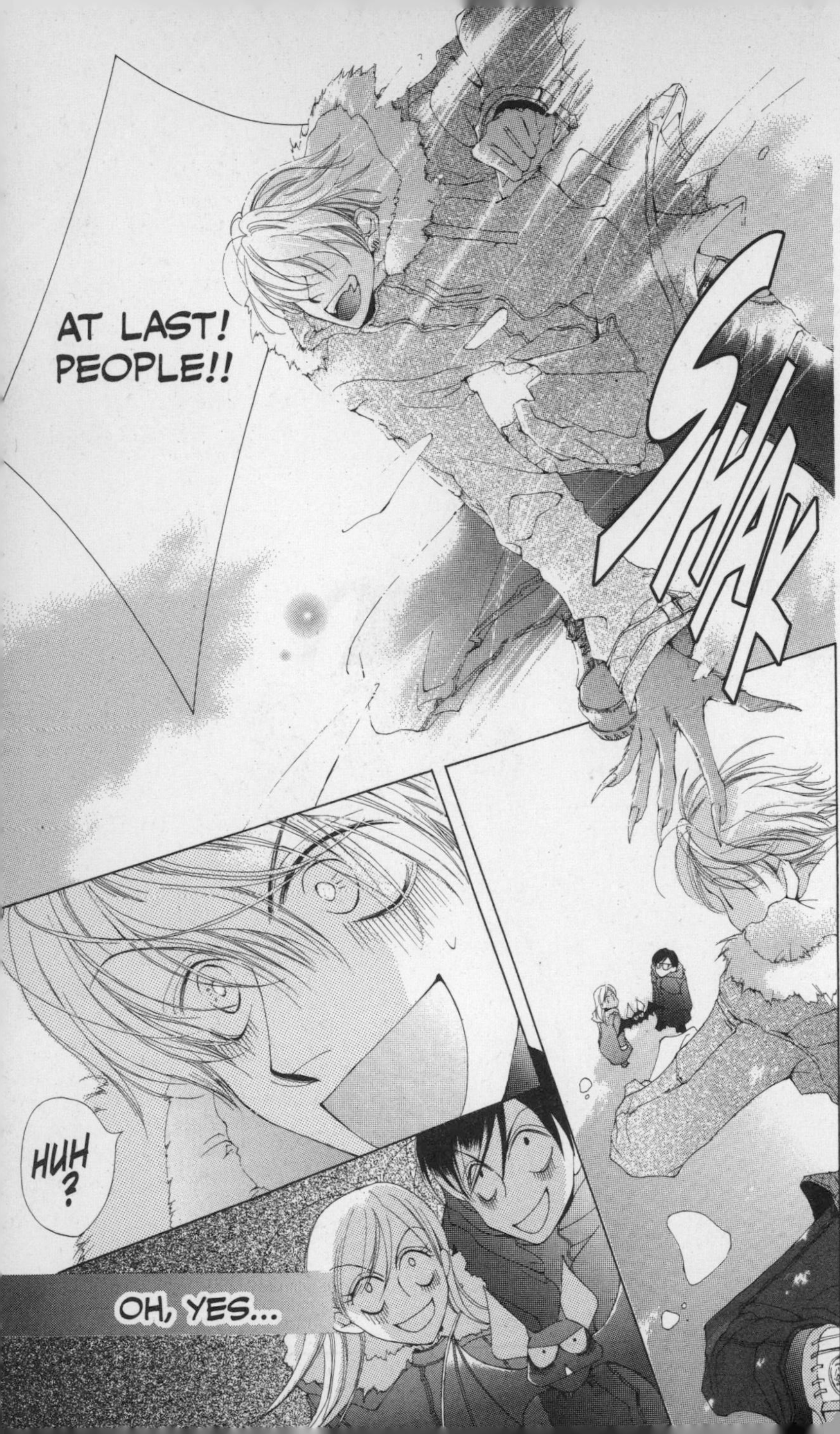
AT LAST! PEOPLE!!
SHAK
HUH?
OH, YES...

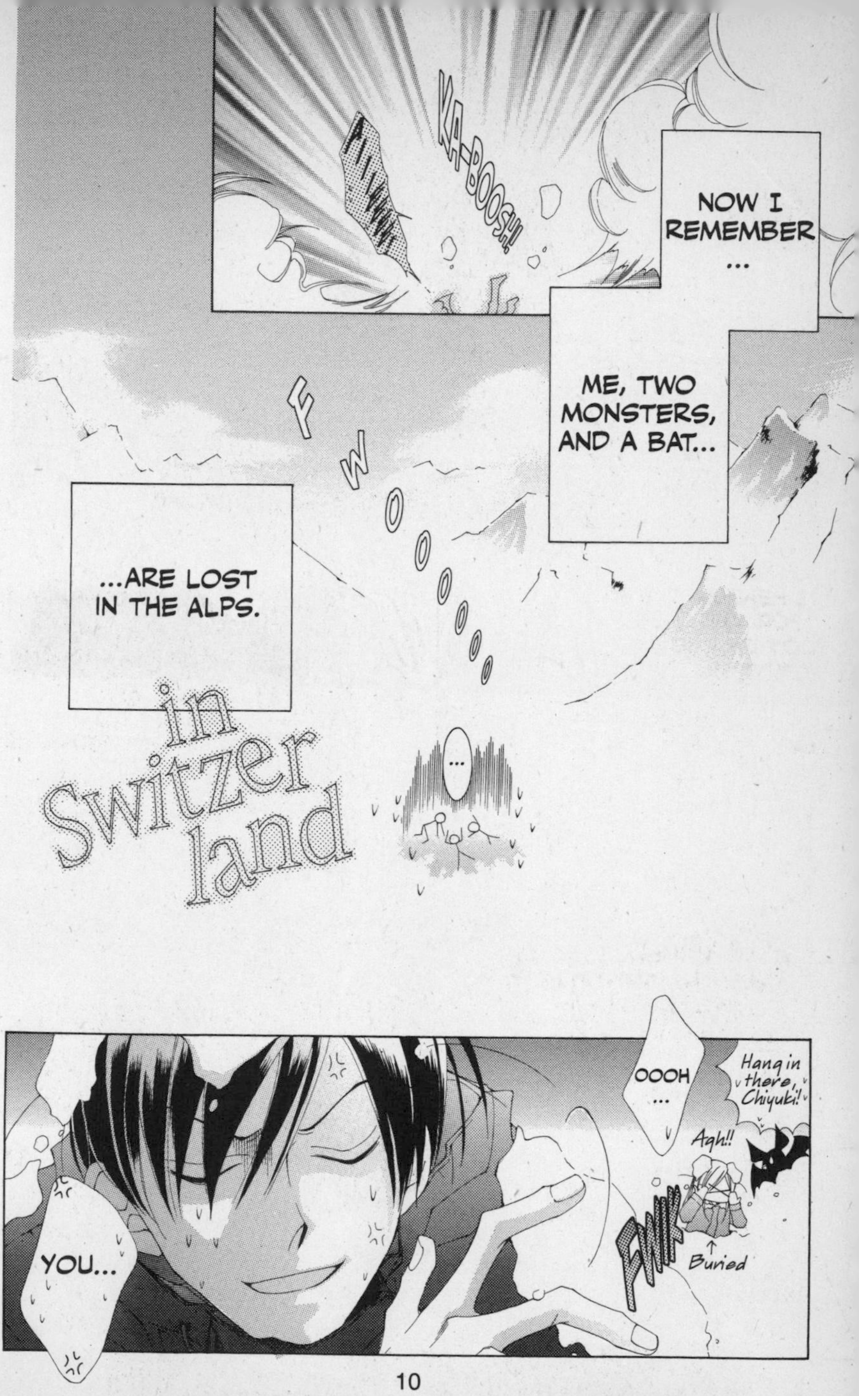
KA-BOOSH!!
NOW I REMEMBER ...
ME, TWO MONSTERS, AND A BAT...
FWOOOOOOO
...ARE LOST IN THE ALPS.
in Switzerland
...
Hang in there, Chiyuki!
Agh!!
OOOH ...
FWIK
Buried
YOU...

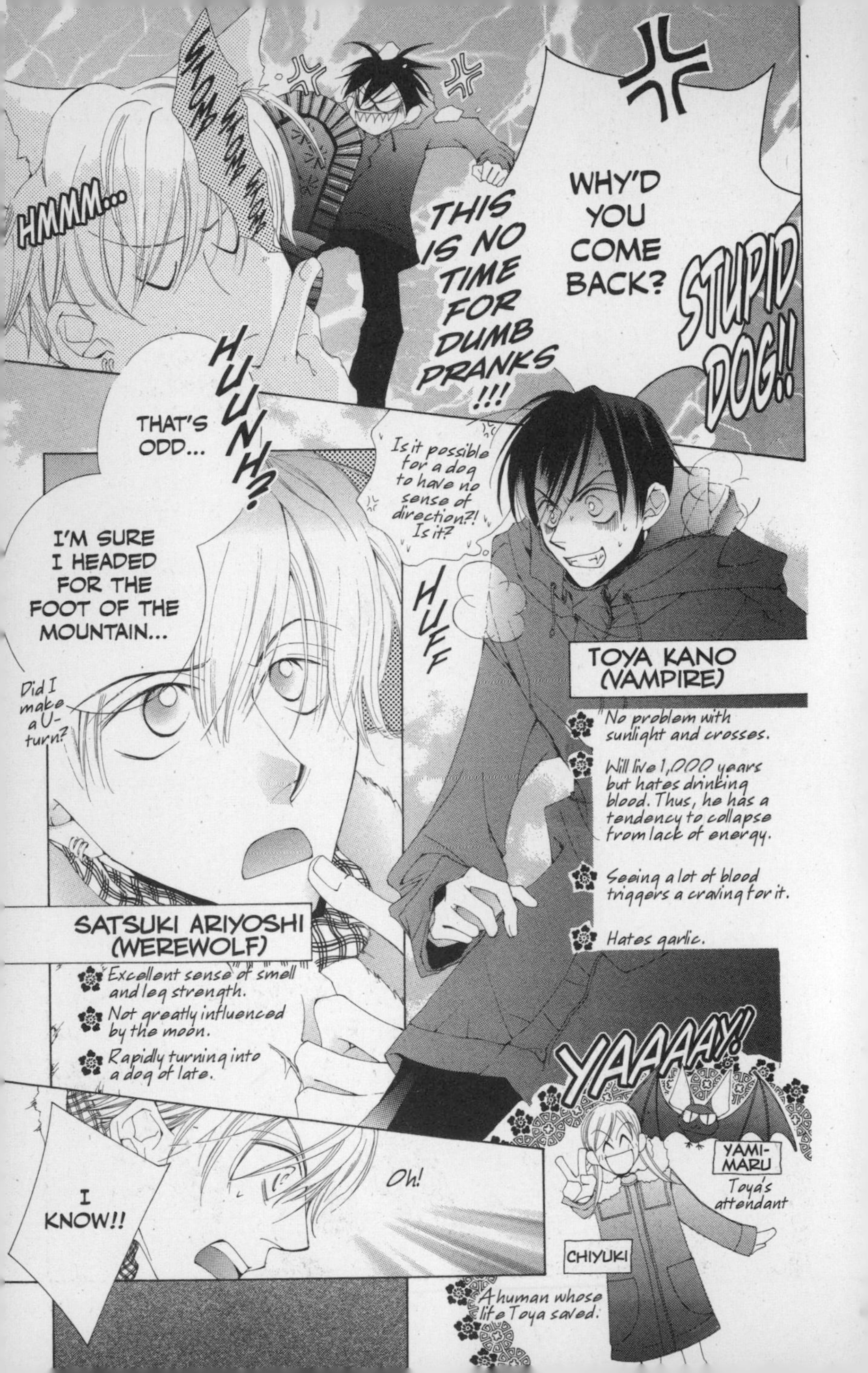
STUPID DOG!!
WHY'D YOU COME BACK?
THIS IS NO TIME FOR DUMB PRANKS!!!
HMMM...
Is it possible for a dog to have no sense of direction?! Is it?
HUFF
TOYA KANO (VAMPIRE)
No problem with sunlight and crosses.
Will live 1,000 years but hates drinking blood. Thus, he has a tendency to collapse from lack of energy.
Seeing a lot of blood triggers a craving for it.
Hates garlic.
HUUNH?
THAT'S ODD...
I'M SURE I HEADED FOR THE FOOT OF THE MOUNTAIN...
Did I make a U-turn?
SATSUKI ARIYOSHI (WEREWOLF)
Excellent sense of smell and leg strength.
Not greatly influenced by the moon.
Rapidly turning into a dog of late.
YAAAAY!
YAMI-MARU
Toya's attendant
CHIYUKI
A human whose life Toya saved.
Oh!
I KNOW!!

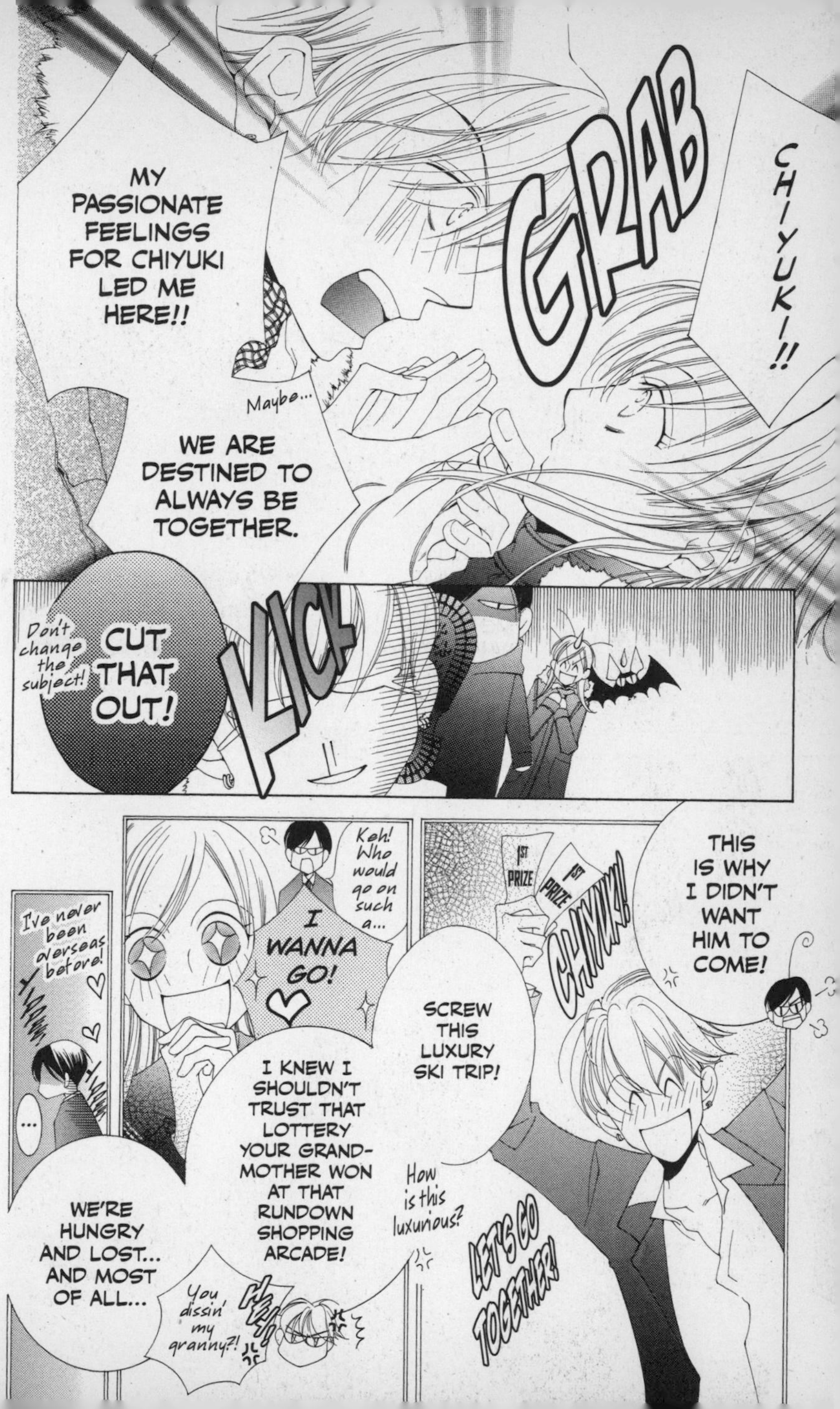
CHIYUKI!!
GRAB
MY PASSIONATE FEELINGS FOR CHIYUKI LED ME HERE!!
Maybe...
WE ARE DESTINED TO ALWAYS BE TOGETHER.
KICK
CUT THAT OUT!
Don't change the subject!
THIS IS WHY I DIDN'T WANT HIM TO COME!
1ST PRIZE
1ST PRIZE
CHIYUKI!!
LET'S GO TOGETHER!
SCREW THIS LUXURY SKI TRIP!
How is this luxurious?
I KNEW I SHOULDN'T TRUST THAT LOTTERY YOUR GRANDMOTHER WON AT THAT RUNDOWN SHOPPING ARCADE!
You dissin' my granny?!
Keh! Who would go on such a...
I WANNA GO!
I've never been overseas before!
...
WE'RE HUNGRY AND LOST... AND MOST OF ALL...

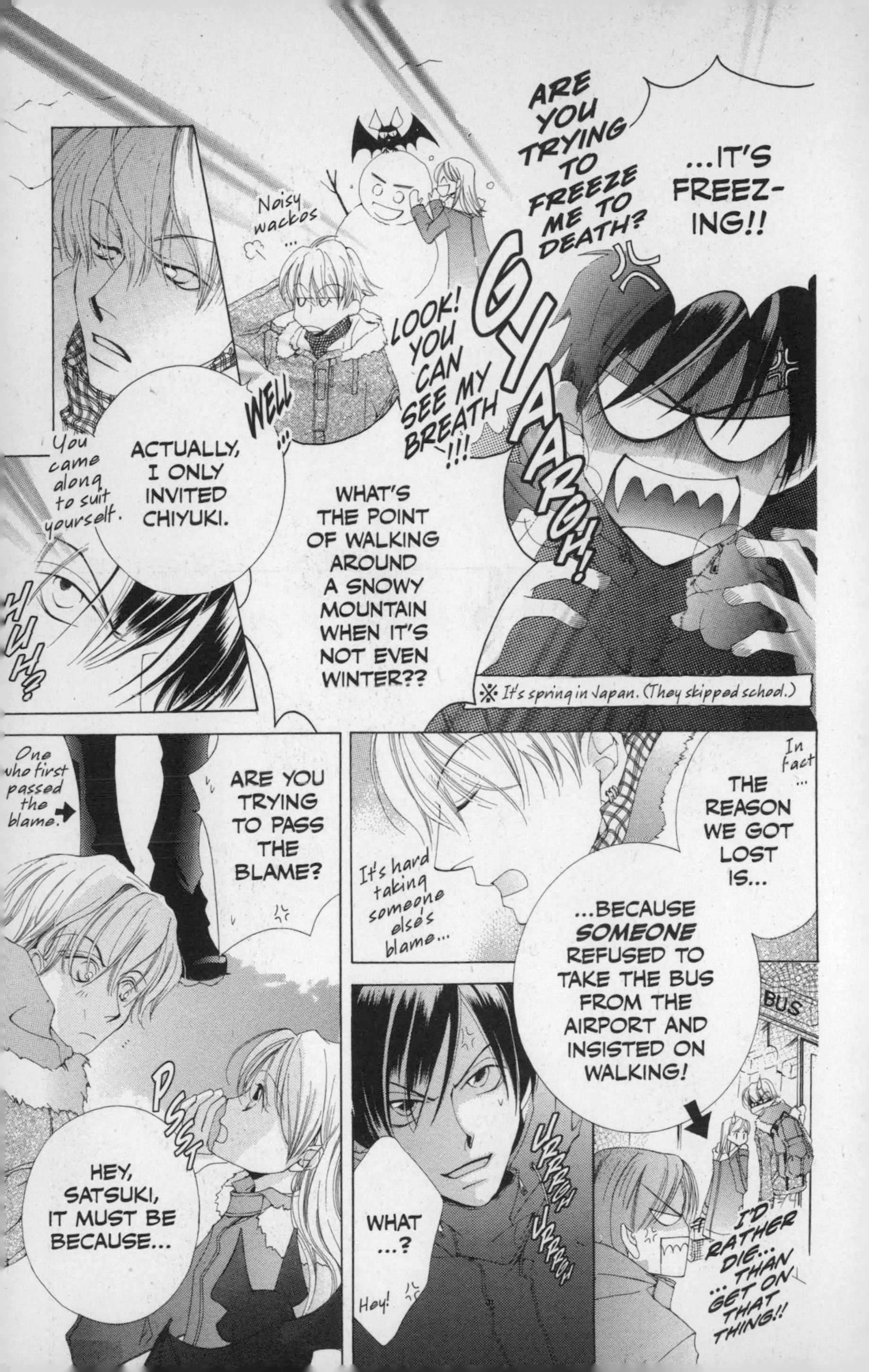
...IT'S FREEZ-ING!!
ARE YOU TRYING TO FREEZE ME TO DEATH?
LOOK! YOU CAN SEE MY BREATH~!!!
Noisy wackos ...
WELL ...
WHAT'S THE POINT OF WALKING AROUND A SNOWY MOUNTAIN WHEN IT'S NOT EVEN WINTER??
ACTUALLY, I ONLY INVITED CHIYUKI.
You came along to suit yourself.
※ It's spring in Japan. (They skipped school.)
In fact ...
THE REASON WE GOT LOST IS...
It's hard taking someone else's blame...
...BECAUSE SOMEONE REFUSED TO TAKE THE BUS FROM THE AIRPORT AND INSISTED ON WALKING!
BUS
I'D RATHER DIE... THAN ... GET ON THAT THING!!
WHAT ...?
Hey!
ARE YOU TRYING TO PASS THE BLAME?
One who first passed the blame.
HEY, SATSUKI, IT MUST BE BECAUSE...

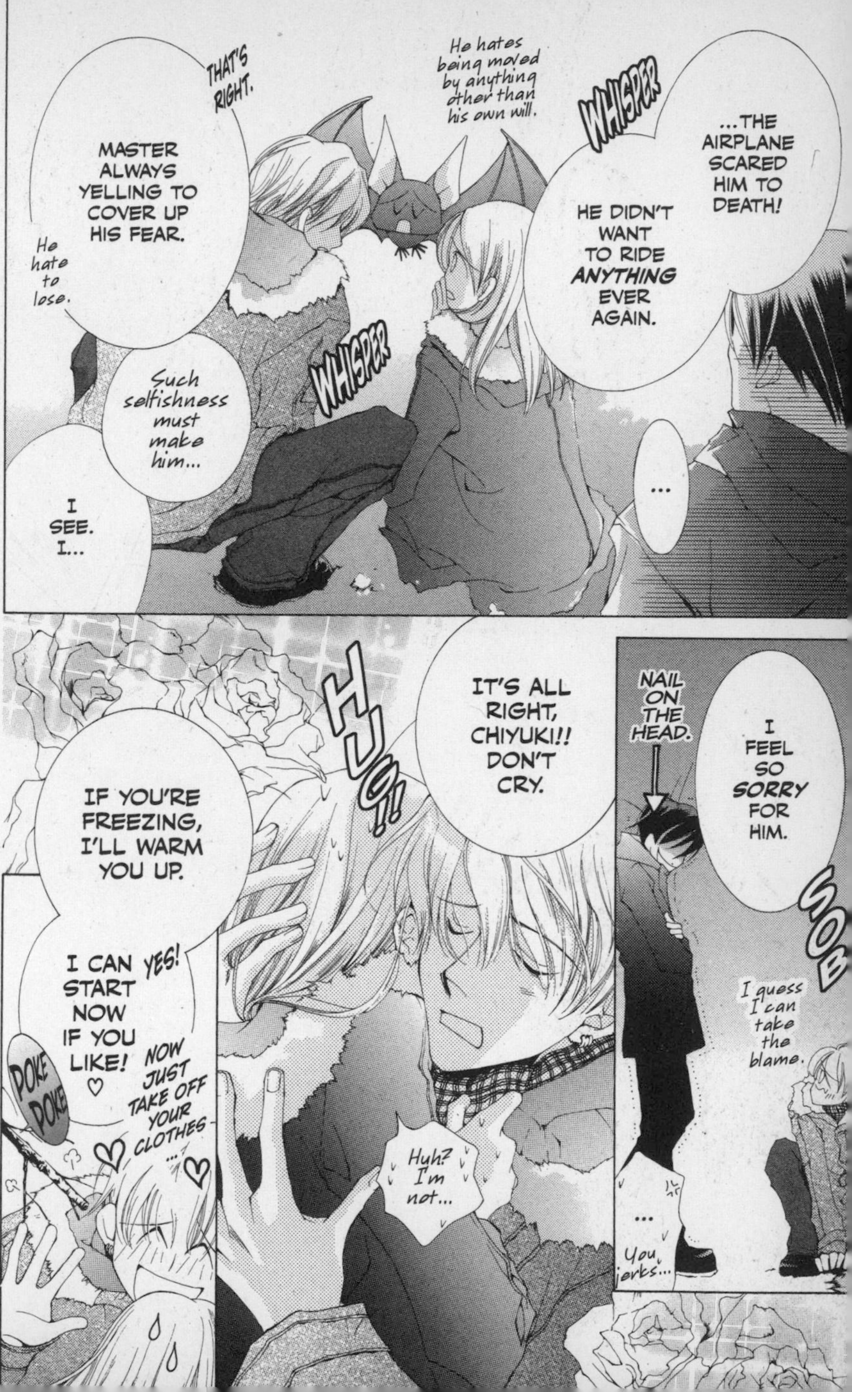

...THE AIRPLANE SCARED HIM TO DEATH!
WHISPER
HE DIDN'T WANT TO RIDE ANYTHING EVER AGAIN.
He hates being moved by anything other than his own will.
THAT'S RIGHT.
MASTER ALWAYS YELLING TO COVER UP HIS FEAR.
He hate to lose.
WHISPER
...
Such selfishness must make him...
I SEE. I...
NAIL ON THE HEAD.
I FEEL SO SORRY FOR HIM.
SOB
I guess I can take the blame.
...
You jerks...
IT'S ALL RIGHT, CHIYUKI!! DON'T CRY.
HUG!!
IF YOU'RE FREEZING, I'LL WARM YOU UP.
YES!
I CAN START NOW IF YOU LIKE! ♡
NOW JUST TAKE OFF YOUR CLOTHES...
Huh? I'm not...
POKE POKE

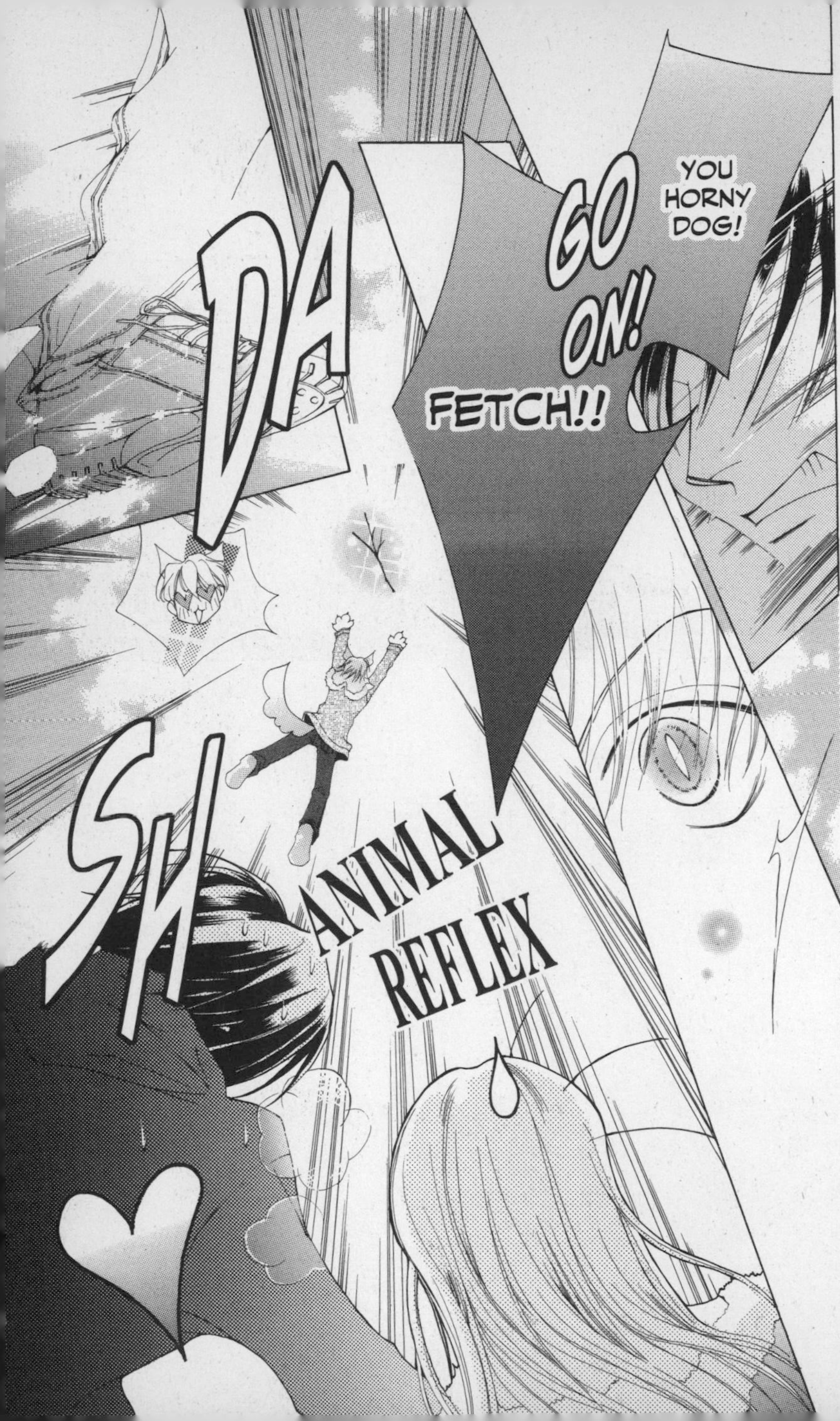
YOU HORNY DOG!
GO ON!
FETCH!!
DA
ANIMAL REFLEX
SH

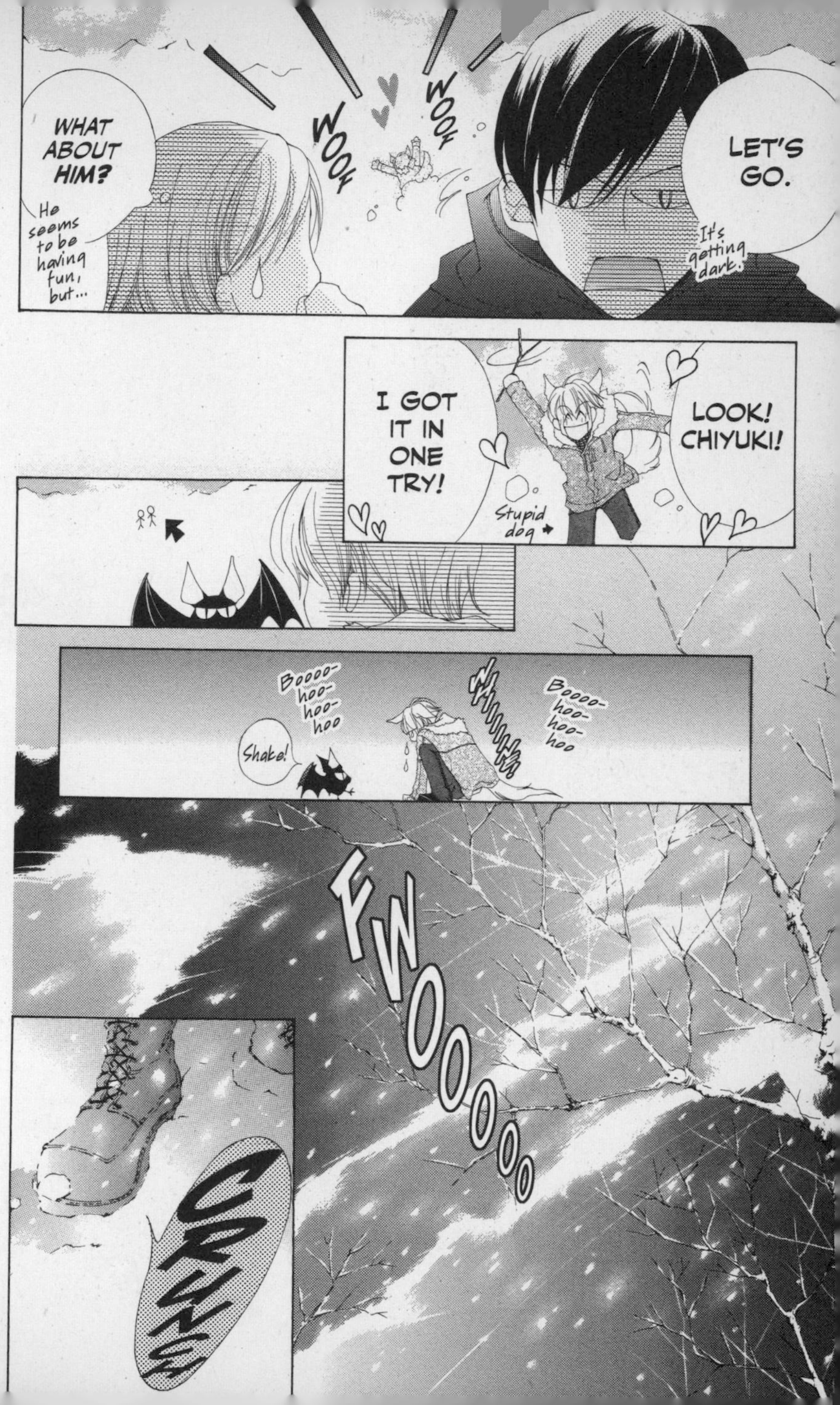
LET'S GO.
It's getting dark.
WOOK
WOOK
WHAT ABOUT HIM?
He seems to be having fun, but...
LOOK! CHIYUKI!
I GOT IT IN ONE TRY!
Stupid dog
Boooo-hoo-hoo-hoo
Boooo-hoo-hoo-hoo
Shake!
FWOOOOOO
CRUNCH

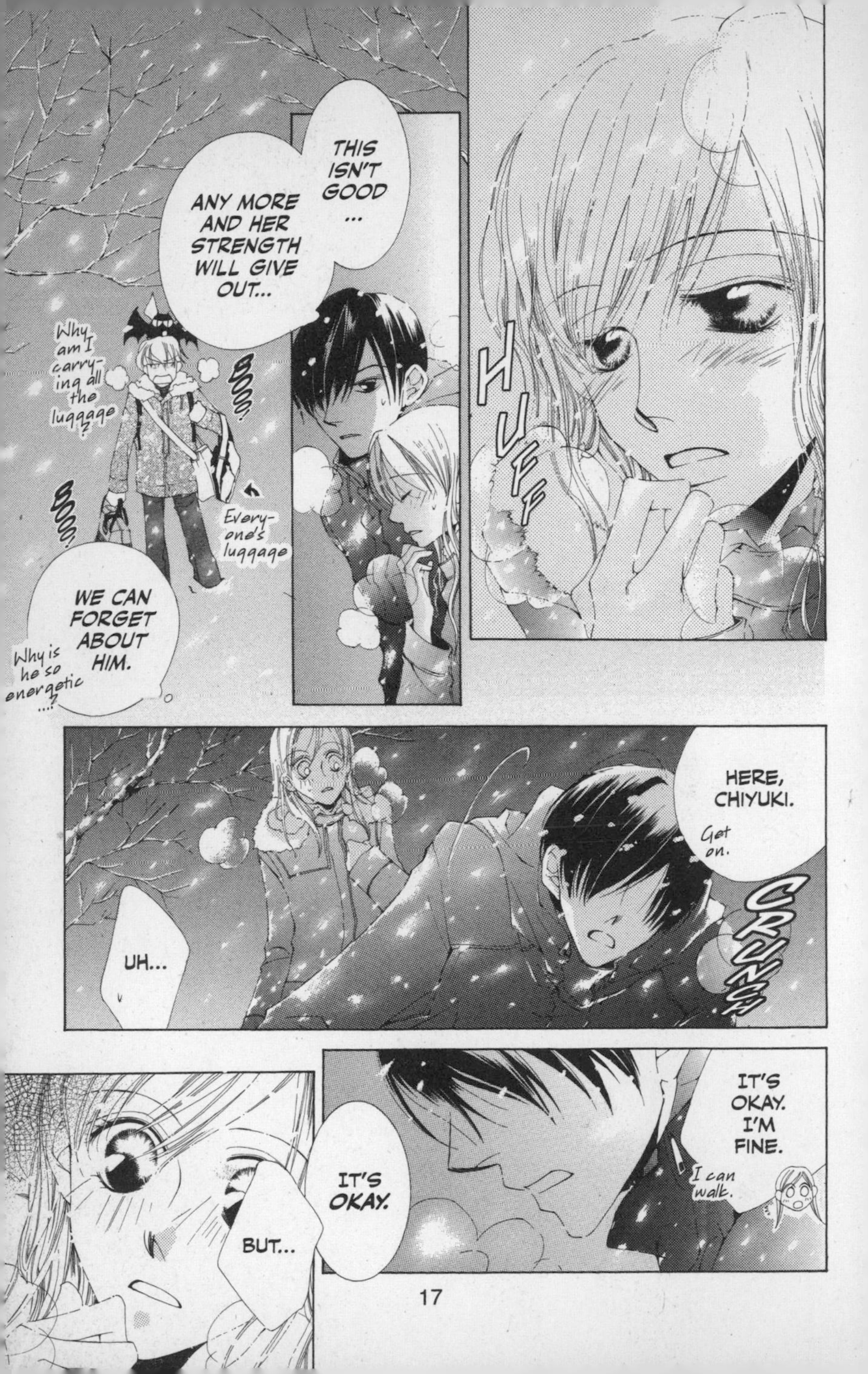
HUFF
THIS ISN'T GOOD ...
ANY MORE AND HER STRENGTH WILL GIVE OUT...
Why am I carrying all the luggage?
Everyone's luggage
WE CAN FORGET ABOUT HIM.
Why is he so energetic ...?
HERE, CHIYUKI.
Get on.
CRUNCH
UH...
IT'S OKAY. I'M FINE.
I can walk.
IT'S OKAY.
BUT...

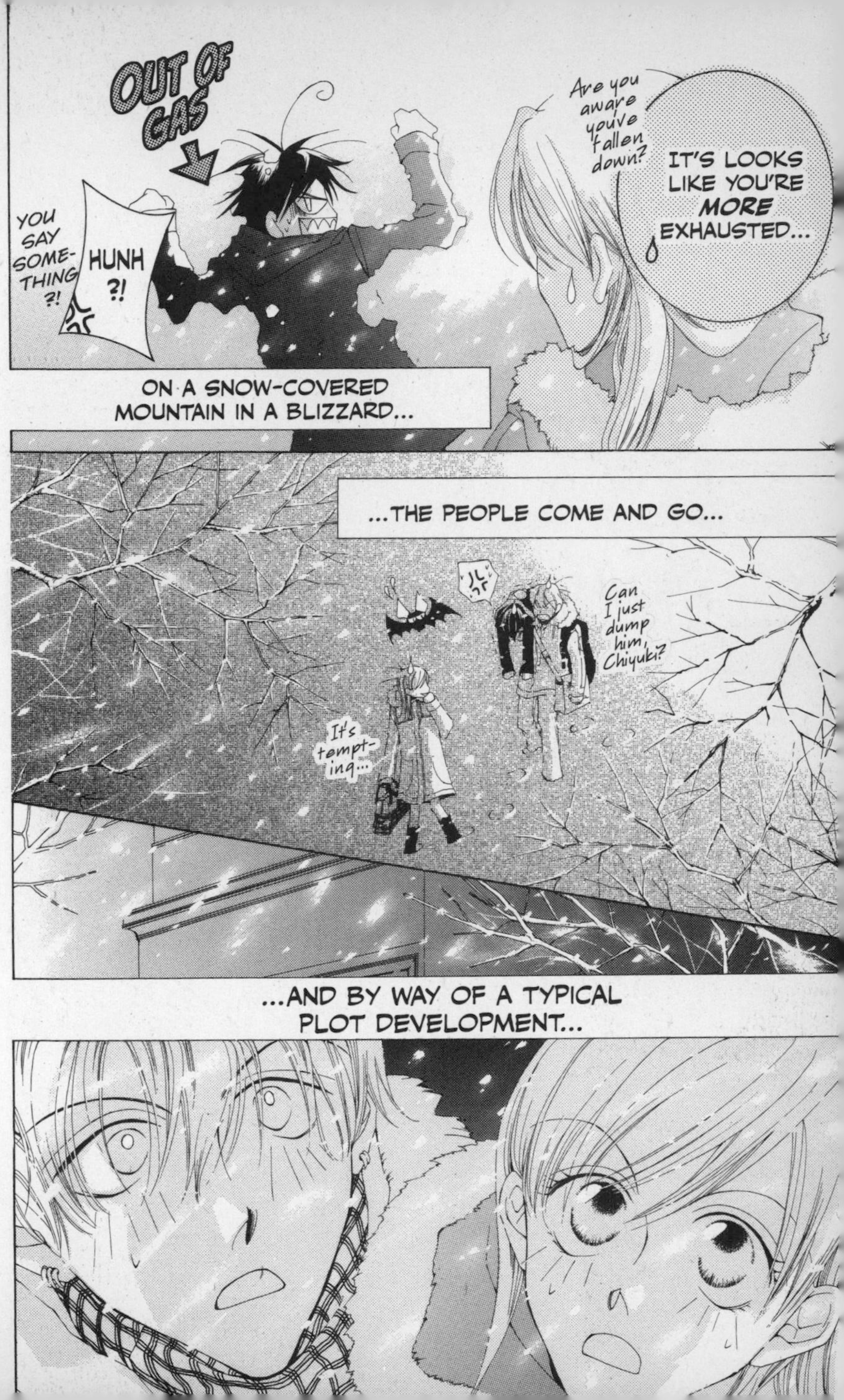
IT'S LOOKS LIKE YOU'RE MORE EXHAUSTED...
Are you aware you've fallen down?
OUT OF GAS
HUNH ?!
YOU SAY SOME-THING ?!
ON A SNOW-COVERED MOUNTAIN IN A BLIZZARD...
...THE PEOPLE COME AND GO...
Can I just dump him, Chiyuki?
It's tempt-ing...
...AND BY WAY OF A TYPICAL PLOT DEVELOPMENT...

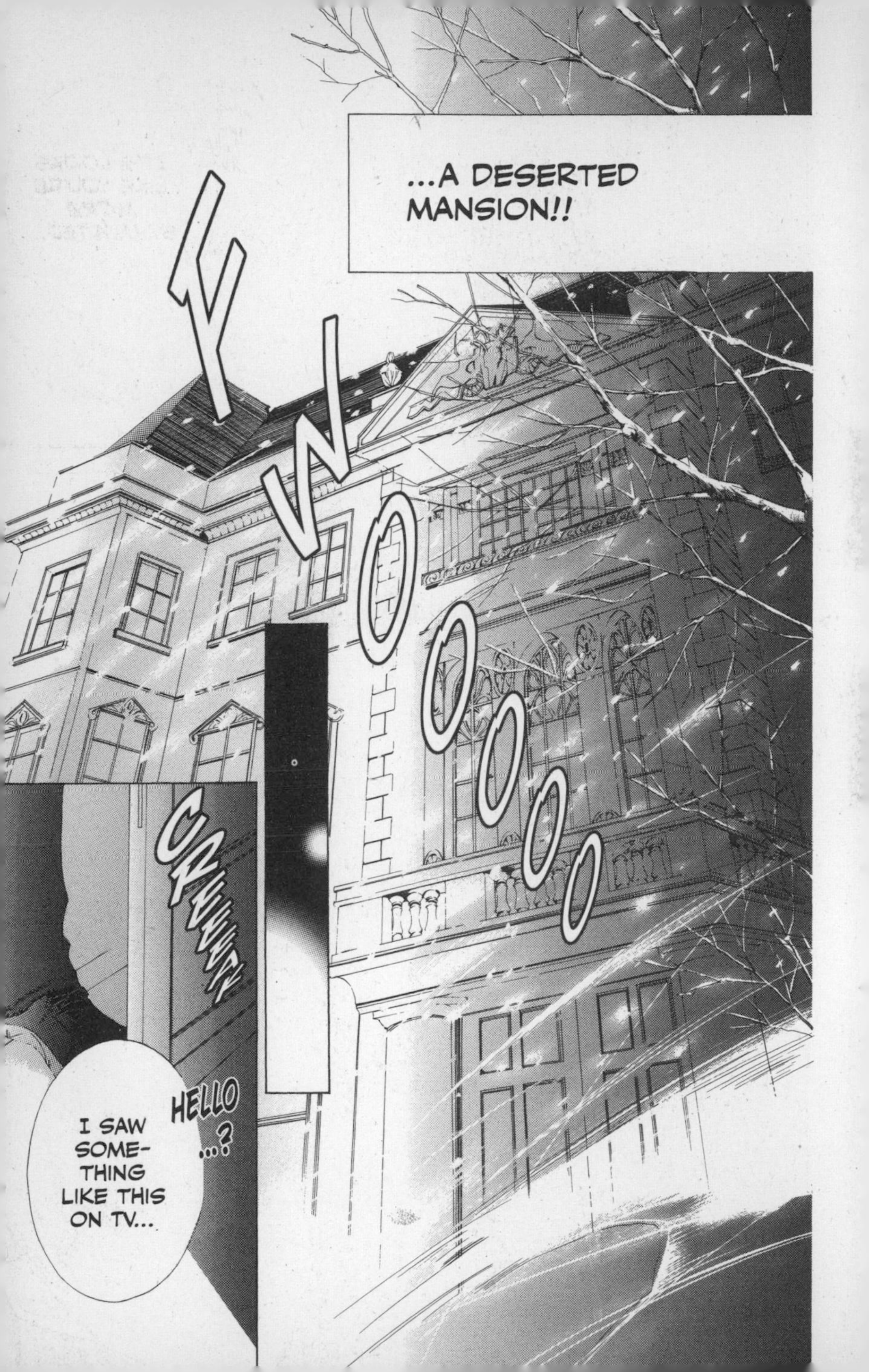
...A DESERTED MANSION!!
FWOOOOO
HELLO ...?
I SAW SOME-THING LIKE THIS ON TV...

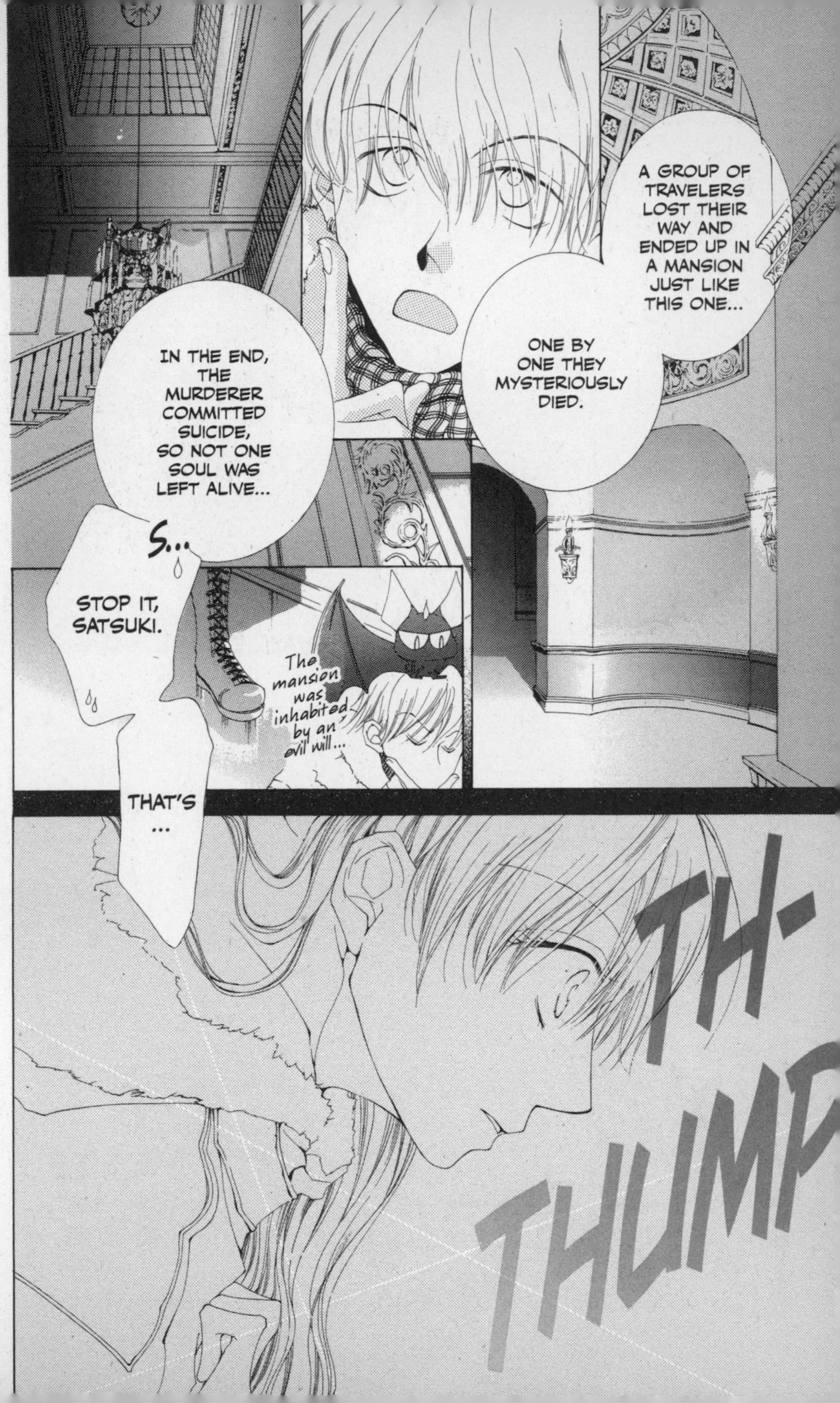
A GROUP OF TRAVELERS LOST THEIR WAY AND ENDED UP IN A MANSION JUST LIKE THIS ONE...
ONE BY ONE THEY MYSTERIOUSLY DIED.
IN THE END, THE MURDERER COMMITTED SUICIDE, SO NOT ONE SOUL WAS LEFT ALIVE...
The mansion was inhabited by an evil will...
S...
STOP IT, SATSUKI.
THAT'S ...
TH-THUMP

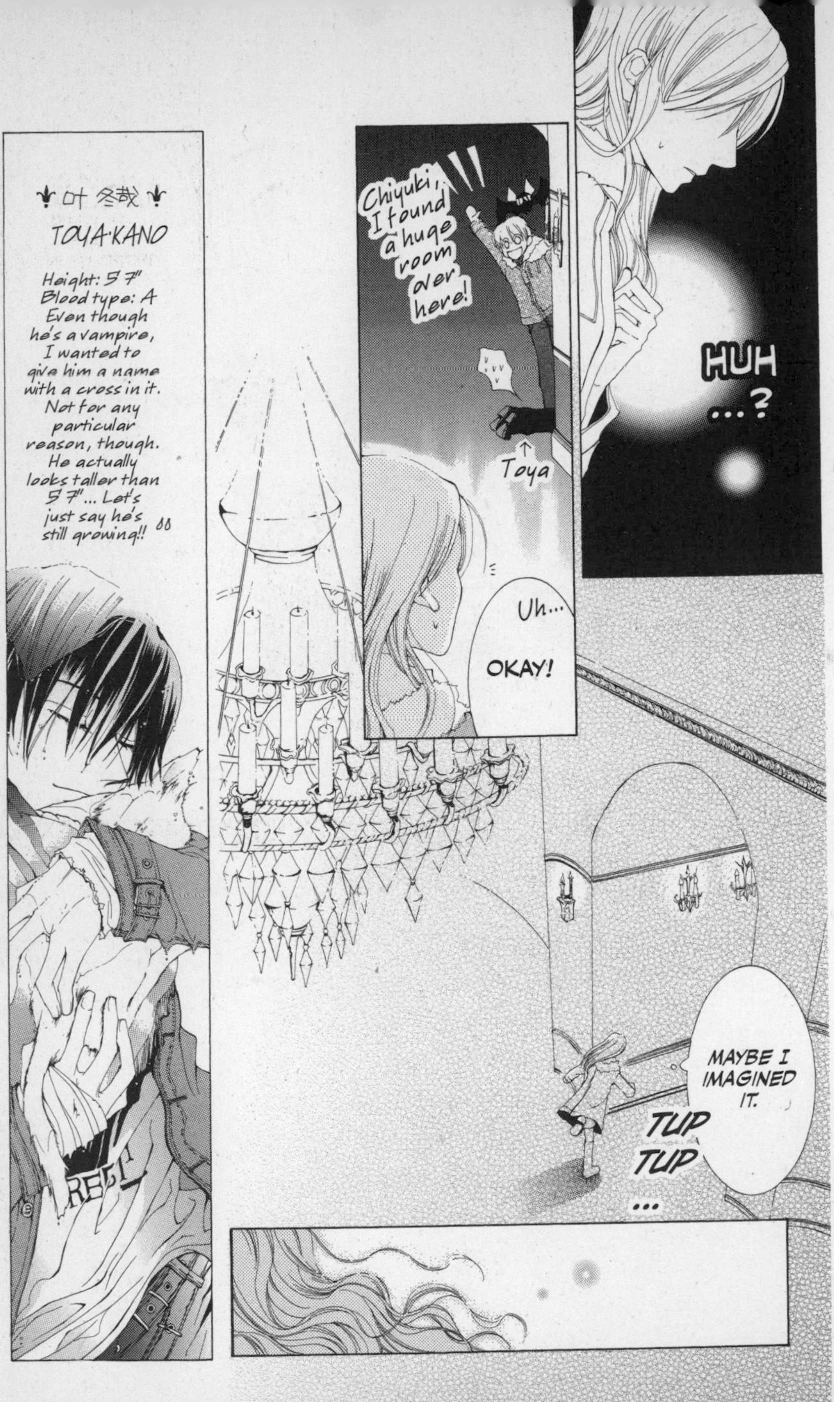

HUH ...?
Chiyuki, I found a huge room over here!
Toya
Uh...
OKAY!
MAYBE I IMAGINED IT.
TUP TUP ...
叶冬哉
TOYA KANO
Height: 5'7"
Blood type: A
Even though he's a vampire, I wanted to give him a name with a cross in it. Not for any particular reason, though. He actually looks taller than 5'7"... Let's just say he's still growing!!

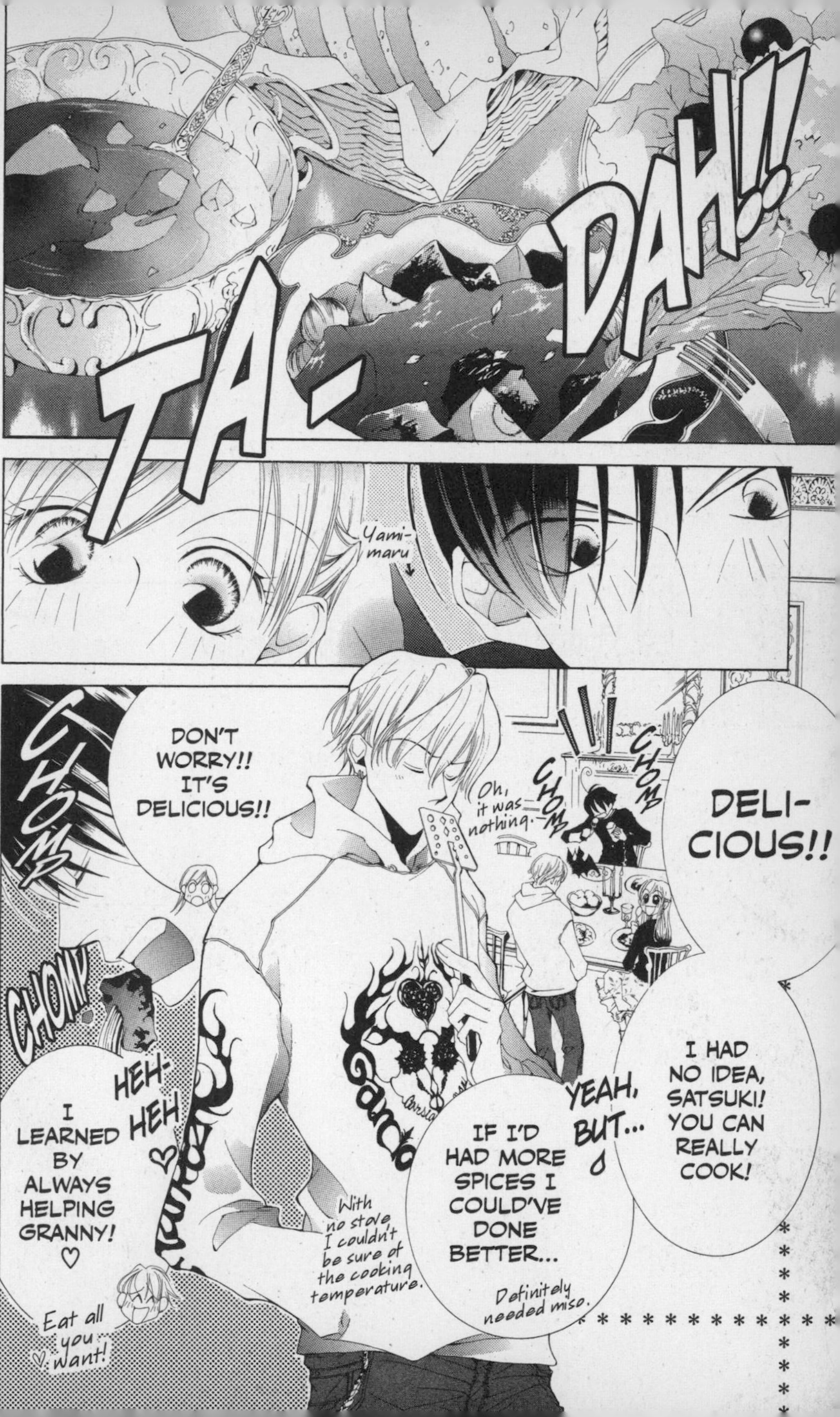
TA-DAH!!
Yami-maru
DELI-CIOUS!!
CHOMP CHOMP
Oh, it was nothing.
DON'T WORRY!! IT'S DELICIOUS!!
CHOMP
CHOMP
I HAD NO IDEA, SATSUKI! YOU CAN REALLY COOK!
YEAH, BUT...
IF I'D HAD MORE SPICES I COULD'VE DONE BETTER...
Definitely needed miso.
With no stove I couldn't be sure of the cooking temperature.
HEH-HEH ♡
I LEARNED BY ALWAYS HELPING GRANNY! ♡
Eat all you want! ♡

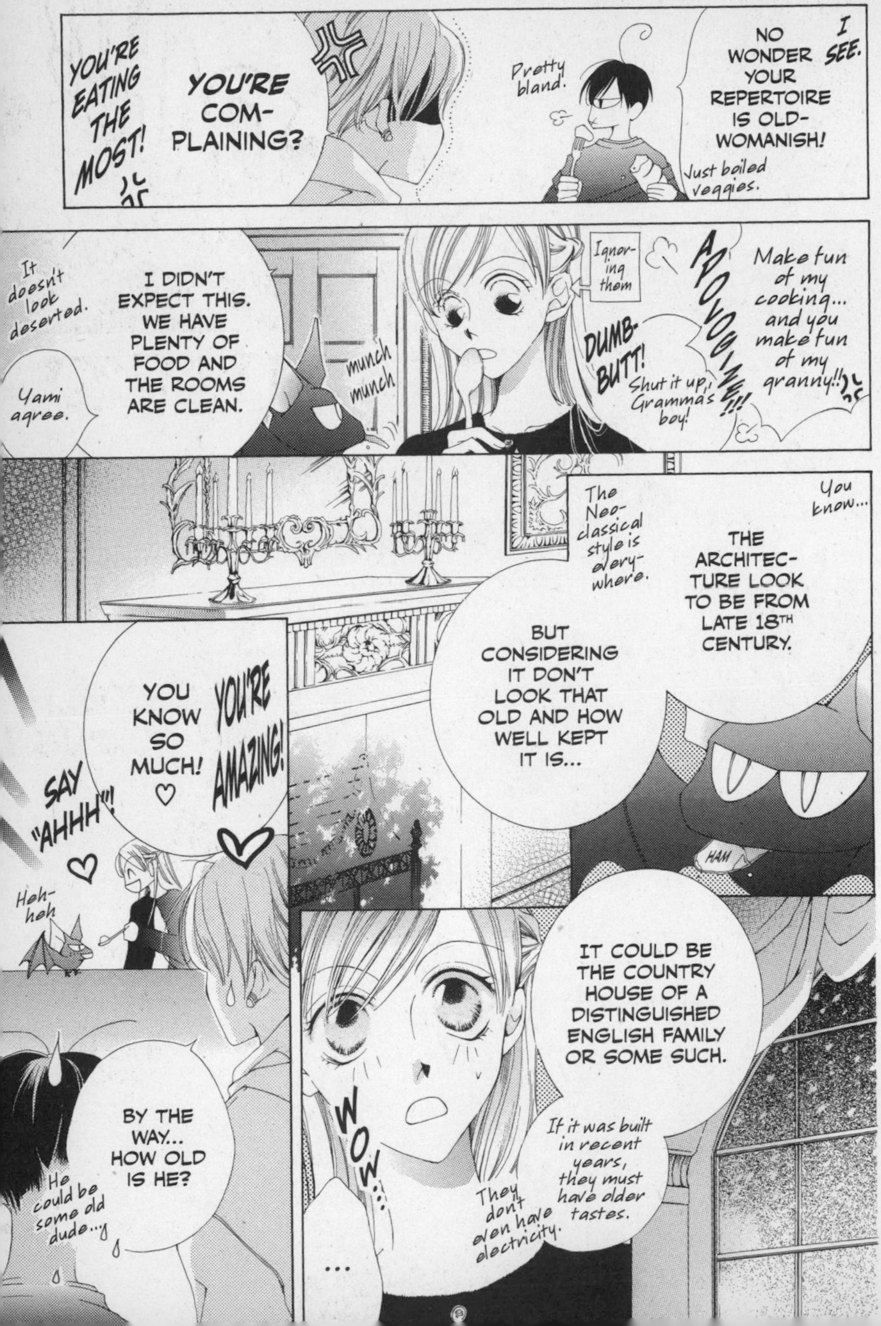
I SEE.
NO WONDER YOUR REPERTOIRE IS OLD-WOMANISH!
Just boiled veggies.
Pretty bland.
YOU'RE COMPLAINING?
YOU'RE EATING THE MOST!
Make fun of my cooking... and you make fun of my granny!!
APOOOOW!!
DUMB-BUTT!
Shut it up, Gramma's boy!
Ignoring them
I DIDN'T EXPECT THIS. WE HAVE PLENTY OF FOOD AND THE ROOMS ARE CLEAN.
munch munch
It doesn't look deserted.
Yami agree.
You know...
THE ARCHITECTURE LOOK TO BE FROM LATE 18TH CENTURY.
The Neo-classical style is everywhere.
BUT CONSIDERING IT DON'T LOOK THAT OLD AND HOW WELL KEPT IT IS...
HAM
YOU'RE AMAZING!
YOU KNOW SO MUCH! ♡
SAY "AHHH"!
Heh-heh
IT COULD BE THE COUNTRY HOUSE OF A DISTINGUISHED ENGLISH FAMILY OR SOME SUCH.
If it was built in recent years, they must have older tastes.
They don't even have electricity.
WOW...
...
BY THE WAY... HOW OLD IS HE?
He could be some old dude...

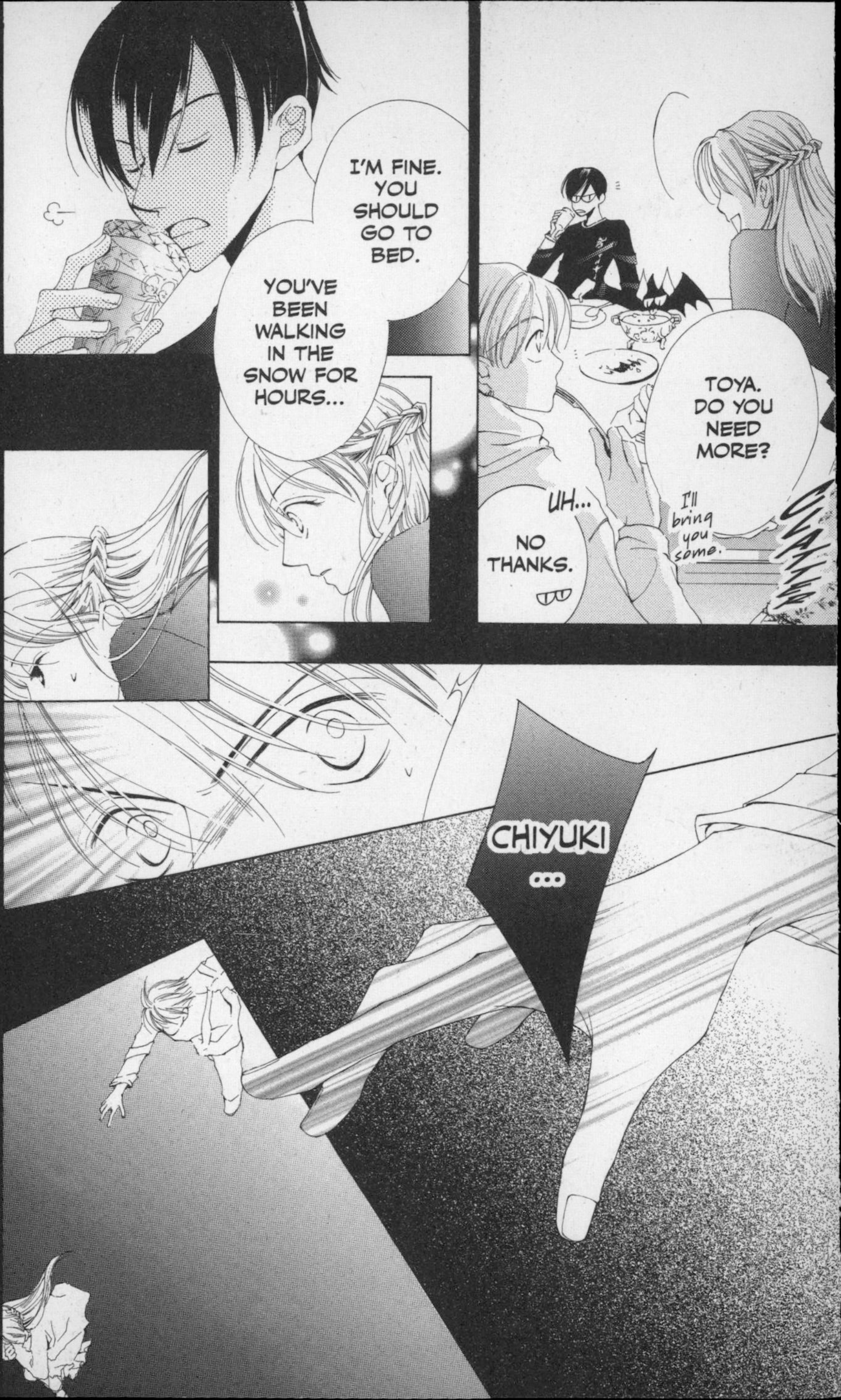
TOYA. DO YOU NEED MORE?
I'll bring you some.
UH...
NO THANKS.
I'M FINE. YOU SHOULD GO TO BED.
YOU'VE BEEN WALKING IN THE SNOW FOR HOURS...
CHIYUKI ...

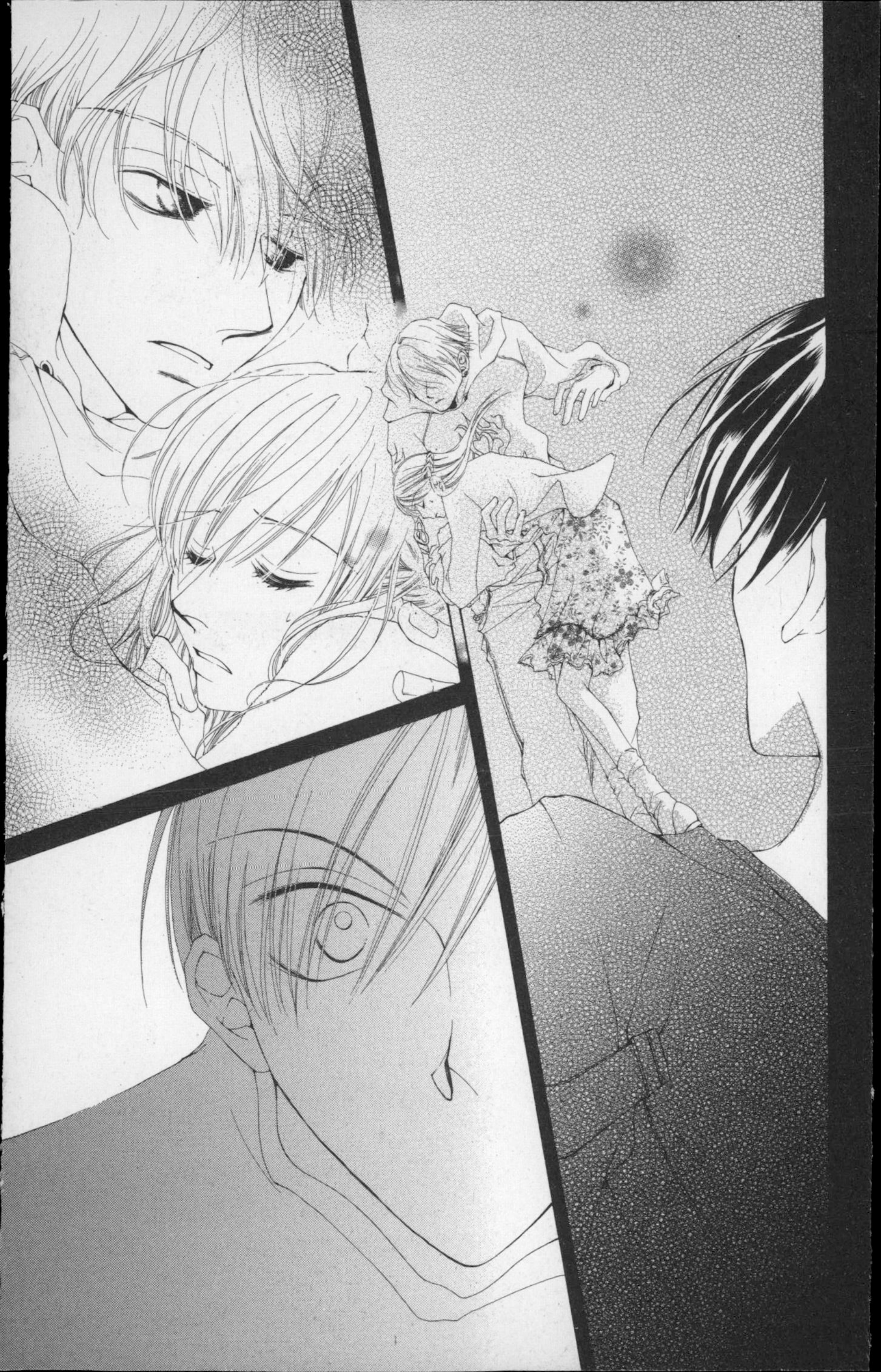

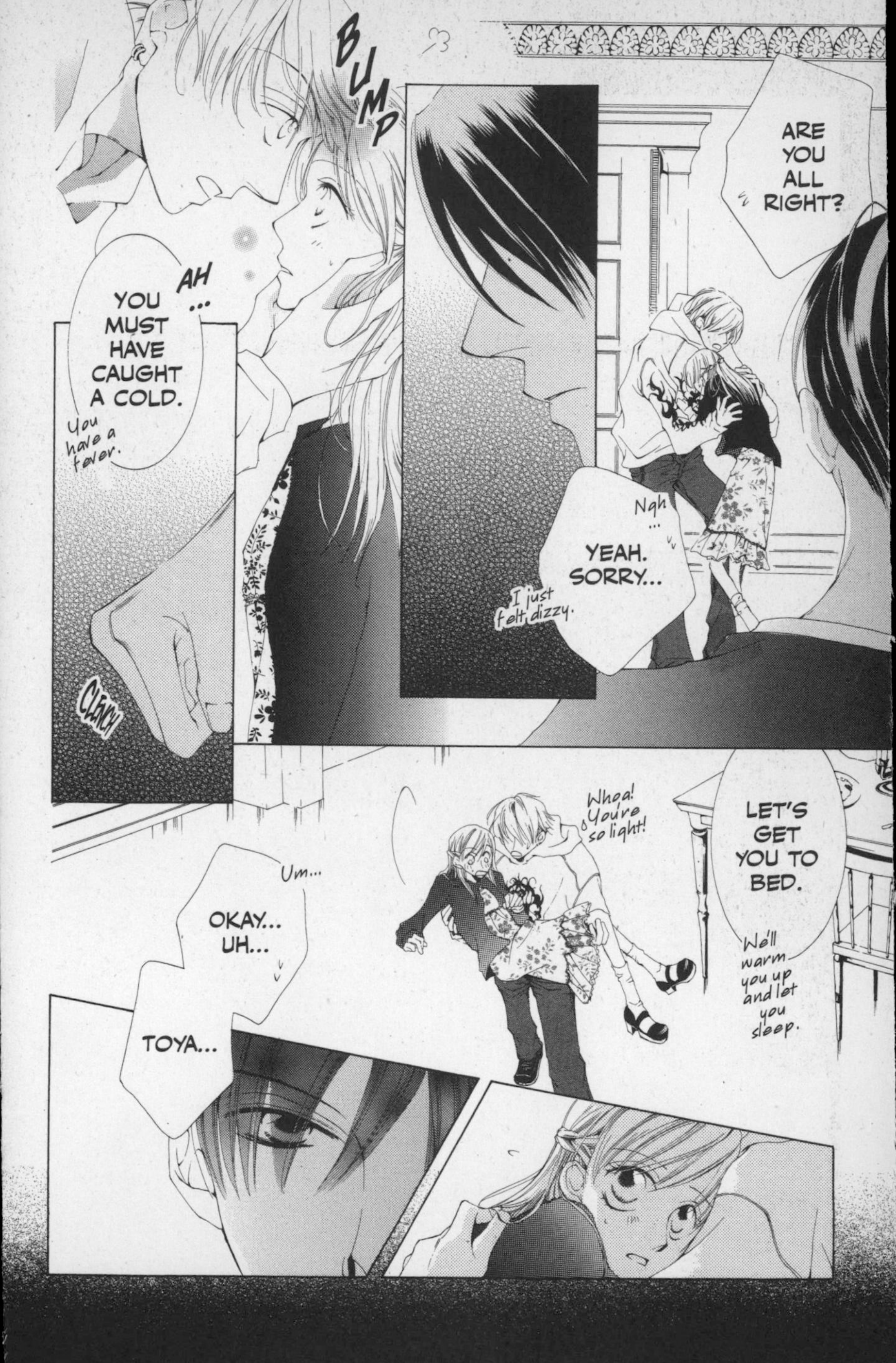
ARE YOU ALL RIGHT?
Ngh...
YEAH. SORRY...
I just felt dizzy.
BUMP
AH...
YOU MUST HAVE CAUGHT A COLD.
You have a fever.
CLENCH
LET'S GET YOU TO BED.
We'll warm you up and let you sleep.
Whoa! You're so light!
Um...
OKAY... UH...
TOYA...

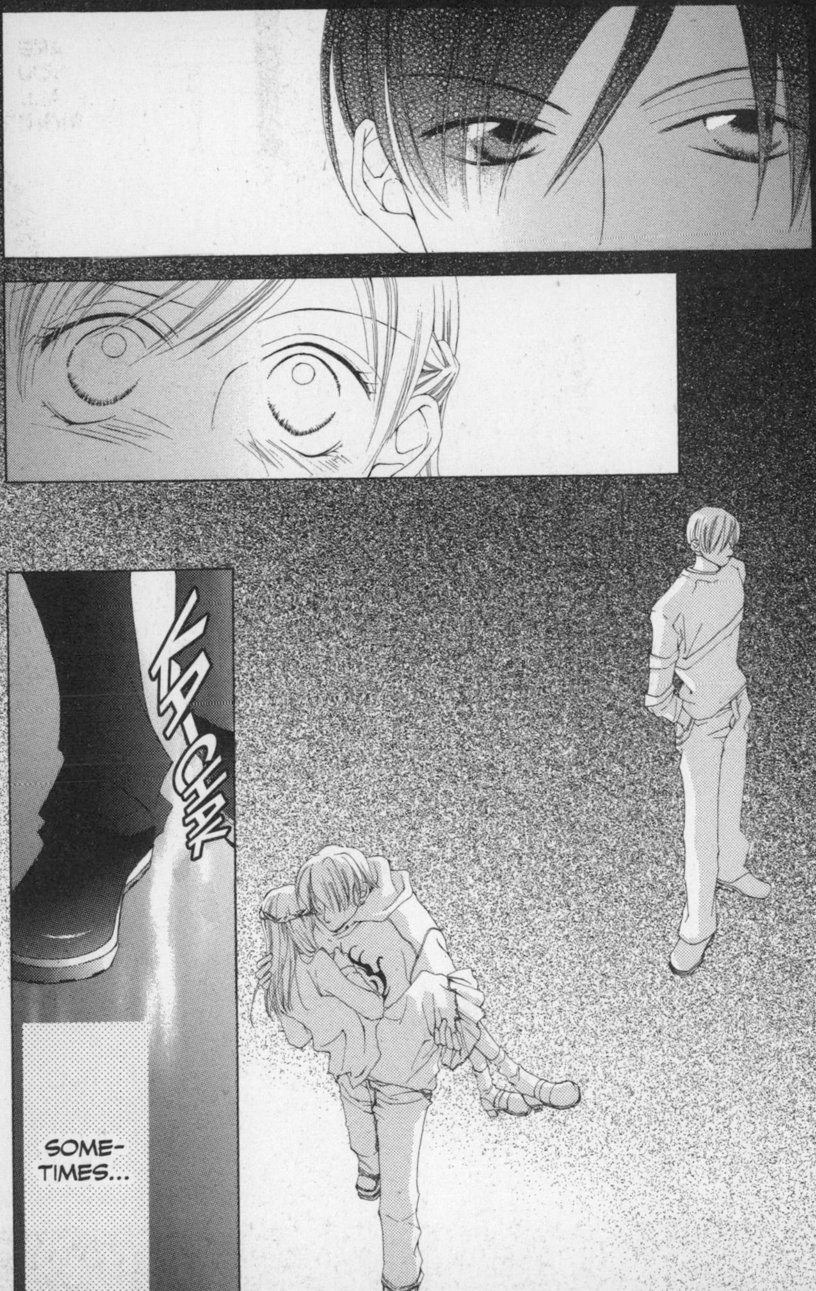
KA-CHAK
SOME-TIMES...

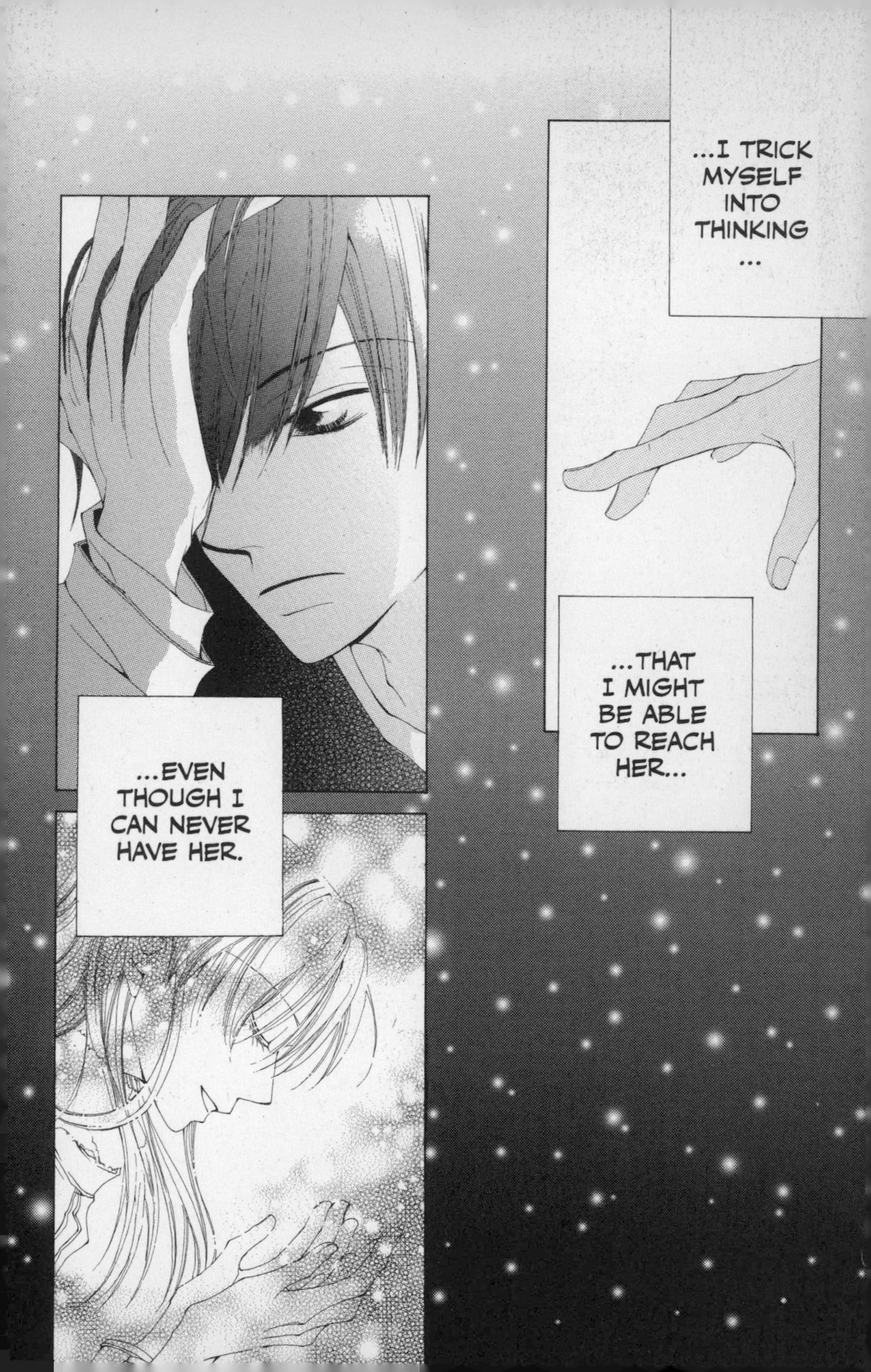
...I TRICK MYSELF INTO THINKING ...
...THAT I MIGHT BE ABLE TO REACH HER...
...EVEN THOUGH I CAN NEVER HAVE HER.

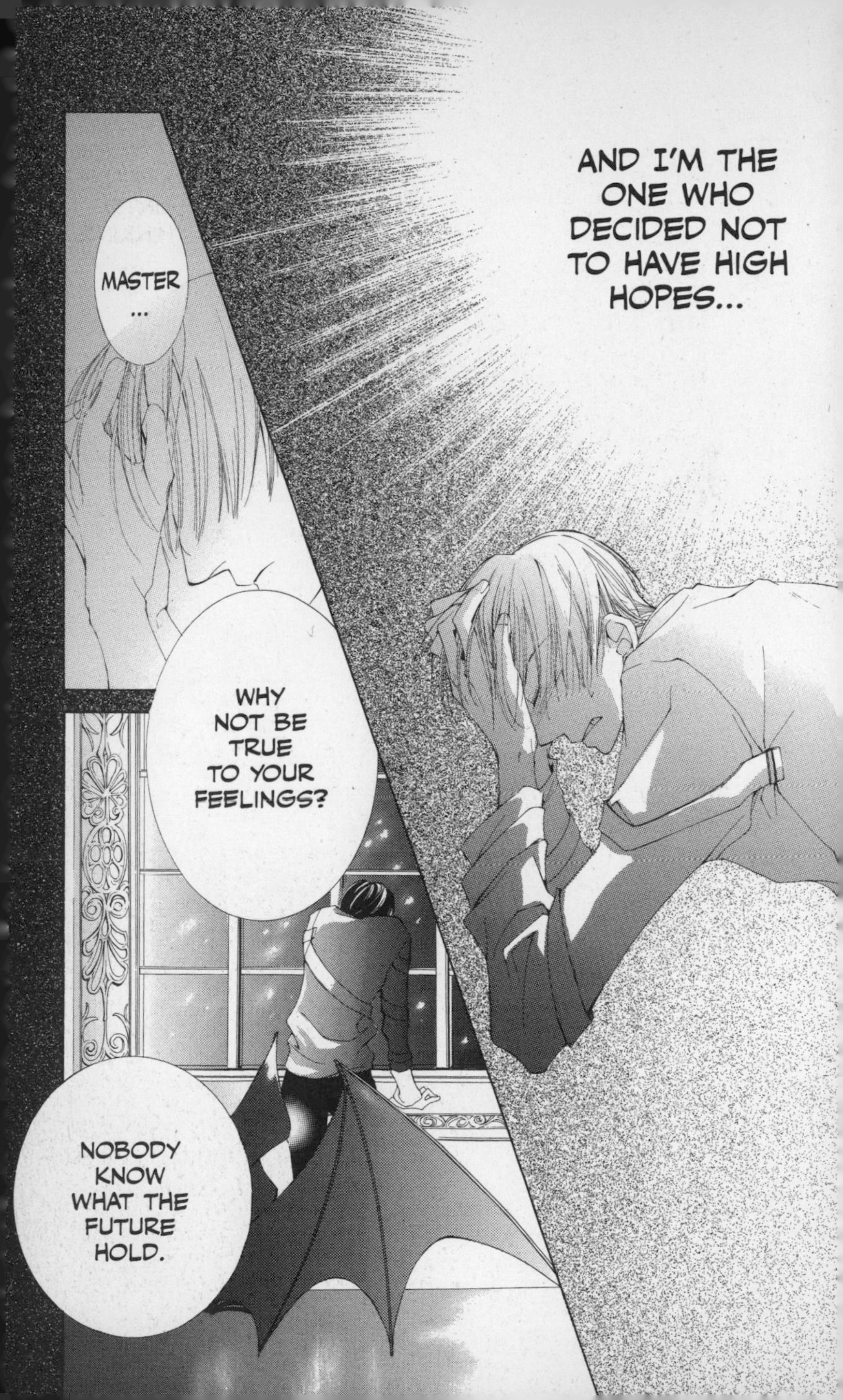

AND I'M THE ONE WHO DECIDED NOT TO HAVE HIGH HOPES...
MASTER ...
WHY NOT BE TRUE TO YOUR FEELINGS?
NOBODY KNOW WHAT THE FUTURE HOLD.

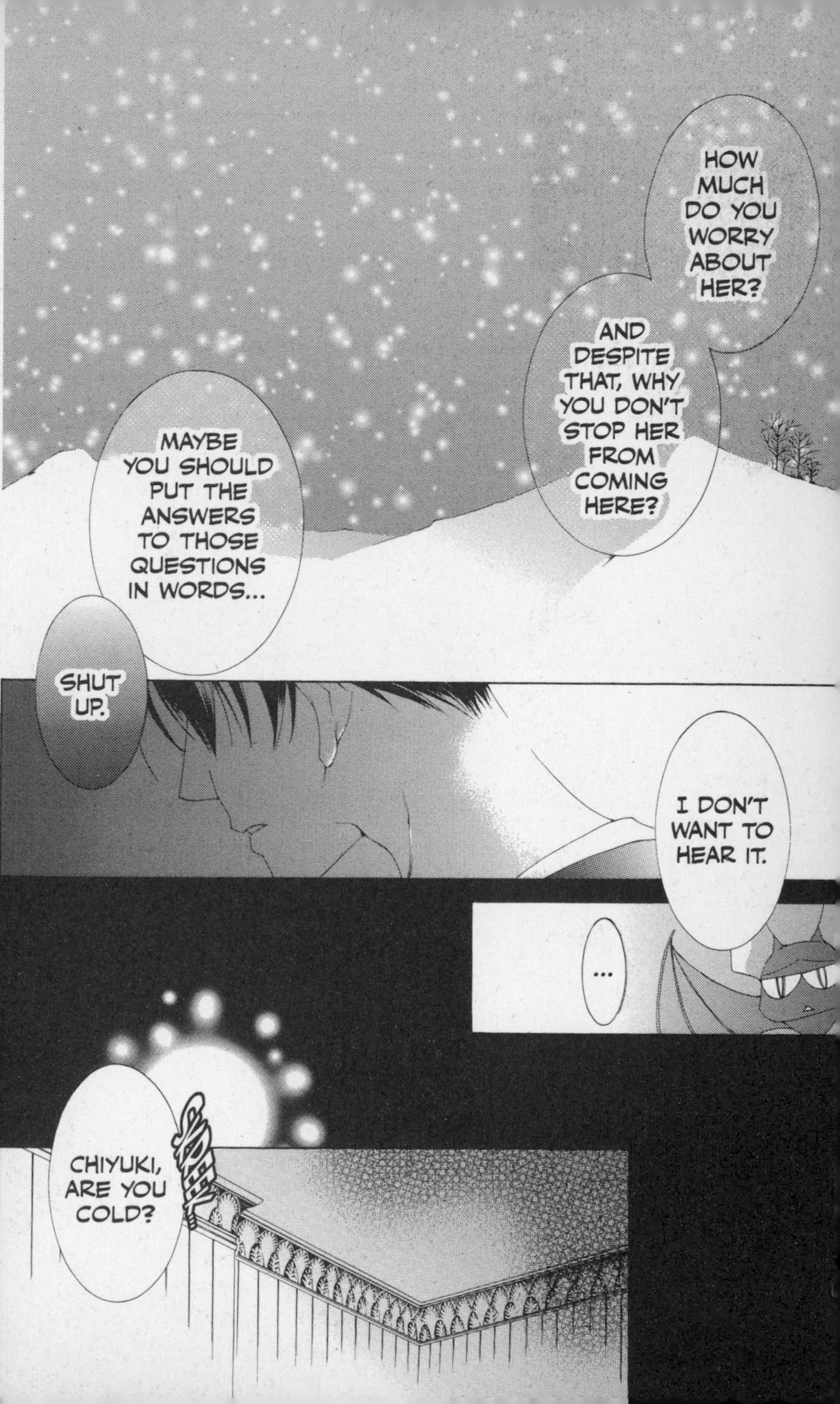
HOW MUCH DO YOU WORRY ABOUT HER?
AND DESPITE THAT, WHY YOU DON'T STOP HER FROM COMING HERE?
MAYBE YOU SHOULD PUT THE ANSWERS TO THOSE QUESTIONS IN WORDS...
SHUT UP.
I DON'T WANT TO HEAR IT.
...
CHIYUKI, ARE YOU COLD?

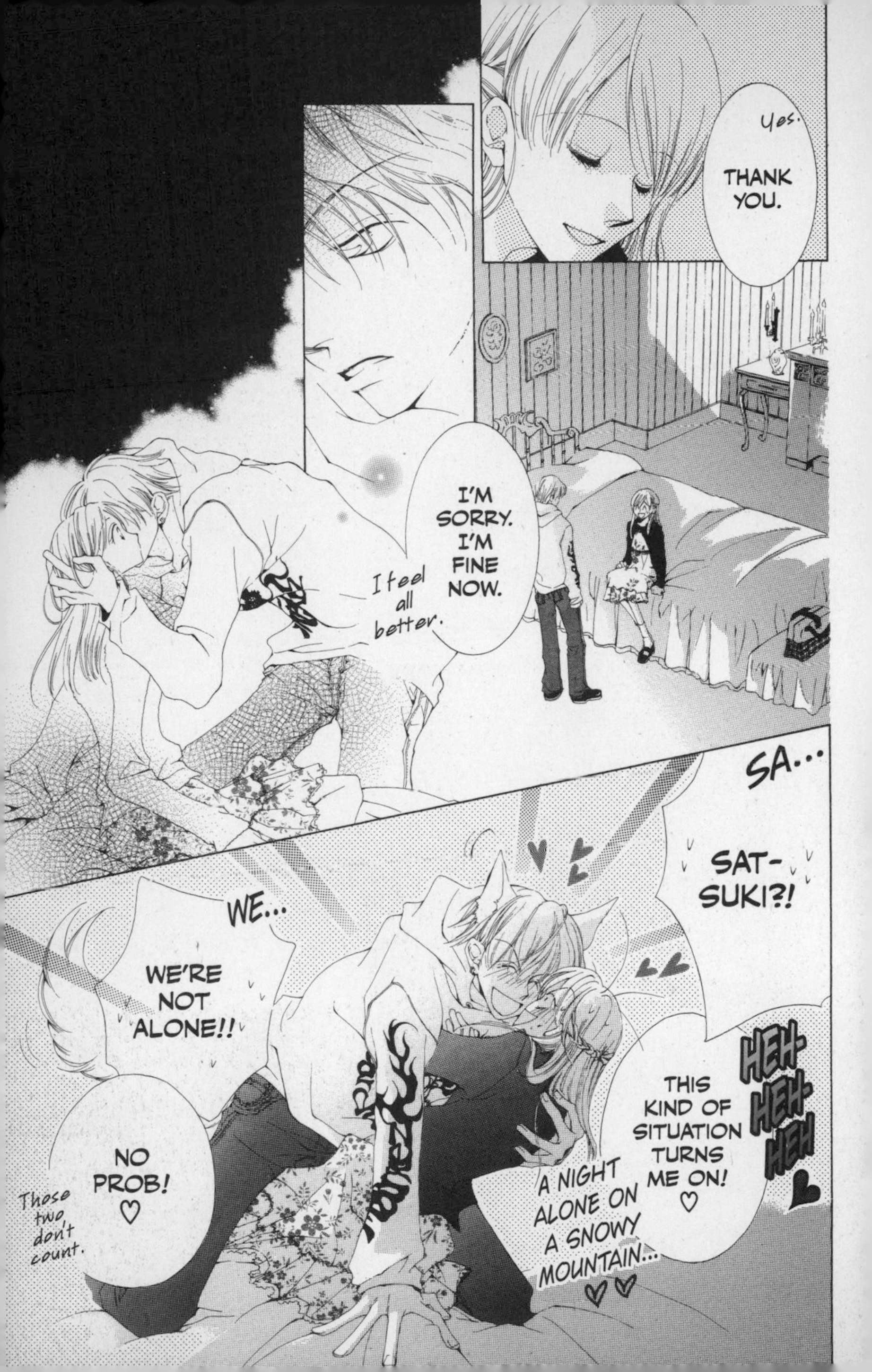
Yes.
THANK YOU.
I'M SORRY. I'M FINE NOW.
I feel all better.
SA...
SAT-SUKI?!
HEH HEH HEH
THIS KIND OF SITUATION TURNS ME ON!
A NIGHT ALONE ON A SNOWY MOUNTAIN...
WE...
WE'RE NOT ALONE!!
NO PROB!
Those two don't count.

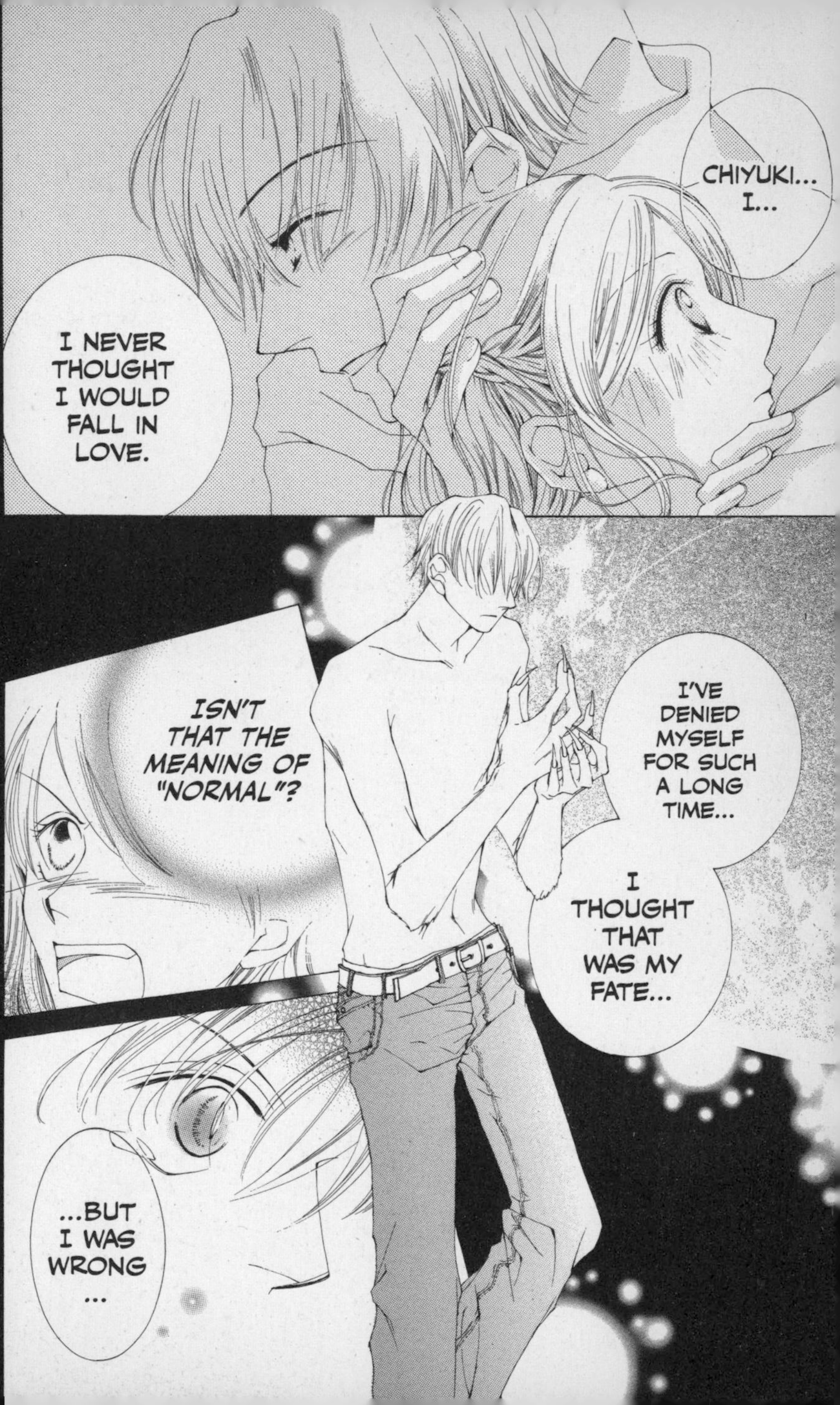
CHIYUKI... I...
I NEVER THOUGHT I WOULD FALL IN LOVE.
I'VE DENIED MYSELF FOR SUCH A LONG TIME...
I THOUGHT THAT WAS MY FATE...
ISN'T THAT THE MEANING OF "NORMAL"?
...BUT I WAS WRONG ...

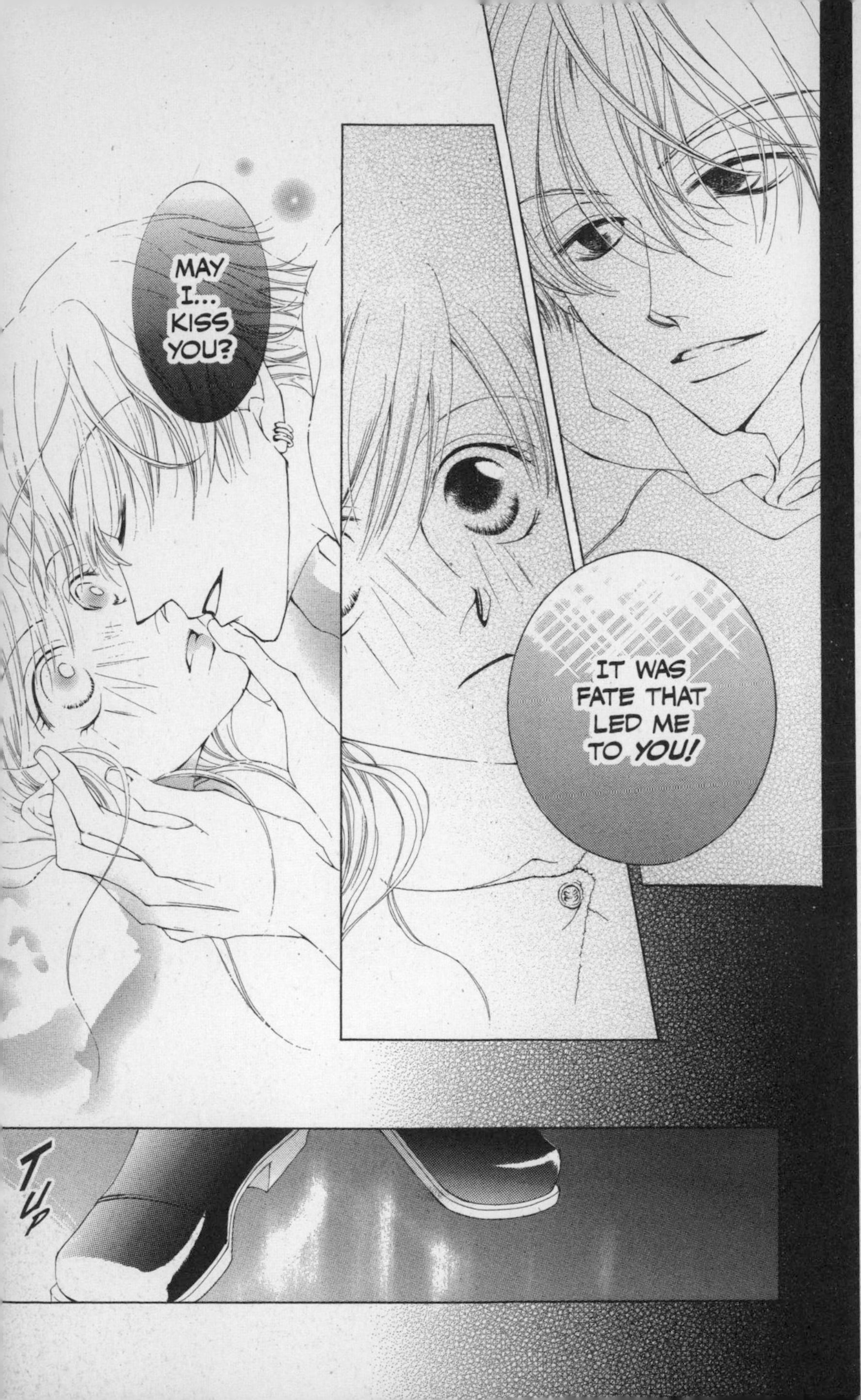
IT WAS FATE THAT LED ME TO YOU!
MAY I... KISS YOU?
TUP

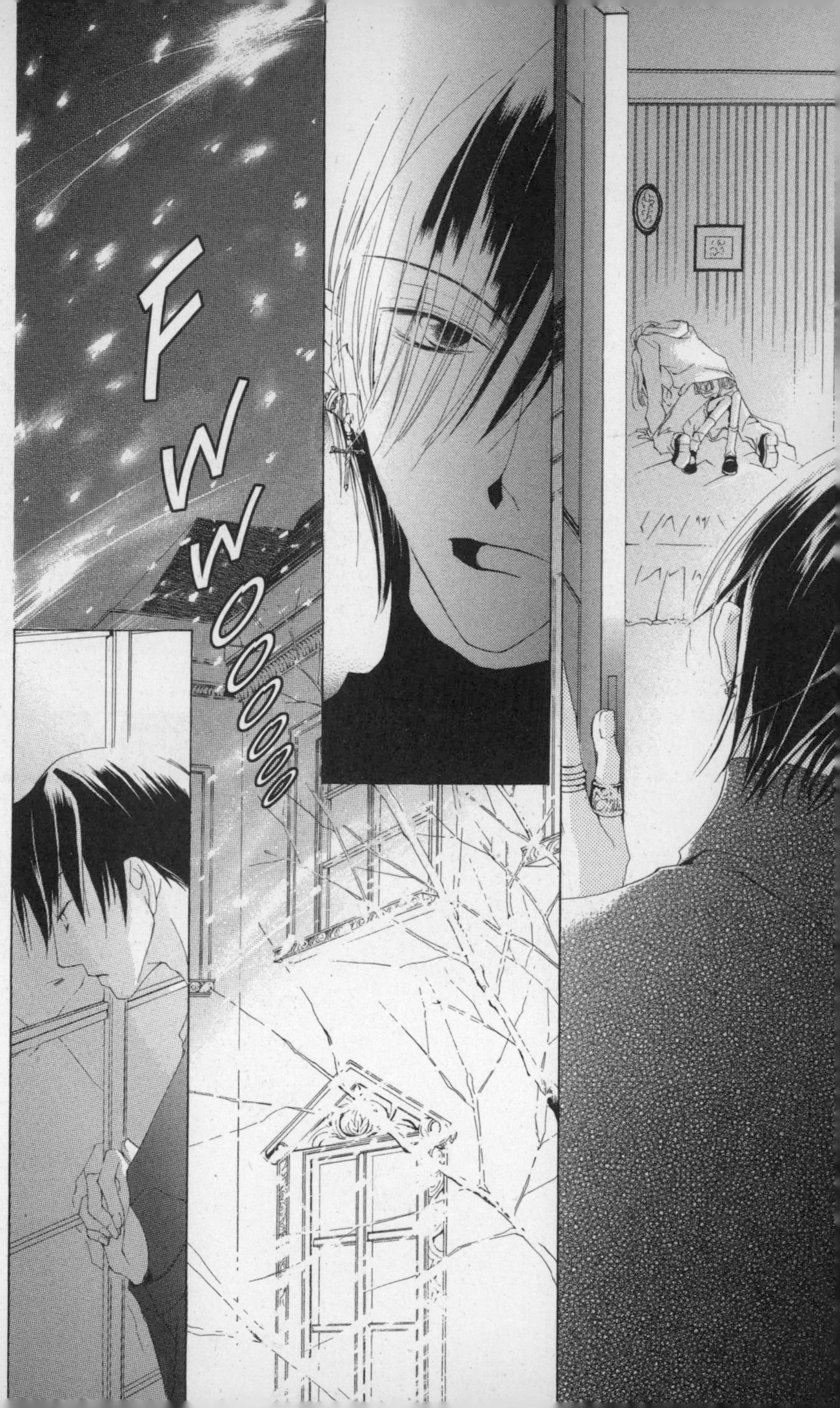
FWOOOOOO

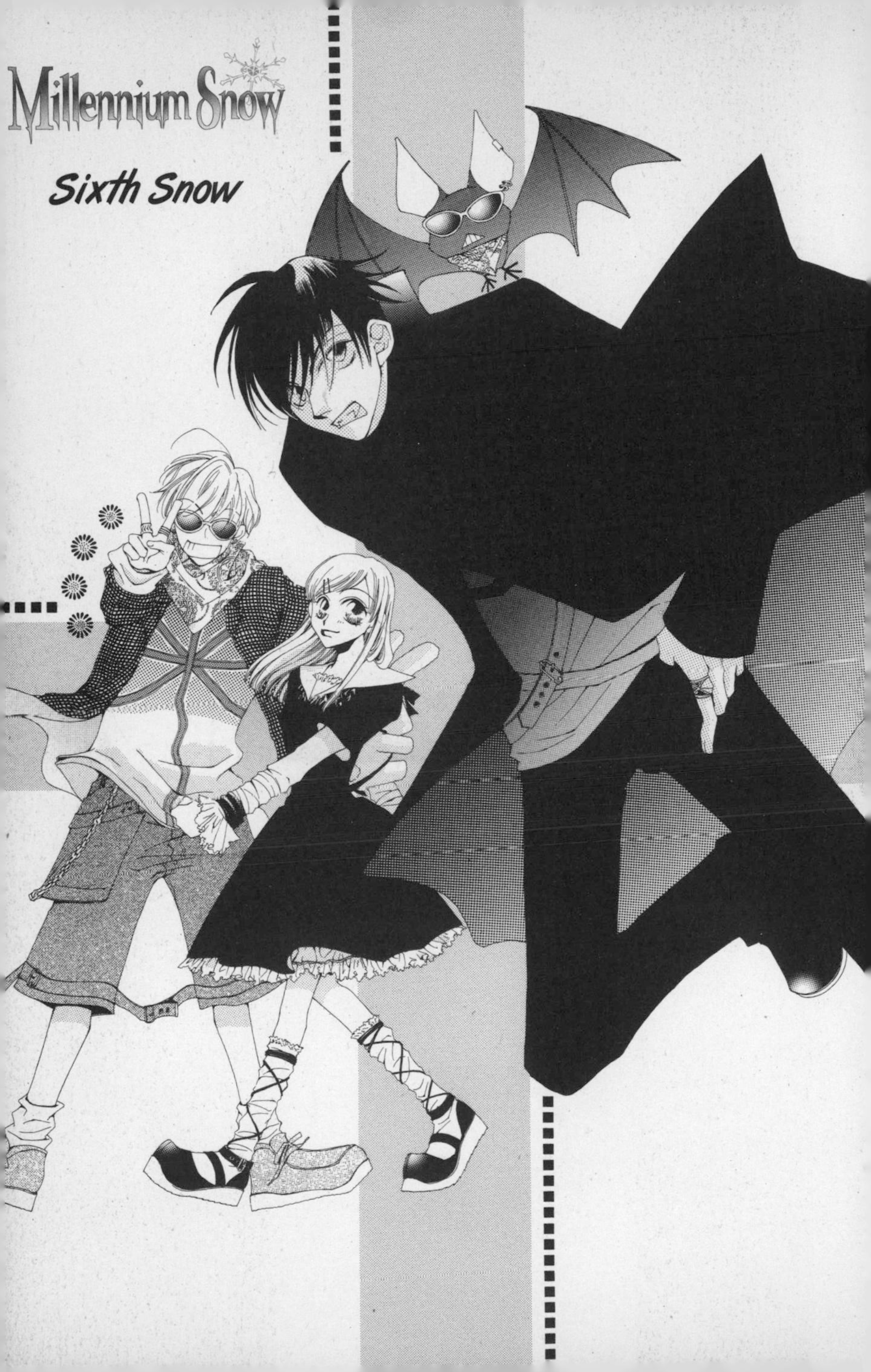
Millennium Snow
Sixth Snow

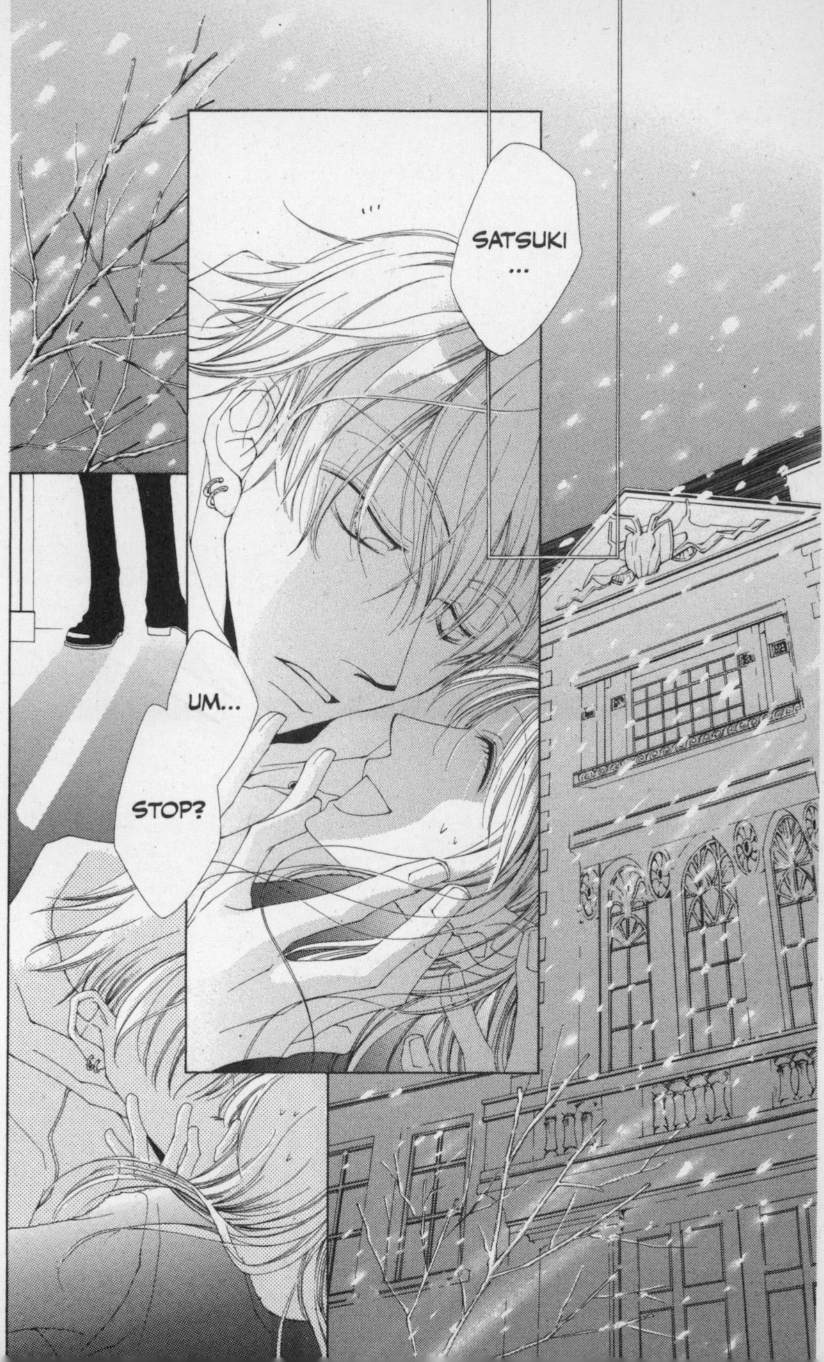
SATSUKI ...
UM...
STOP?

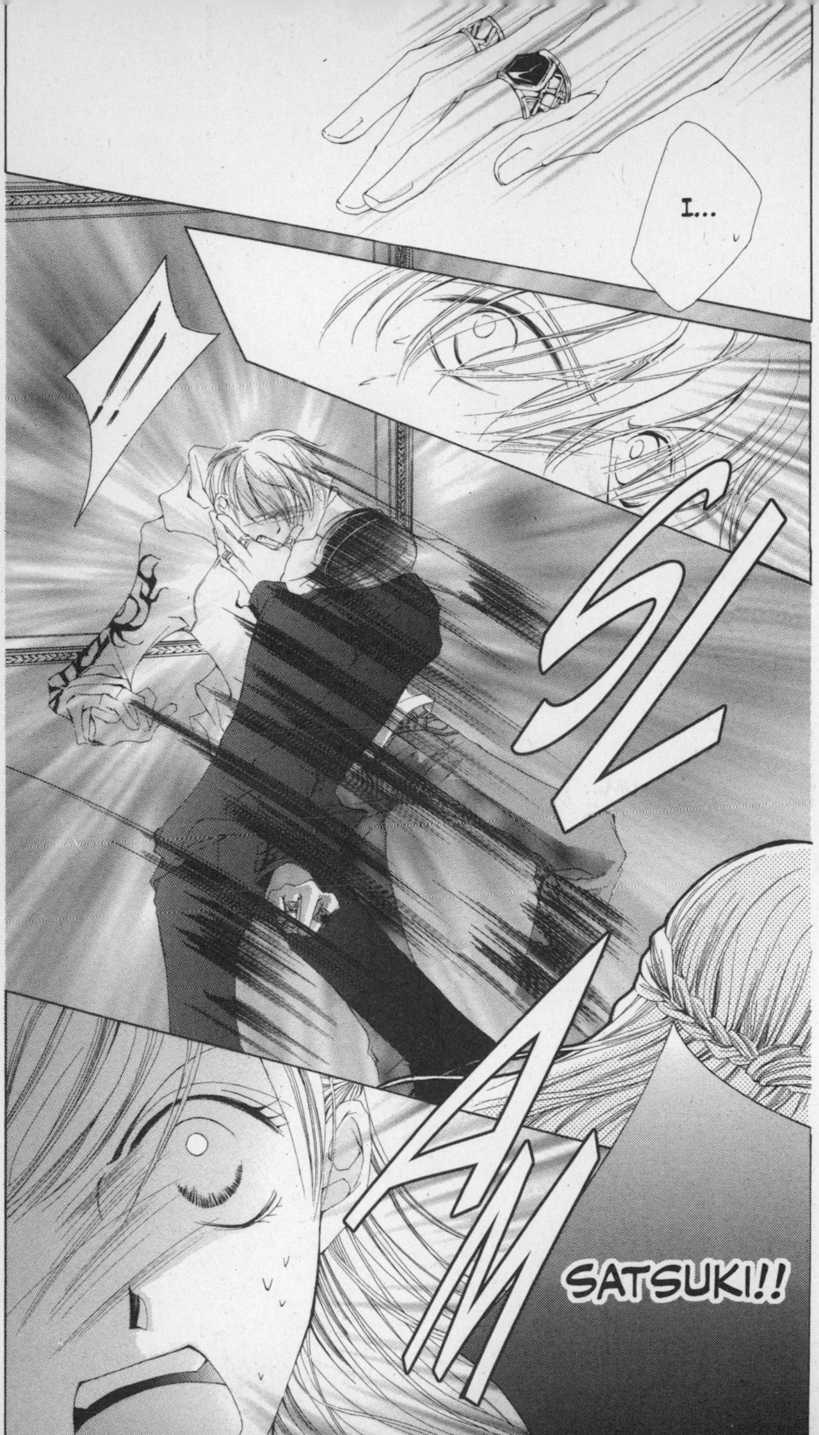
I...
SLAM
SATSUKI!!

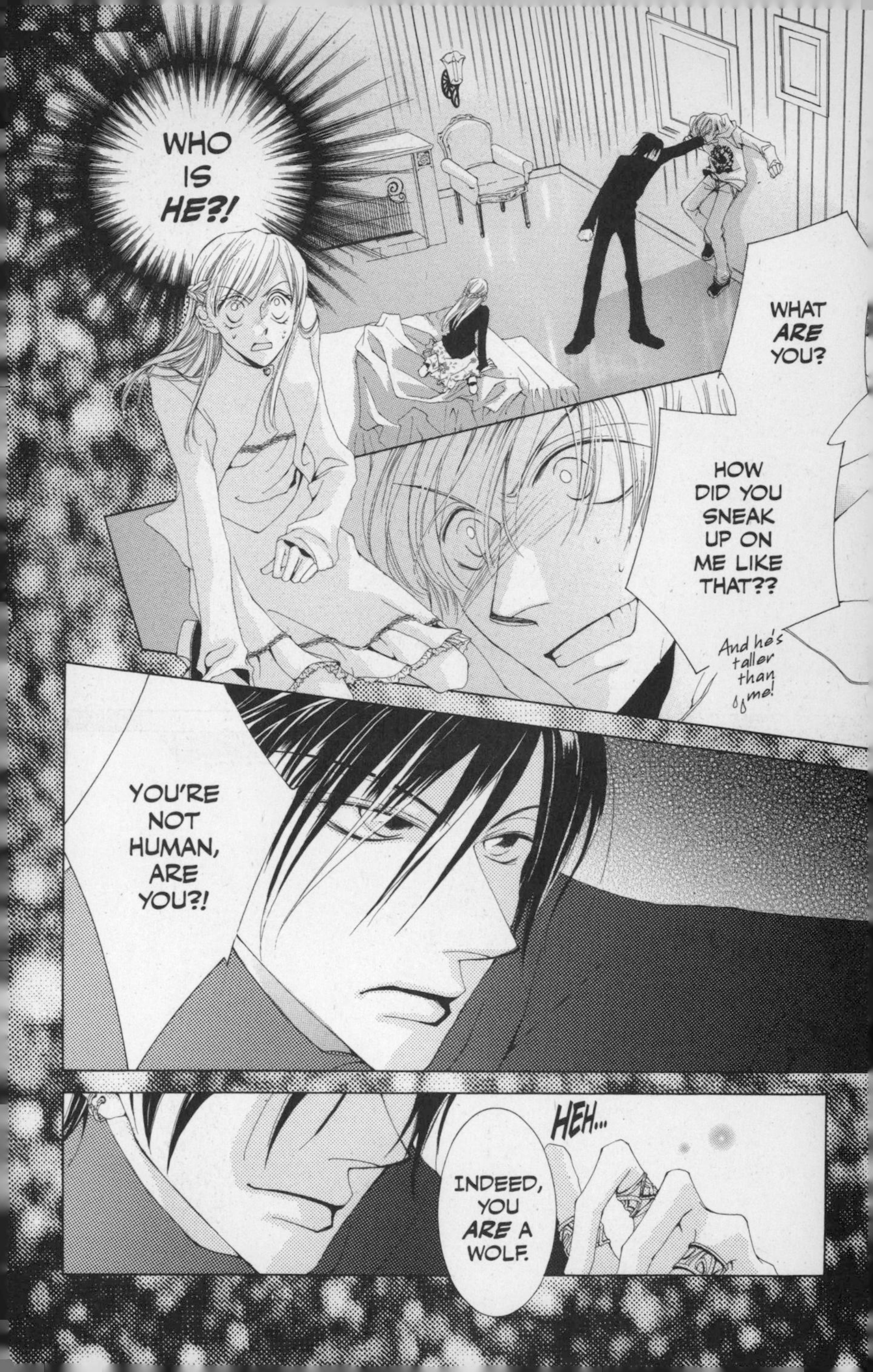
WHO IS HE?!
WHAT ARE YOU?
HOW DID YOU SNEAK UP ON ME LIKE THAT??
And he's taller than me!
YOU'RE NOT HUMAN, ARE YOU?!
HEH...
INDEED, YOU ARE A WOLF.

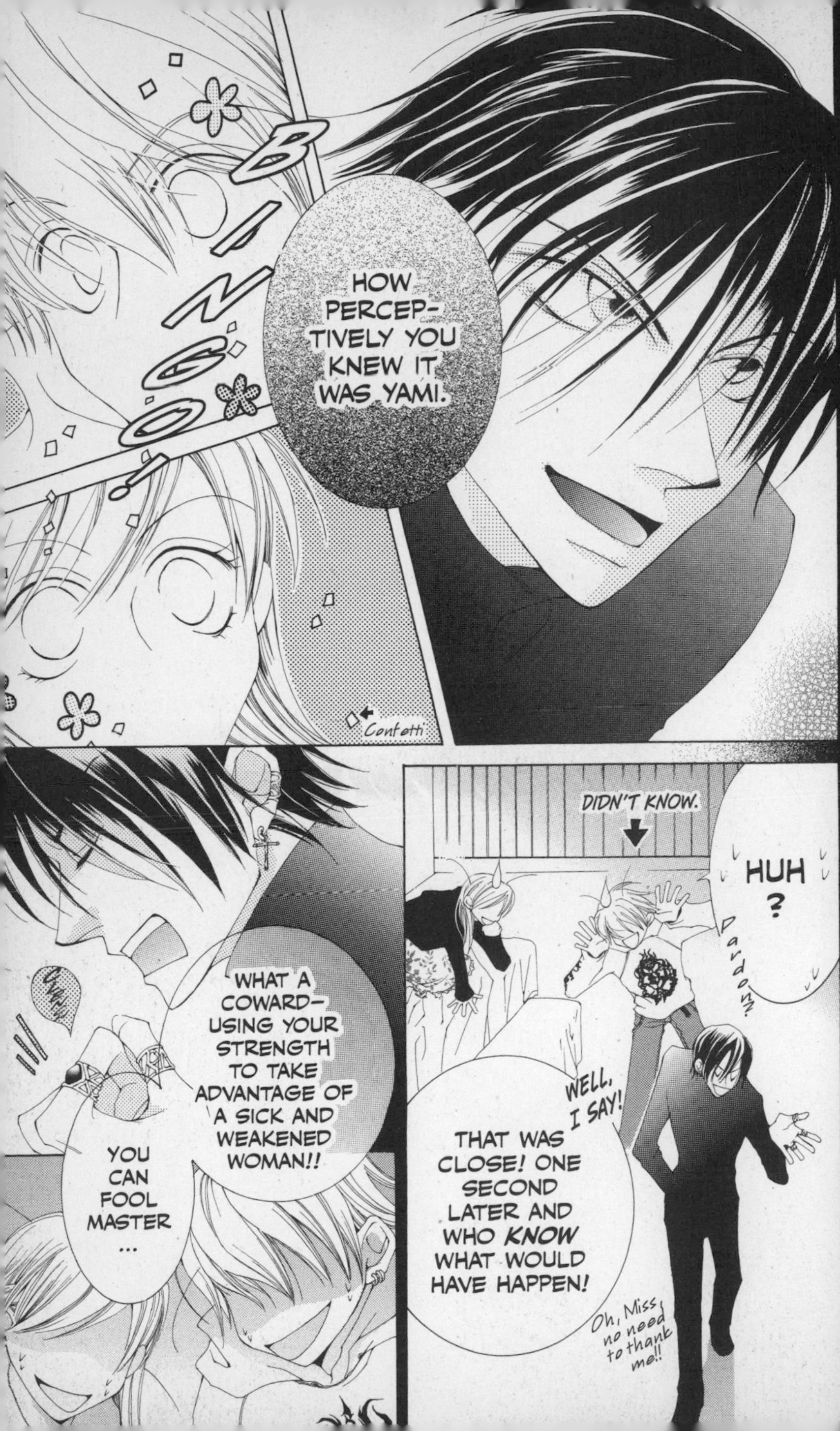
HOW PERCEPTIVELY YOU KNEW IT WAS YAMI.
BINGO!
Confetti
HUH?
Pardon?
DIDN'T KNOW.
WELL, I SAY!
THAT WAS CLOSE! ONE SECOND LATER AND WHO KNOW WHAT WOULD HAVE HAPPEN!
Oh, Miss, no need to thank me!!
WHAT A COWARD– USING YOUR STRENGTH TO TAKE ADVANTAGE OF A SICK AND WEAKENED WOMAN!!
YOU CAN FOOL MASTER ...

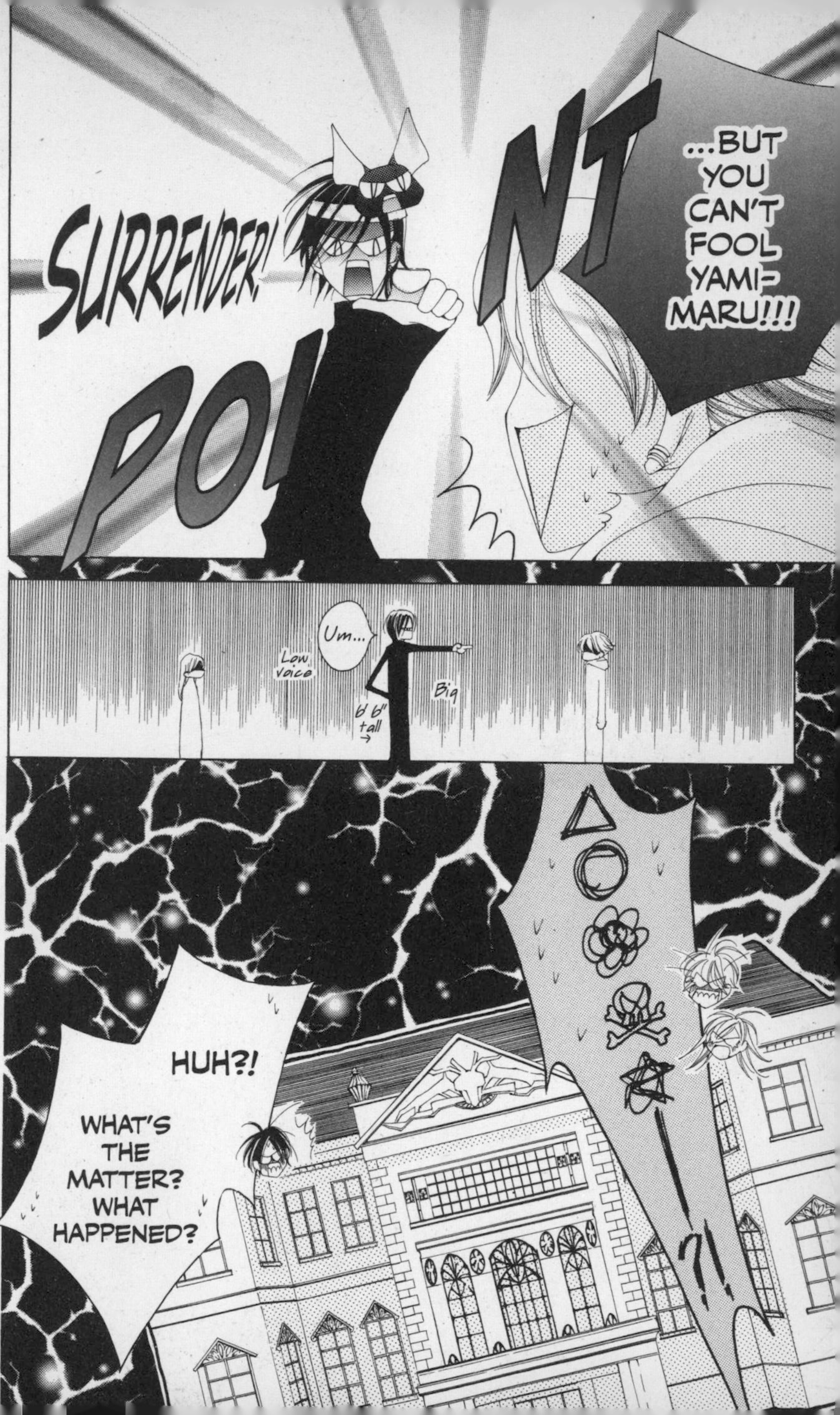
...BUT YOU CAN'T FOOL YAMI-MARU!!!
POINT
SURRENDER!
Um...
Low voice
Big
6'6" tall
?!
HUH?!
WHAT'S THE MATTER? WHAT HAPPENED?

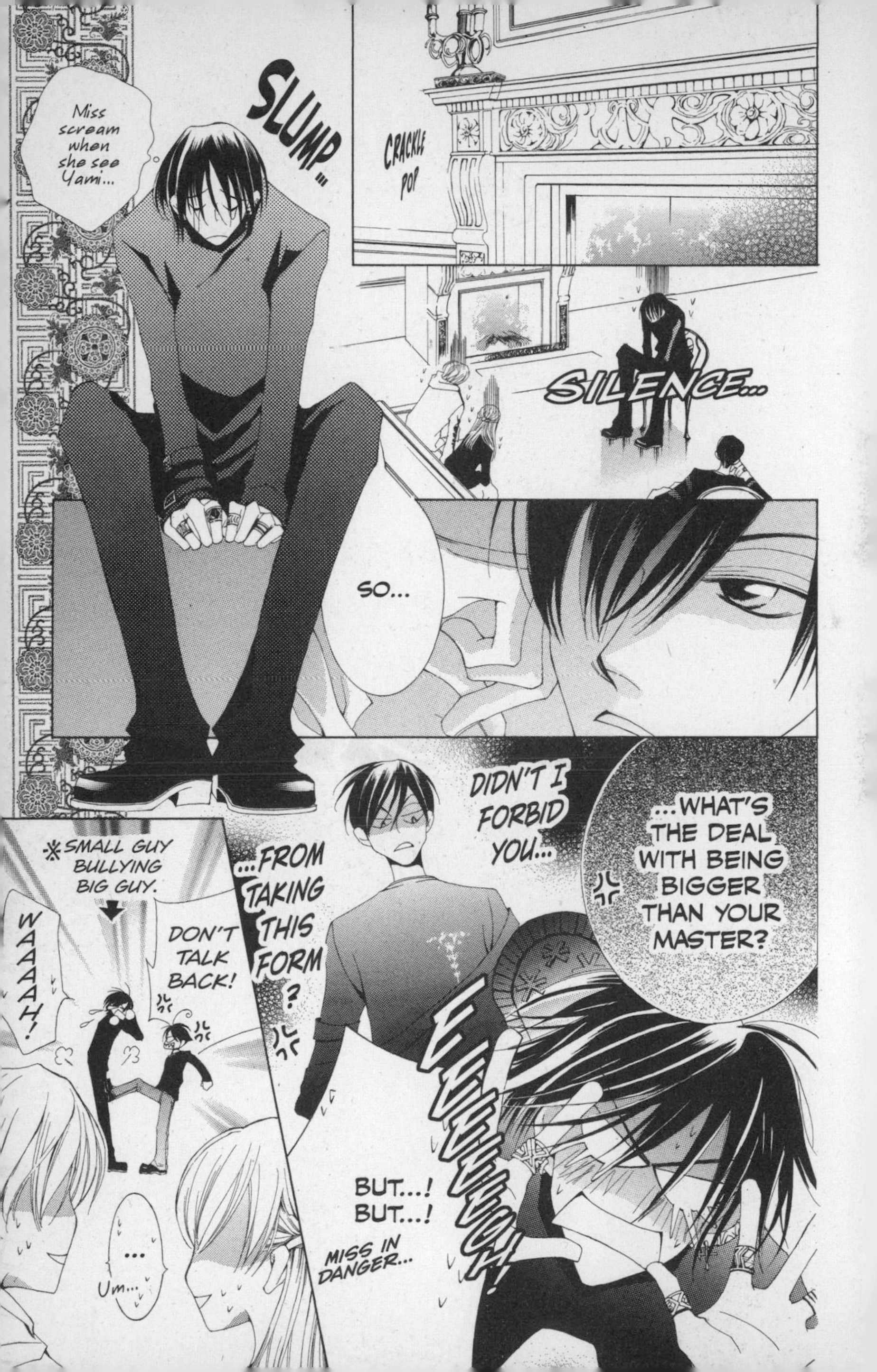
CRACKLE POP
SILENCE...
SO...
SLUMP...
Miss scream when she see Yami...
...WHAT'S THE DEAL WITH BEING BIGGER THAN YOUR MASTER?
DIDN'T I FORBID YOU...
...FROM TAKING THIS FORM?
BUT...! BUT...!
MISS IN DANGER...
※SMALL GUY BULLYING BIG GUY.
DON'T TALK BACK!
WAAAAAH!
...
Um...

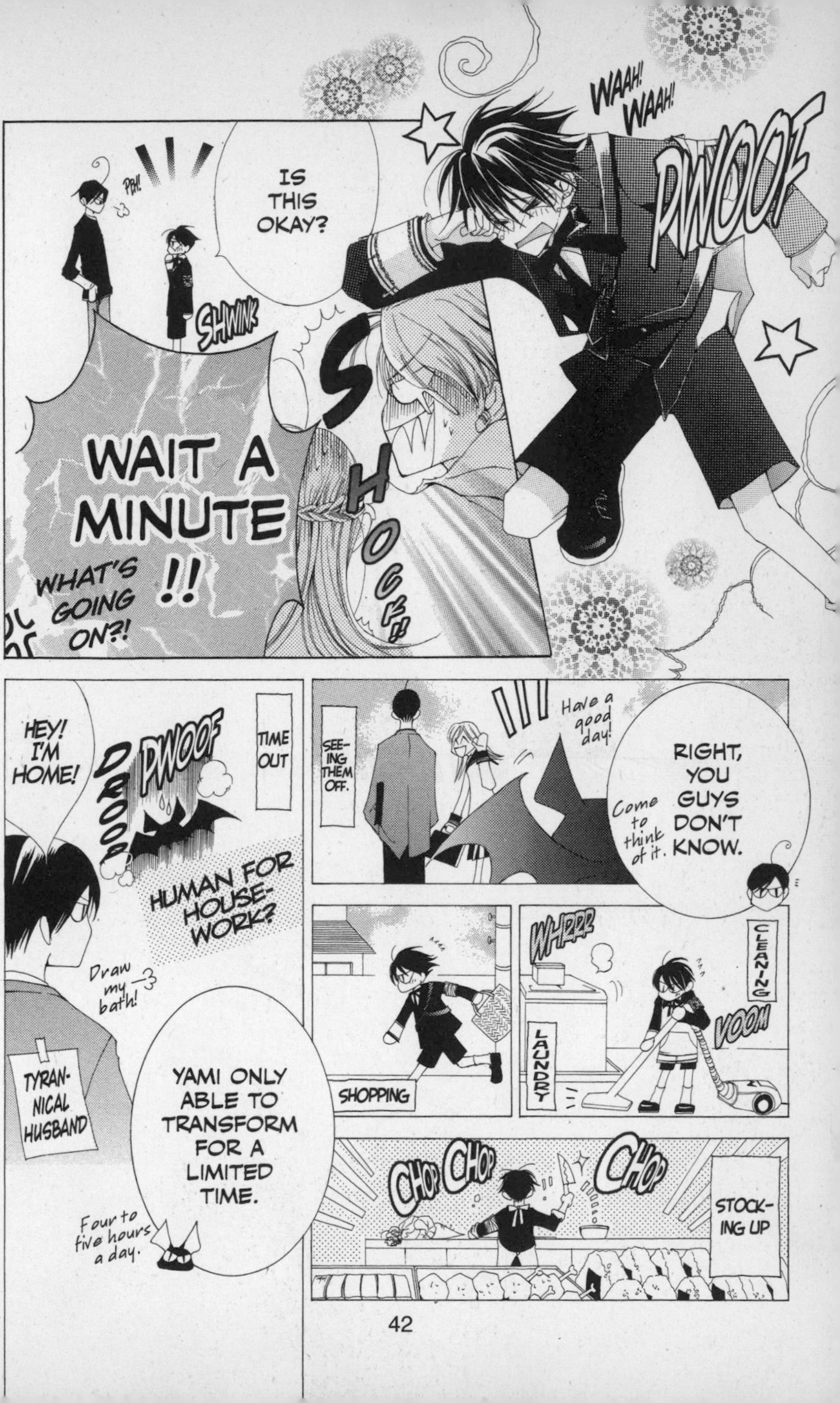
WAAH! WAAH!
PWOOF
IS THIS OKAY?
PBH!
SHWINK
SHOCK!!
WAIT A MINUTE !!
WHAT'S GOING ON?!
Have a good day!
RIGHT, YOU GUYS DON'T KNOW.
Come to think of it.
SEEING THEM OFF.
WHRRR
CLEANING
VOOM
LAUNDRY
SHOPPING
CHOP CHOP
CHOP
STOCKING UP
TIME OUT
HEY! I'M HOME!
PWOOF
DROOP
HUMAN FOR HOUSEWORK?
Draw my bath!
TYRANNICAL HUSBAND
YAMI ONLY ABLE TO TRANSFORM FOR A LIMITED TIME.
Four to five hours a day.

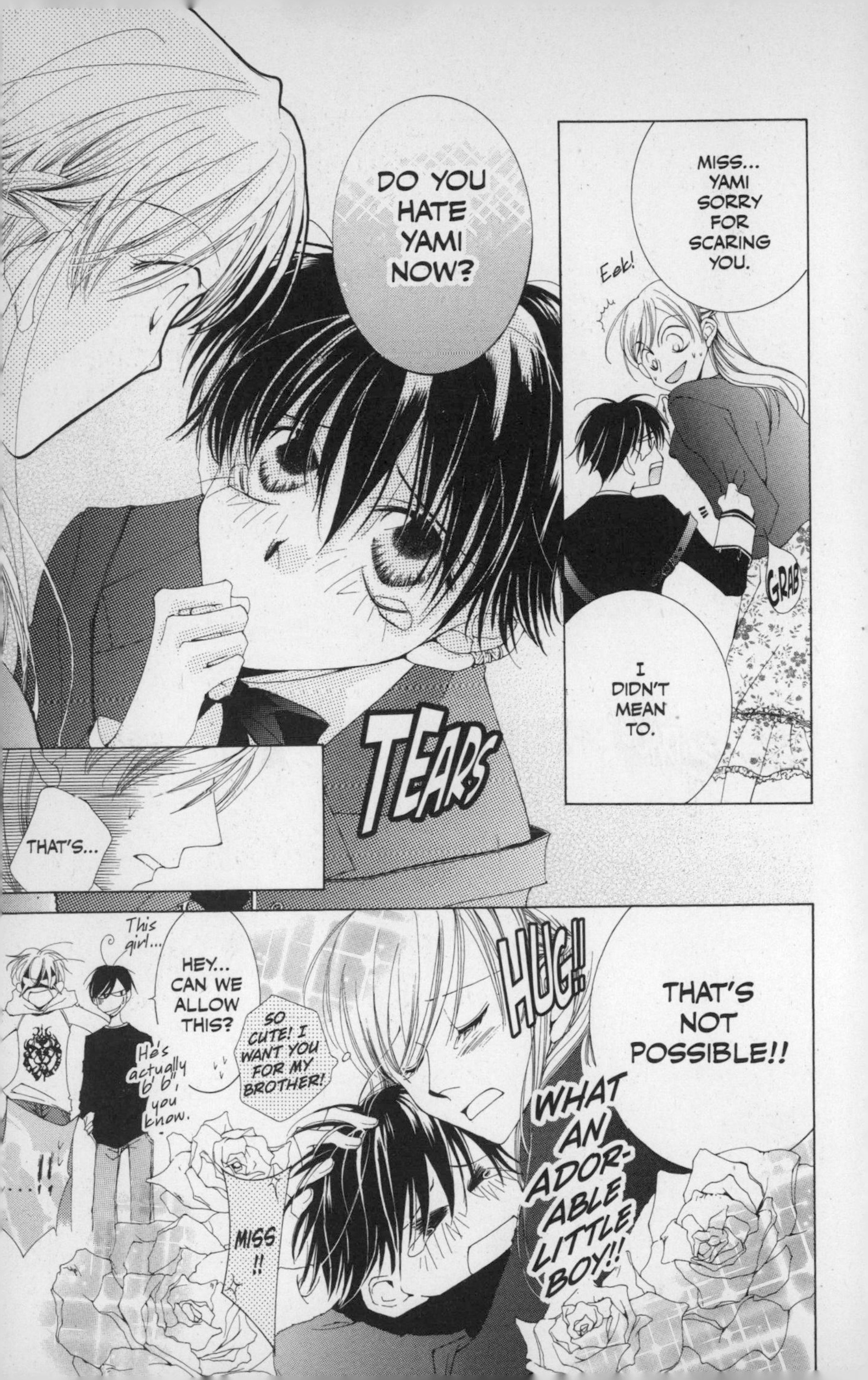
MISS... YAMI SORRY FOR SCARING YOU.
Eek!
GRAB
I DIDN'T MEAN TO.
DO YOU HATE YAMI NOW?
TEARS
THAT'S...
THAT'S NOT POSSIBLE!!
HUG!!
WHAT AN ADORABLE LITTLE BOY!!
MISS!!
SO CUTE! I WANT YOU FOR MY BROTHER!
HEY... CAN WE ALLOW THIS?
This girl...
He's actually 6'6", you know.

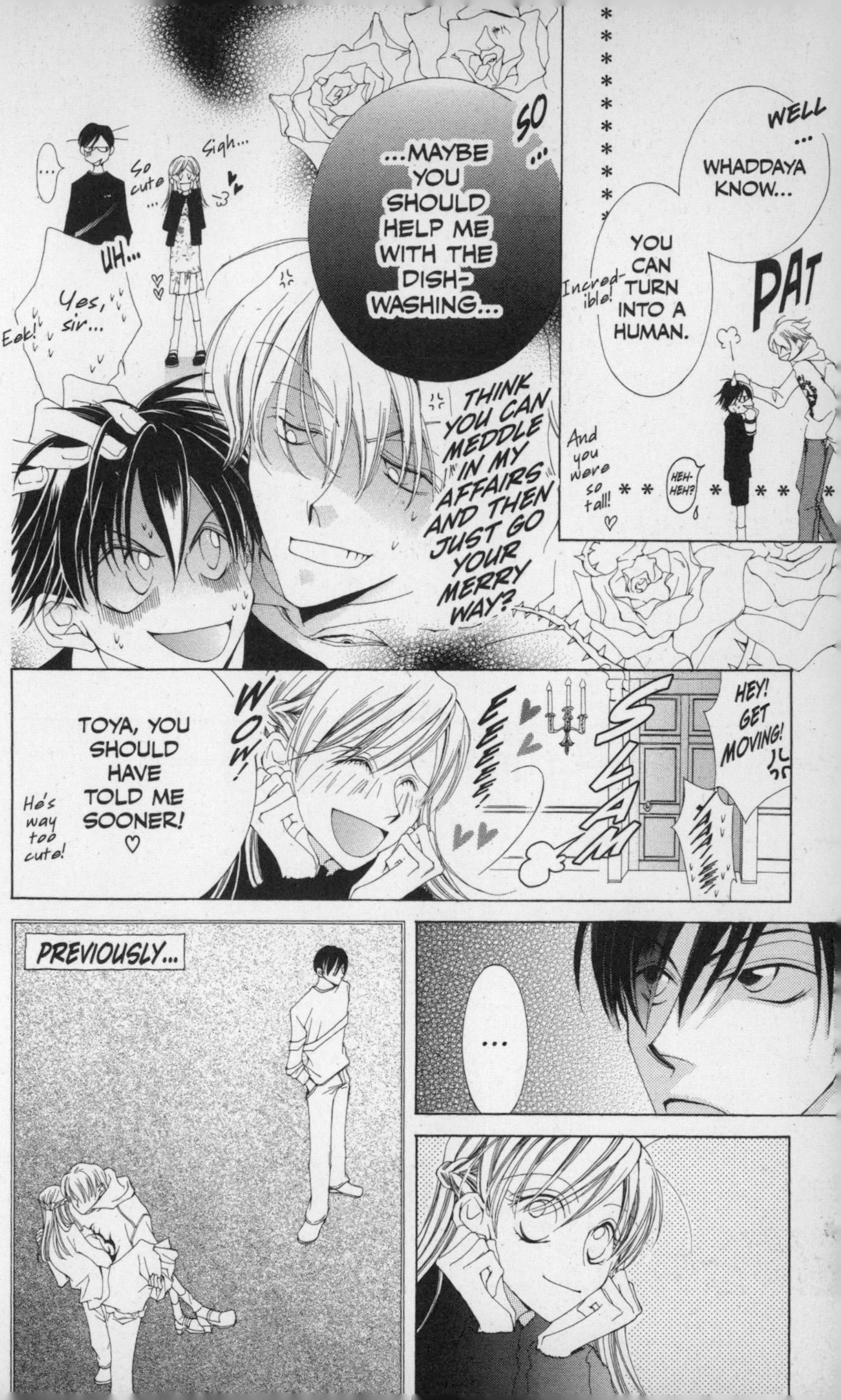
WELL ... WHADDAYA KNOW...
YOU CAN TURN INTO A HUMAN.
Incred-ible!
PAT
And you were so tall! ♡
HEH-HEH?
SO ...
...MAYBE YOU SHOULD HELP ME WITH THE DISH-WASHING...
THINK YOU CAN MEDDLE IN MY AFFAIRS AND THEN JUST GO YOUR MERRY WAY?
...
Sigh...
So cute ...
UH...
Yes, sir...
Eek!
HEY! GET MOVING!
SLAM
EEEEE!
WOW!
TOYA, YOU SHOULD HAVE TOLD ME SOONER! ♡
He's way too cute!
...
PREVIOUSLY...

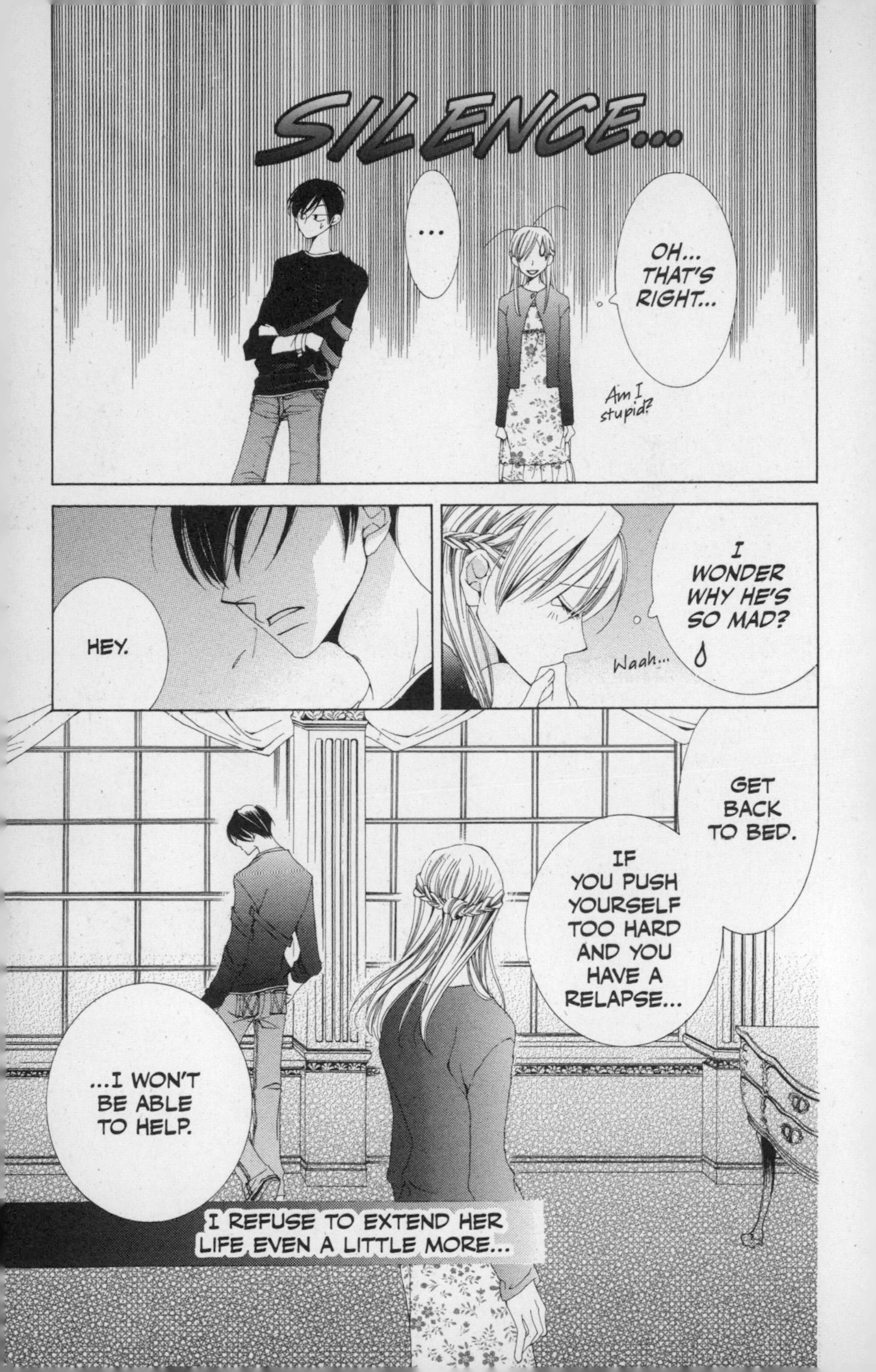
SILENCE...
OH... THAT'S RIGHT...
Am I stupid?
...
I WONDER WHY HE'S SO MAD?
Waah...
HEY.
GET BACK TO BED.
IF YOU PUSH YOURSELF TOO HARD AND YOU HAVE A RELAPSE...
...I WON'T BE ABLE TO HELP.
I REFUSE TO EXTEND HER LIFE EVEN A LITTLE MORE...

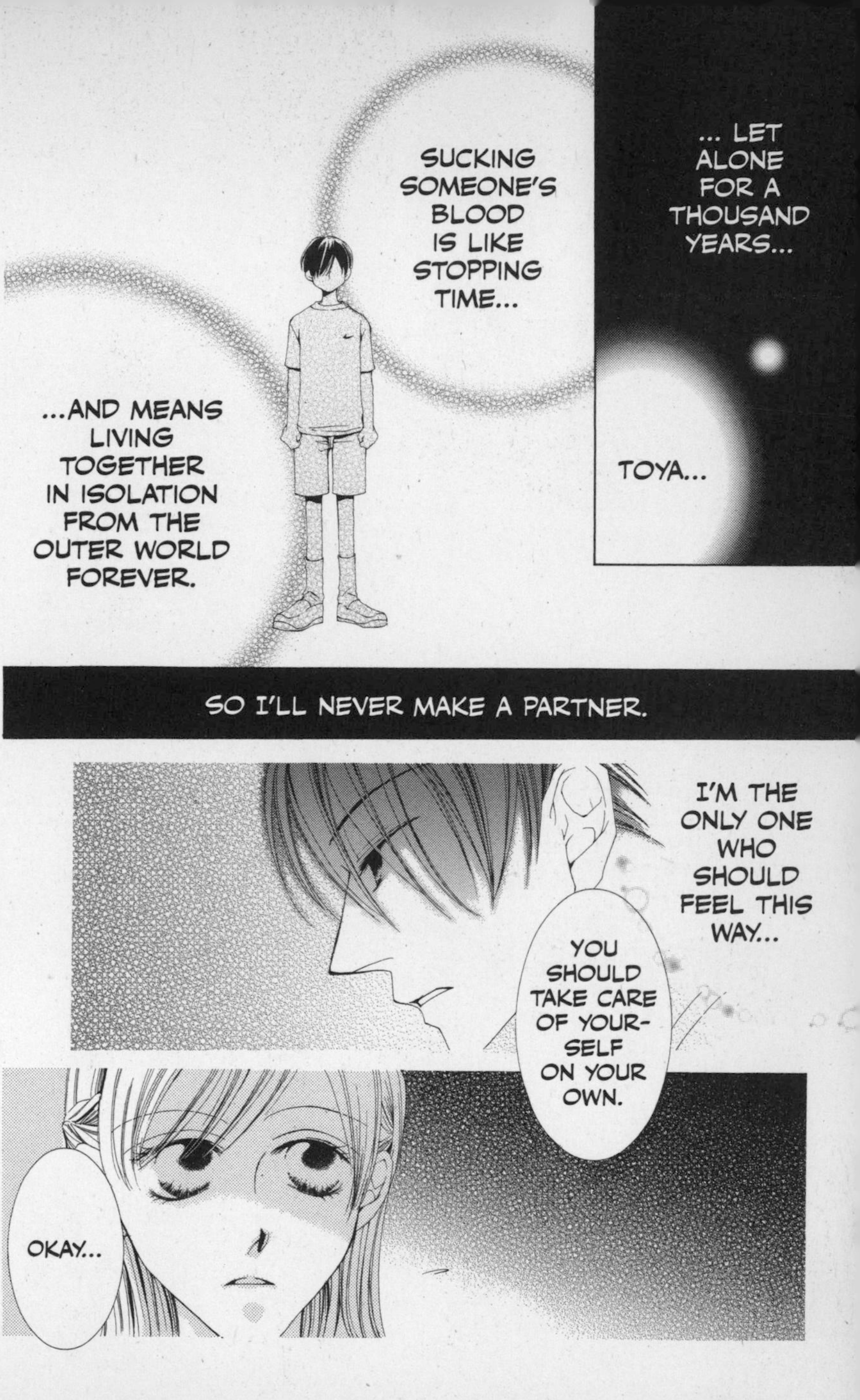
... LET ALONE FOR A THOUSAND YEARS...
TOYA...
SUCKING SOMEONE'S BLOOD IS LIKE STOPPING TIME...
...AND MEANS LIVING TOGETHER IN ISOLATION FROM THE OUTER WORLD FOREVER.
SO I'LL NEVER MAKE A PARTNER.
I'M THE ONLY ONE WHO SHOULD FEEL THIS WAY...
YOU SHOULD TAKE CARE OF YOUR-SELF ON YOUR OWN.
OKAY...

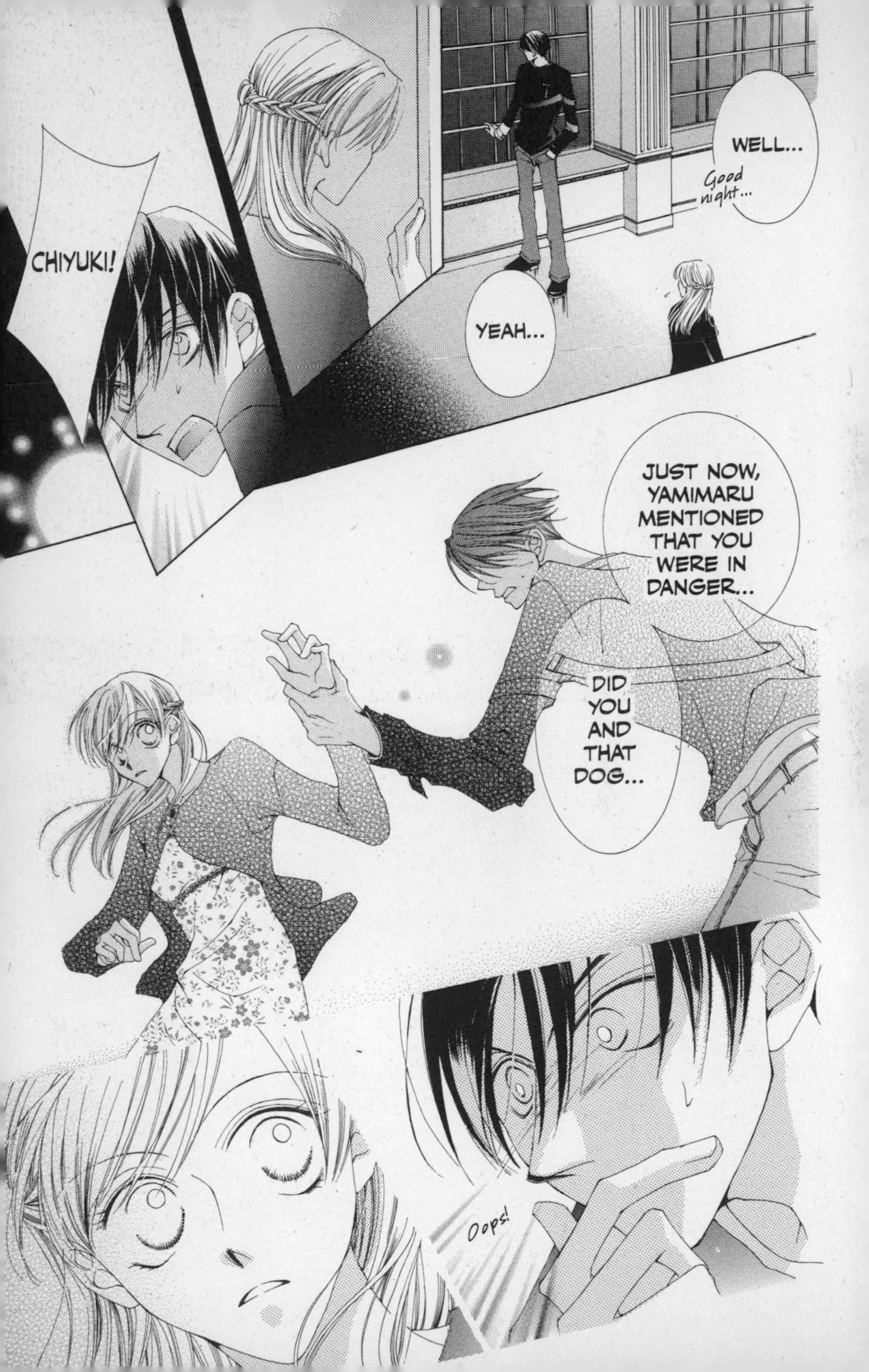
WELL...
Good night...
YEAH...
CHIYUKI!
JUST NOW, YAMIMARU MENTIONED THAT YOU WERE IN DANGER...
DID YOU AND THAT DOG...
Oops!

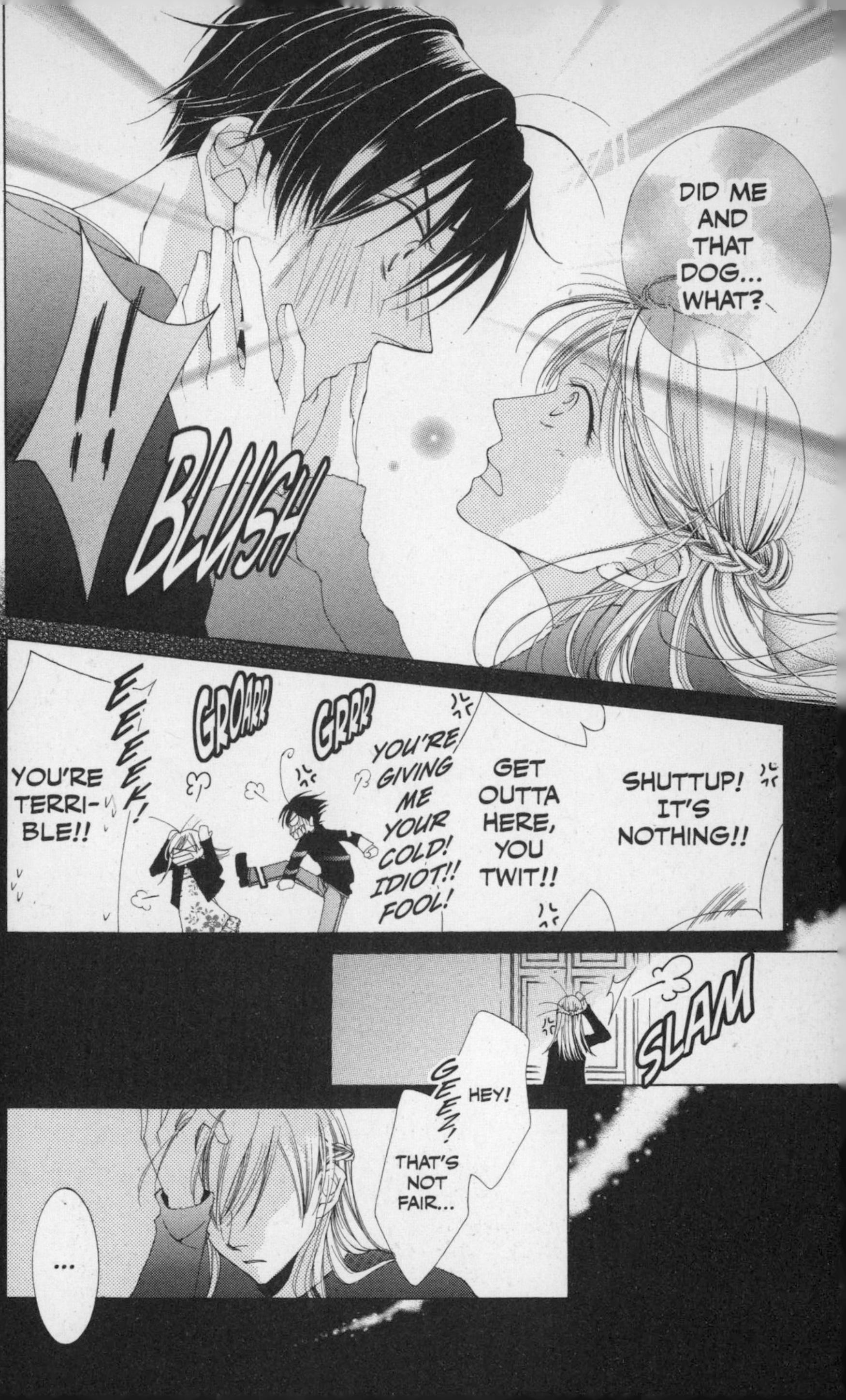
DID ME AND THAT DOG... WHAT?
!!
BLUSH
SHUTTUP! IT'S NOTHING!!
GET OUTTA HERE, YOU TWIT!!
YOU'RE GIVING ME YOUR COLD! IDIOT!! FOOL!
GRRR
GROARR
EEEEK!
YOU'RE TERRI-BLE!!
SLAM
HEY!
GEEZ!
THAT'S NOT FAIR...
...

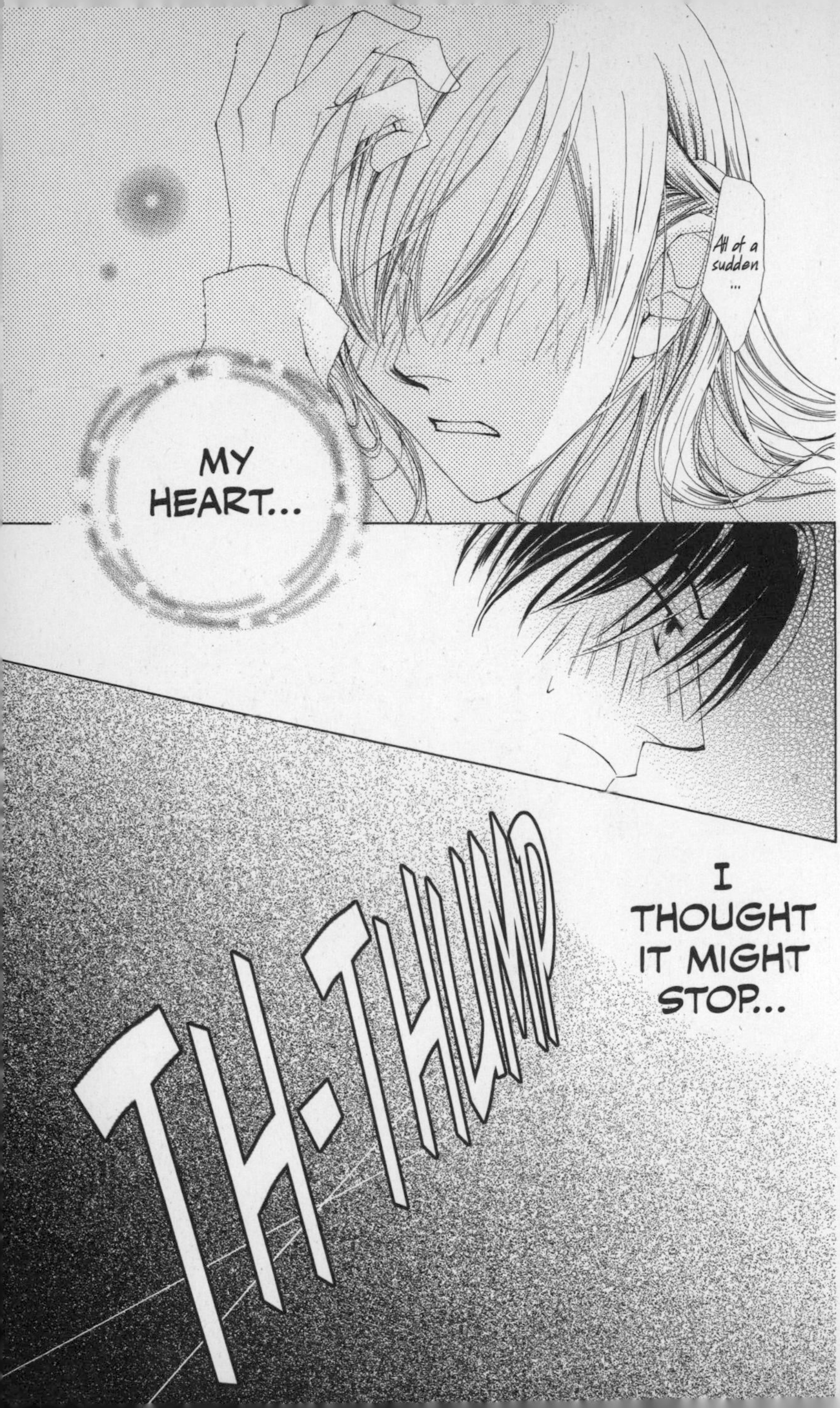
All of a sudden ...
MY HEART...
I THOUGHT IT MIGHT STOP...
TH-THUMP

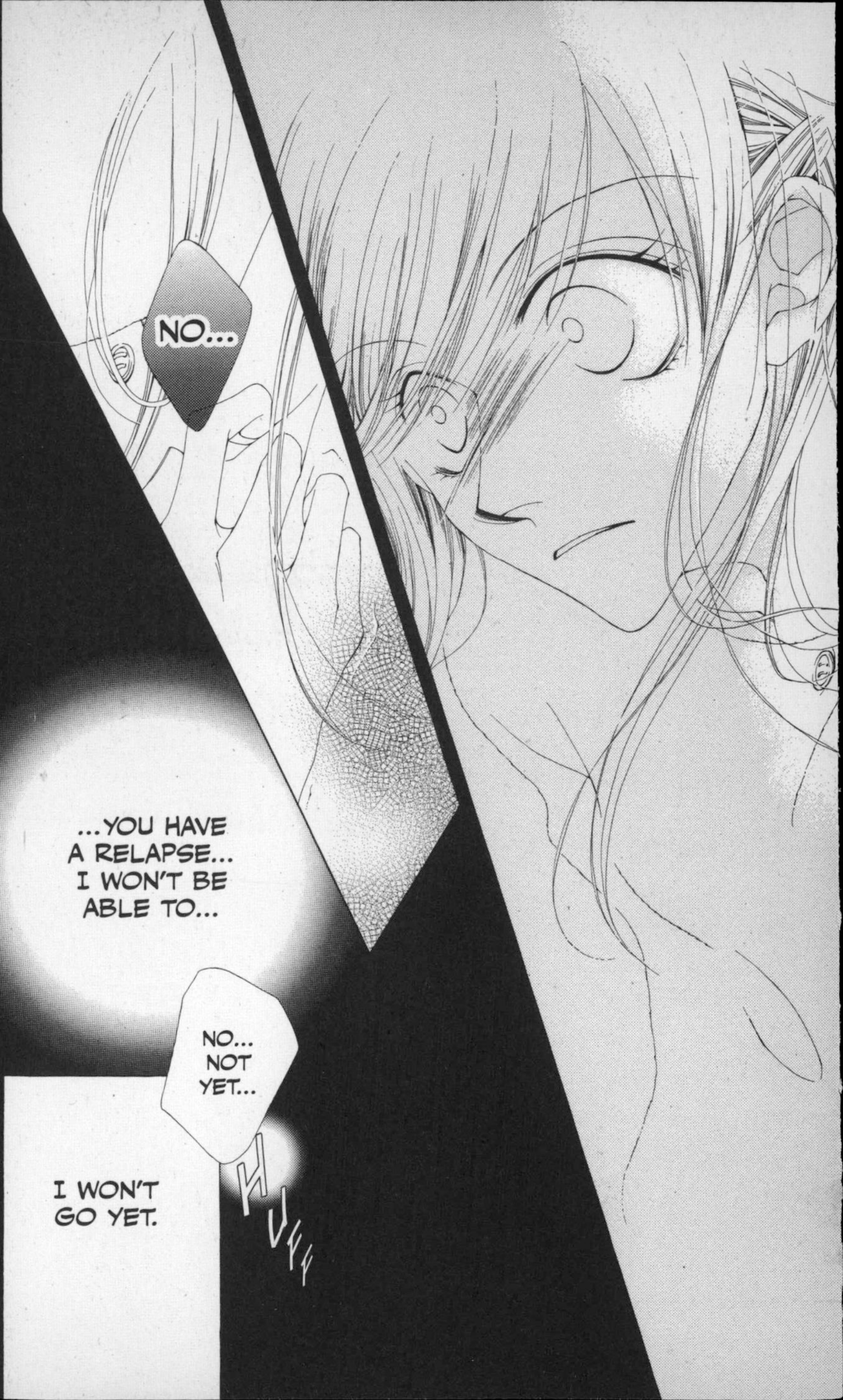
NO...
...YOU HAVE A RELAPSE... I WON'T BE ABLE TO...
NO... NOT YET...
HUFF
I WON'T GO YET.

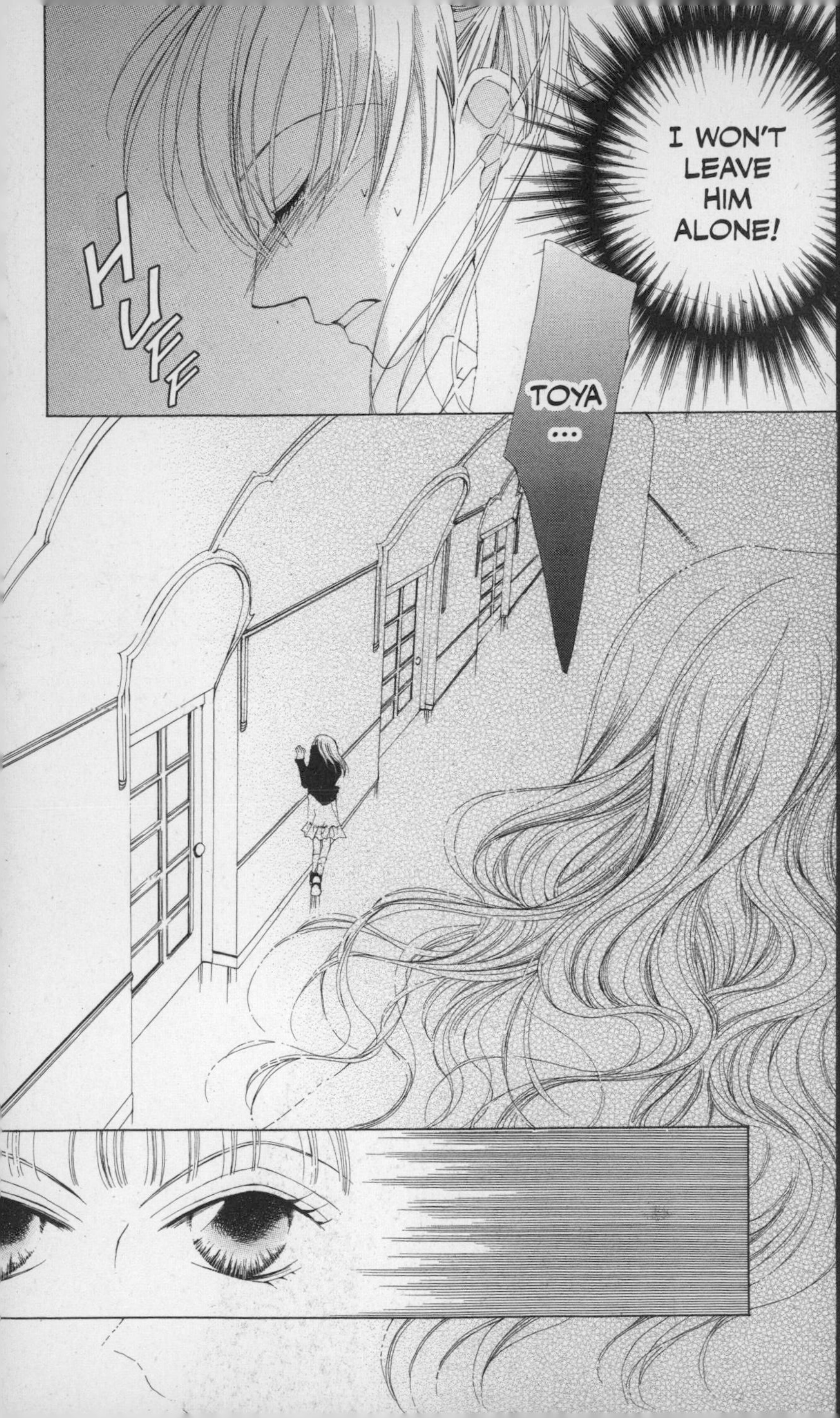
I WON'T LEAVE HIM ALONE!
HUFF
TOYA ...

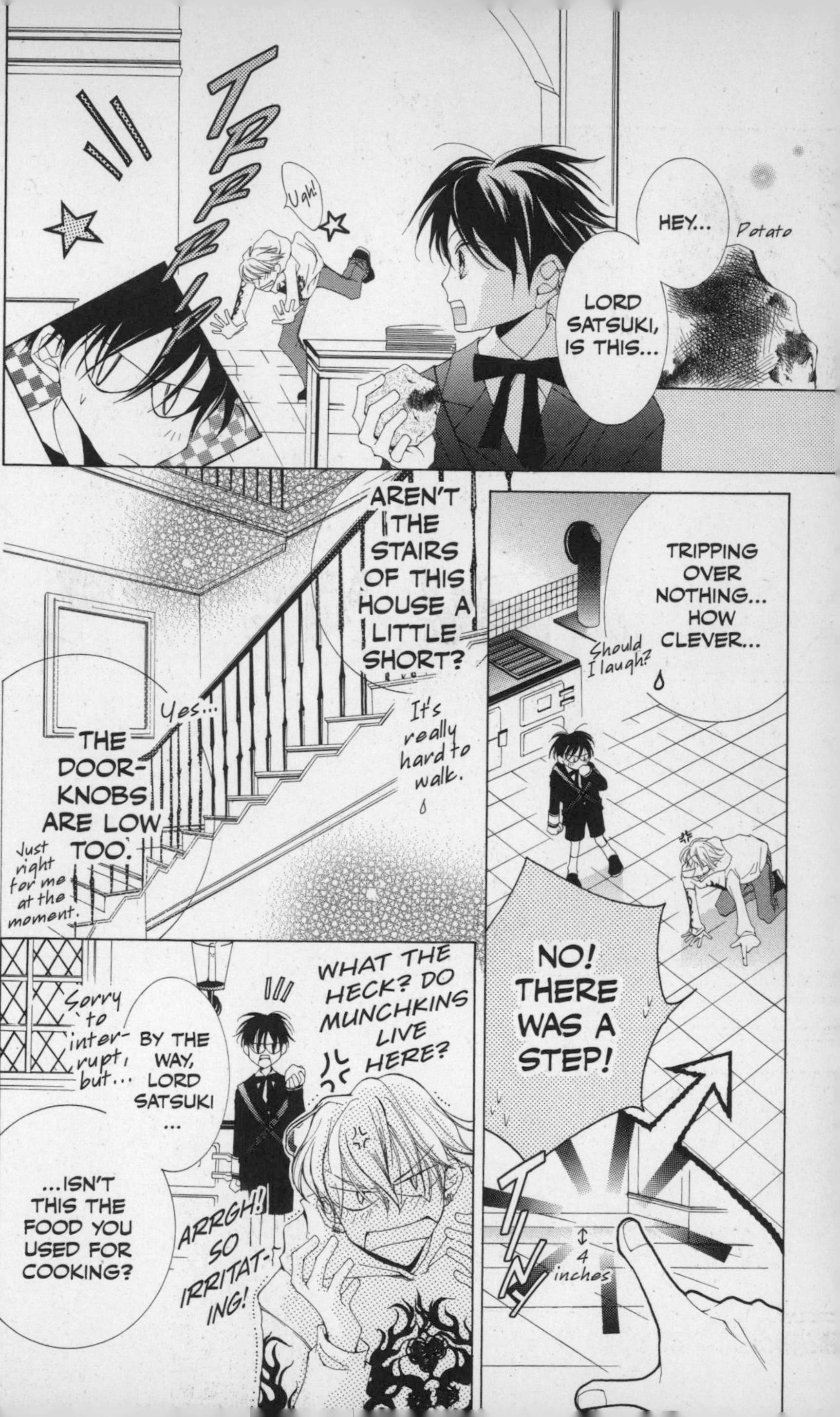
HEY...
LORD SATSUKI, IS THIS...
Potato
Ugh!
TRIPPING OVER NOTHING... HOW CLEVER...
Should I laugh?
AREN'T THE STAIRS OF THIS HOUSE A LITTLE SHORT?
It's really hard to walk.
Yes...
THE DOOR-KNOBS ARE LOW TOO.
Just right for me at the moment.
NO! THERE WAS A STEP!
4 inches
WHAT THE HECK? DO MUNCHKINS LIVE HERE?
Sorry to interrupt, but...
BY THE WAY, LORD SATSUKI...
...ISN'T THIS THE FOOD YOU USED FOR COOKING?
ARRGH! SO IRRITAT-ING!

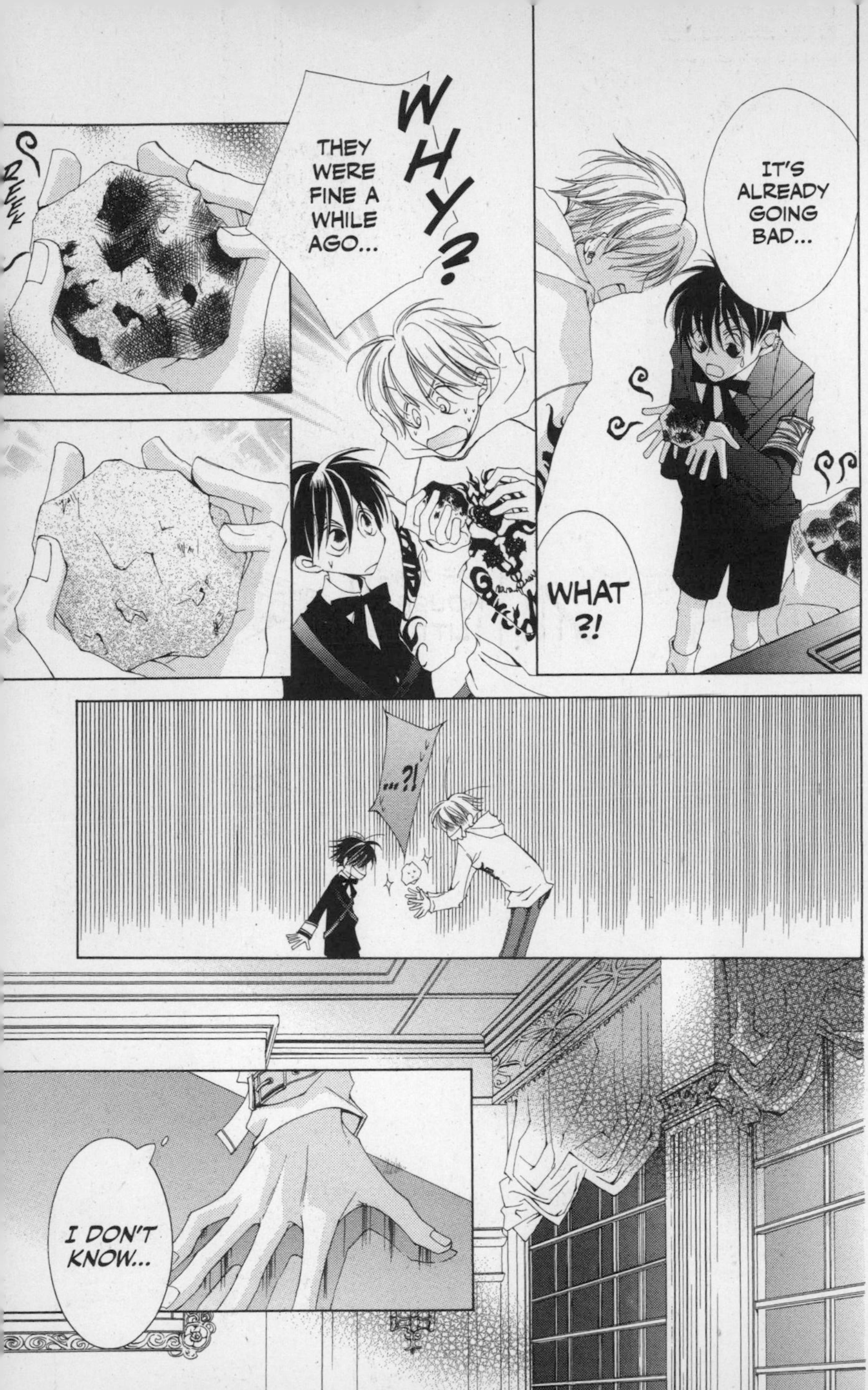
IT'S ALREADY GOING BAD...
WHAT?!
WHY?
THEY WERE FINE A WHILE AGO...
...?!
I DON'T KNOW...

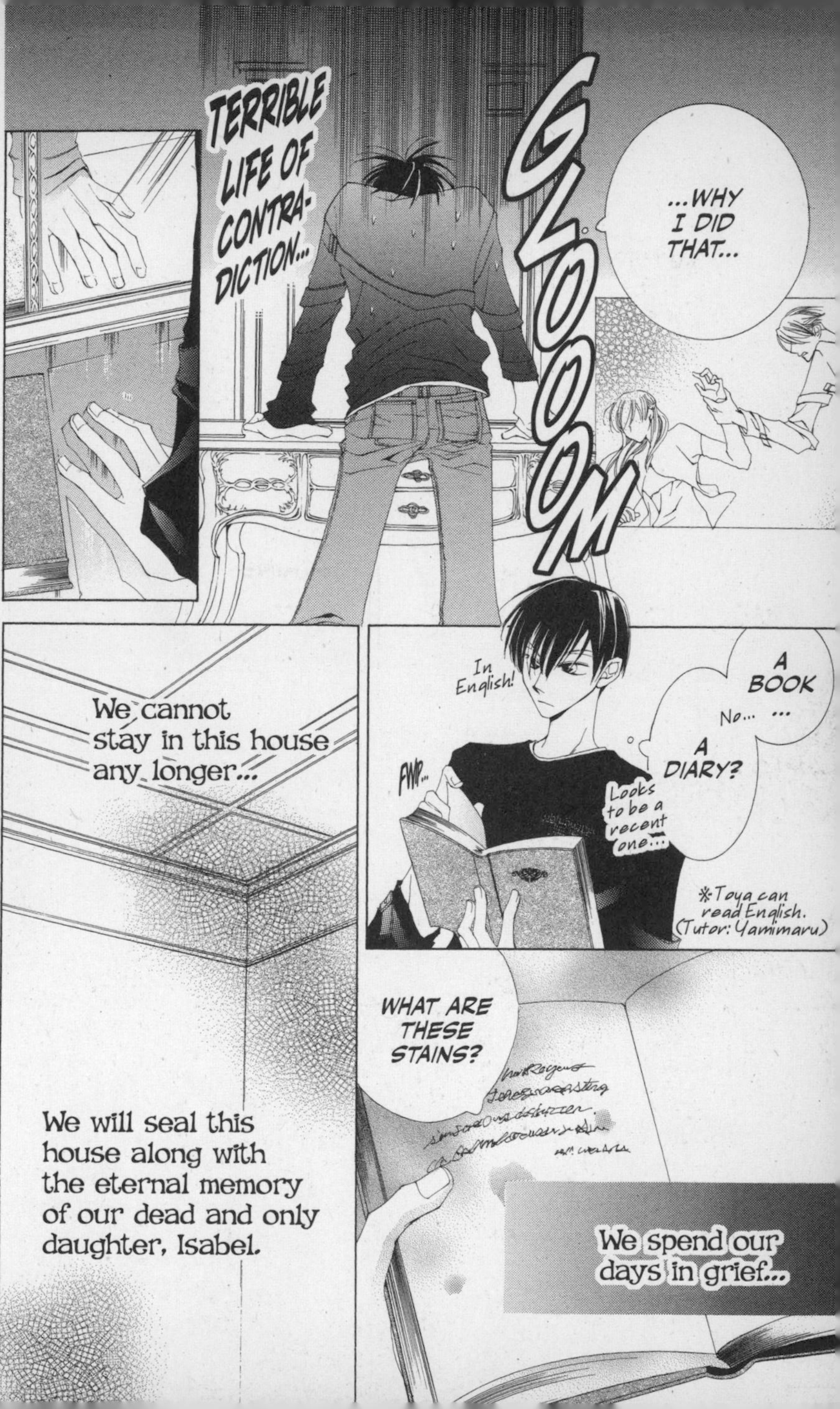
...WHY I DID THAT...
GLOOOOM
TERRIBLE LIFE OF CONTRA-DICTION...
A BOOK ... No... A DIARY?
In English!
FWP...
Looks to be a recent one...
※Toya can read English. (Tutor: Yamimaru)
WHAT ARE THESE STAINS?
We spend our days in grief...
We cannot stay in this house any longer...
We will seal this house along with the eternal memory of our dead and only daughter, Isabel.

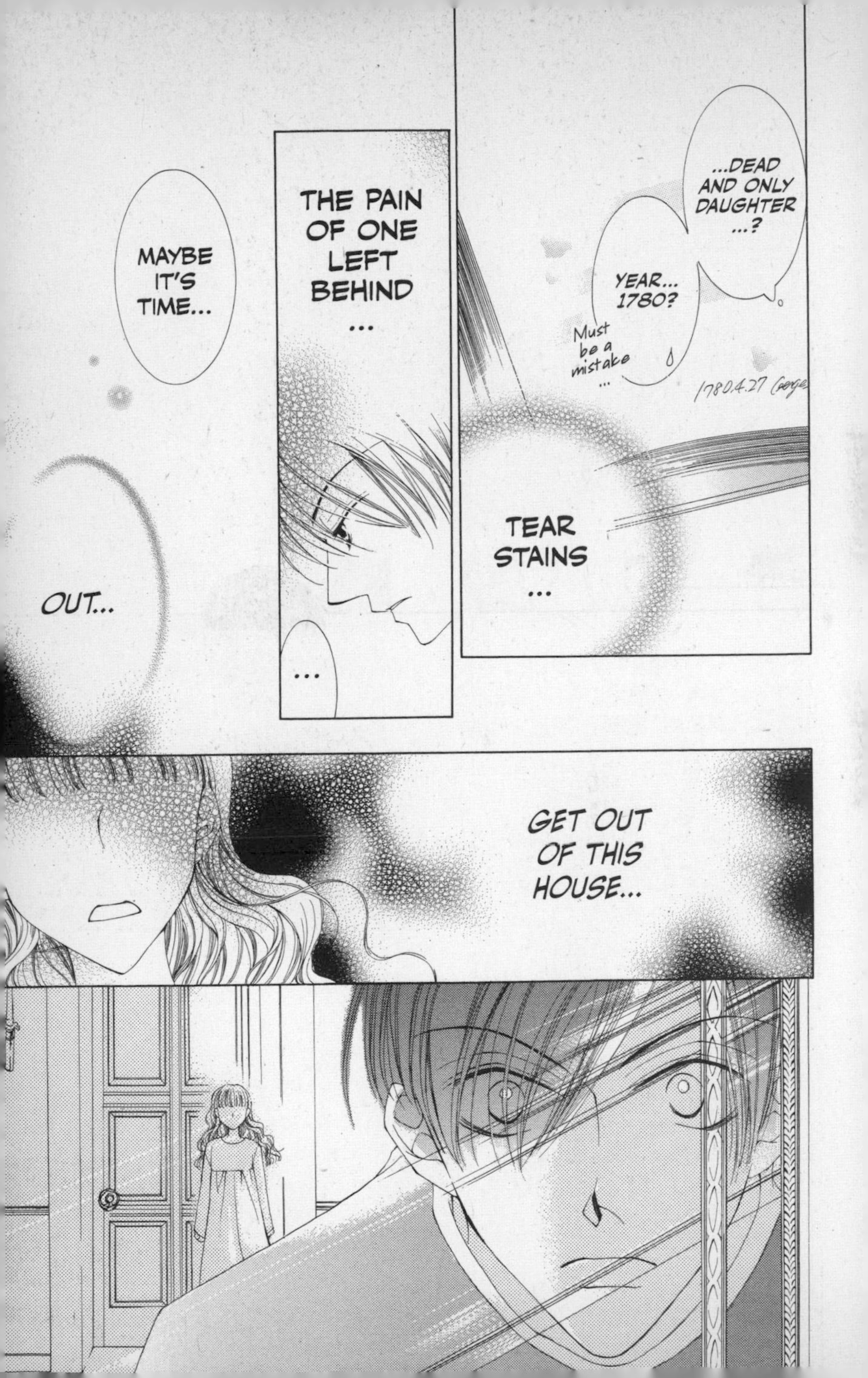
...DEAD AND ONLY DAUGHTER ...?
YEAR... 1780?
Must be a mistake ...
1780.4.27
TEAR STAINS ...
THE PAIN OF ONE LEFT BEHIND ...
...
MAYBE IT'S TIME...
OUT...
GET OUT OF THIS HOUSE...

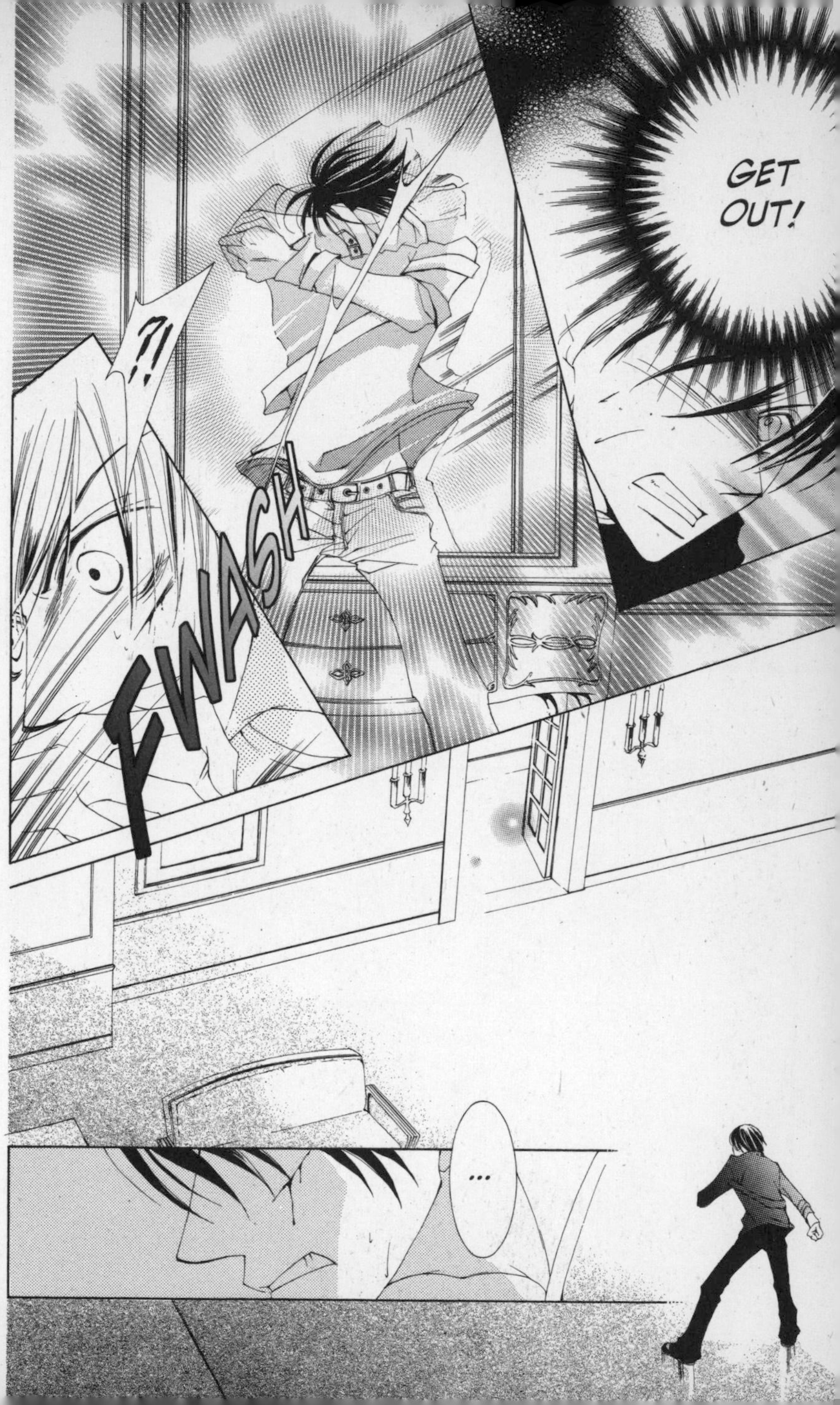
GET OUT!
?!
FWASH
...

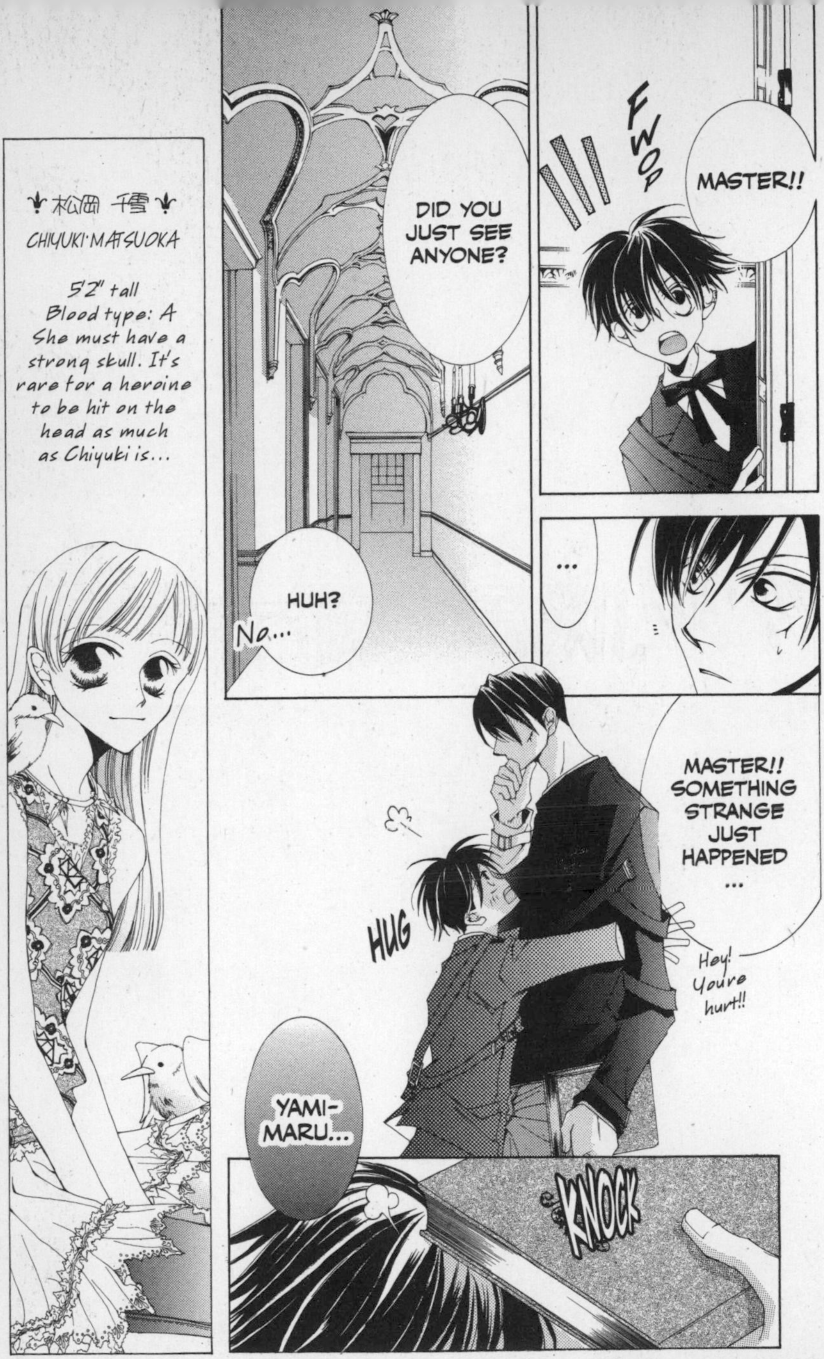
FWOP
MASTER!!
DID YOU JUST SEE ANYONE?
HUH?
No...
...
MASTER!! SOMETHING STRANGE JUST HAPPENED ...
HUG
Hey! You're hurt!!
YAMI-MARU...
KNOCK
松岡 千雪
CHIYUKI·MATSUOKA
5'2" tall
Blood type: A
She must have a strong skull. It's rare for a heroine to be hit on the head as much as Chiyuki is...

I HAVE A BAD FEELING ABOUT THIS.
INVESTI-GATE THE HOUSE.
ROGER!
THE PAIN... MY CHEST...

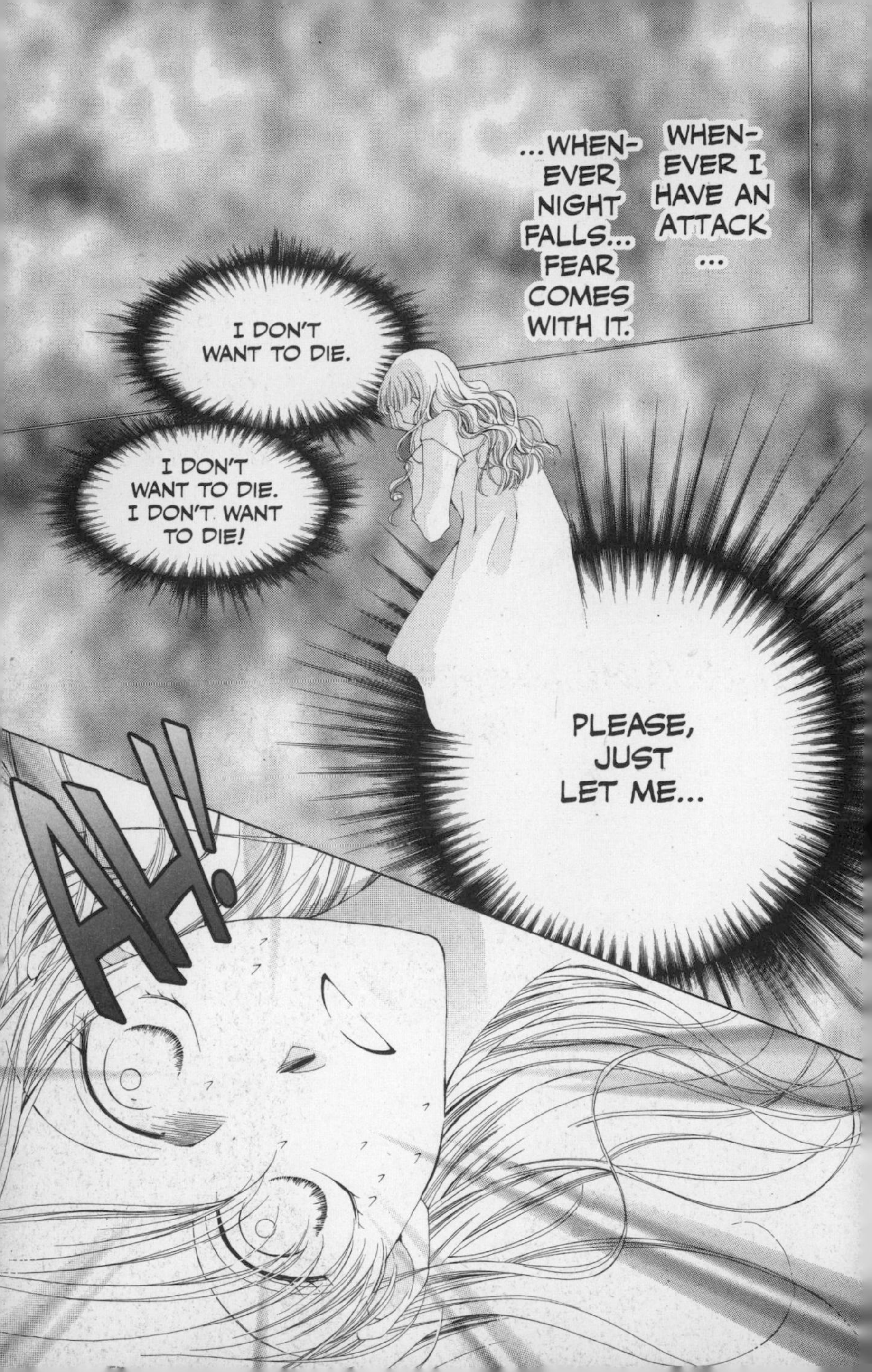
WHENEVER I HAVE AN ATTACK...
...WHENEVER NIGHT FALLS... FEAR COMES WITH IT.
I DON'T WANT TO DIE.
I DON'T WANT TO DIE. I DON'T WANT TO DIE!
PLEASE, JUST LET ME...
AH!!

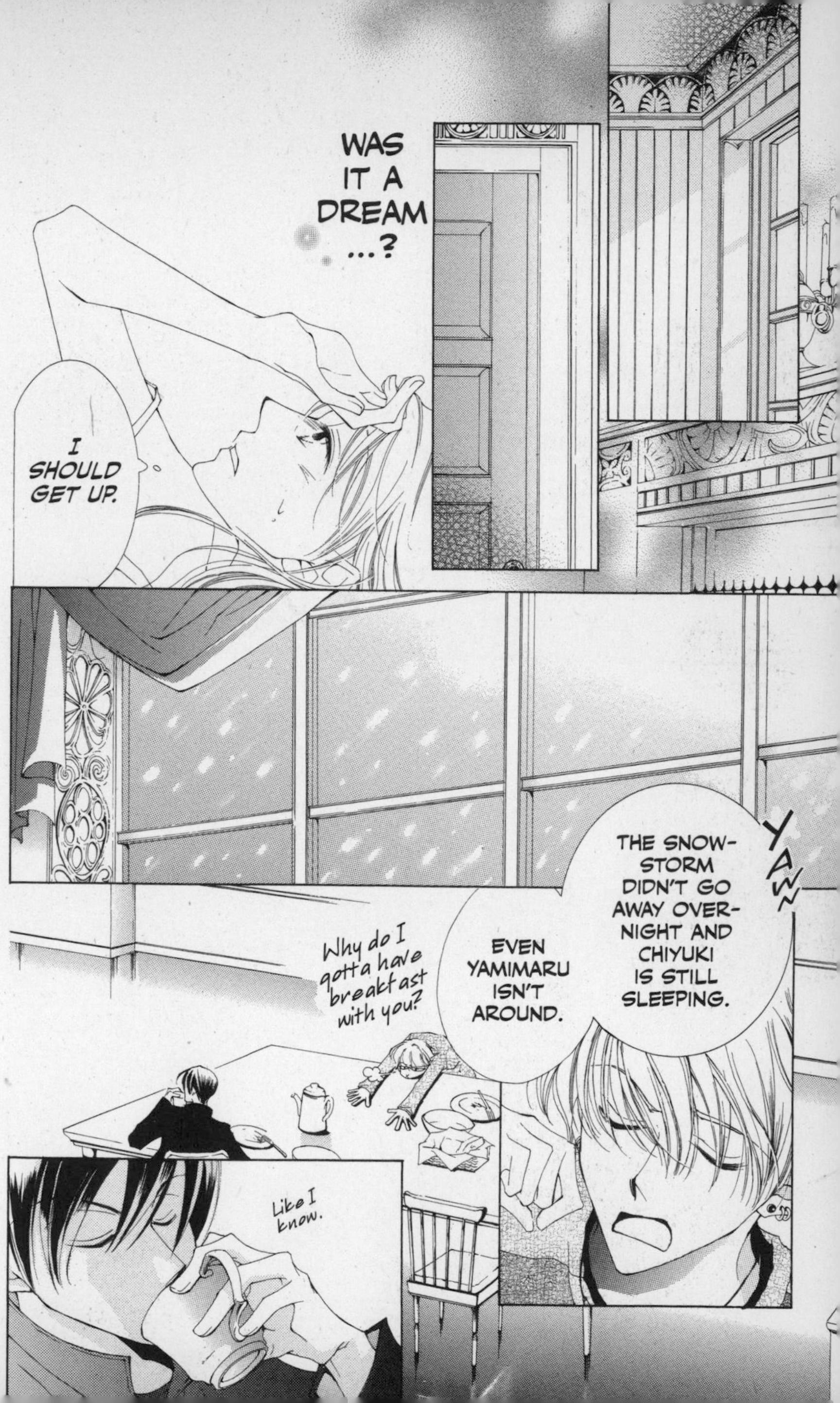
WAS IT A DREAM ...?
I SHOULD GET UP.
YAWN
THE SNOW-STORM DIDN'T GO AWAY OVER-NIGHT AND CHIYUKI IS STILL SLEEPING.
EVEN YAMIMARU ISN'T AROUND.
Why do I gotta have breakfast with you?
Like I know.

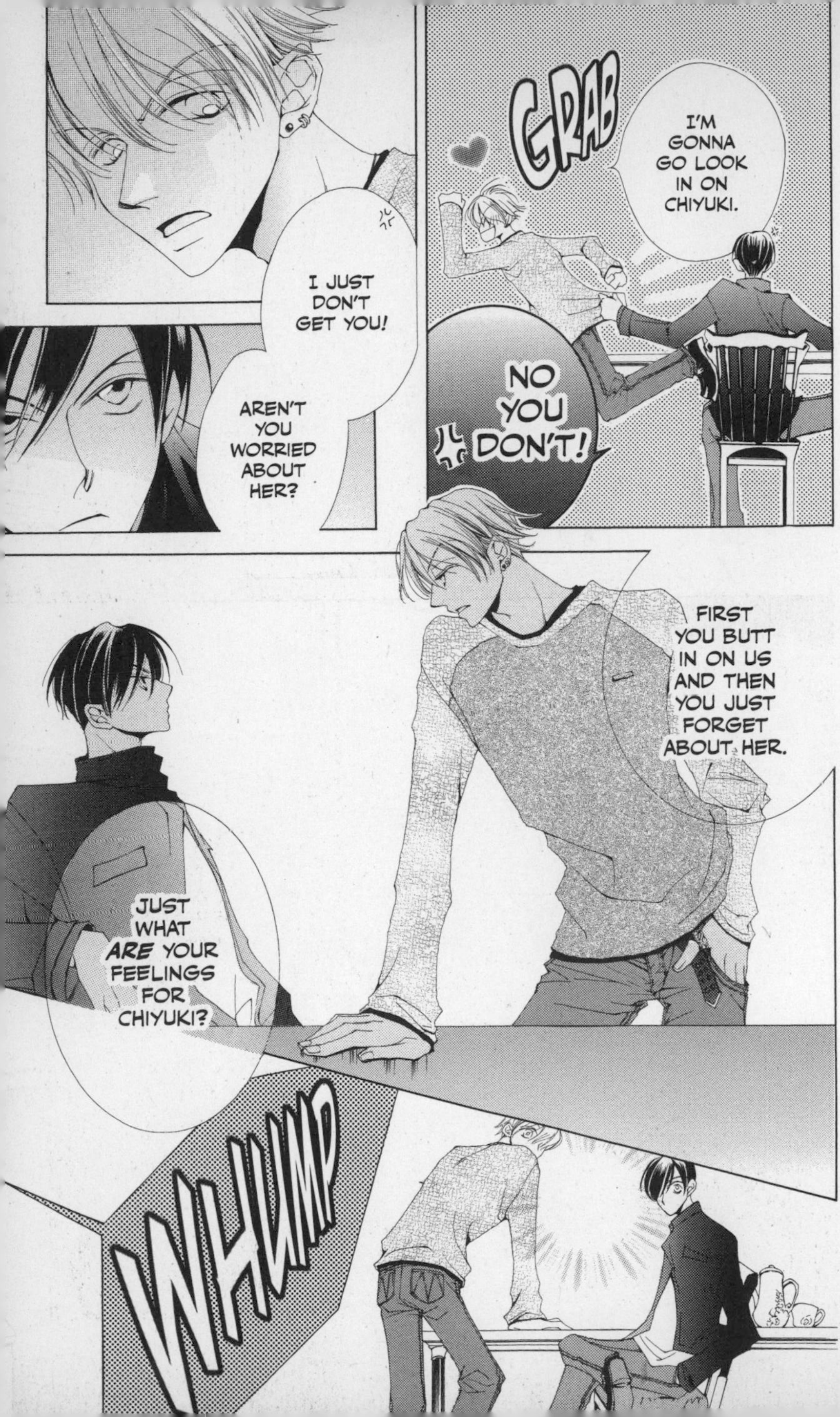
GRAB
I'M GONNA GO LOOK IN ON CHIYUKI.
NO YOU DON'T!
I JUST DON'T GET YOU!
AREN'T YOU WORRIED ABOUT HER?
FIRST YOU BUTT IN ON US AND THEN YOU JUST FORGET ABOUT HER.
JUST WHAT *ARE* YOUR FEELINGS FOR CHIYUKI?
WHUMP

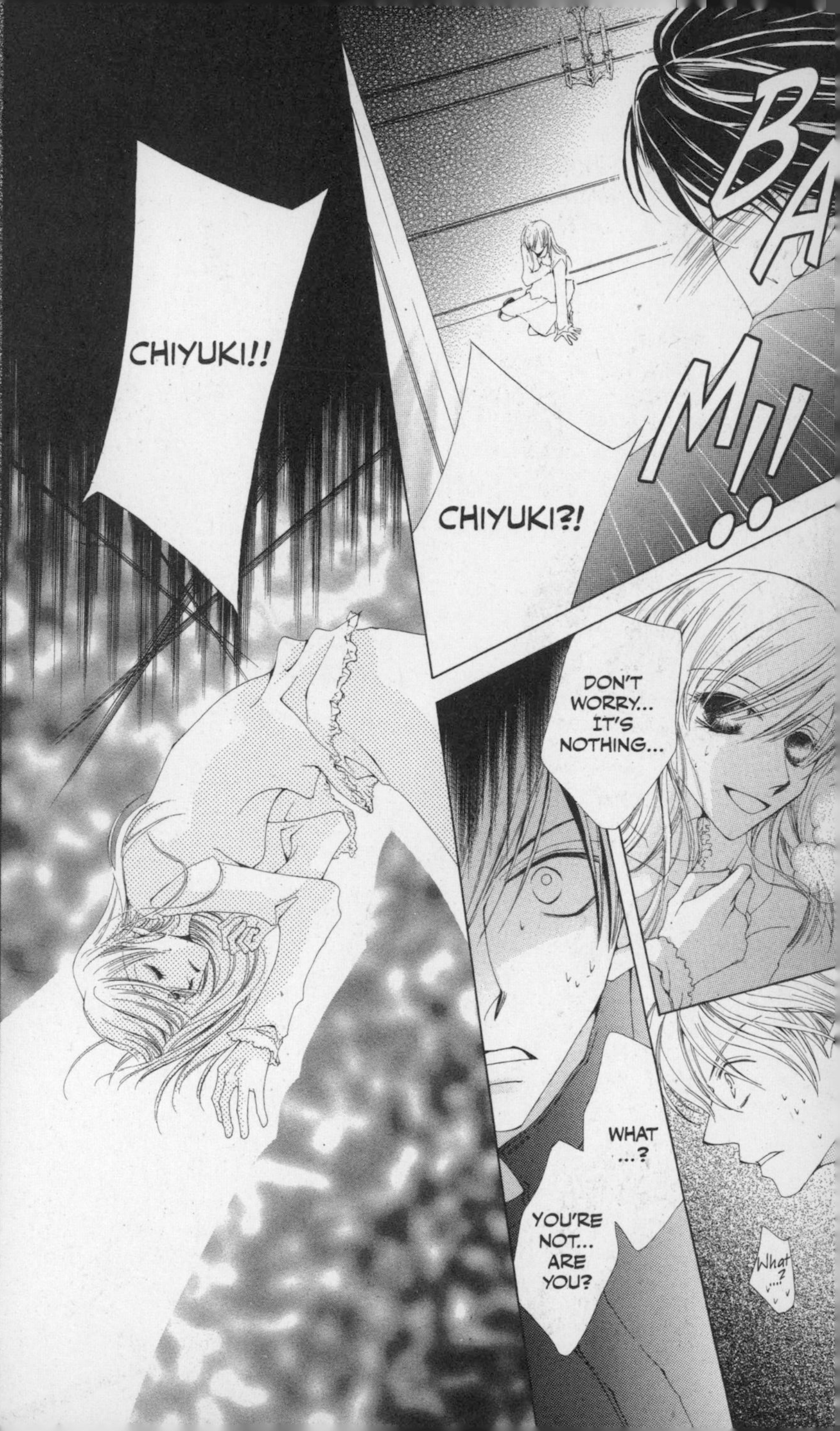
BAM!!
CHIYUKI?!
DON'T WORRY... IT'S NOTHING...
WHAT ...?
YOU'RE NOT... ARE YOU?
What ...?
CHIYUKI!!

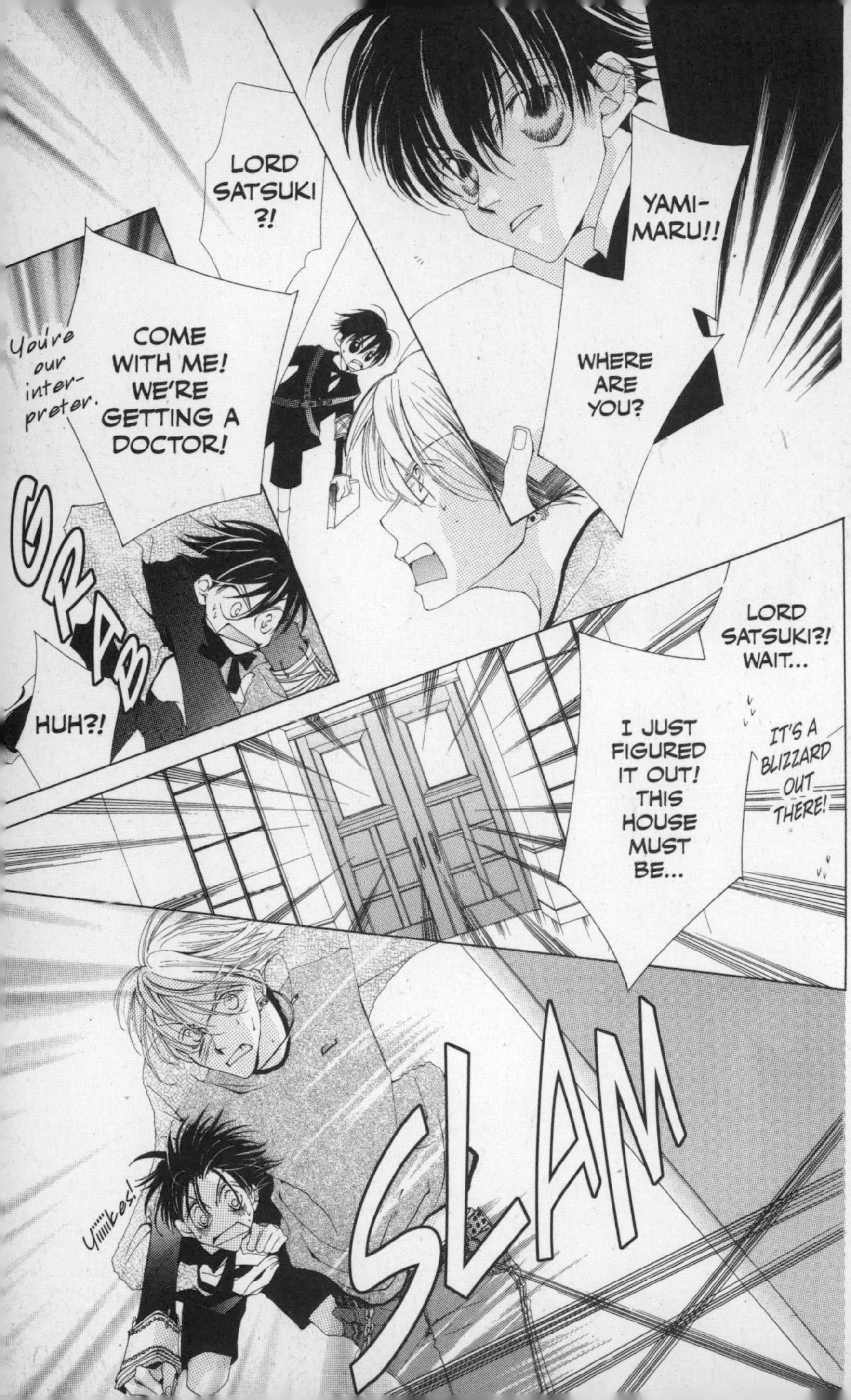
YAMI-MARU!!
WHERE ARE YOU?
LORD SATSUKI ?!
COME WITH ME! WE'RE GETTING A DOCTOR!
You're our inter-preter.
GRAB
HUH?!
LORD SATSUKI?! WAIT...
IT'S A BLIZZARD OUT THERE!
I JUST FIGURED IT OUT! THIS HOUSE MUST BE...
SLAM
Yiiiikes!

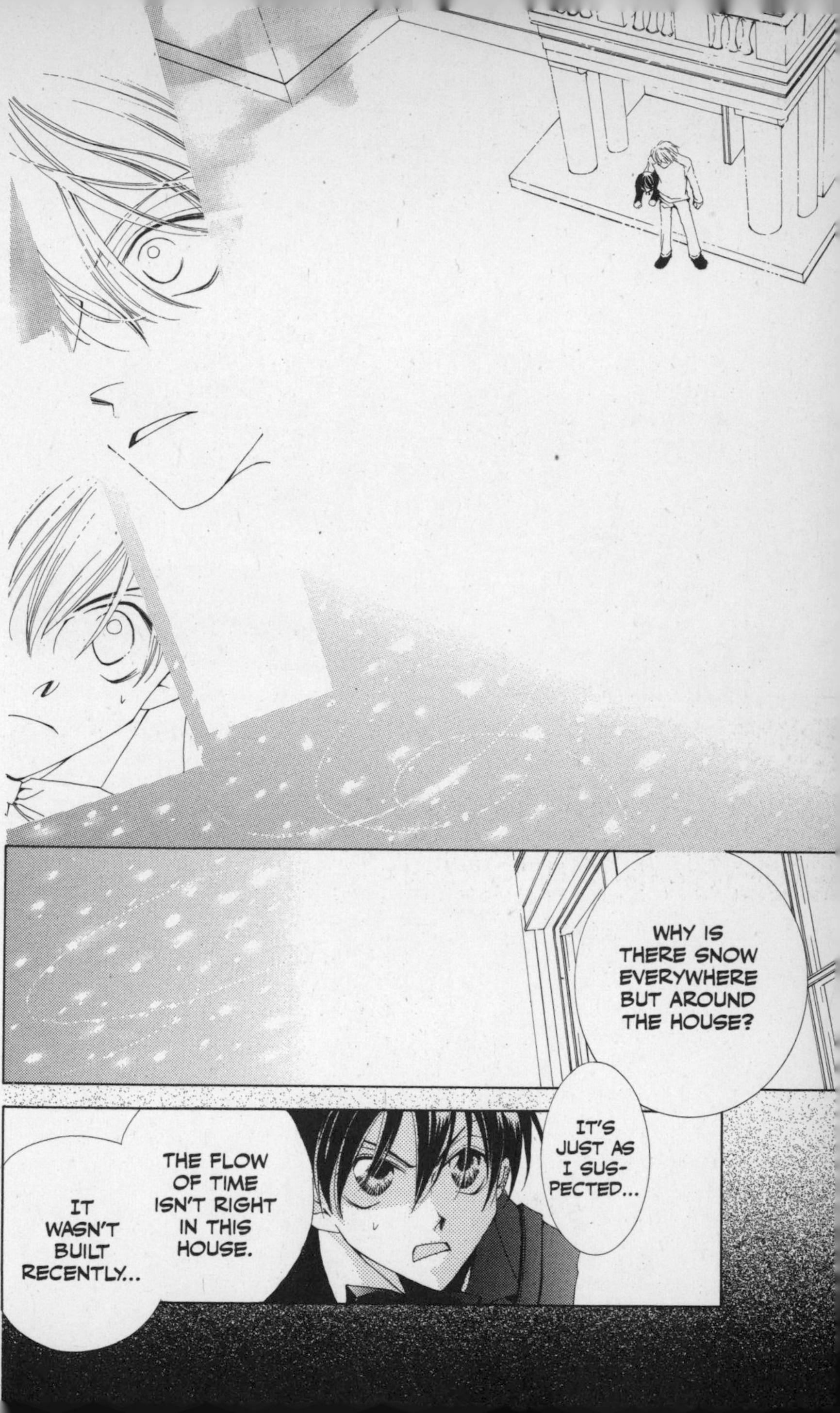
WHY IS THERE SNOW EVERYWHERE BUT AROUND THE HOUSE?
IT'S JUST AS I SUS-PECTED...
THE FLOW OF TIME ISN'T RIGHT IN THIS HOUSE.
IT WASN'T BUILT RECENTLY...

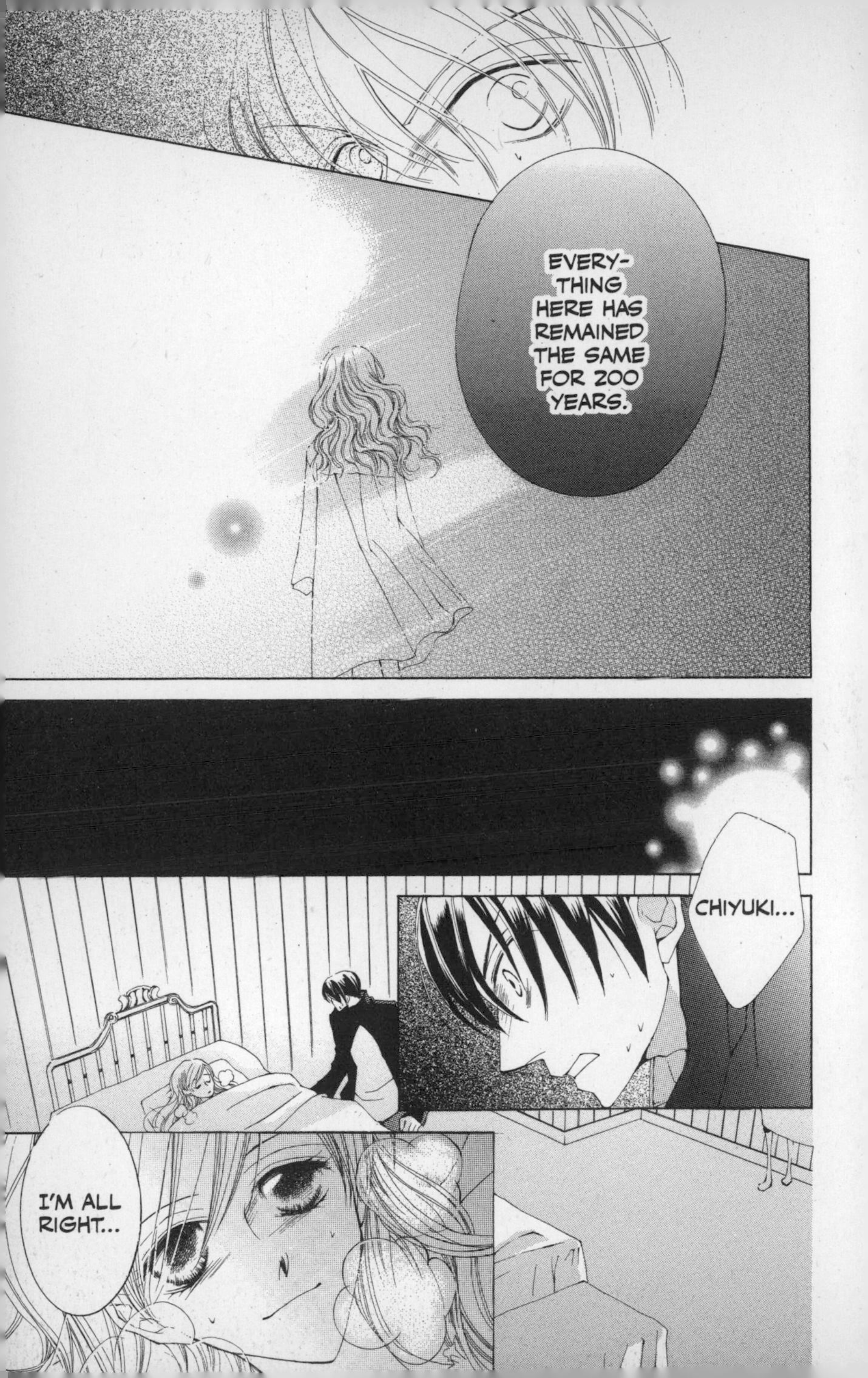
EVERY-THING HERE HAS REMAINED THE SAME FOR 200 YEARS.
CHIYUKI...
I'M ALL RIGHT...

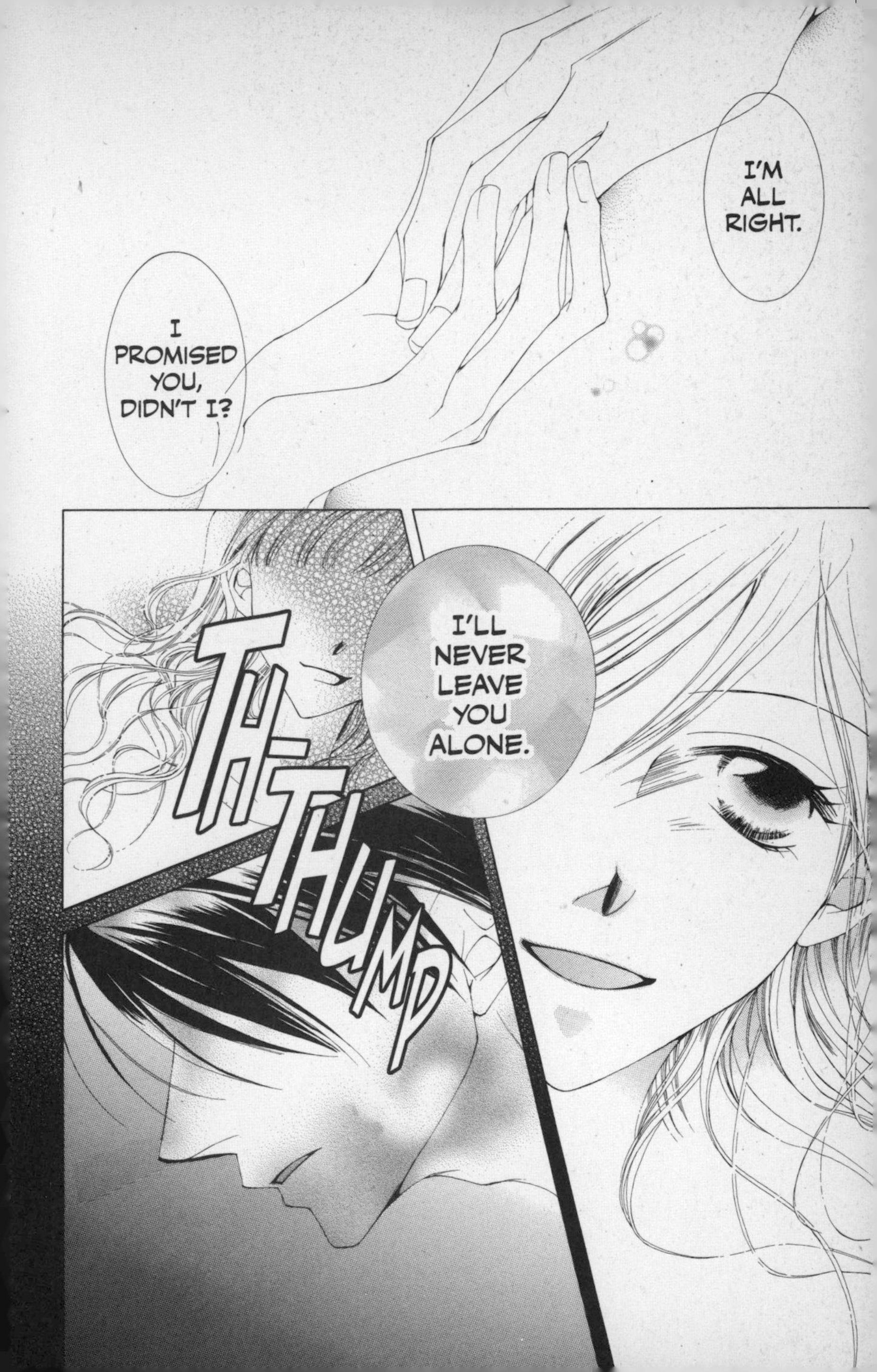
I'M ALL RIGHT.
I PROMISED YOU, DIDN'T I?
I'LL NEVER LEAVE YOU ALONE.
TH-THUMP

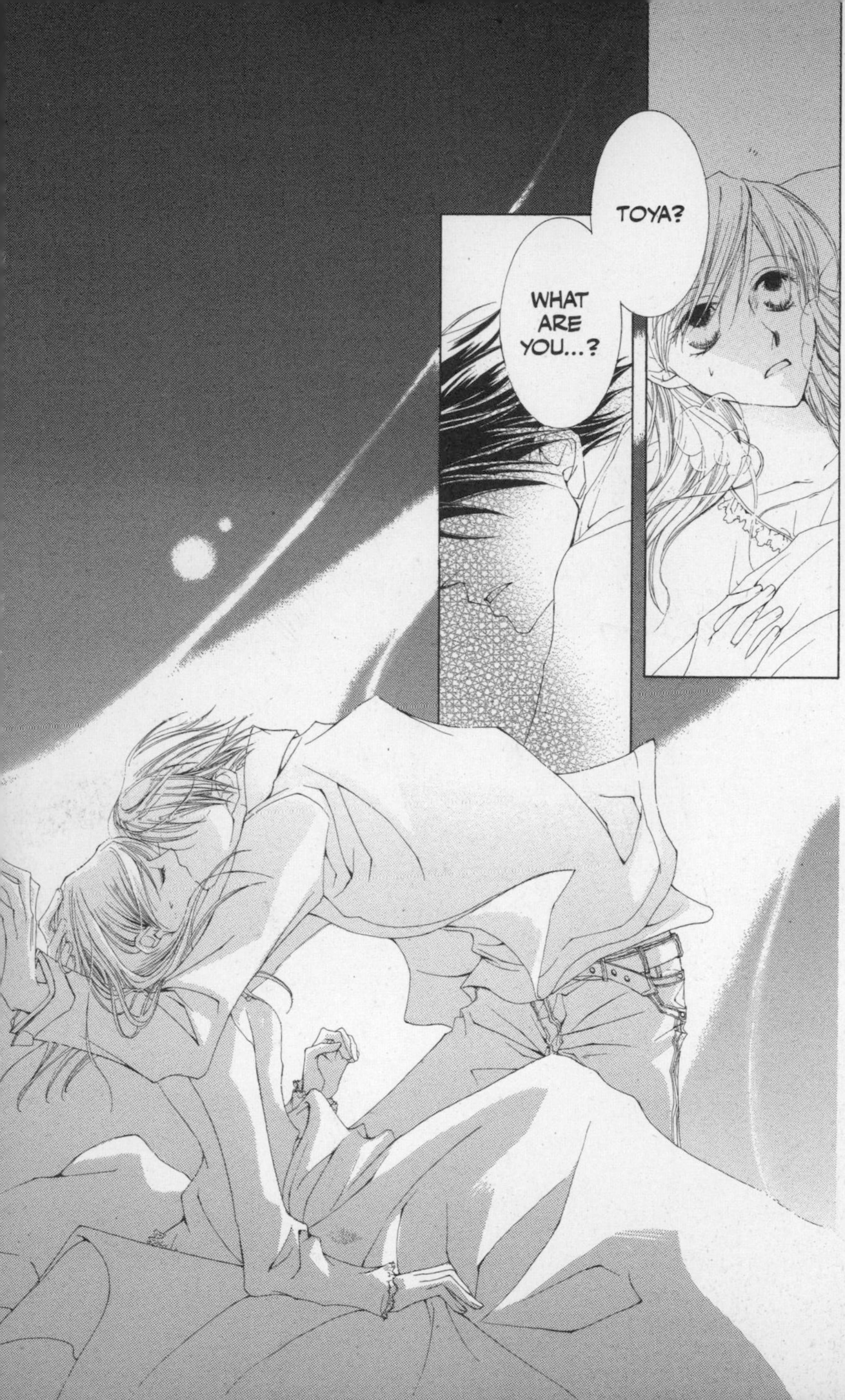
TOYA?
WHAT ARE YOU...?

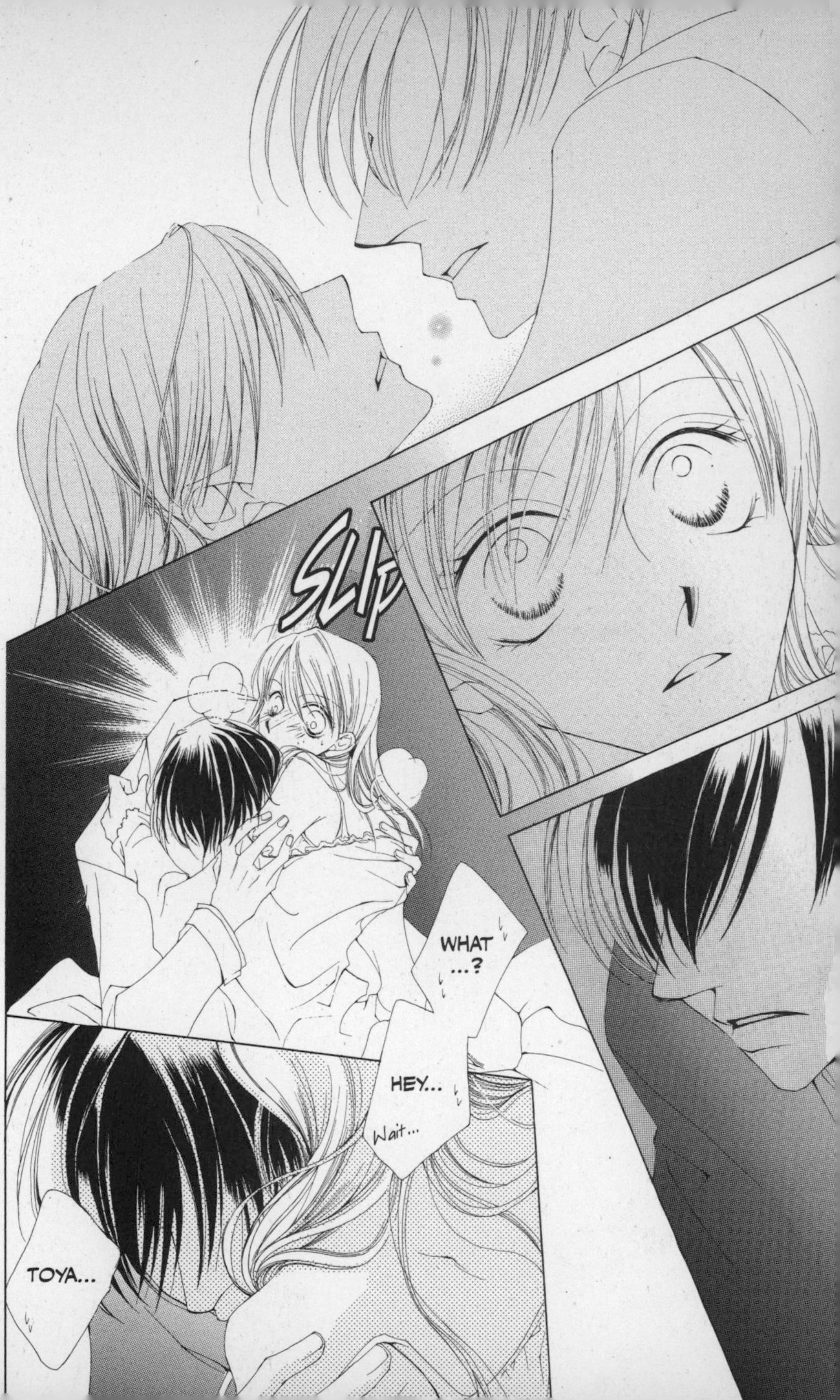
SLIP
WHAT ...?
HEY...
Wait...
TOYA...

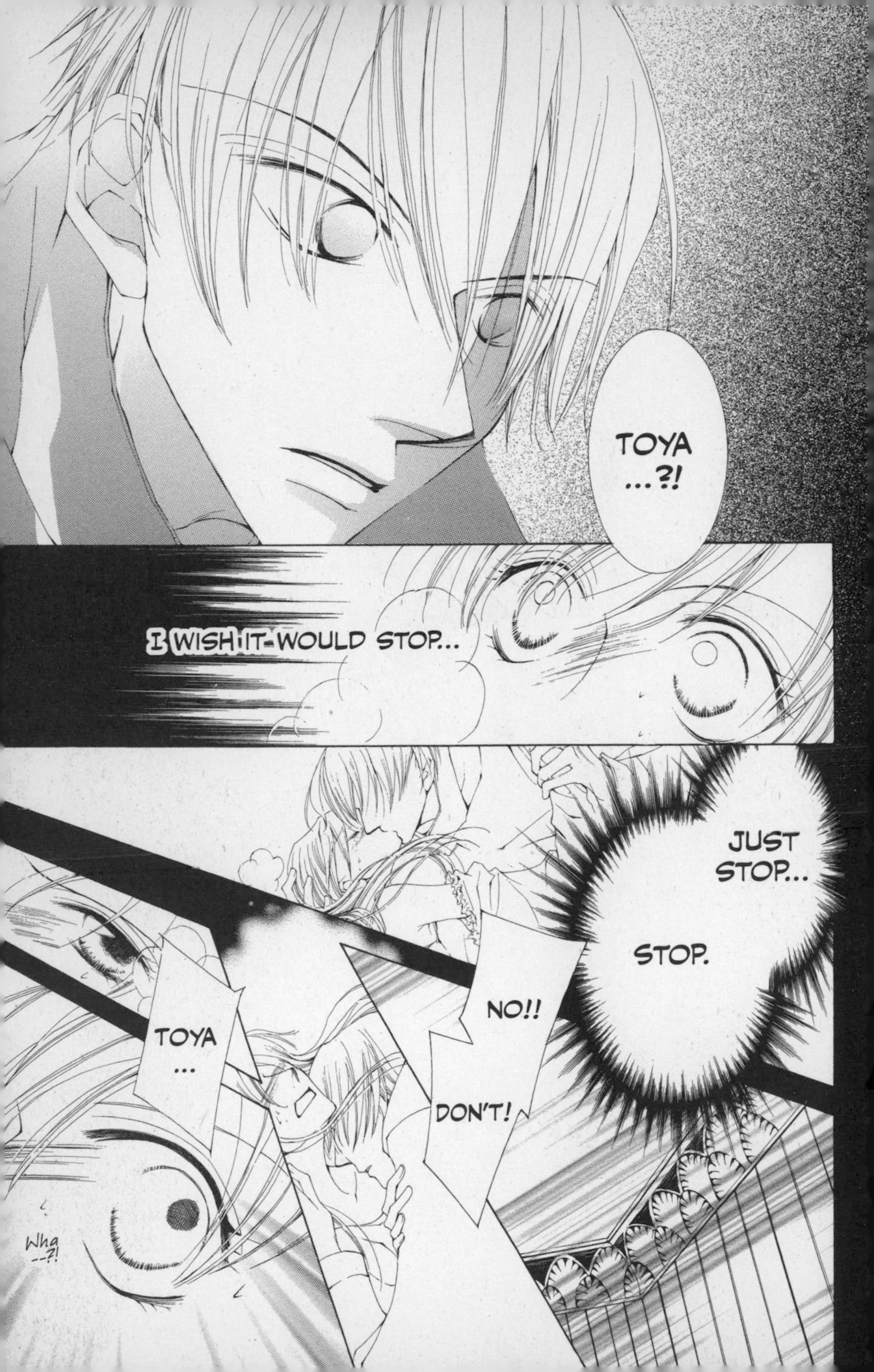
TOYA ...?!
I WISH IT WOULD STOP...
JUST STOP...
STOP.
NO!!
DON'T!
TOYA ...
Wha --?!

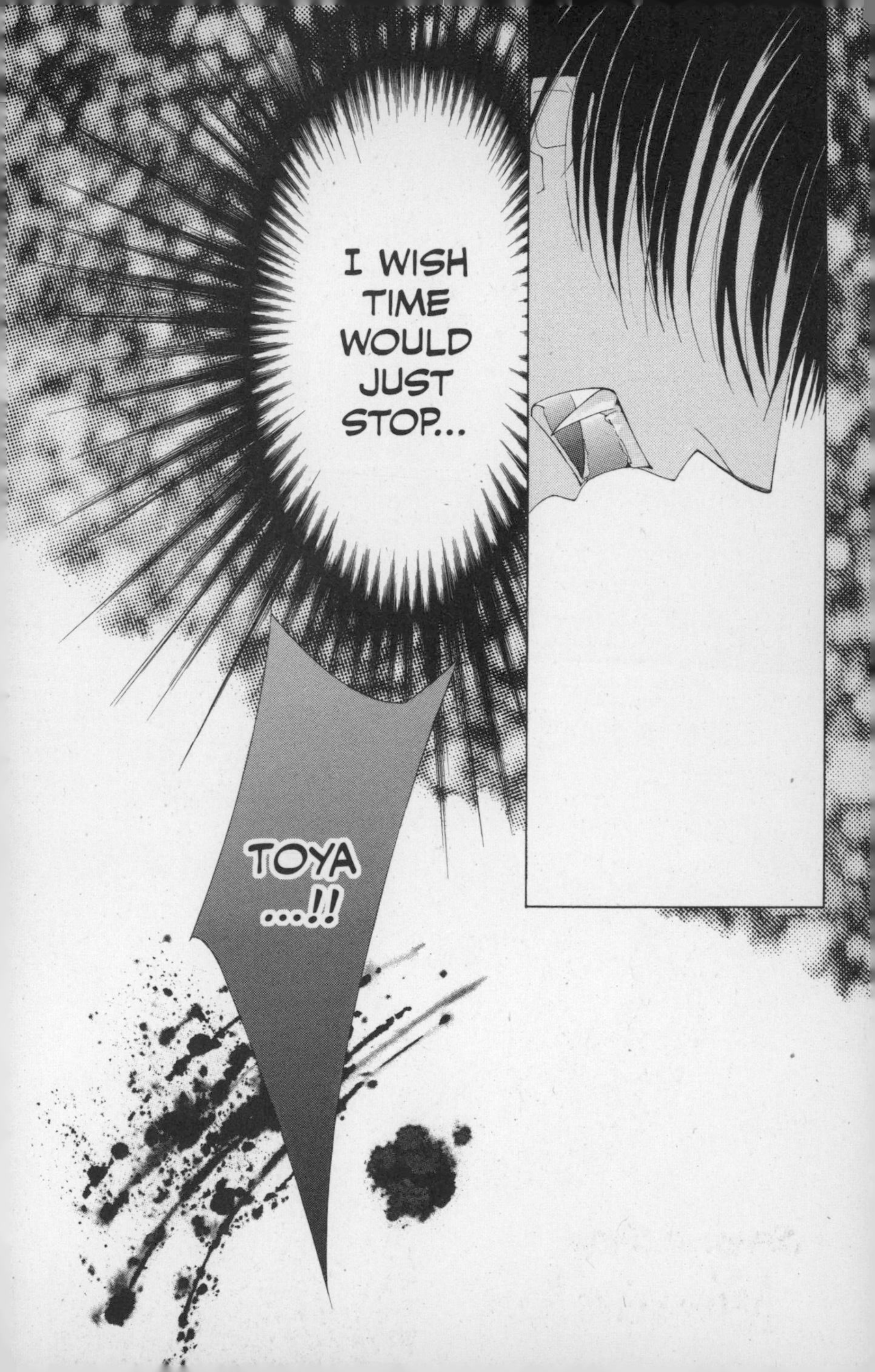
I WISH TIME WOULD JUST STOP...
TOYA ...!!

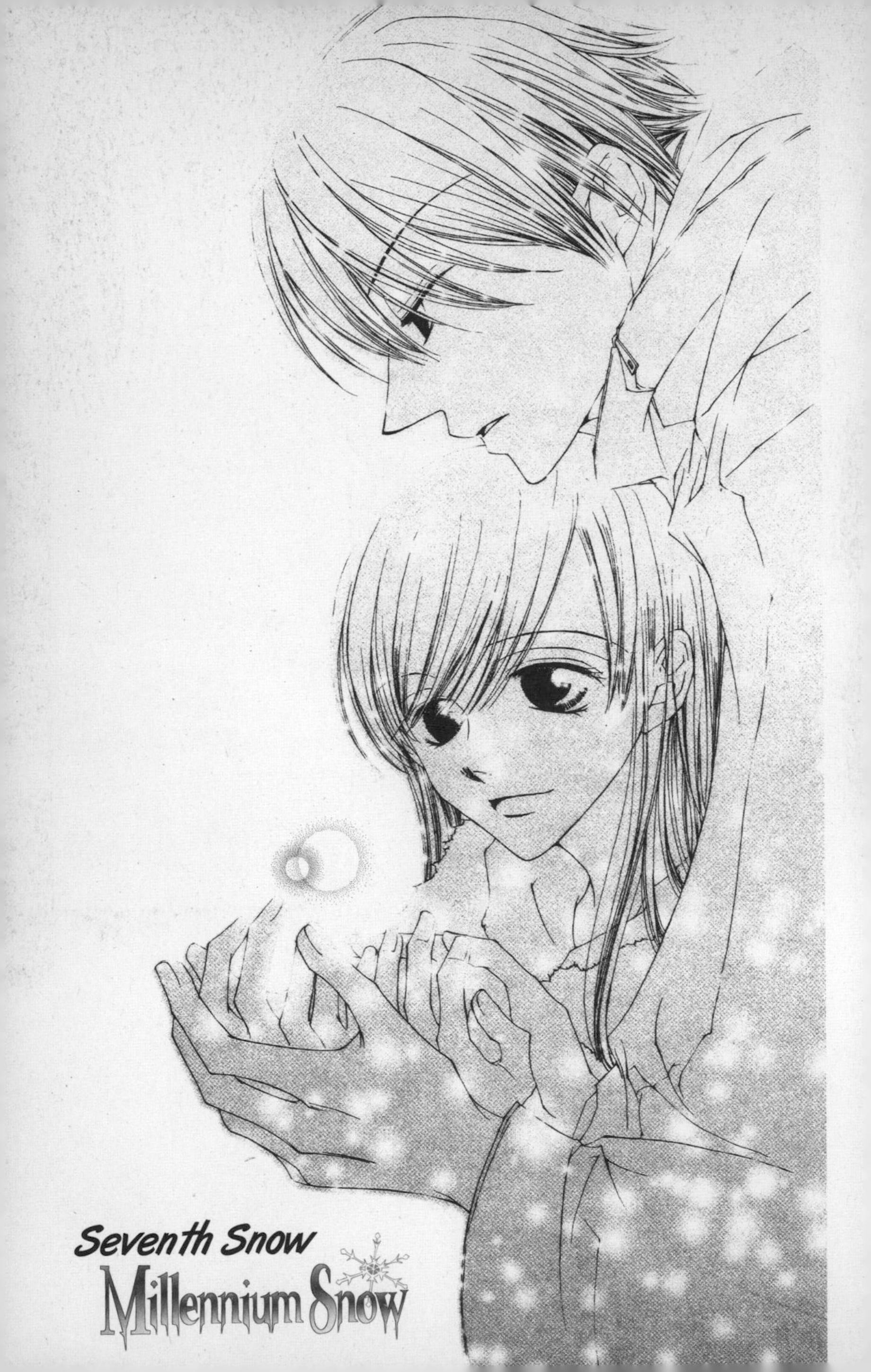
Seventh Snow
Millennium Snow

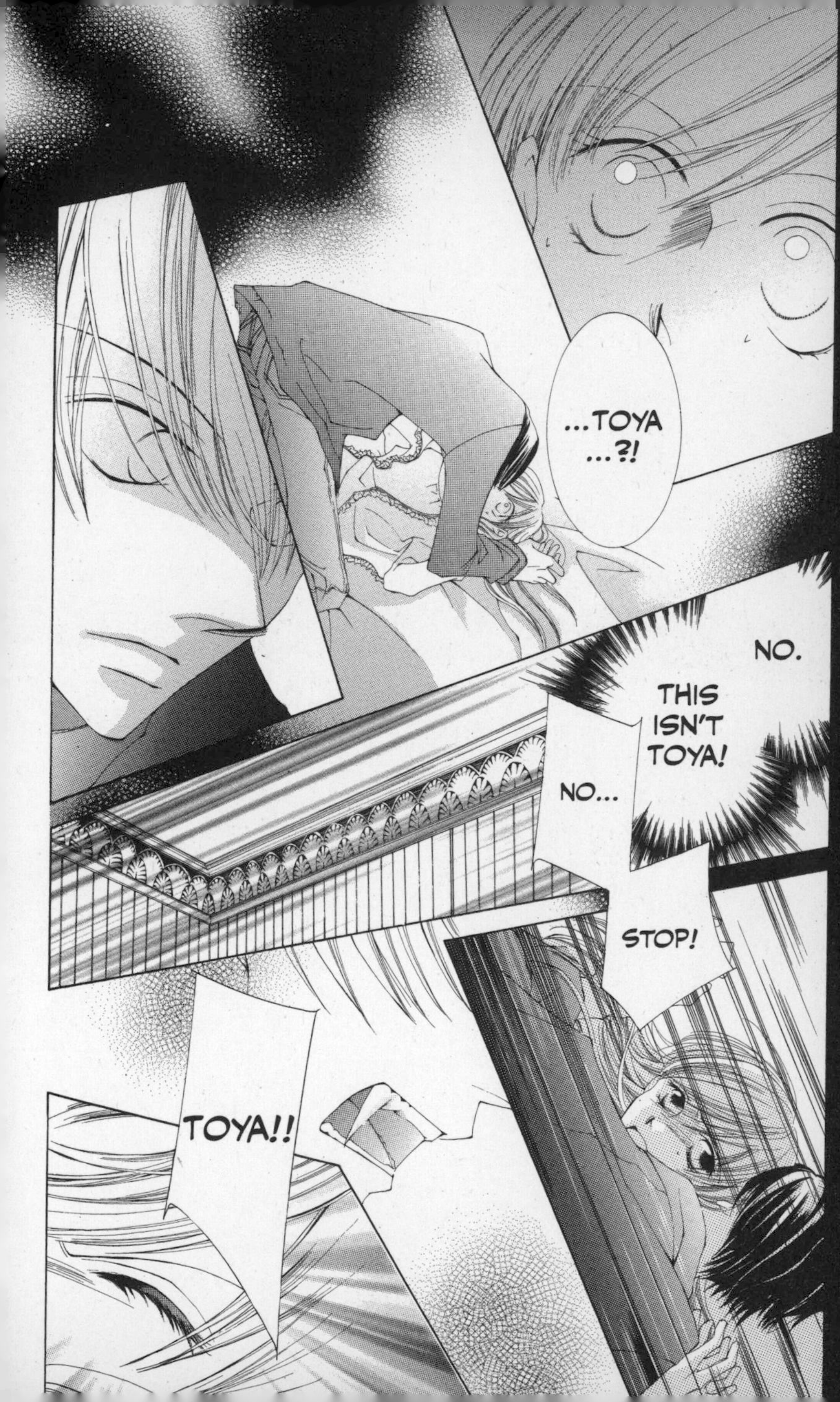
...TOYA ...?!
NO.
THIS ISN'T TOYA!
NO...
STOP!
TOYA!!

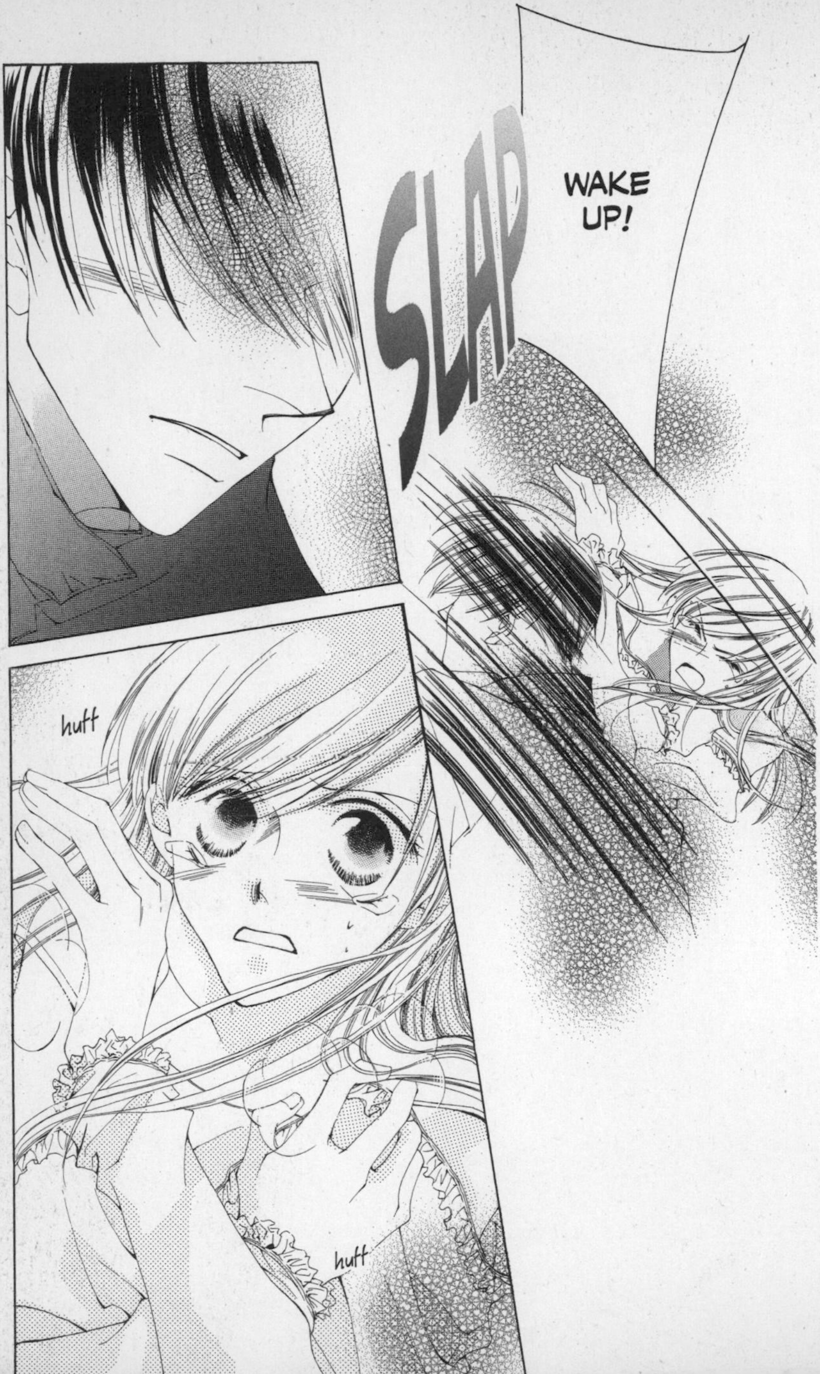
WAKE UP!
SLAP
huff
huff

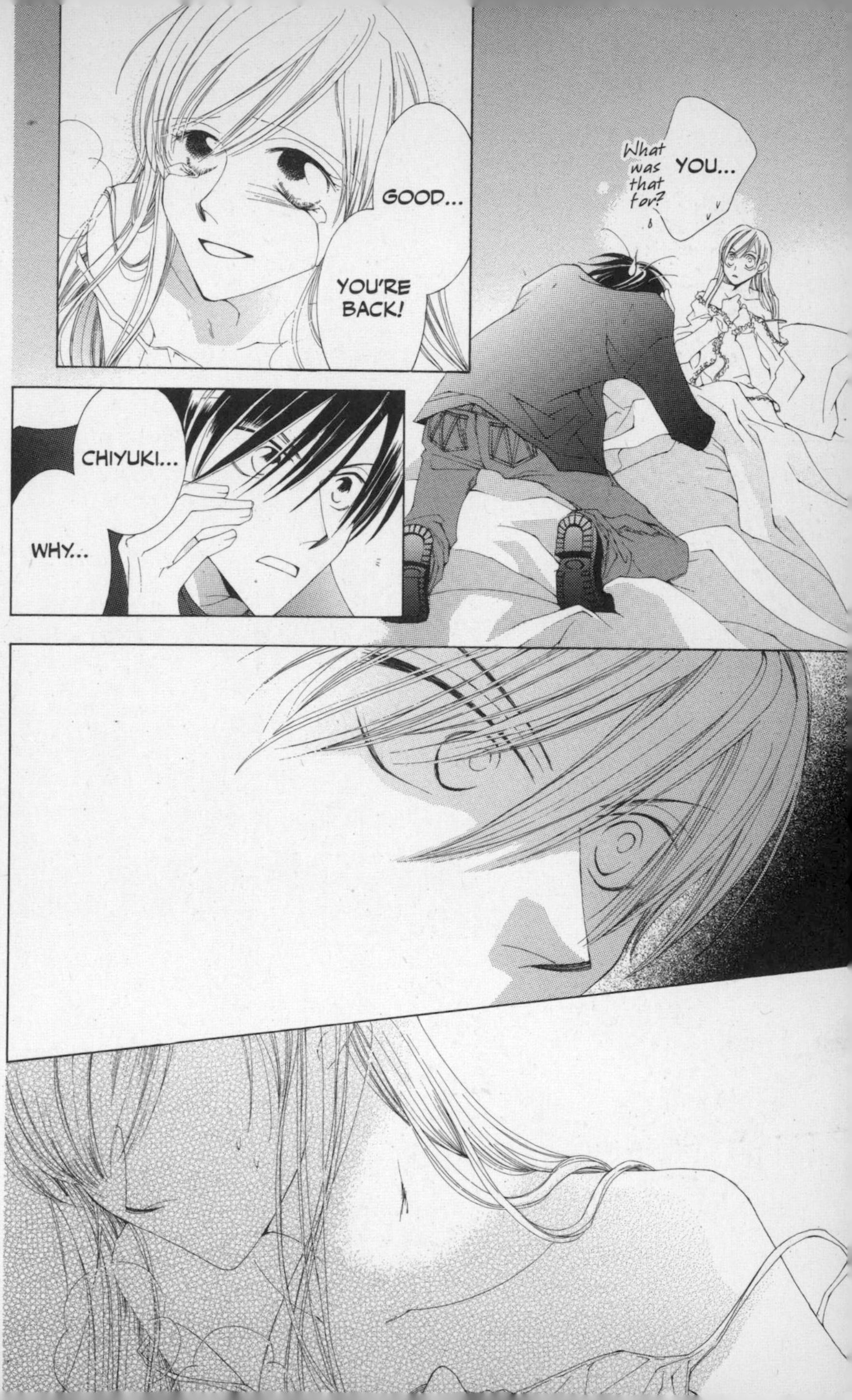
YOU...
What was that for?
GOOD...
YOU'RE BACK!
CHIYUKI...
WHY...

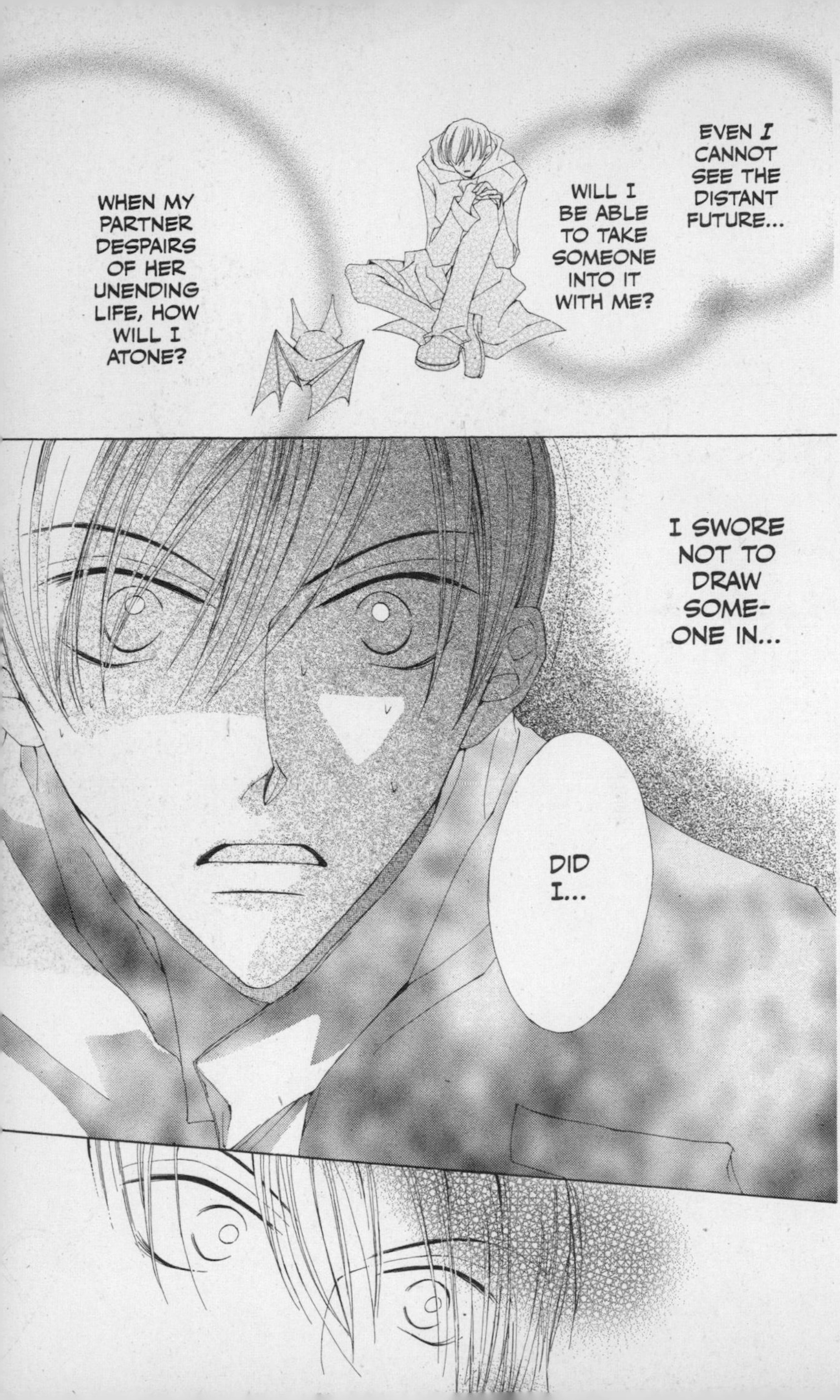
EVEN I CANNOT SEE THE DISTANT FUTURE...
WILL I BE ABLE TO TAKE SOMEONE INTO IT WITH ME?
WHEN MY PARTNER DESPAIRS OF HER UNENDING LIFE, HOW WILL I ATONE?
I SWORE NOT TO DRAW SOME-ONE IN...
DID I...

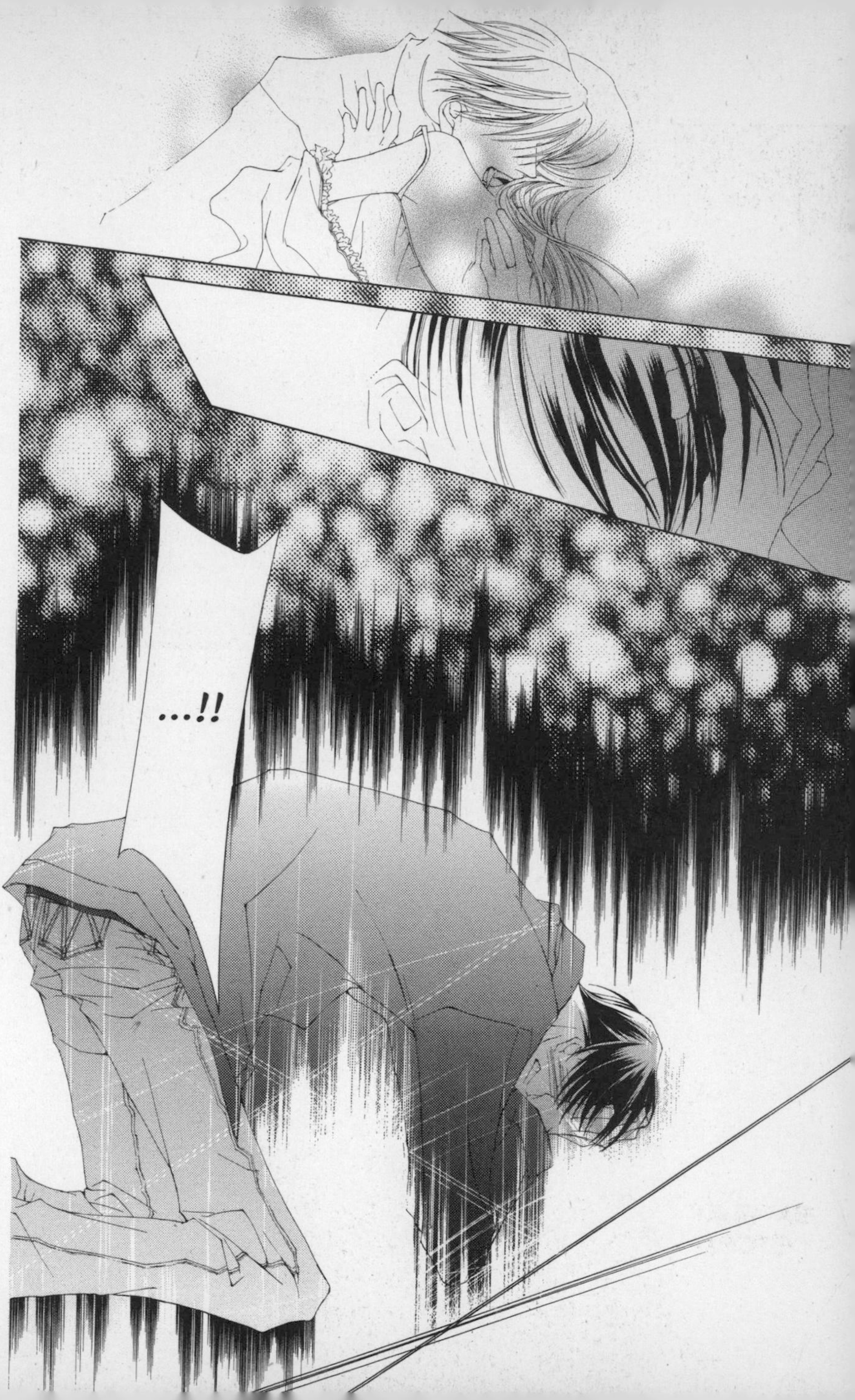
...!!

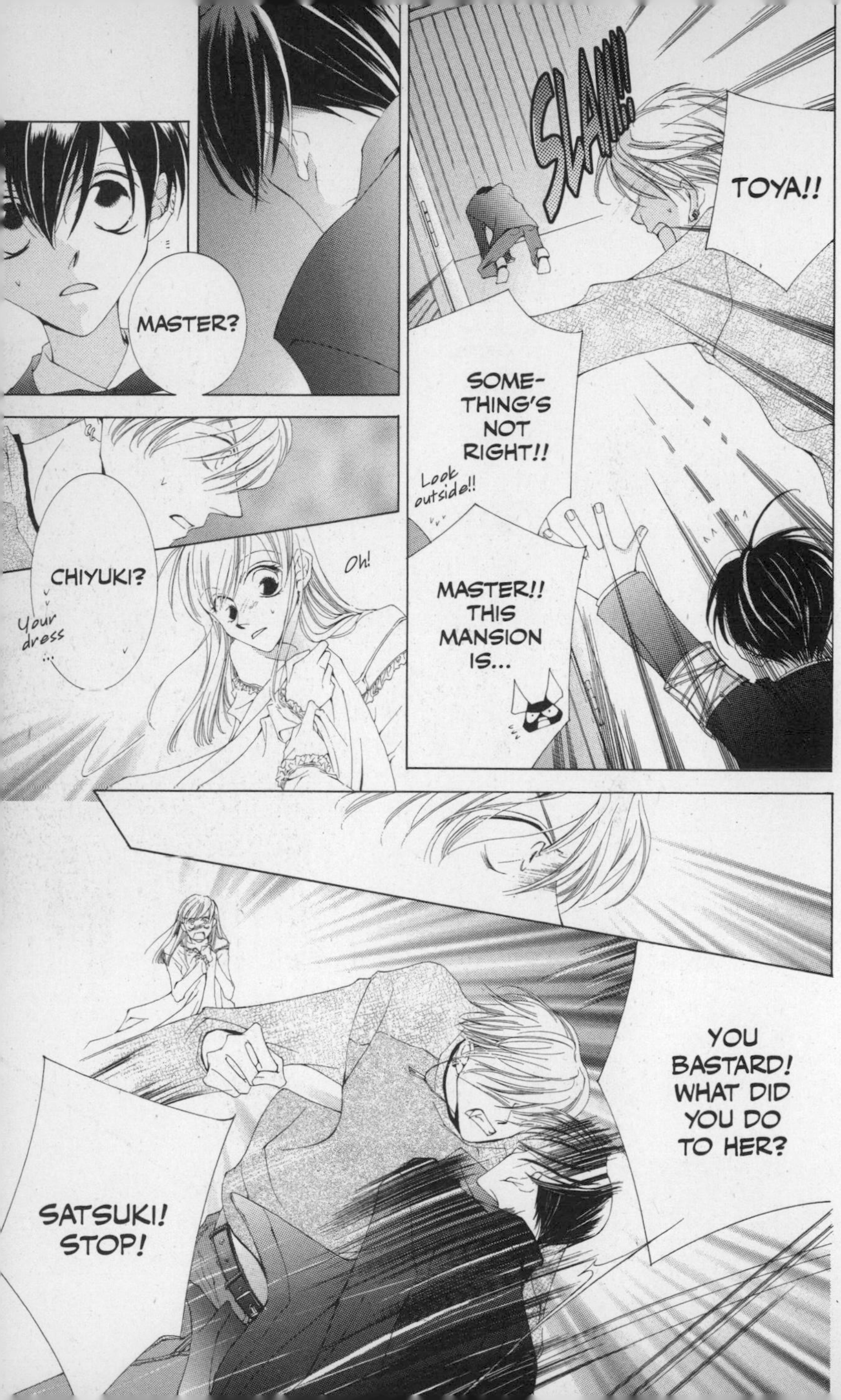

SLAM!!
TOYA!!
SOME-THING'S NOT RIGHT!!
Look outside!!
MASTER!! THIS MANSION IS...
MASTER?
CHIYUKI?
Your dress ...
Oh!
YOU BASTARD! WHAT DID YOU DO TO HER?
SATSUKI! STOP!

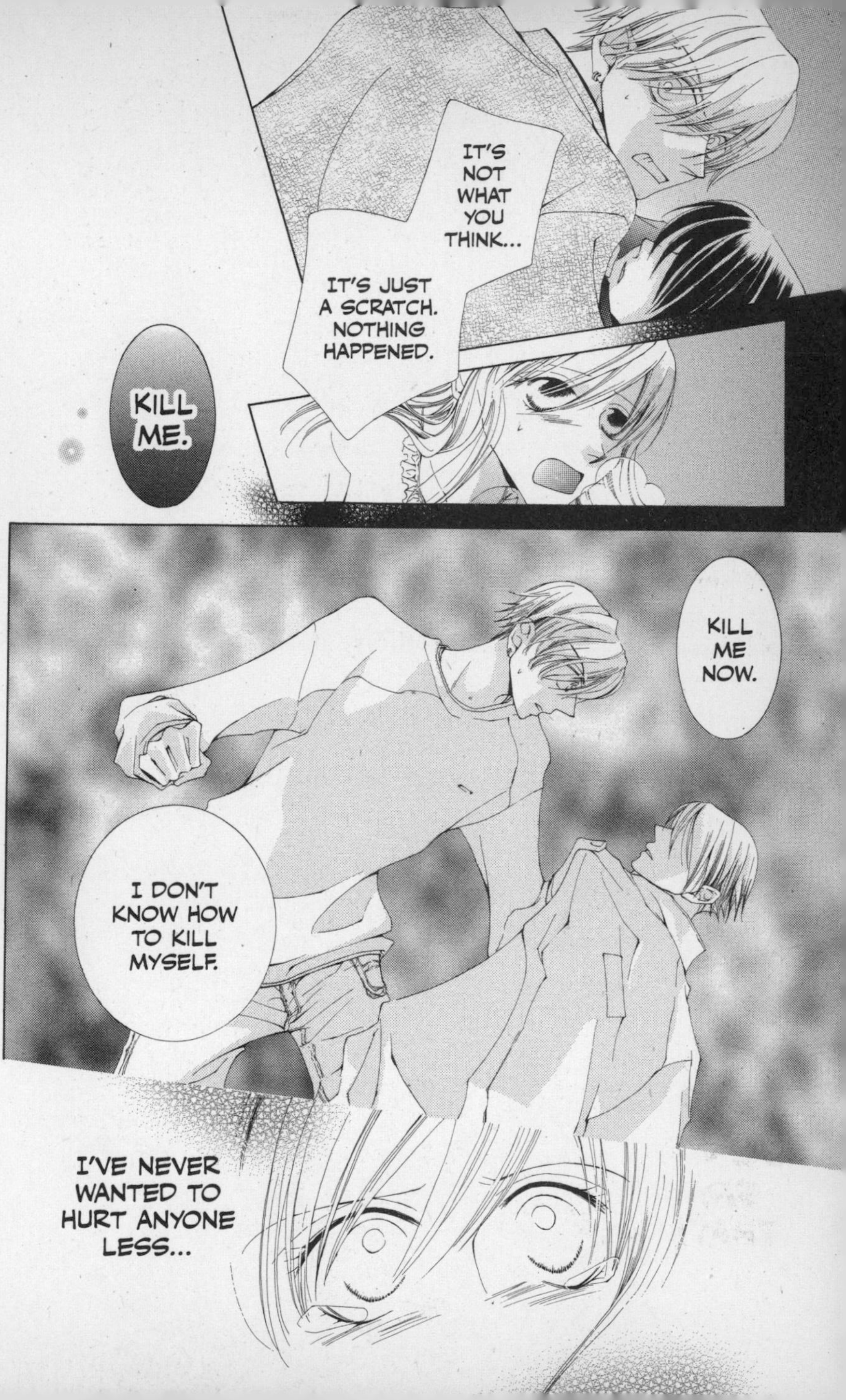
IT'S NOT WHAT YOU THINK...
IT'S JUST A SCRATCH. NOTHING HAPPENED.
KILL ME.
KILL ME NOW.
I DON'T KNOW HOW TO KILL MYSELF.
I'VE NEVER WANTED TO HURT ANYONE LESS...

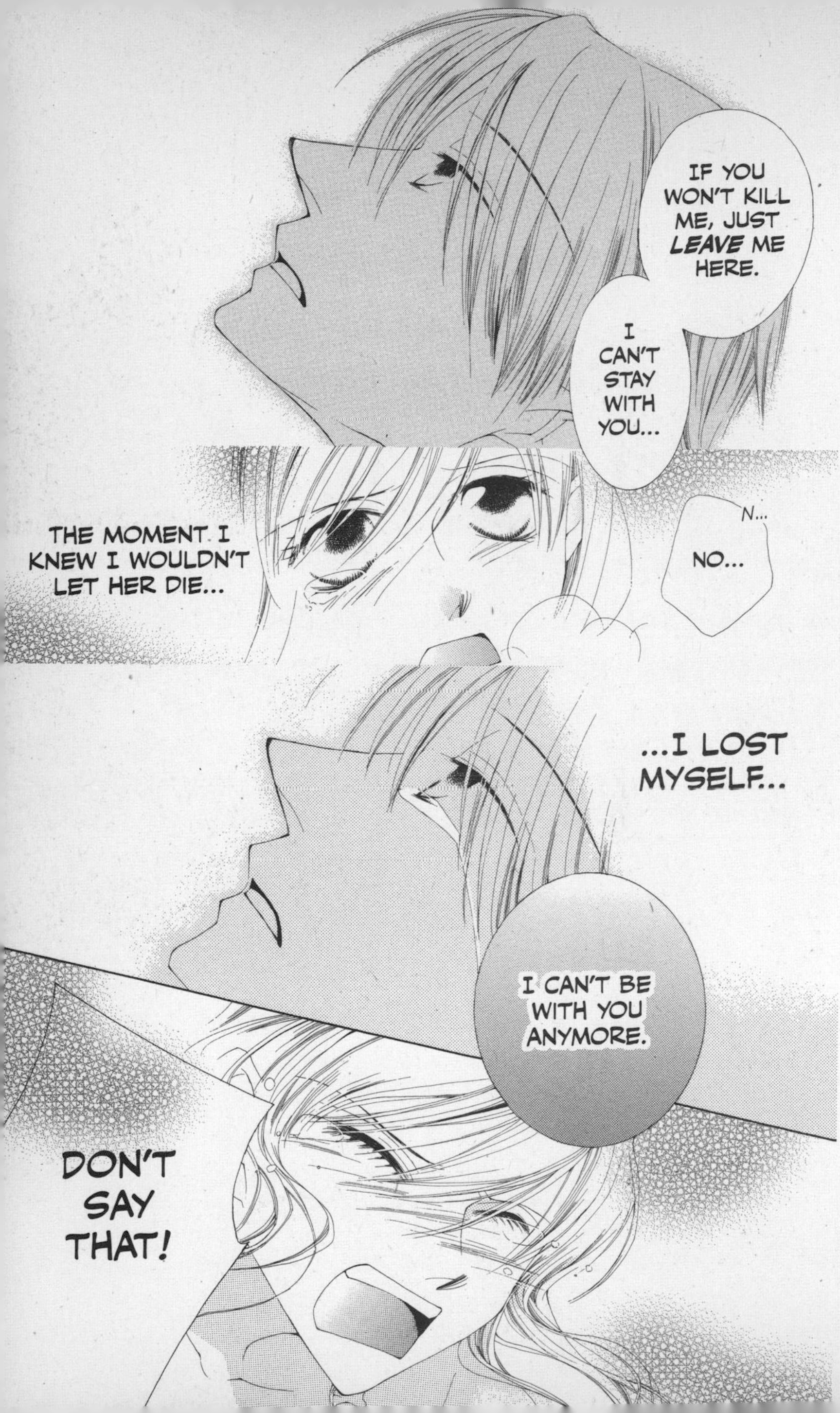
IF YOU WON'T KILL ME, JUST *LEAVE* ME HERE.
I CAN'T STAY WITH YOU...
N... NO...
THE MOMENT I KNEW I WOULDN'T LET HER DIE...
...I LOST MYSELF...
I CAN'T BE WITH YOU ANYMORE.
DON'T SAY THAT!

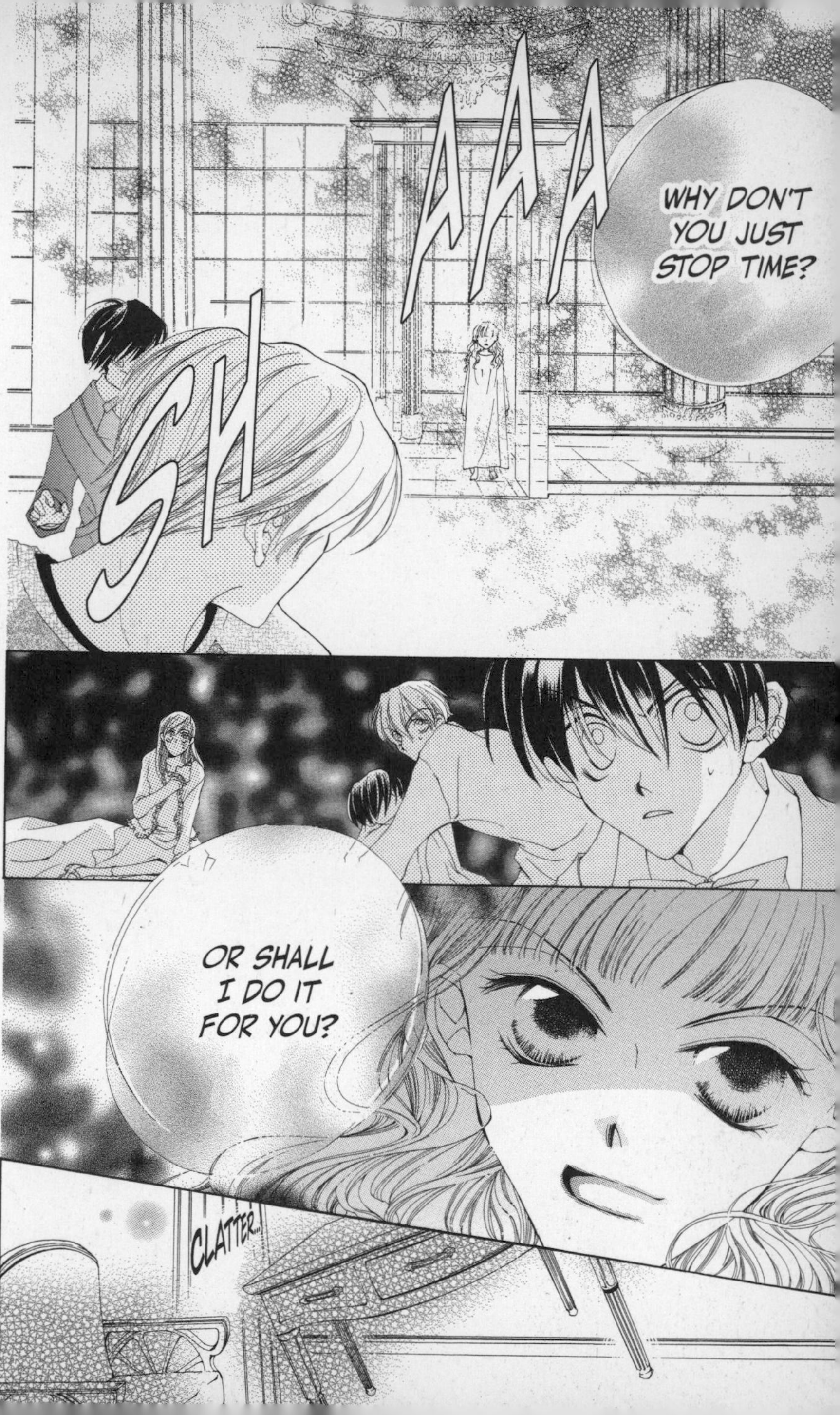
WHY DON'T YOU JUST STOP TIME?
AAA
SH
OR SHALL I DO IT FOR YOU?
CLATTER...

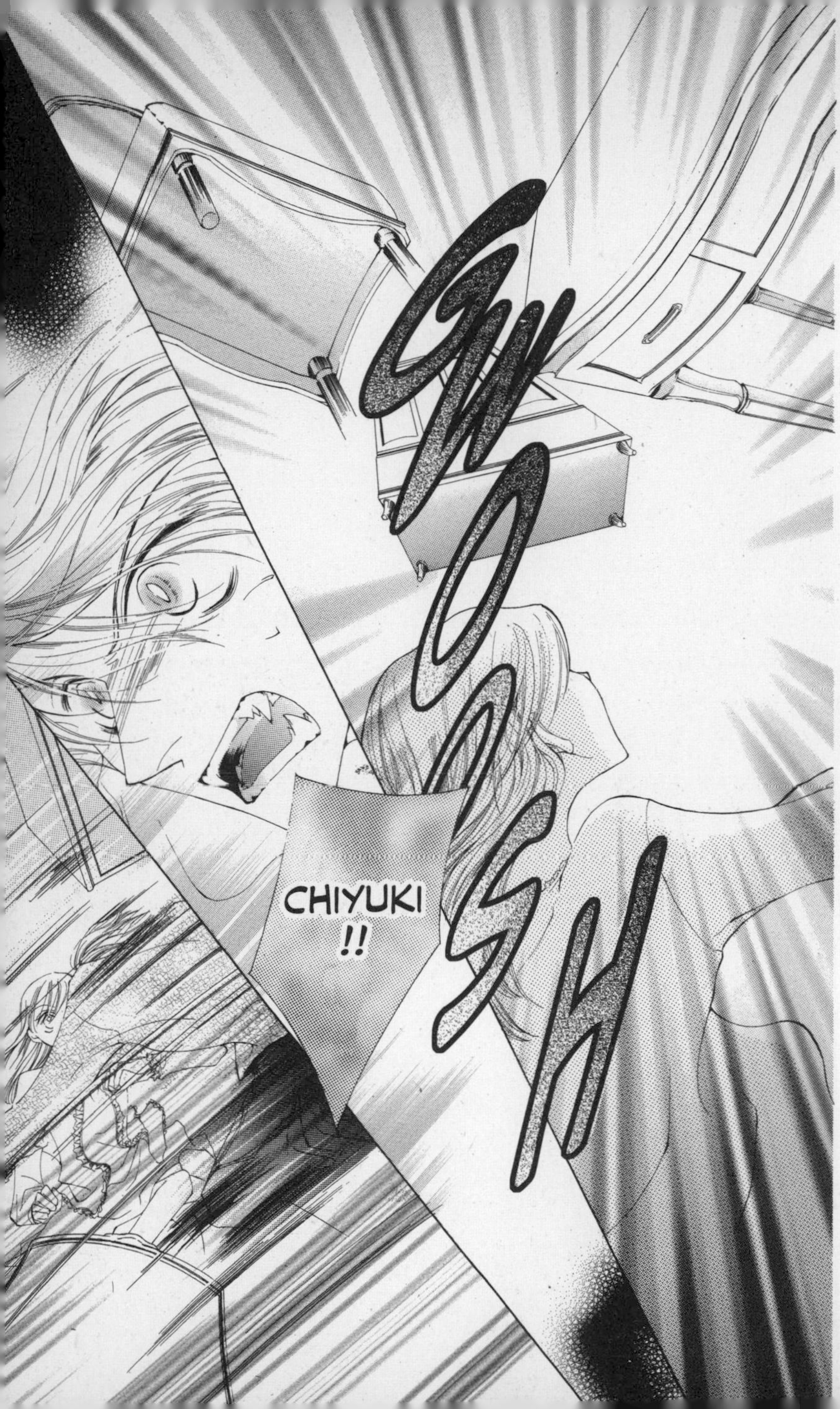
GWOOSH
CHIYUKI !!

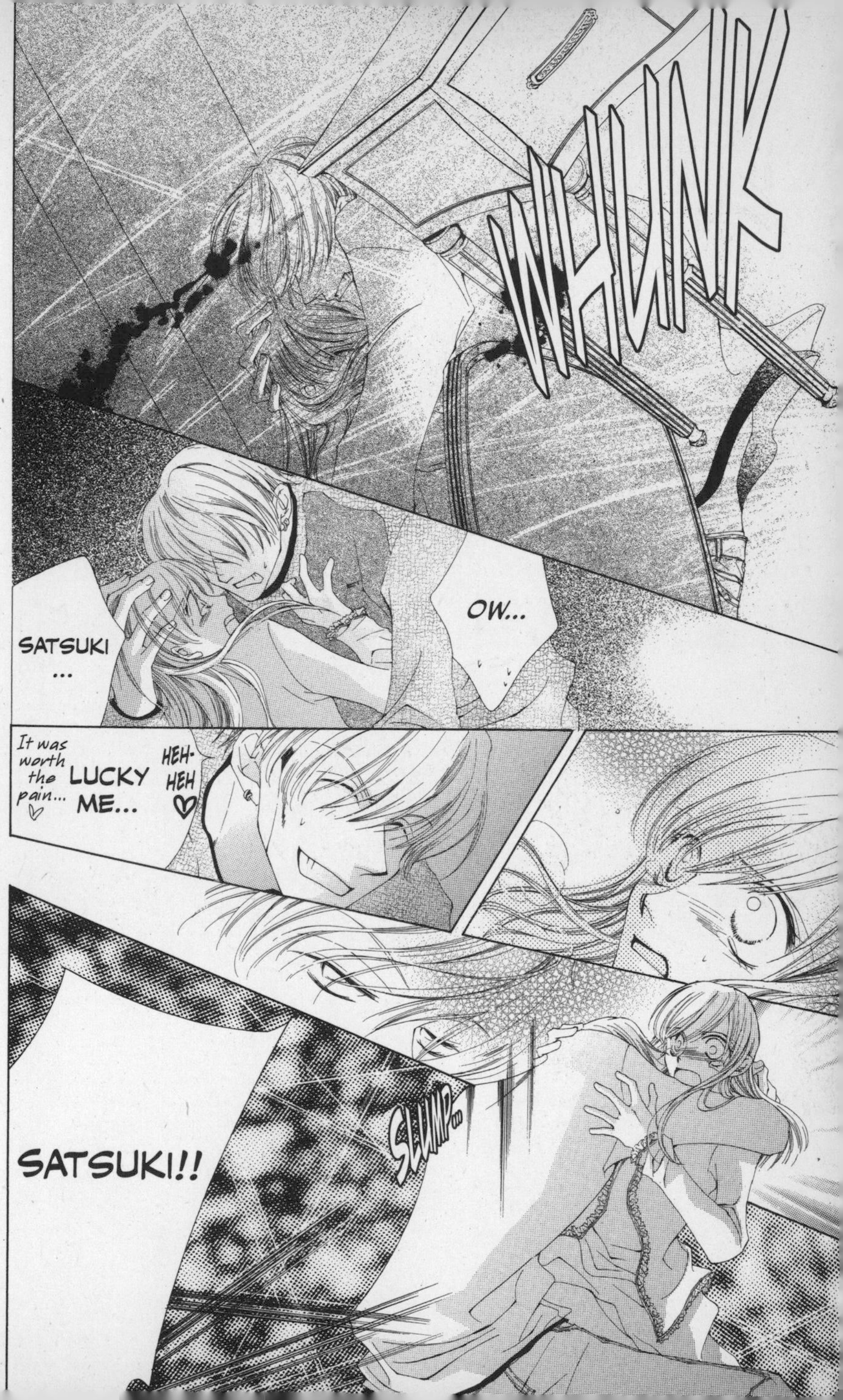
WHUNK
OW...
SATSUKI ...
HEH-HEH ♥
LUCKY ME...
It was worth the pain... ♥
SLUMP...
SATSUKI!!

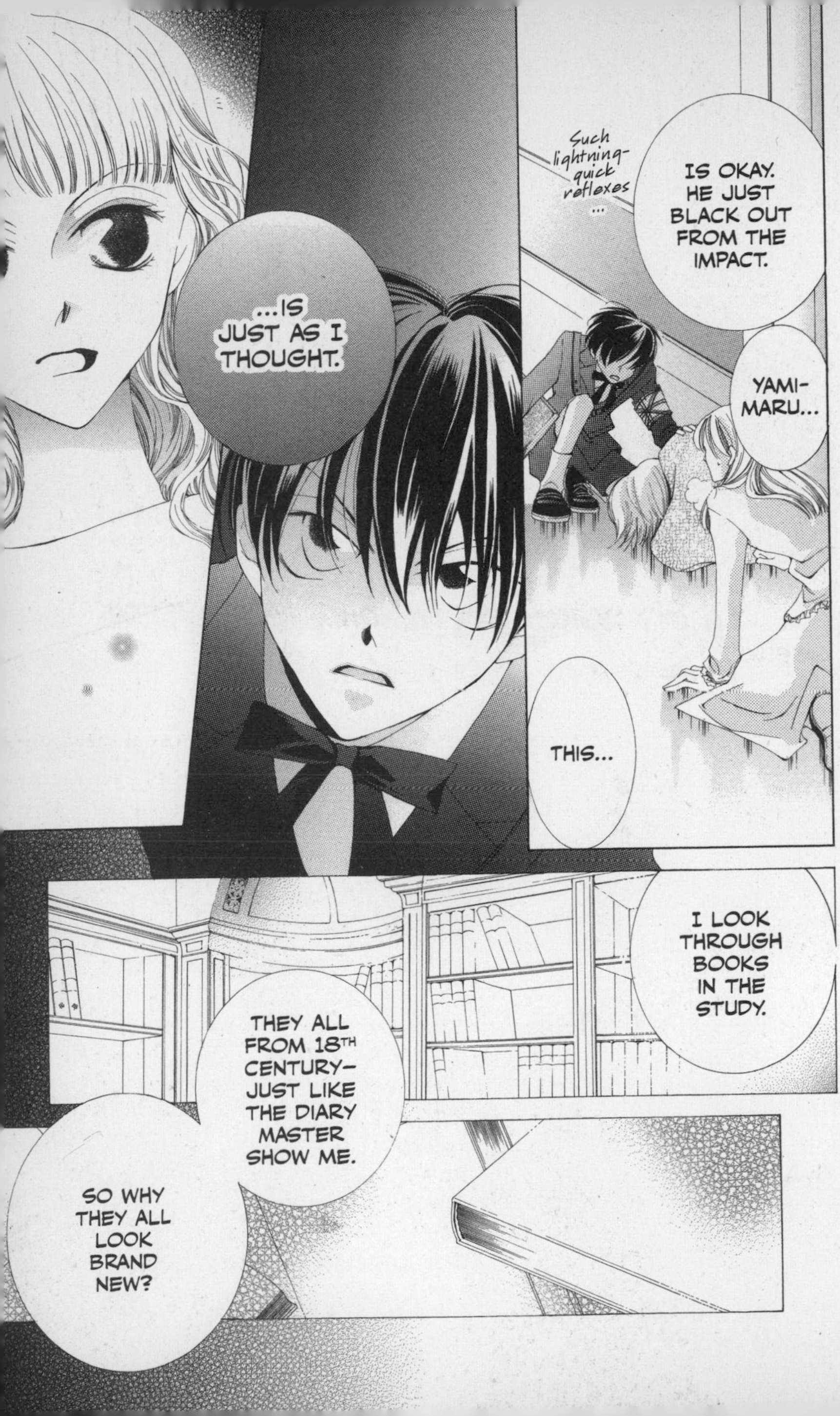
IS OKAY. HE JUST BLACK OUT FROM THE IMPACT.
Such lightning-quick reflexes ...
YAMI-MARU...
THIS...
...IS JUST AS I THOUGHT.
I LOOK THROUGH BOOKS IN THE STUDY.
THEY ALL FROM 18TH CENTURY—JUST LIKE THE DIARY MASTER SHOW ME.
SO WHY THEY ALL LOOK BRAND NEW?

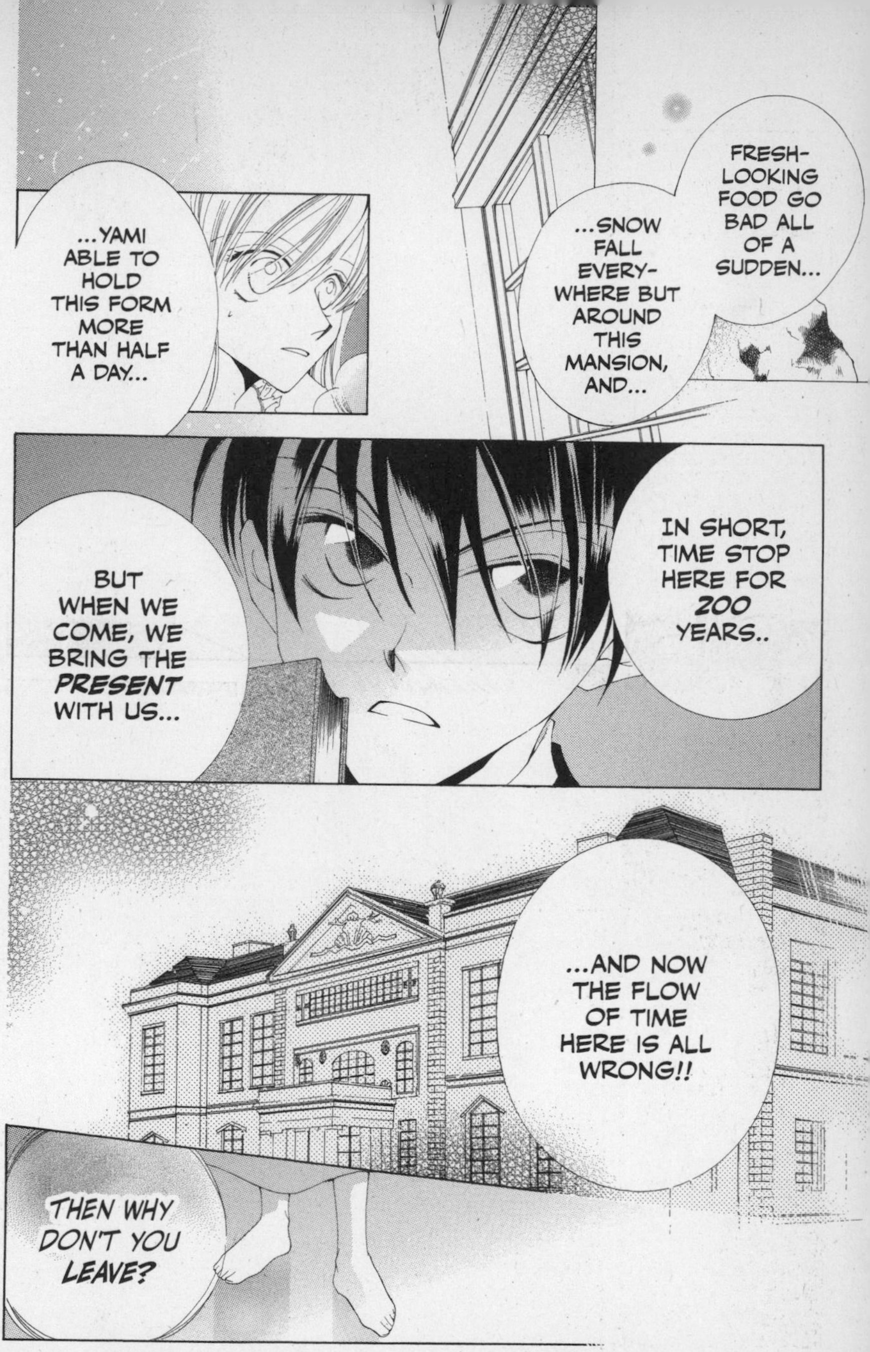
FRESH-LOOKING FOOD GO BAD ALL OF A SUDDEN...
...SNOW FALL EVERY-WHERE BUT AROUND THIS MANSION, AND...
...YAMI ABLE TO HOLD THIS FORM MORE THAN HALF A DAY...
IN SHORT, TIME STOP HERE FOR 200 YEARS..
BUT WHEN WE COME, WE BRING THE PRESENT WITH US...
...AND NOW THE FLOW OF TIME HERE IS ALL WRONG!!
THEN WHY DON'T YOU LEAVE?

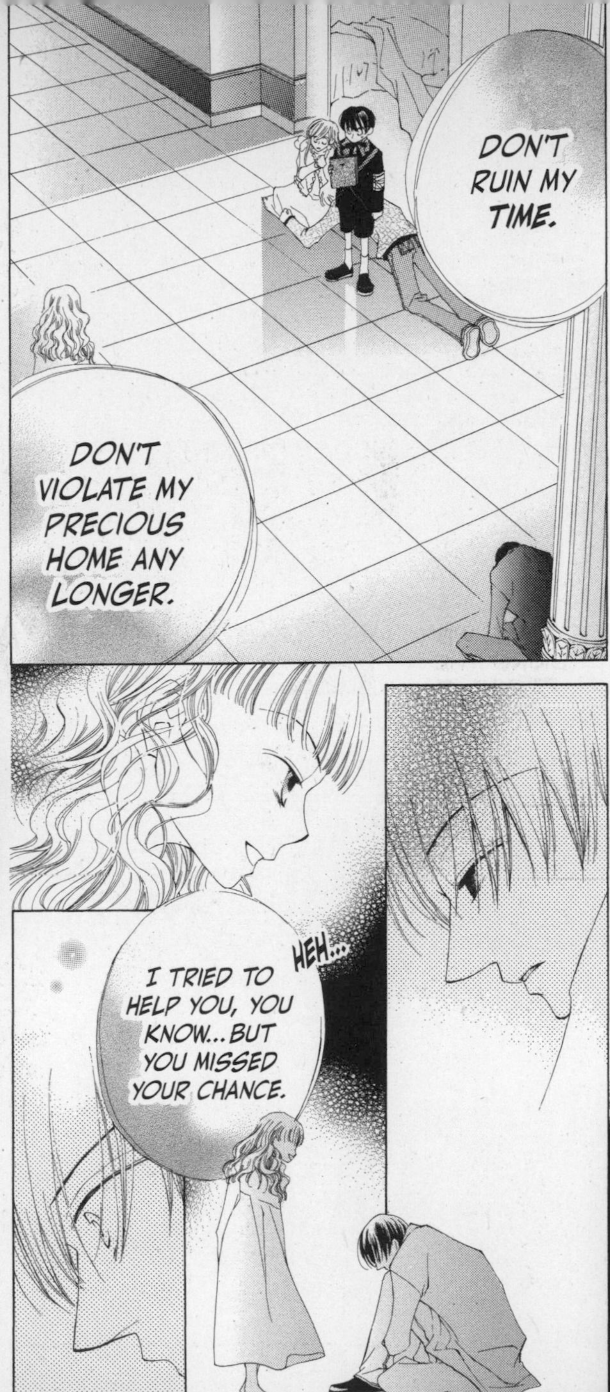
DON'T RUIN MY TIME.
DON'T VIOLATE MY PRECIOUS HOME ANY LONGER.
HEH...
I TRIED TO HELP YOU, YOU KNOW...BUT YOU MISSED YOUR CHANCE.

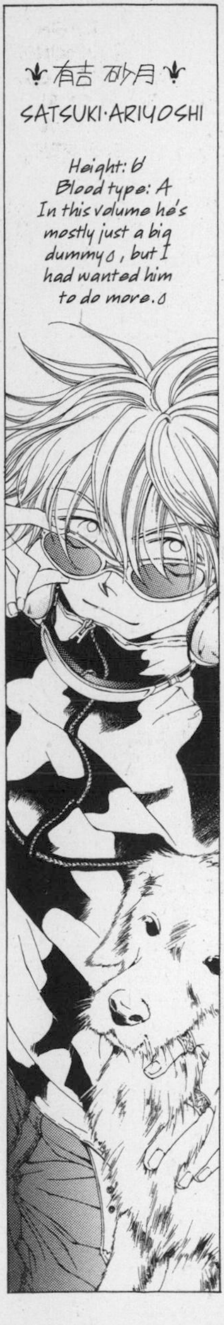
有吉 砂月
SATSUKI·ARIYOSHI
Height: 6'
Blood type: A
In this volume he's mostly just a big dummy♪, but I had wanted him to do more.♪

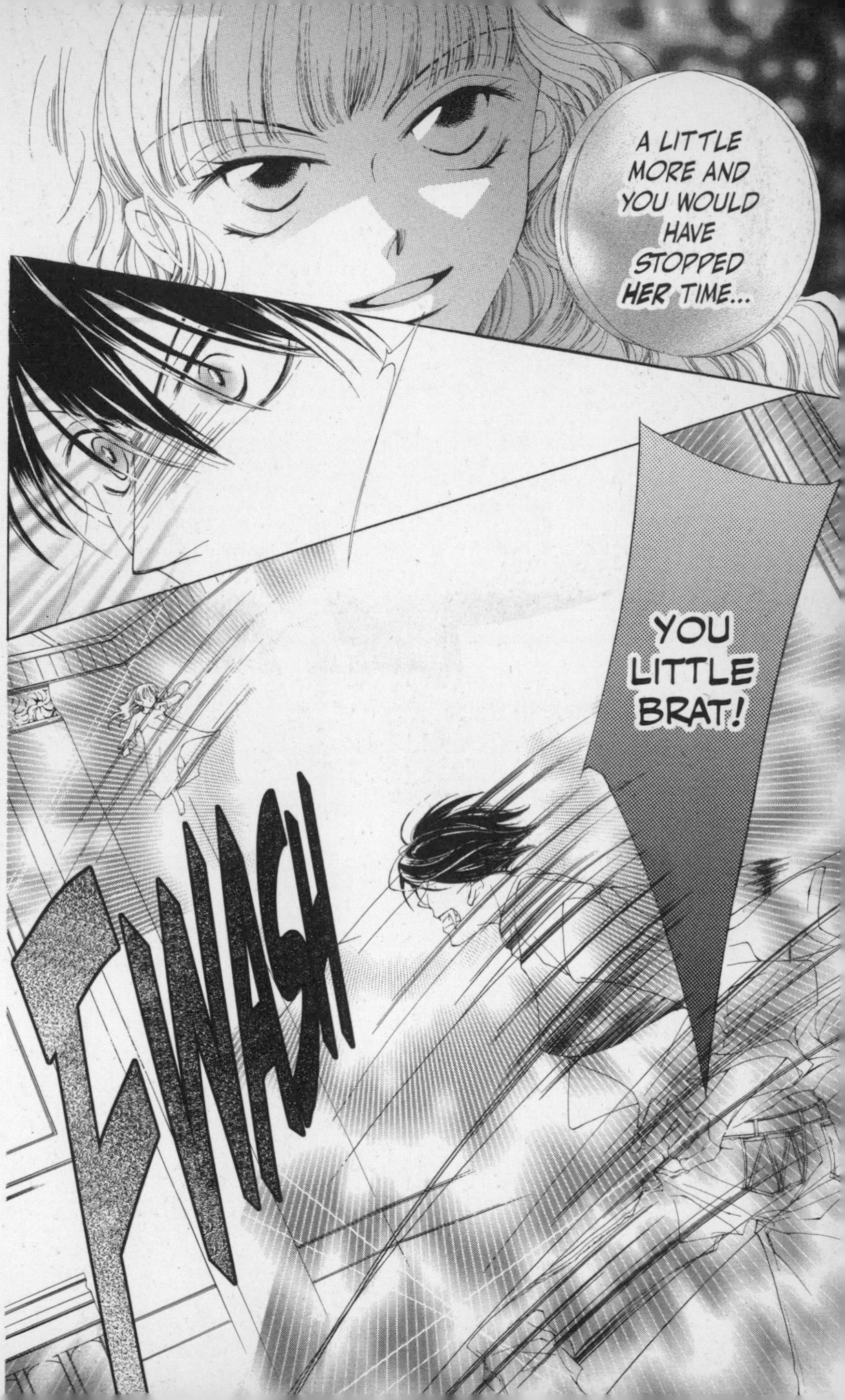
A LITTLE MORE AND YOU WOULD HAVE STOPPED HER TIME...
YOU LITTLE BRAT!
SMASH

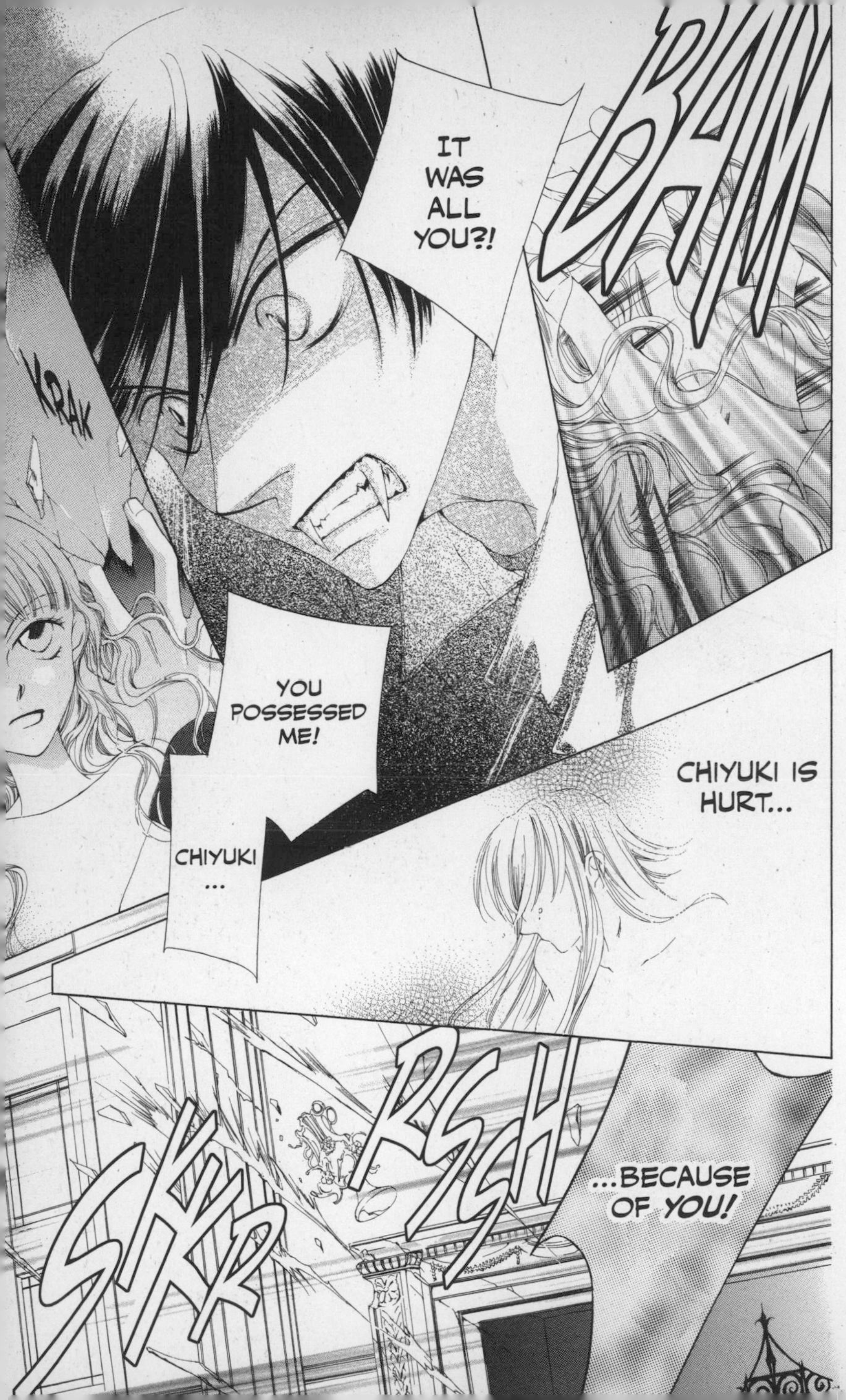
BAM
BAM
IT WAS ALL YOU?!
KRAK
YOU POSSESSED ME!
CHIYUKI ...
CHIYUKI IS HURT...
...BECAUSE OF YOU!
RSCH
SKR

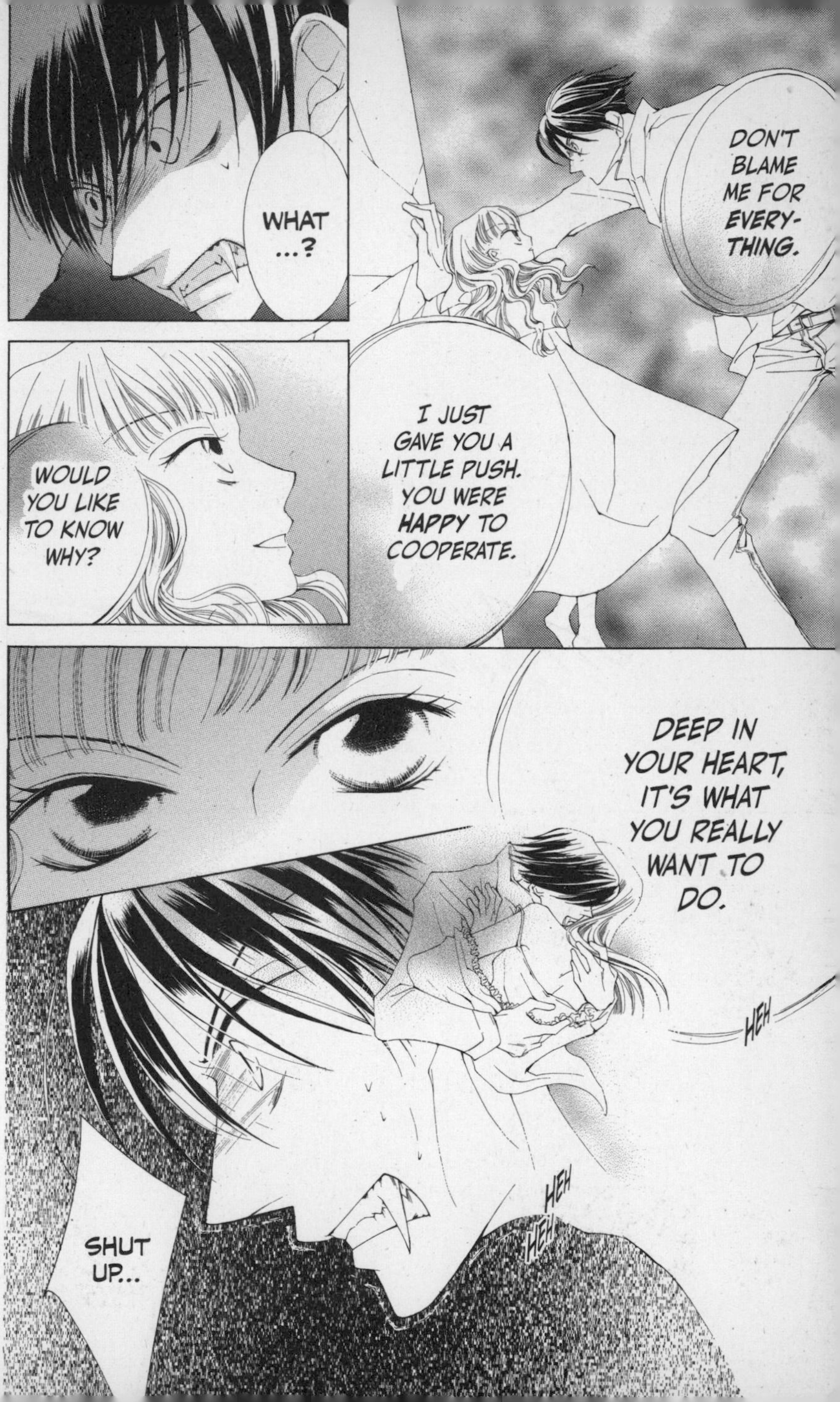
DON'T BLAME ME FOR EVERY-THING.
I JUST GAVE YOU A LITTLE PUSH. YOU WERE HAPPY TO COOPERATE.
WHAT ...?
WOULD YOU LIKE TO KNOW WHY?
DEEP IN YOUR HEART, IT'S WHAT YOU REALLY WANT TO DO.
HEH
HEH
HEH
SHUT UP...

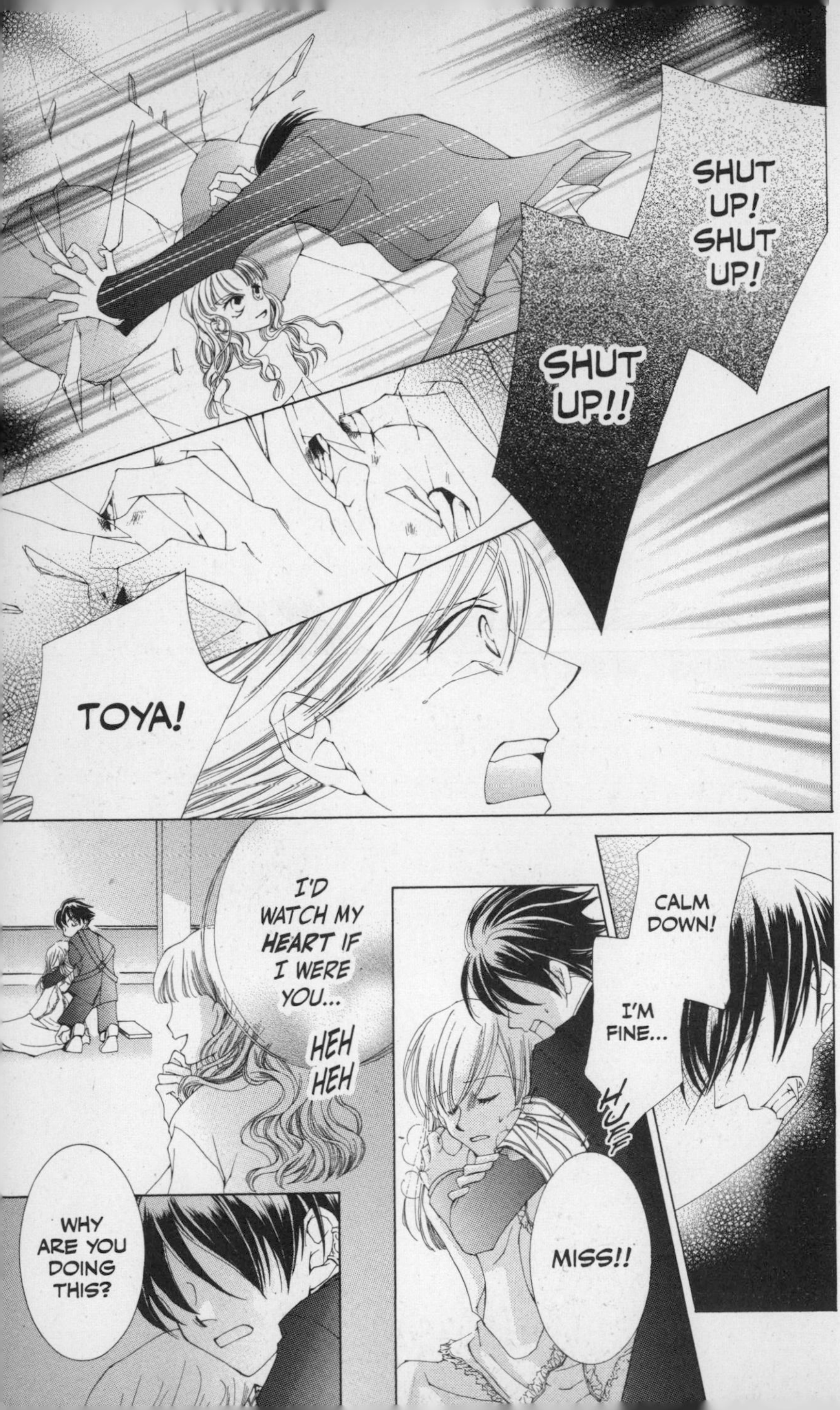
SHUT UP! SHUT UP!
SHUT UP!!
TOYA!
CALM DOWN!
I'M FINE...
MISS!!
I'D WATCH MY HEART IF I WERE YOU...
HEH HEH
WHY ARE YOU DOING THIS?

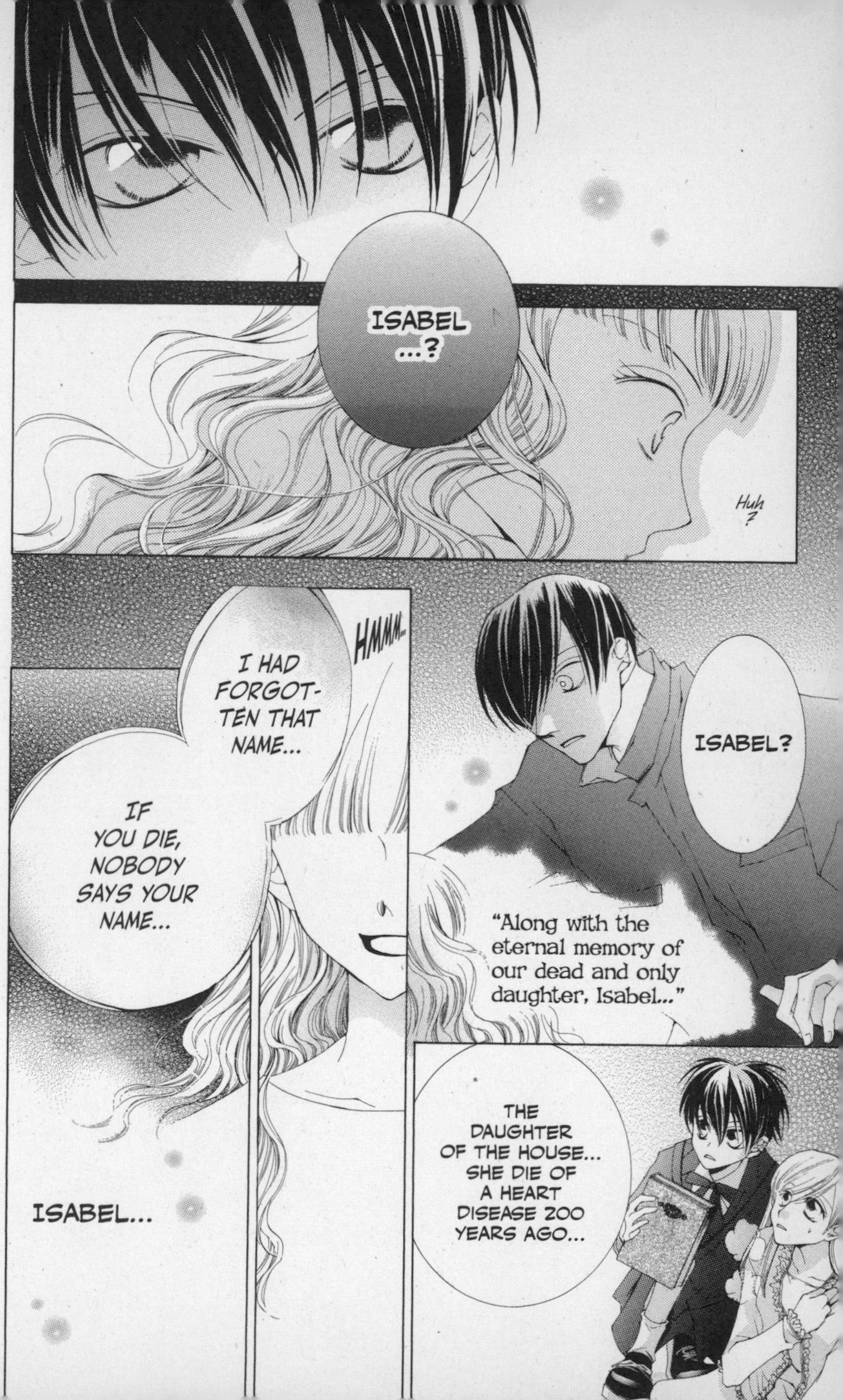
ISABEL ...?
Huh?
ISABEL?
"Along with the eternal memory of our dead and only daughter, Isabel..."
THE DAUGHTER OF THE HOUSE... SHE DIE OF A HEART DISEASE 200 YEARS AGO...
HMMM...
I HAD FORGOT-TEN THAT NAME...
IF YOU DIE, NOBODY SAYS YOUR NAME...
ISABEL...

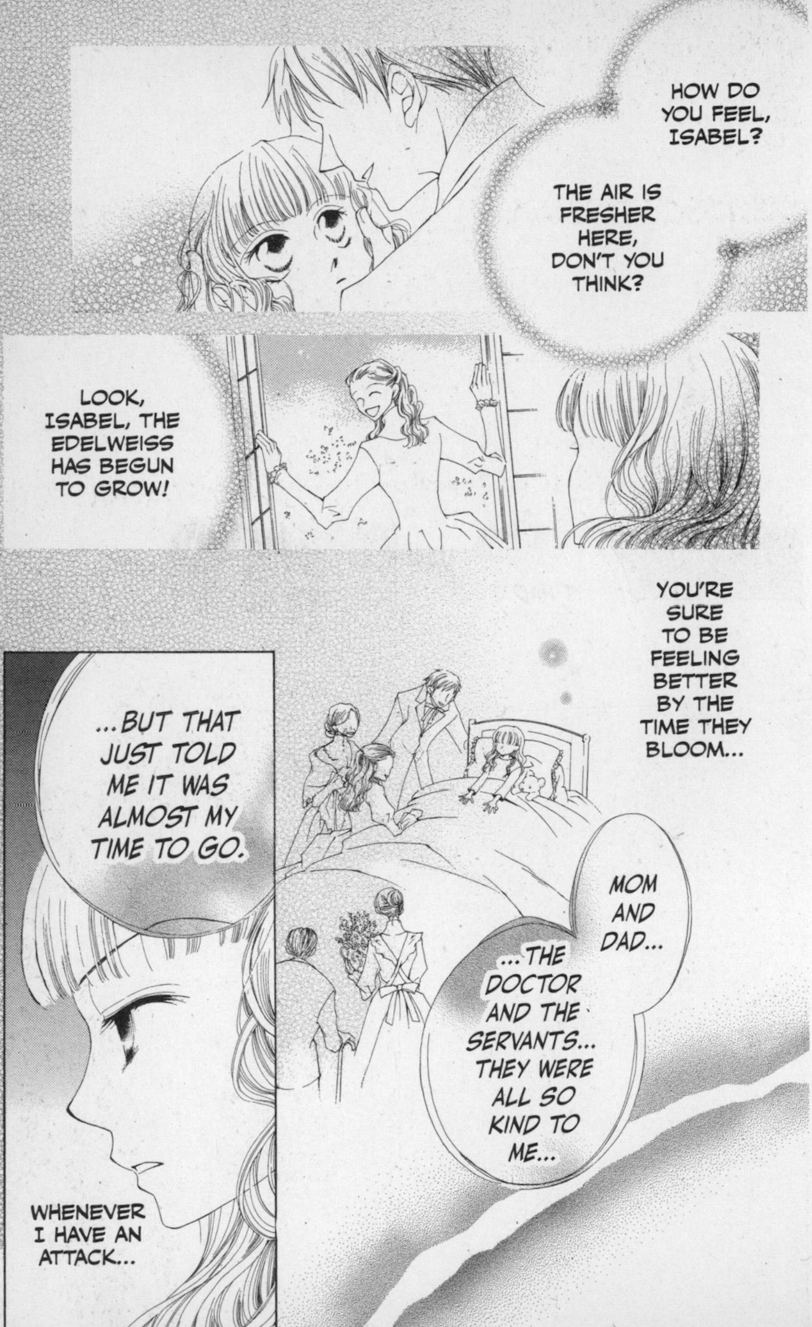
HOW DO YOU FEEL, ISABEL?
THE AIR IS FRESHER HERE, DON'T YOU THINK?
LOOK, ISABEL, THE EDELWEISS HAS BEGUN TO GROW!
YOU'RE SURE TO BE FEELING BETTER BY THE TIME THEY BLOOM...
MOM AND DAD...
...THE DOCTOR AND THE SERVANTS... THEY WERE ALL SO KIND TO ME...
...BUT THAT JUST TOLD ME IT WAS ALMOST MY TIME TO GO.
WHENEVER I HAVE AN ATTACK...

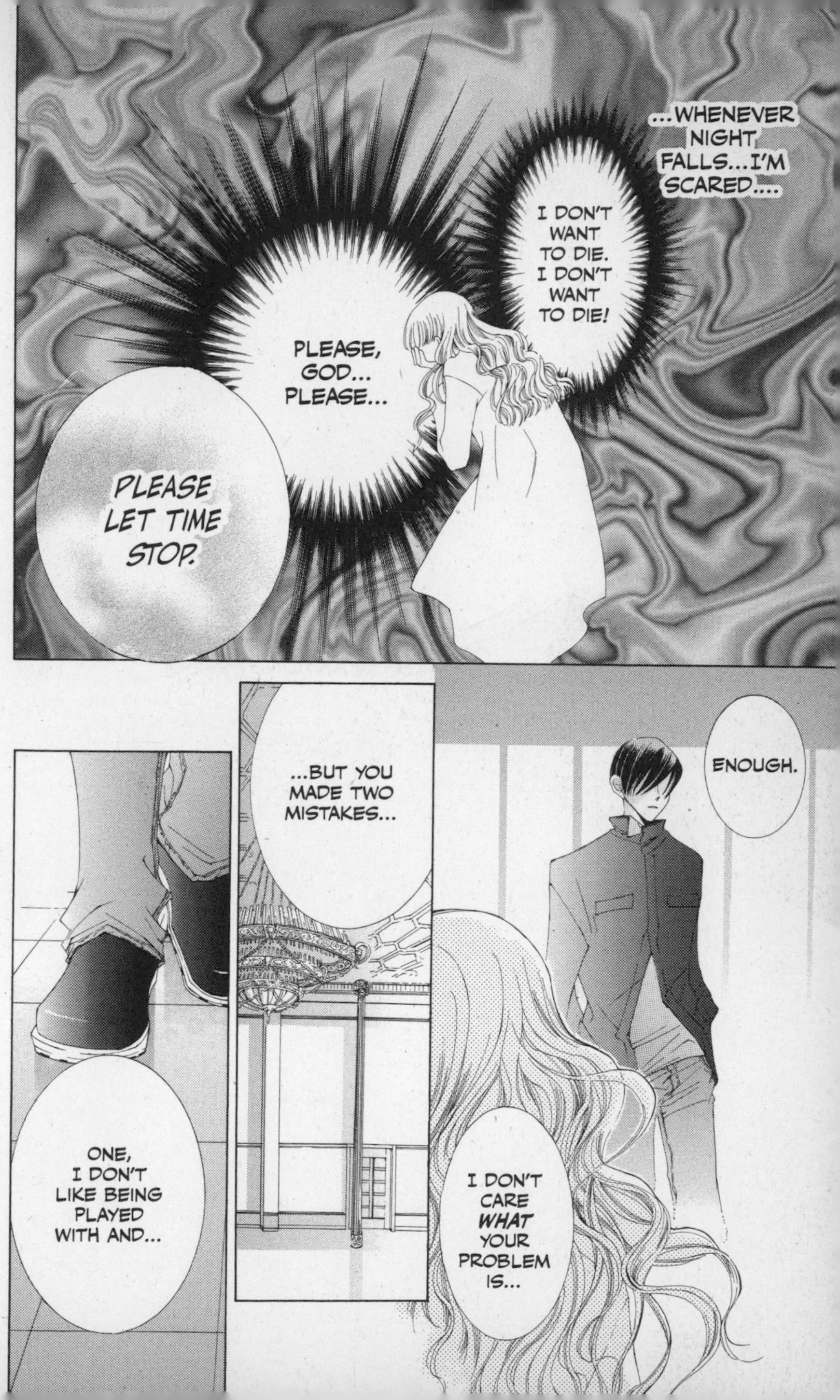
...WHENEVER NIGHT FALLS...I'M SCARED....
I DON'T WANT TO DIE. I DON'T WANT TO DIE!
PLEASE, GOD... PLEASE...
PLEASE LET TIME STOP.
ENOUGH.
I DON'T CARE *WHAT* YOUR PROBLEM IS...
...BUT YOU MADE TWO MISTAKES...
ONE, I DON'T LIKE BEING PLAYED WITH AND...

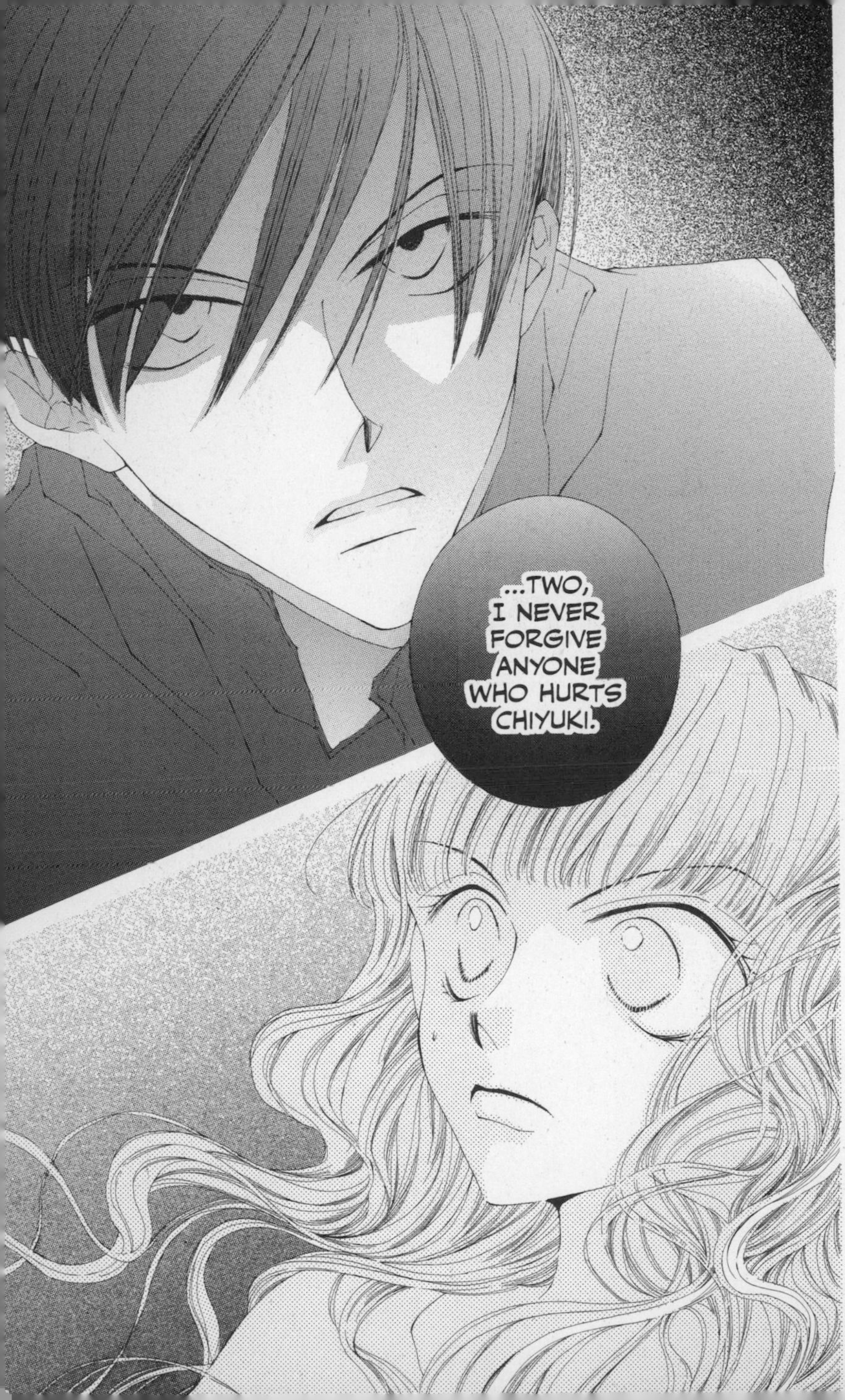
...TWO, I NEVER FORGIVE ANYONE WHO HURTS CHIYUKI.

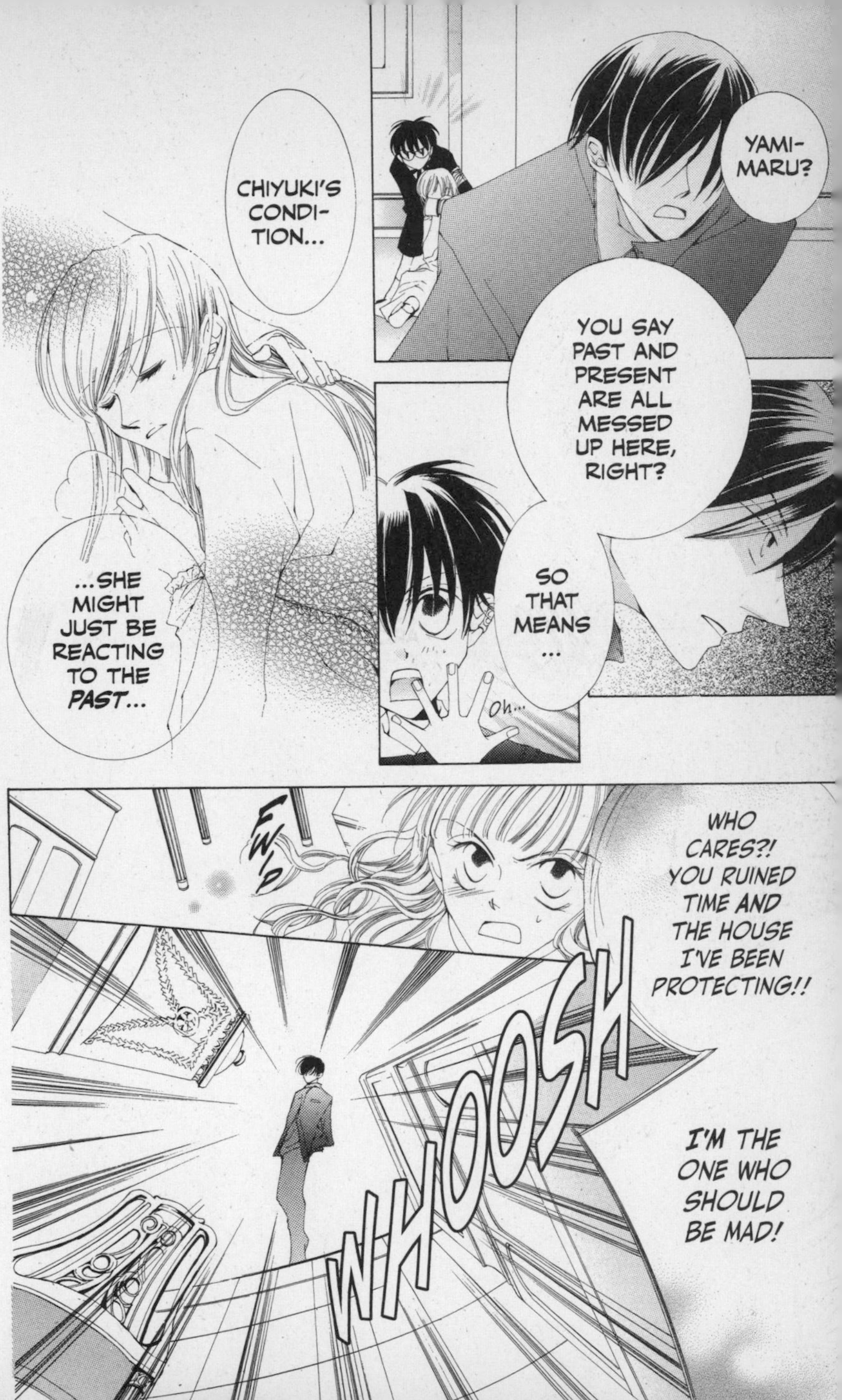
YAMI-MARU?
YOU SAY PAST AND PRESENT ARE ALL MESSED UP HERE, RIGHT?
SO THAT MEANS...
Oh...
CHIYUKI'S CONDITION...
...SHE MIGHT JUST BE REACTING TO THE *PAST*...
FWIP
WHO CARES?! YOU RUINED TIME AND THE HOUSE I'VE BEEN PROTECTING!!
WHOOSH
I'M THE ONE WHO SHOULD BE MAD!

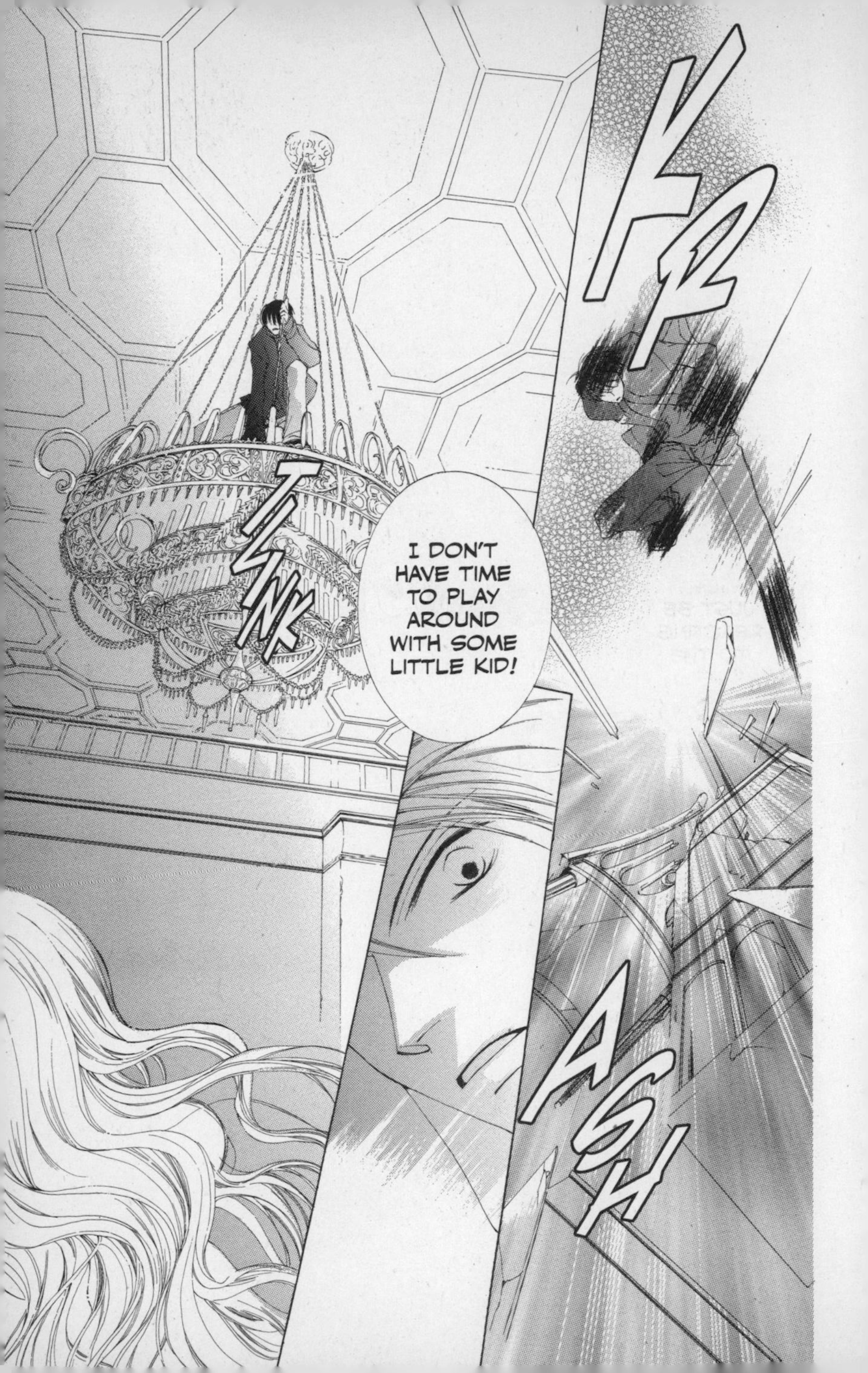
KRASH
I DON'T HAVE TIME TO PLAY AROUND WITH SOME LITTLE KID!
TINK

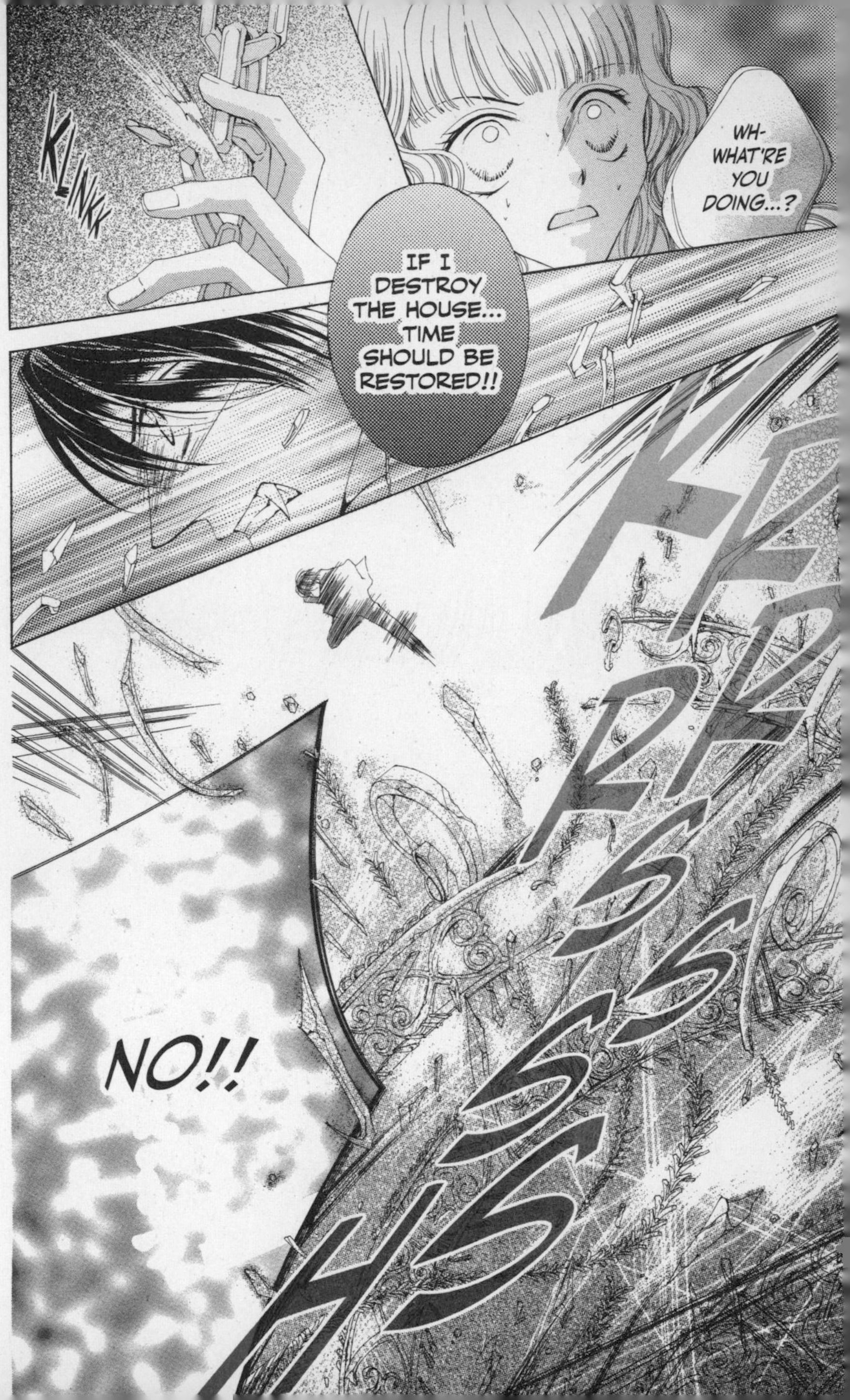
WH-
WHAT'RE
YOU
DOING...?
KLINKK
IF I DESTROY THE HOUSE... TIME SHOULD BE RESTORED!!
NO!!

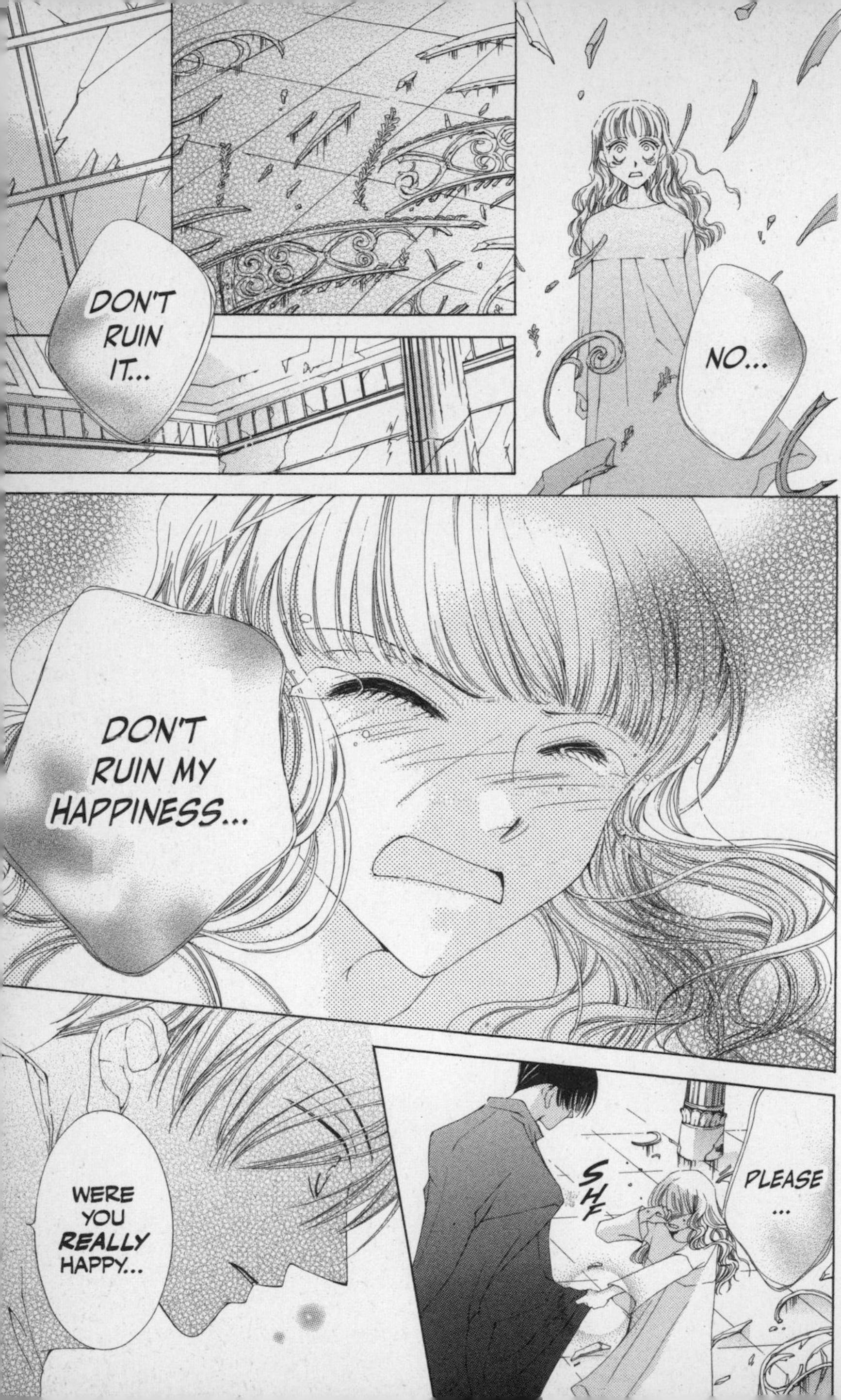
NO...
DON'T RUIN IT...
DON'T RUIN MY HAPPINESS...
PLEASE ...
SHF
WERE YOU **REALLY** HAPPY...

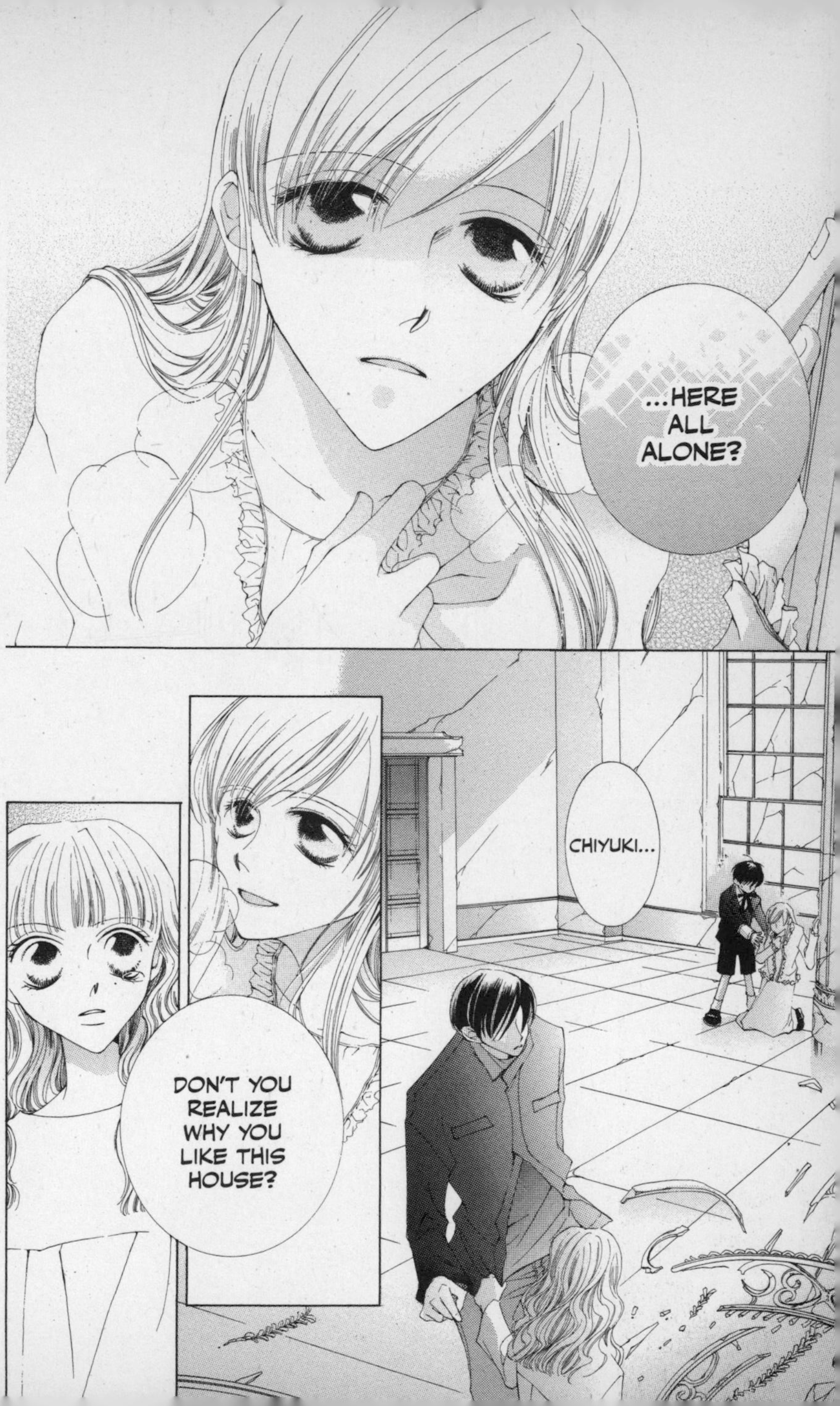
...HERE ALL ALONE?
CHIYUKI...
DON'T YOU REALIZE WHY YOU LIKE THIS HOUSE?

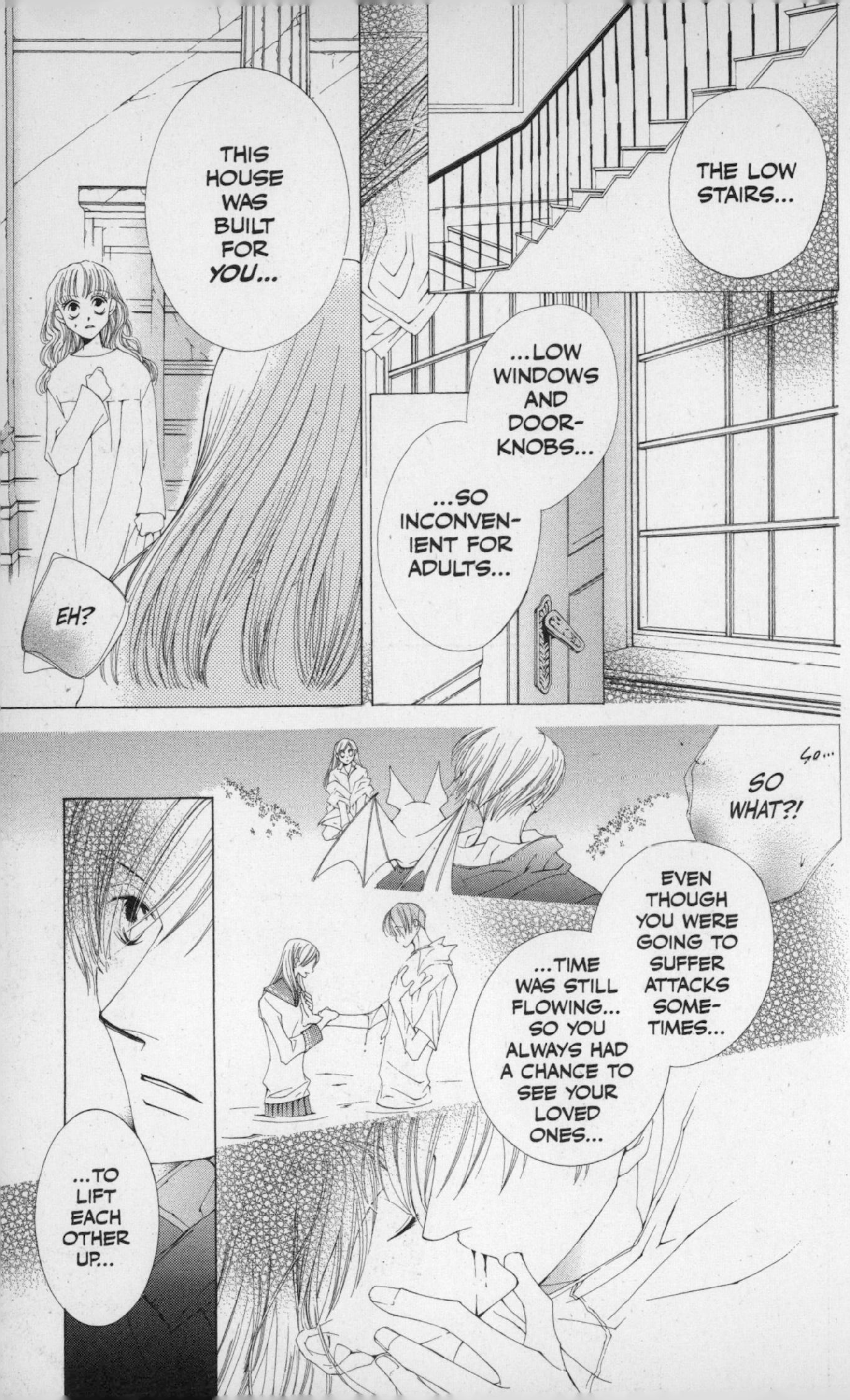
THE LOW STAIRS...
...LOW WINDOWS AND DOOR-KNOBS...
...SO INCONVEN-IENT FOR ADULTS...
THIS HOUSE WAS BUILT FOR YOU...
EH?
So...
SO WHAT?!
EVEN THOUGH YOU WERE GOING TO SUFFER ATTACKS SOME-TIMES...
...TIME WAS STILL FLOWING... SO YOU ALWAYS HAD A CHANCE TO SEE YOUR LOVED ONES...
...TO LIFT EACH OTHER UP...

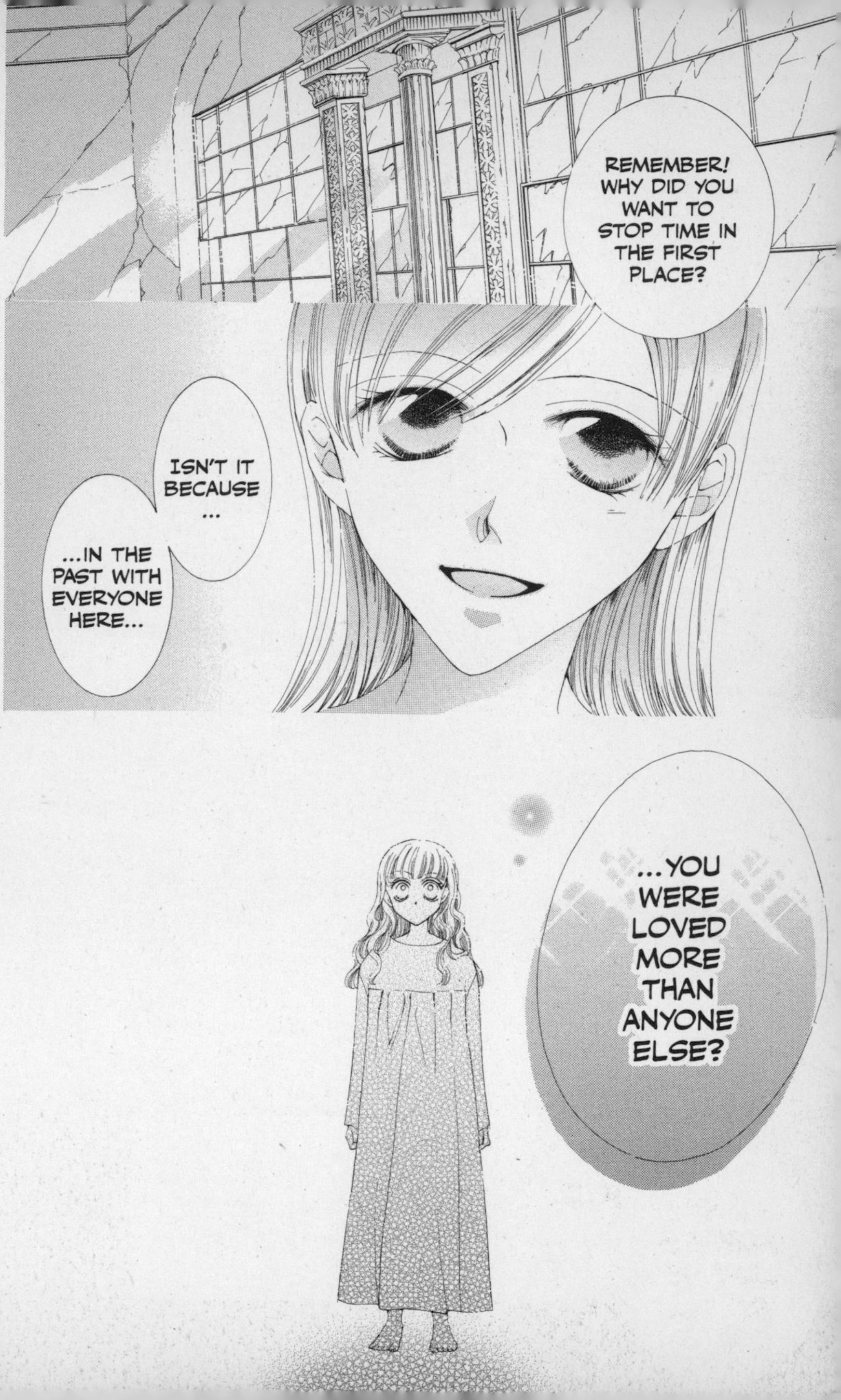
REMEMBER! WHY DID YOU WANT TO STOP TIME IN THE FIRST PLACE?
ISN'T IT BECAUSE ...
...IN THE PAST WITH EVERYONE HERE...
...YOU WERE LOVED MORE THAN ANYONE ELSE?

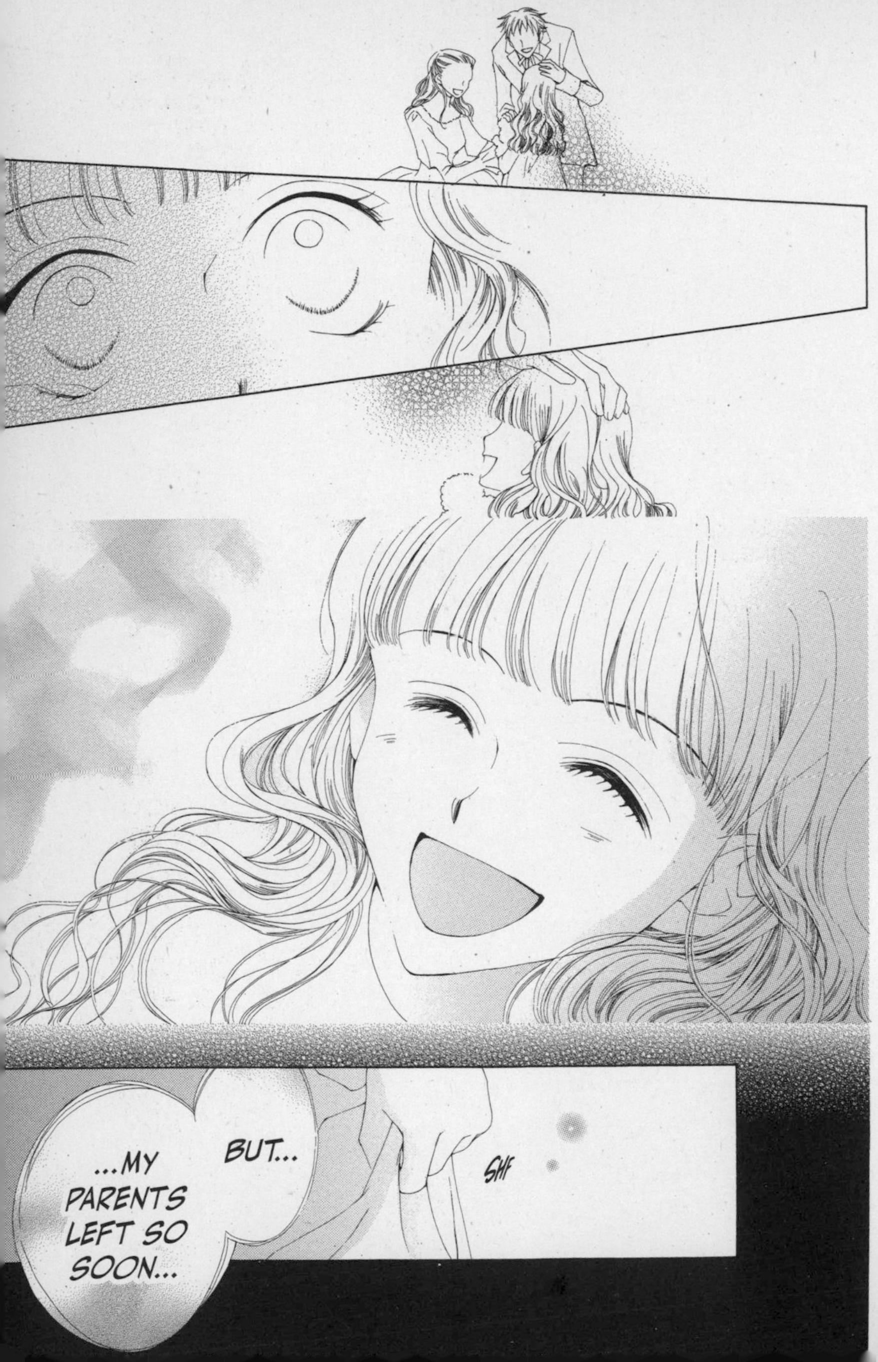
SHF
BUT...
...MY PARENTS LEFT SO SOON...

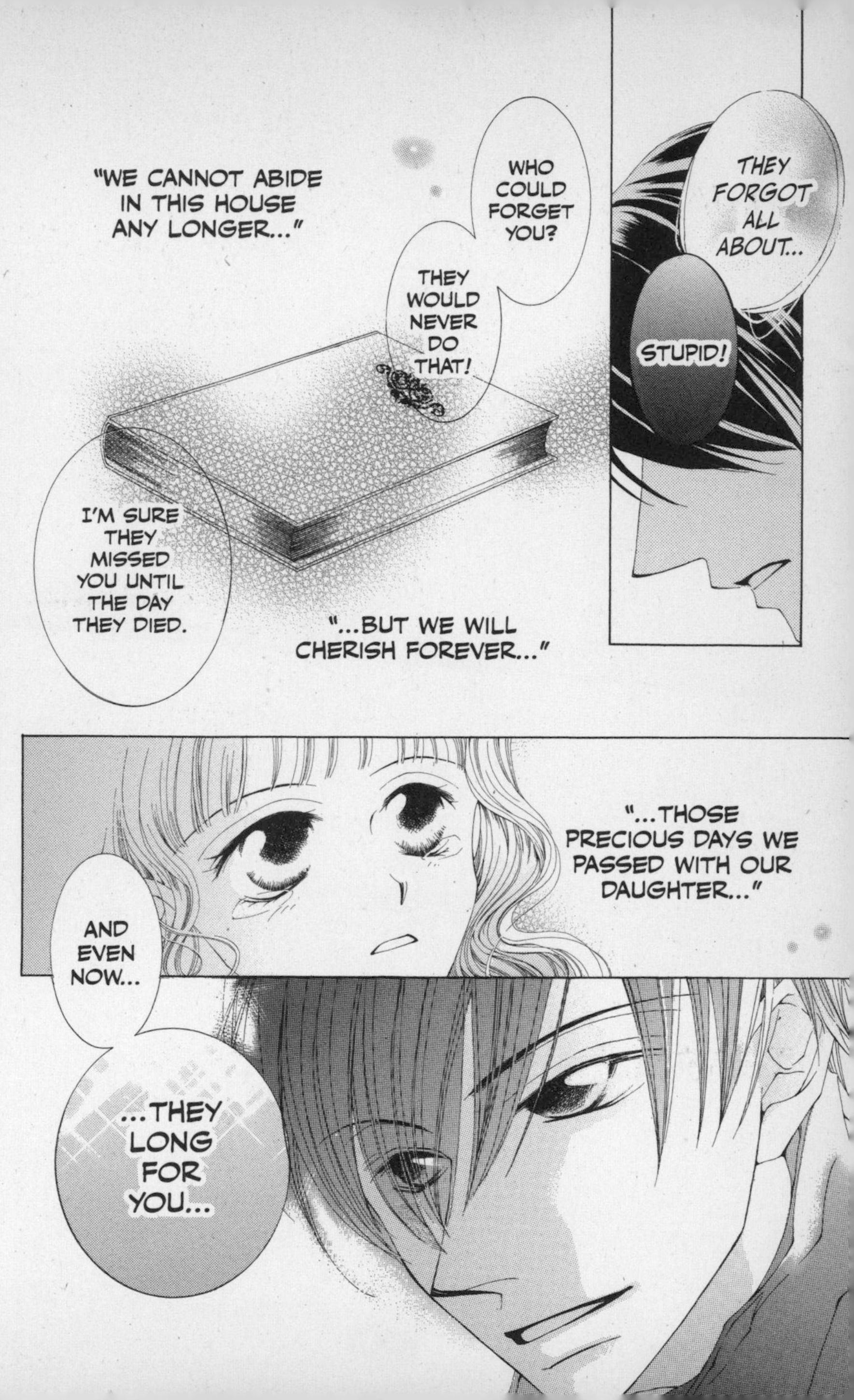
THEY FORGOT ALL ABOUT...
STUPID!
WHO COULD FORGET YOU?
THEY WOULD NEVER DO THAT!
"WE CANNOT ABIDE IN THIS HOUSE ANY LONGER..."
I'M SURE THEY MISSED YOU UNTIL THE DAY THEY DIED.
"...BUT WE WILL CHERISH FOREVER..."
"...THOSE PRECIOUS DAYS WE PASSED WITH OUR DAUGHTER..."
AND EVEN NOW...
...THEY LONG FOR YOU...

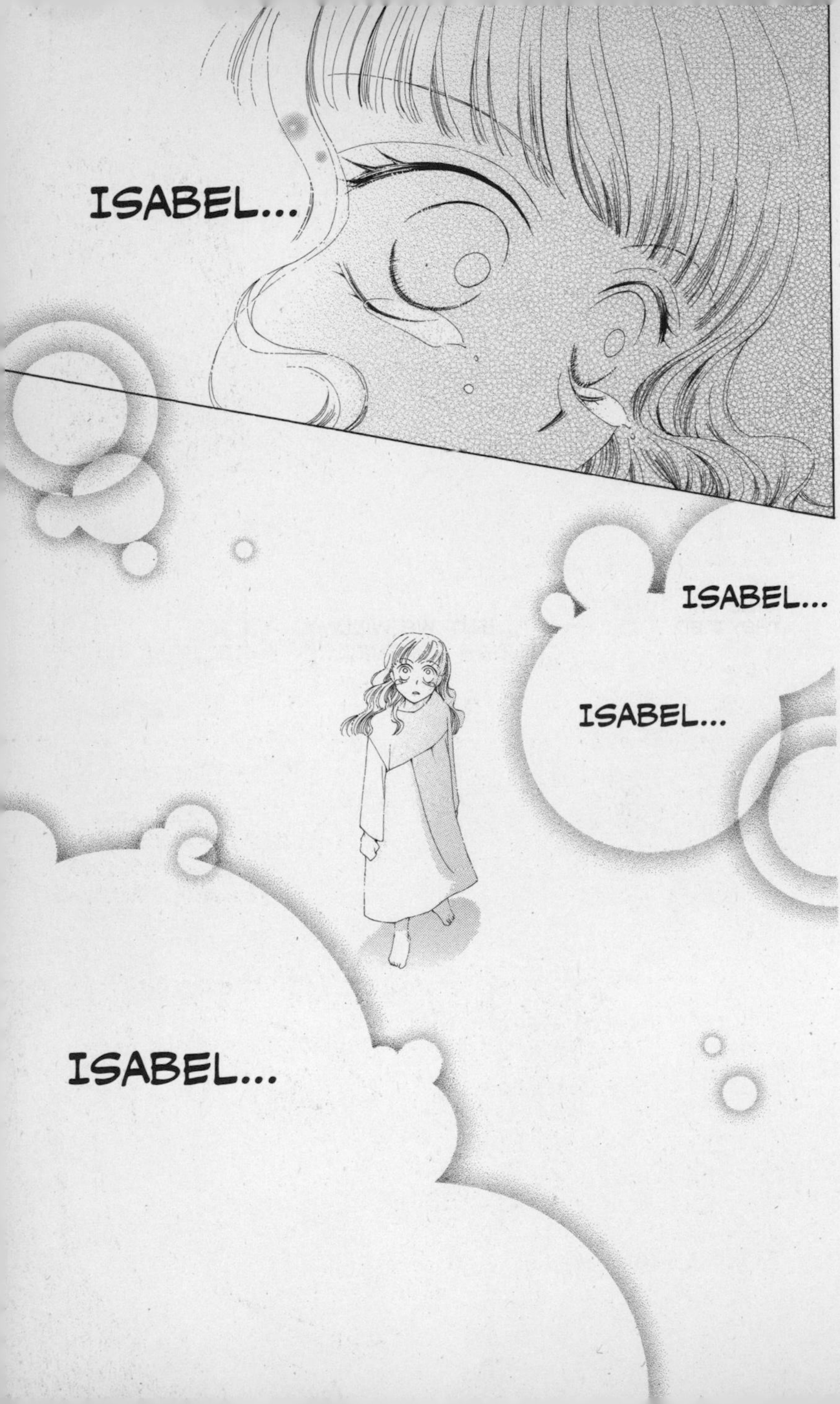
ISABEL...
ISABEL...
ISABEL...
ISABEL...

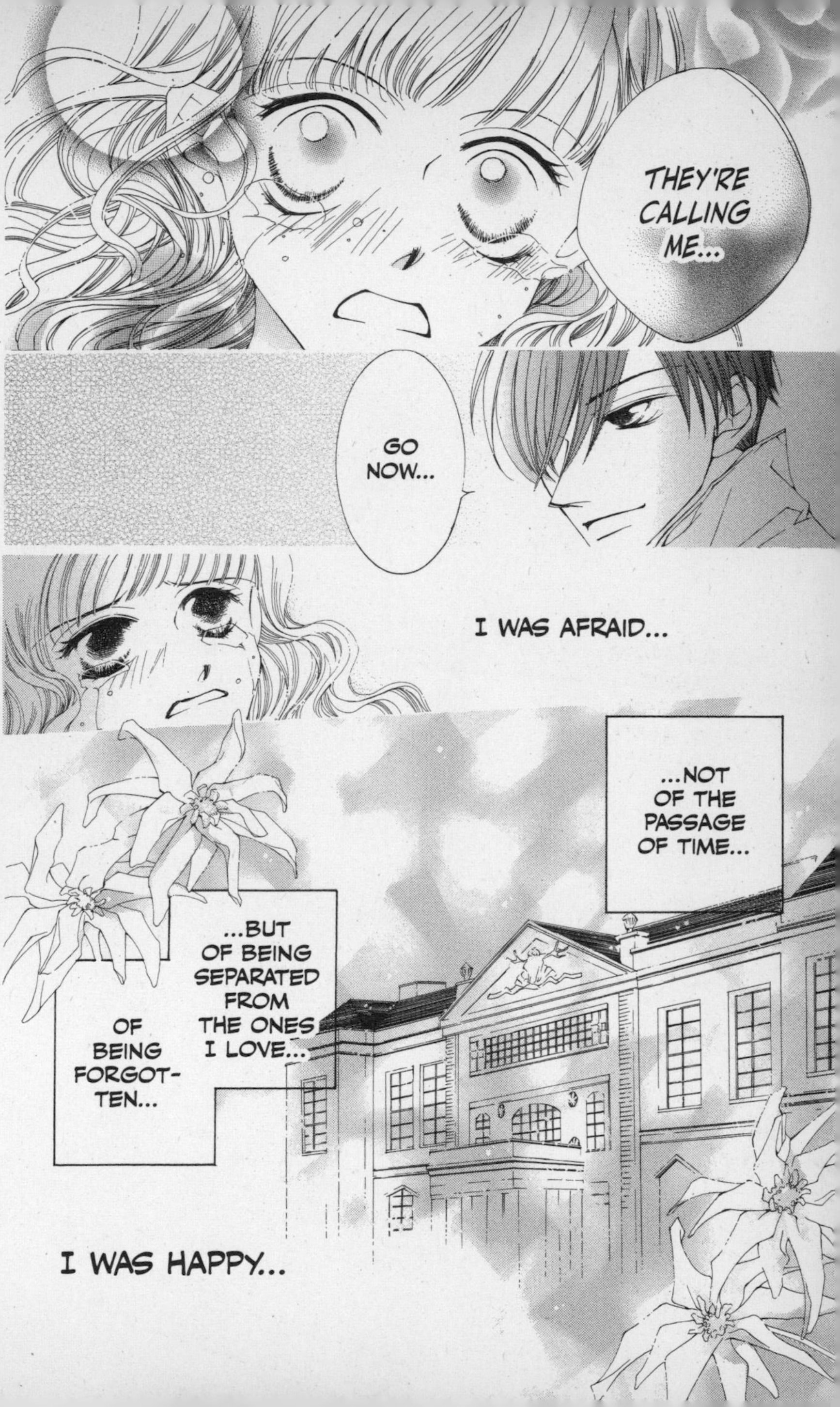
THEY'RE CALLING ME...
GO NOW...
I WAS AFRAID...
...NOT OF THE PASSAGE OF TIME...
...BUT OF BEING SEPARATED FROM THE ONES I LOVE...
OF BEING FORGOT-TEN...
I WAS HAPPY...

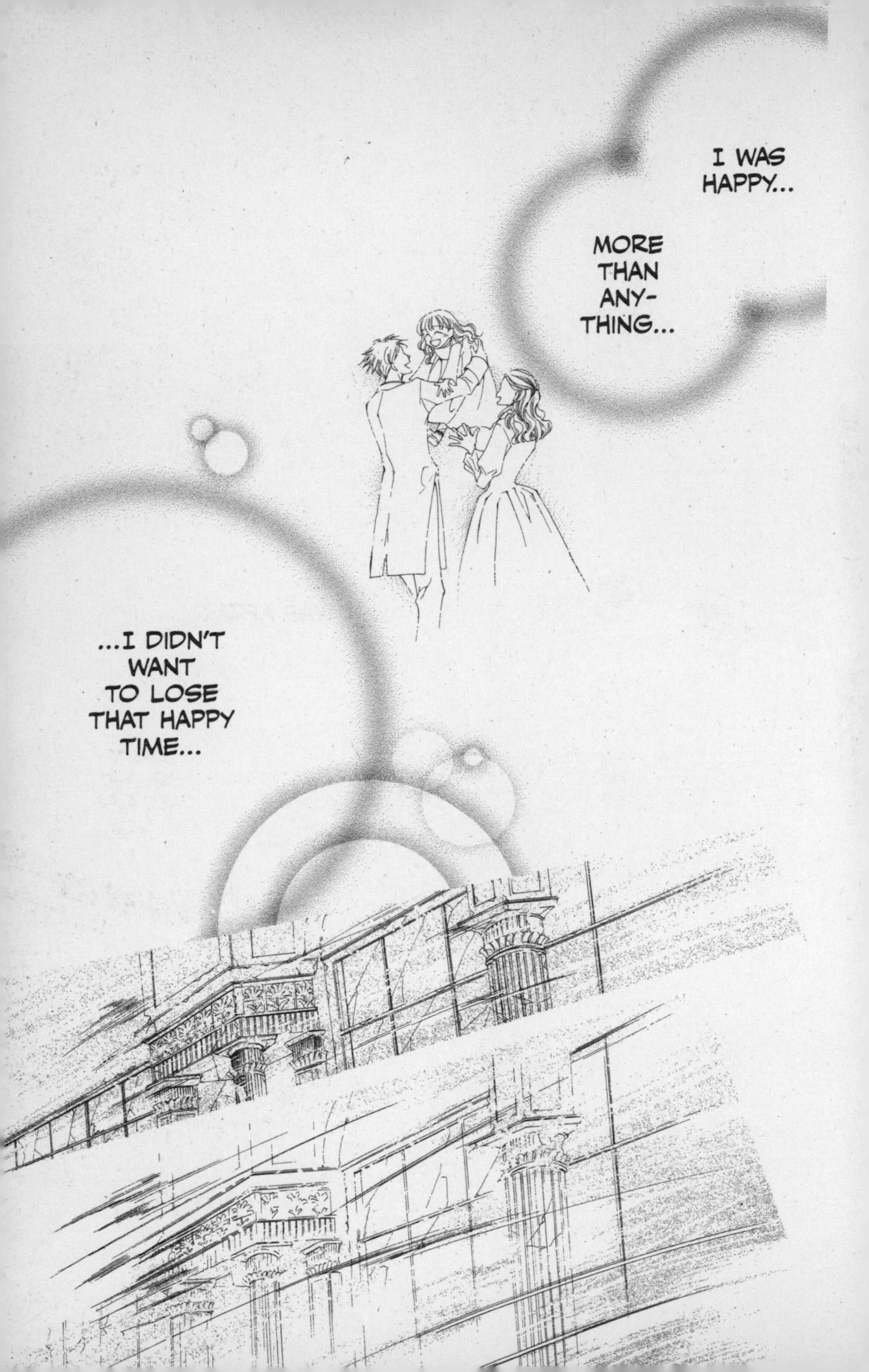
I WAS HAPPY...
MORE THAN ANY-THING...
...I DIDN'T WANT TO LOSE THAT HAPPY TIME...

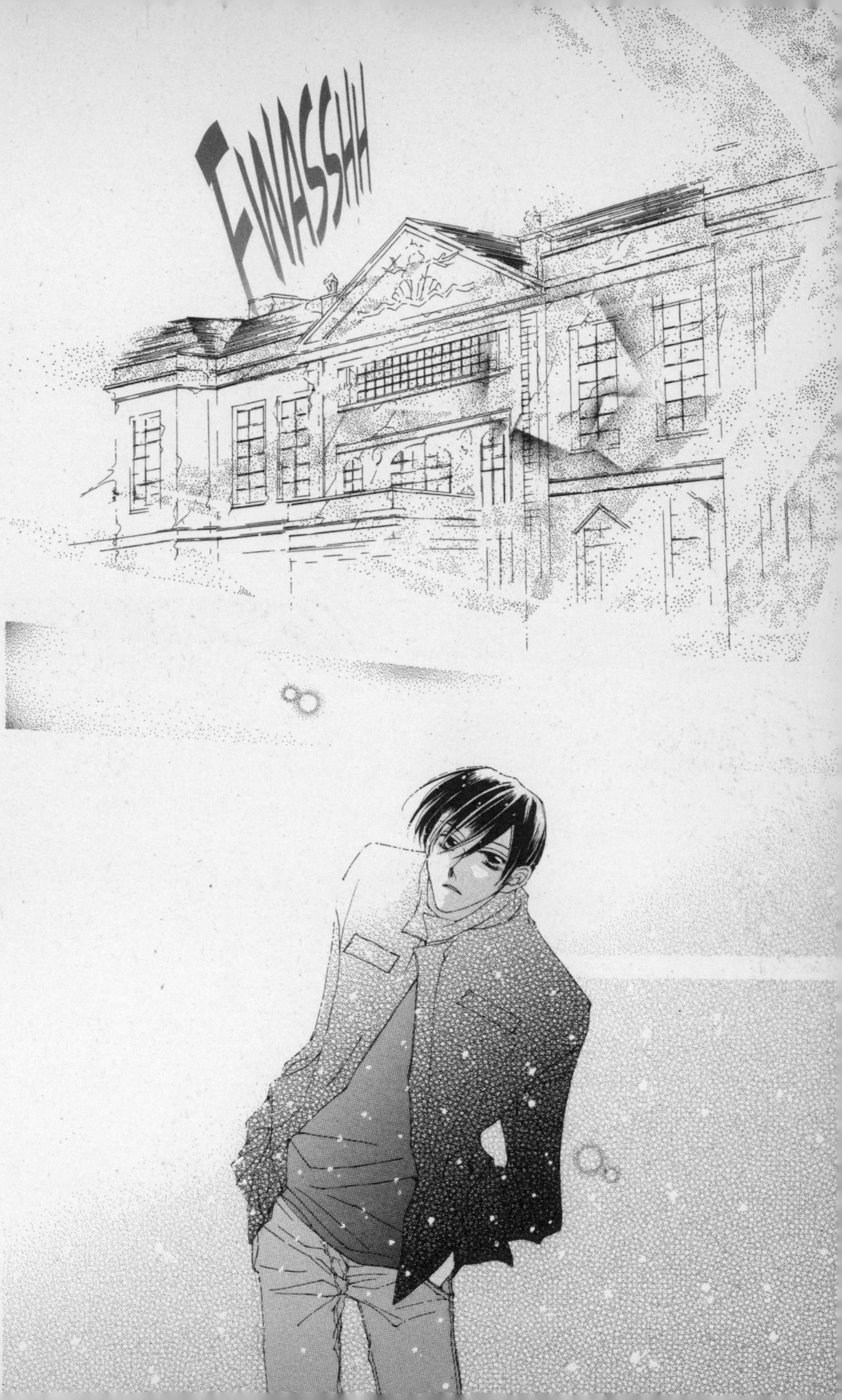
FWASSHH

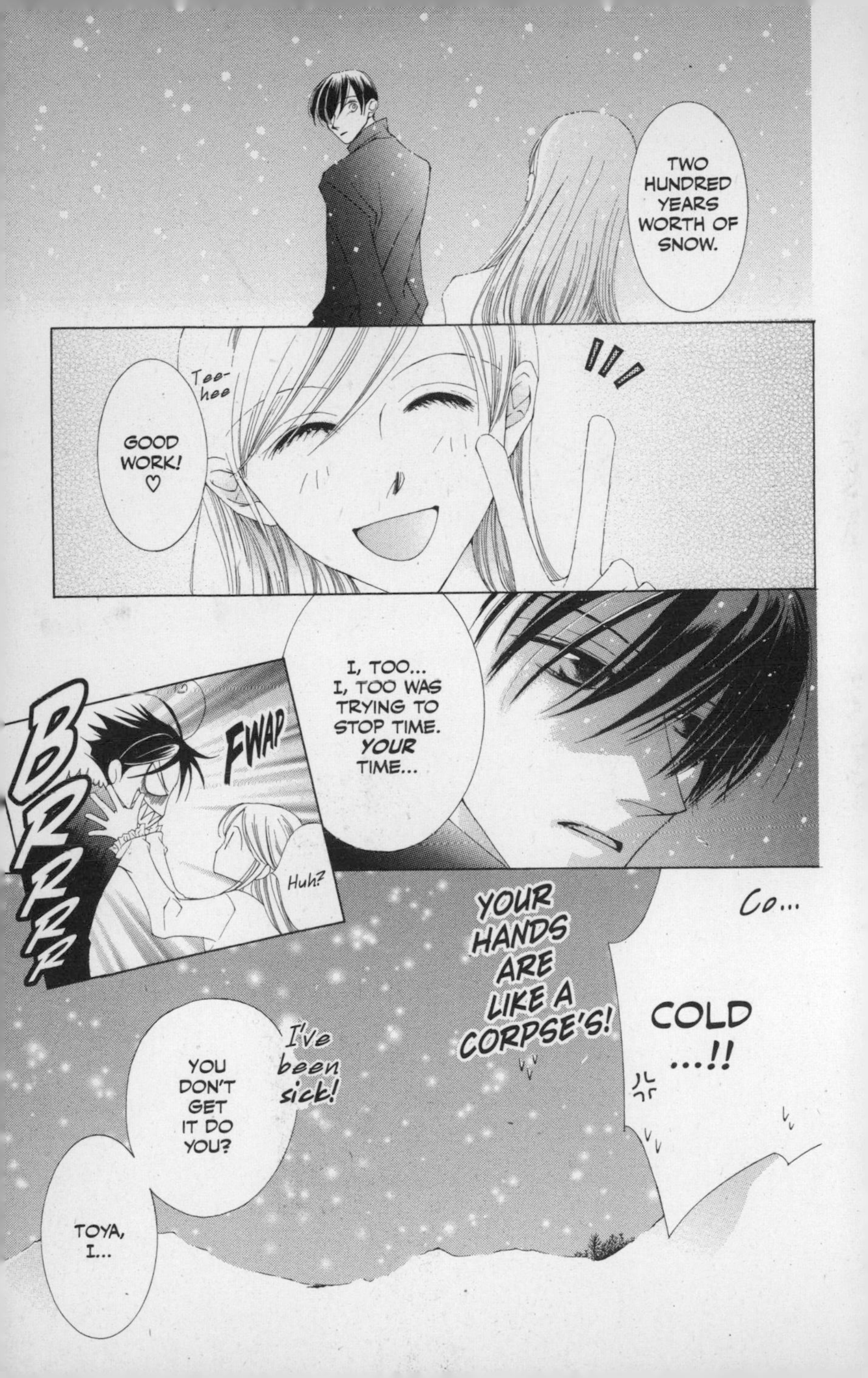
TWO HUNDRED YEARS WORTH OF SNOW.
Tee-hee
GOOD WORK! ♡
I, TOO... I, TOO WAS TRYING TO STOP TIME. *YOUR* TIME...
FWAP
Huh?
BRRRR
Co...
COLD ...!!
YOUR HANDS ARE LIKE A CORPSE'S!
I've been sick!
YOU DON'T GET IT DO YOU?
TOYA, I...

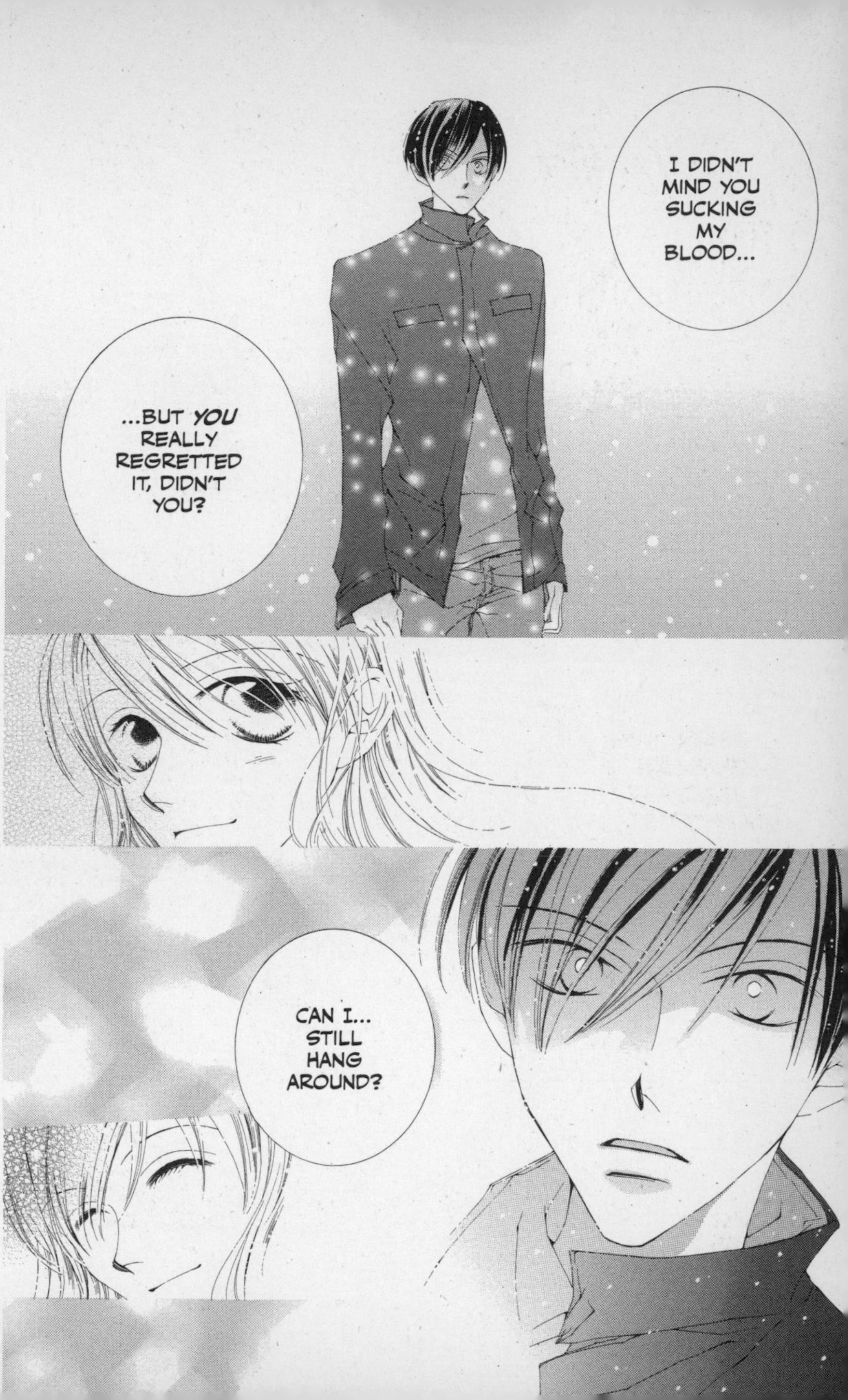
I DIDN'T MIND YOU SUCKING MY BLOOD...
...BUT *YOU* REALLY REGRETTED IT, DIDN'T YOU?
CAN I... STILL HANG AROUND?

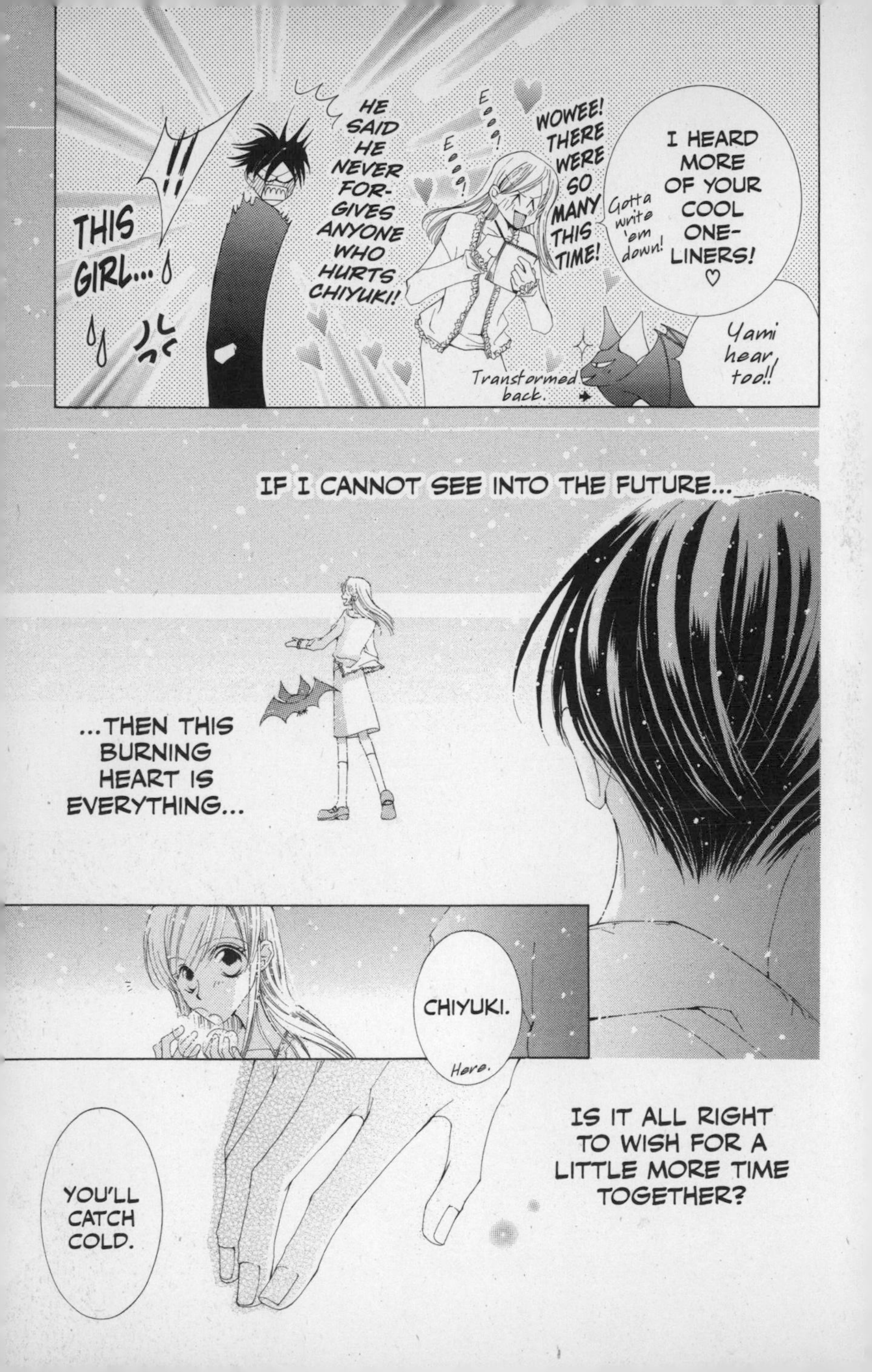
I HEARD MORE OF YOUR COOL ONE-LINERS! ♡
Yami hear, too!!
Gotta write 'em down!
WOWEE! THERE WERE SO MANY THIS TIME!
Eeee!
Eeee!
Transformed back.
HE SAID HE NEVER FORGIVES ANYONE WHO HURTS CHIYUKI!
!!
THIS GIRL...
IF I CANNOT SEE INTO THE FUTURE...
...THEN THIS BURNING HEART IS EVERYTHING...
CHIYUKI.
Here.
IS IT ALL RIGHT TO WISH FOR A LITTLE MORE TIME TOGETHER?
YOU'LL CATCH COLD.

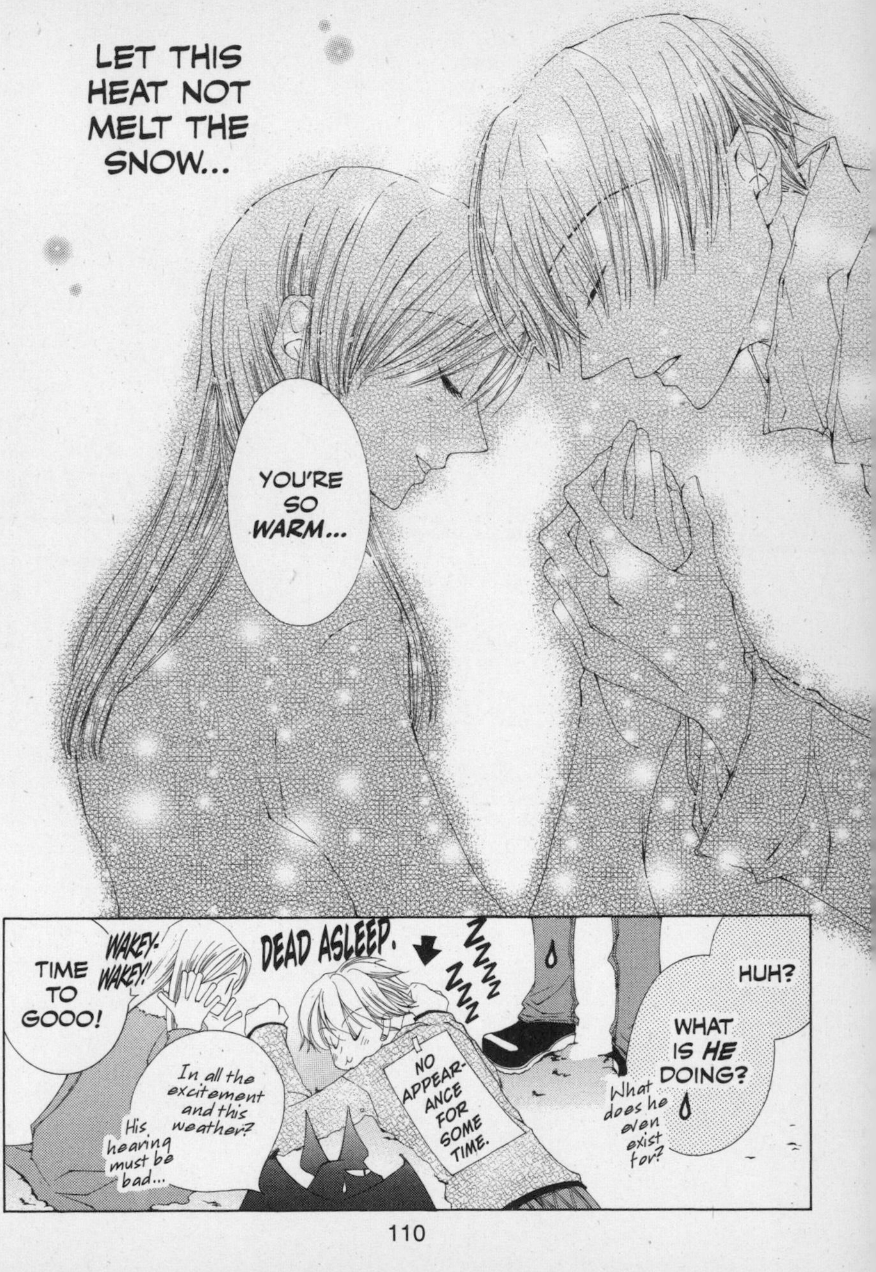

LET THIS HEAT NOT MELT THE SNOW...
YOU'RE SO WARM...
HUH?
WHAT IS HE DOING?
What does he even exist for?
ZZZZ ZZZ
DEAD ASLEEP.
NO APPEARANCE FOR SOME TIME.
WAKEY-WAKEY!
TIME TO GOOO!
In all the excitement and this weather?
His hearing must be bad...

After-bath cake.
The last snack of the day.

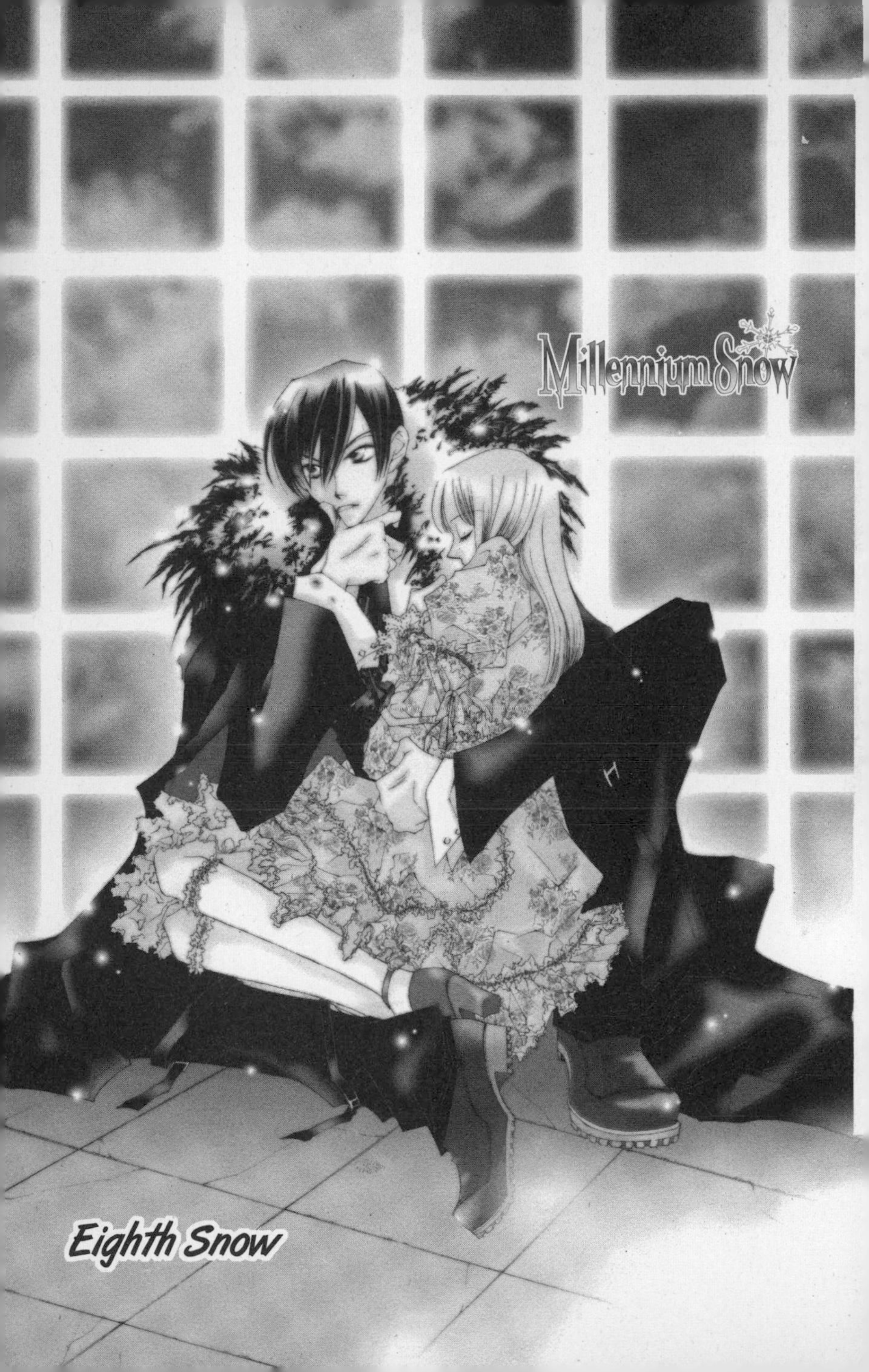
Millennium Snow
Eighth Snow

Go Go Shopping

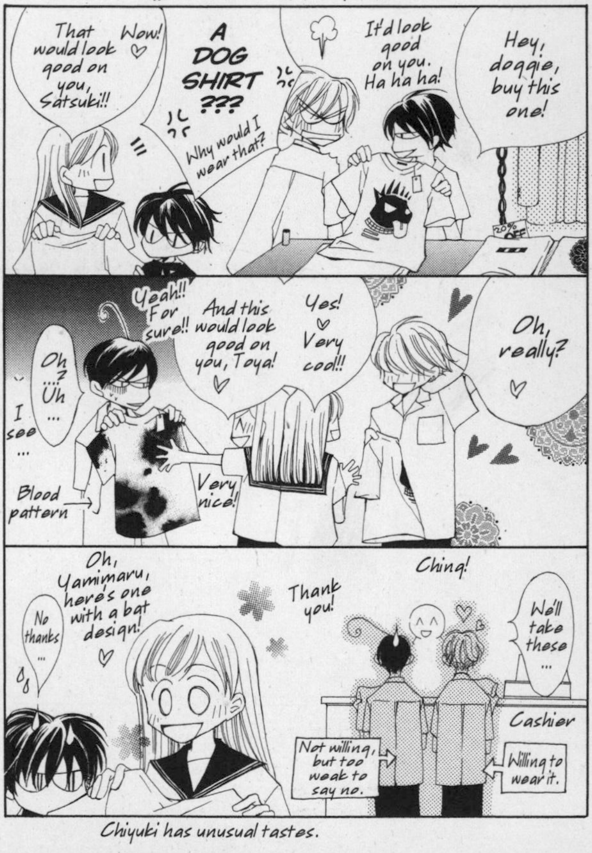
Hey, doggie, buy this one!
It'd look good on you. Ha ha ha!
A DOG SHIRT ???
Why would I wear that?
Wow! ♡
That would look good on you, Satsuki!!
Oh, really? ♡
Yes! ♡ Very cool!!
And this would look good on you, Toya! ♡
Yeah!! For sure!!
Oh ...? Uh ...
I see ...
Very nice!
Blood pattern
We'll take these ...
Ching!
Thank you!
Cashier
Willing to wear it.
Not willing, but too weak to say no.
Oh, Yamimaru, here's one with a bat design! ♡
No thanks ...

Chiyuki has unusual tastes.

And now ...

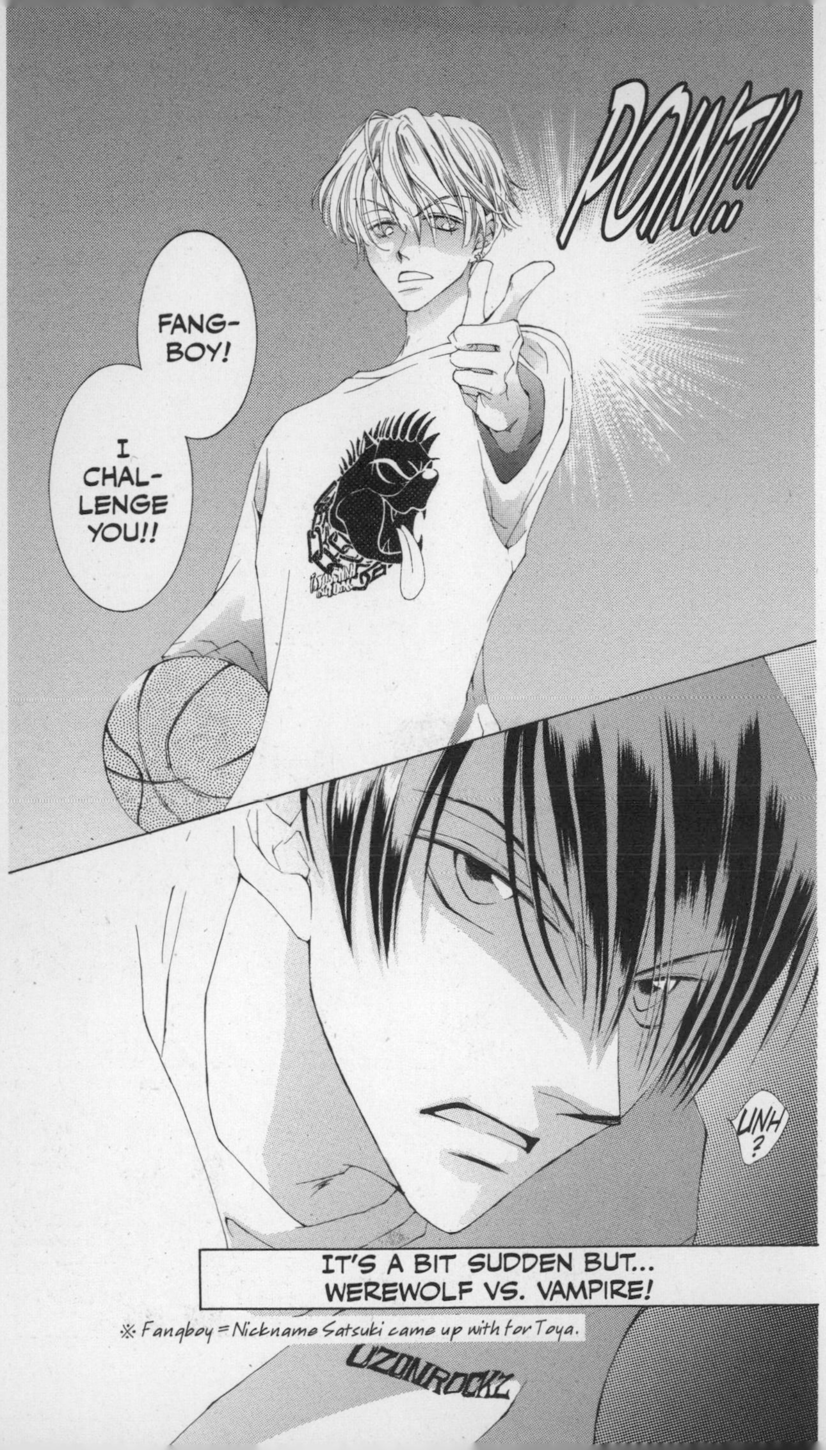
PON!!
FANG-BOY!
I CHAL-LENGE YOU!!
UNH?
IT'S A BIT SUDDEN BUT... WEREWOLF VS. VAMPIRE!
UZONROCKZ

※ Fangboy = Nickname Satsuki came up with for Toya.

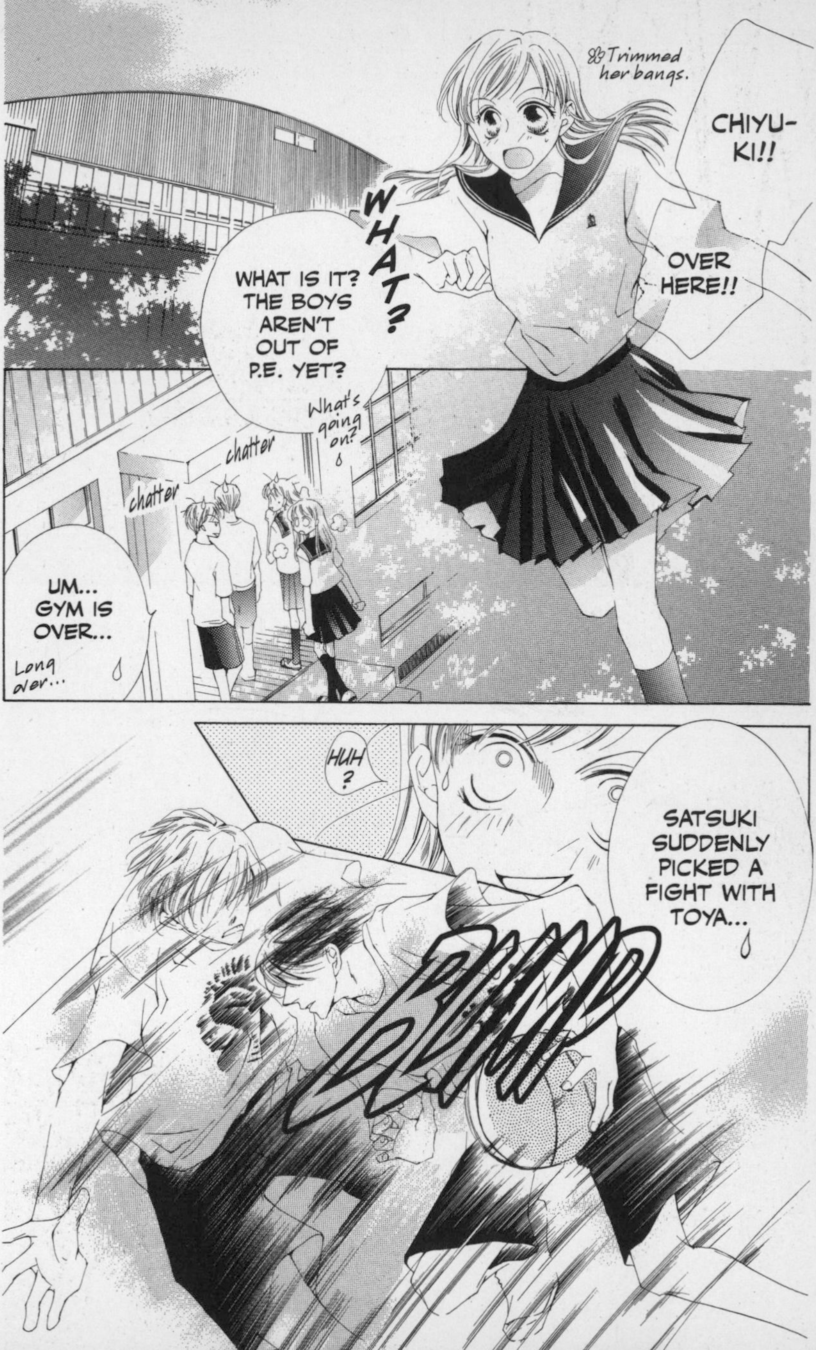
CHIYU-KI!!
OVER HERE!!
Trimmed her bangs.
WHAT?
WHAT IS IT? THE BOYS AREN'T OUT OF P.E. YET?
What's going on?
chatter
chatter
UM... GYM IS OVER...
Long over...
SATSUKI SUDDENLY PICKED A FIGHT WITH TOYA...
HUH?

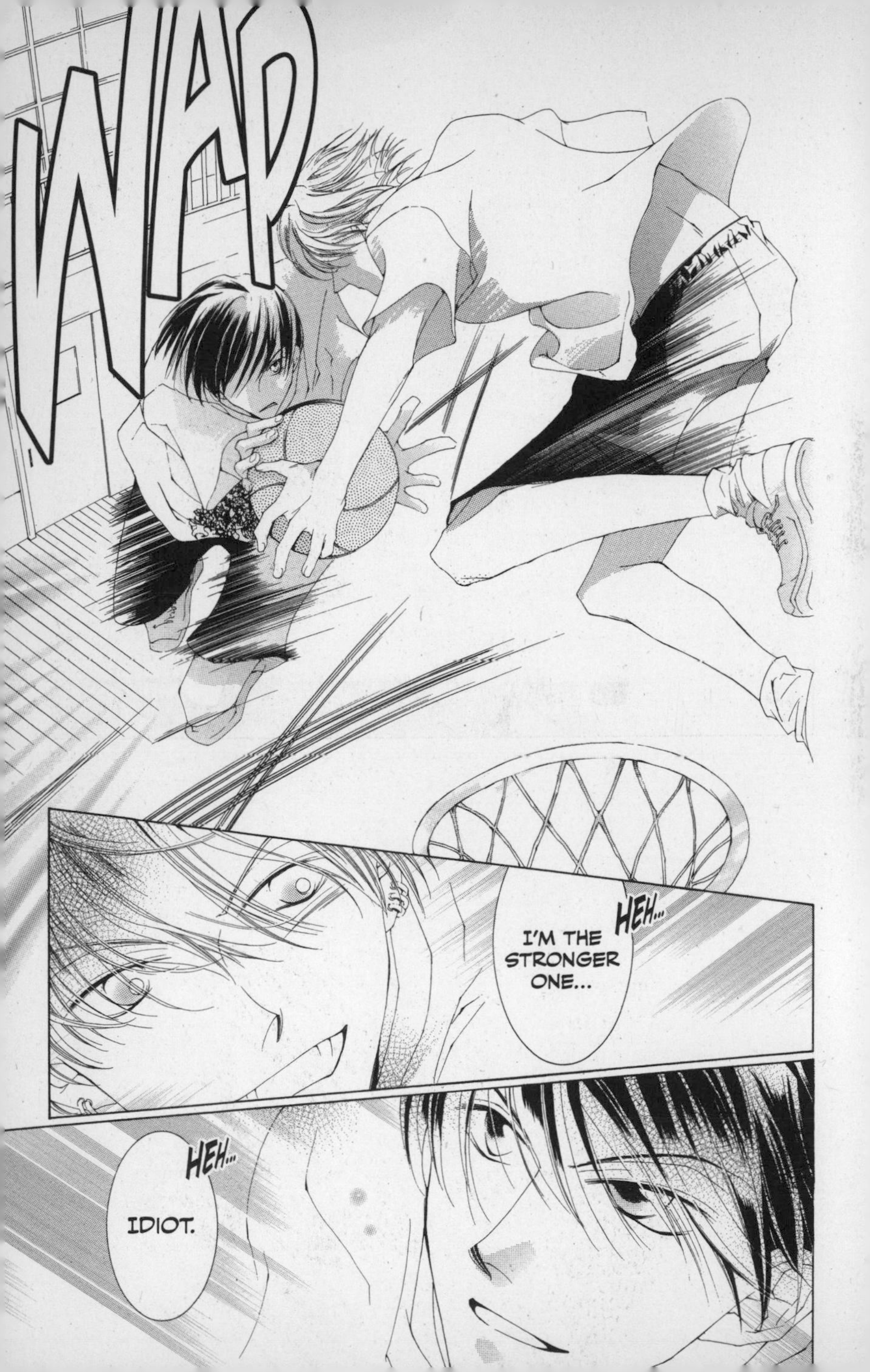
WAP
HEH...
I'M THE STRONGER ONE...
HEH...
IDIOT.

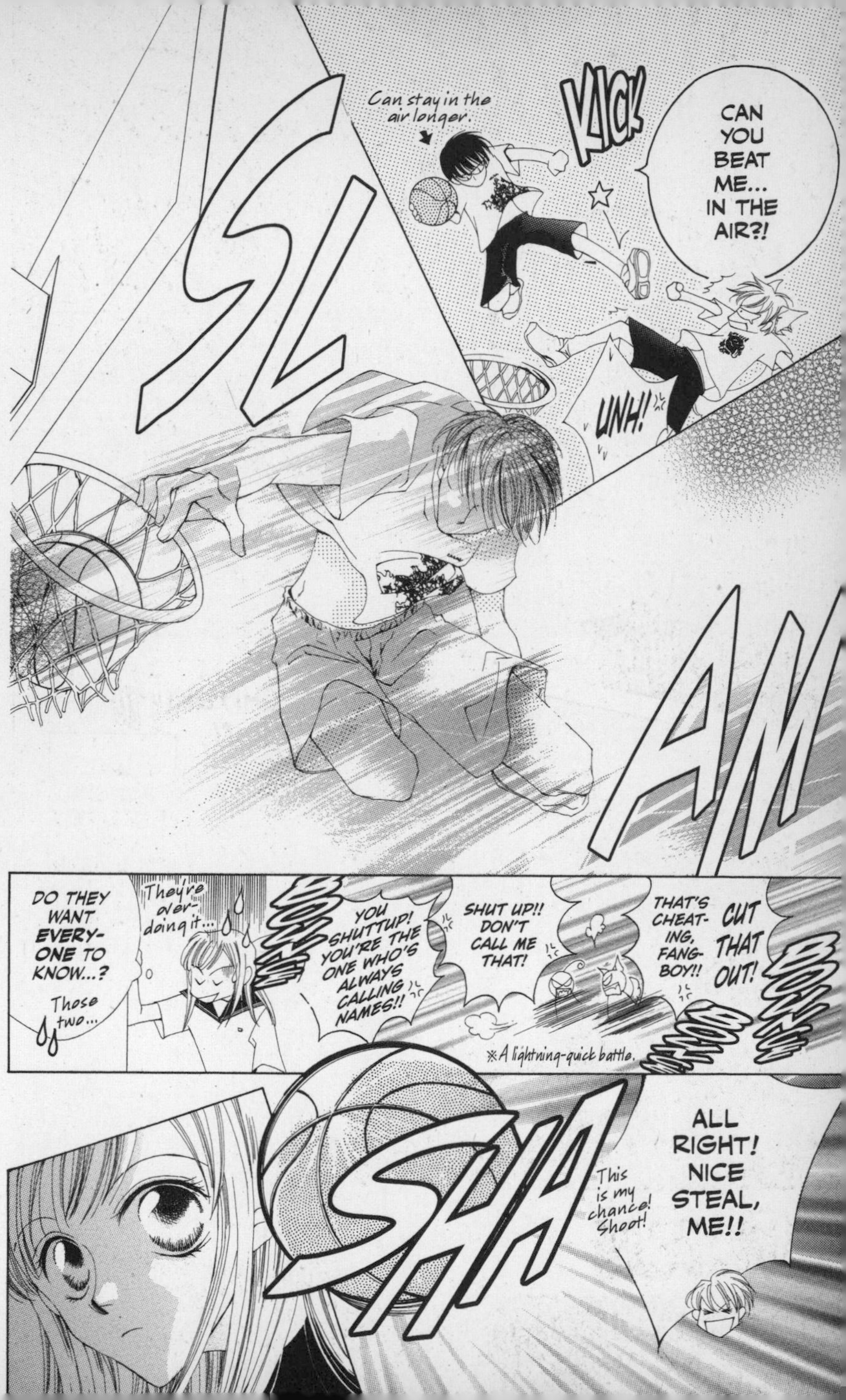
CAN YOU BEAT ME... IN THE AIR?!
KICK
Can stay in the air longer.
UNH!
SL
AM
CUT THAT OUT!
THAT'S CHEAT-ING, FANG-BOY!!
SHUT UP!! DON'T CALL ME THAT!
YOU SHUTTUP! YOU'RE THE ONE WHO'S ALWAYS CALLING NAMES!!
※A lightning-quick battle.
They're over-doing it...
DO THEY WANT EVERY-ONE TO KNOW...?
Those two...
ALL RIGHT! NICE STEAL, ME!!
This is my chance! Shoot!
SHA

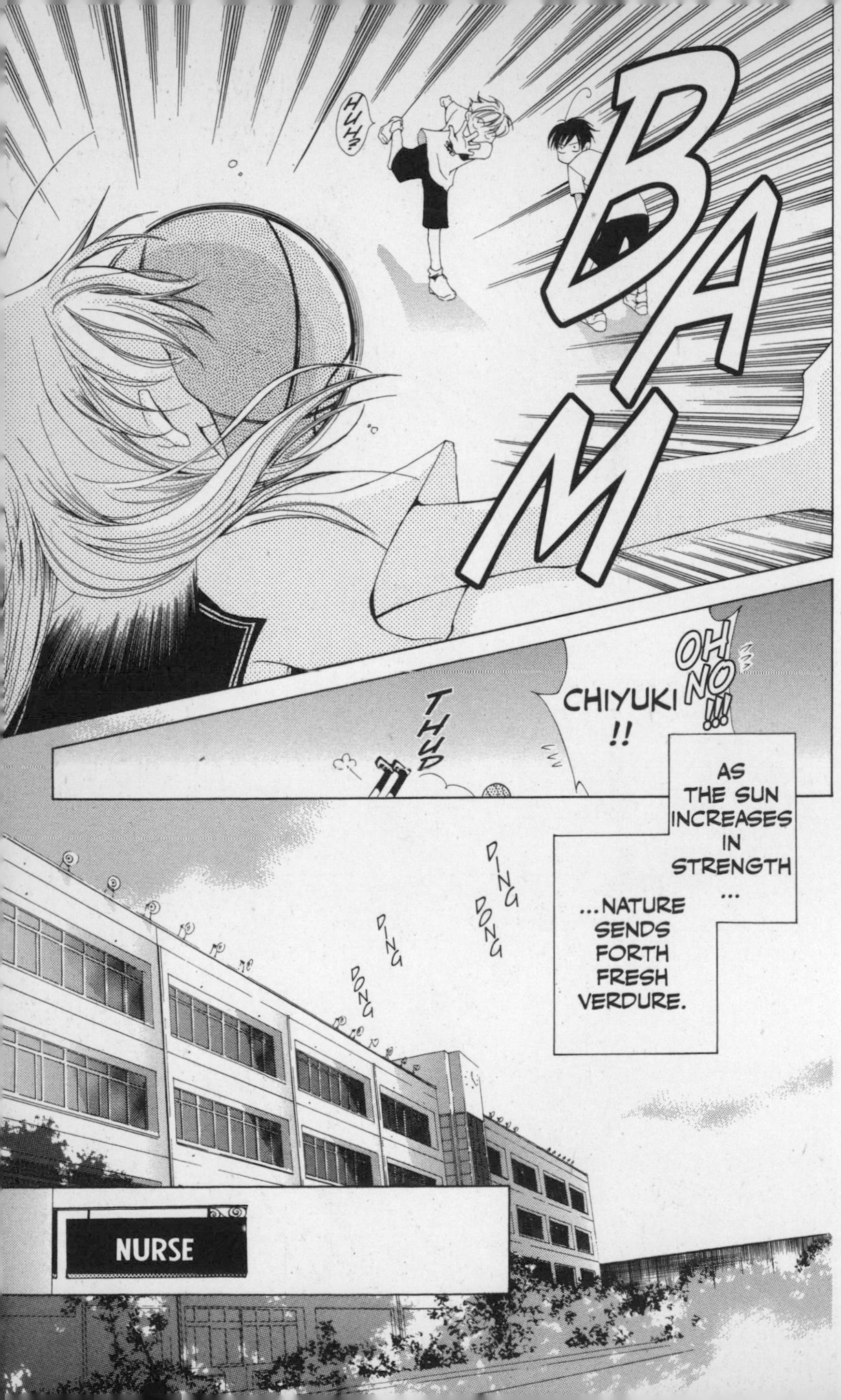
BAM
HUH?
OH NO!!!
CHIYUKI!!
THUD
AS THE SUN INCREASES IN STRENGTH...
...NATURE SENDS FORTH FRESH VERDURE.
DING DONG
DING DONG
NURSE

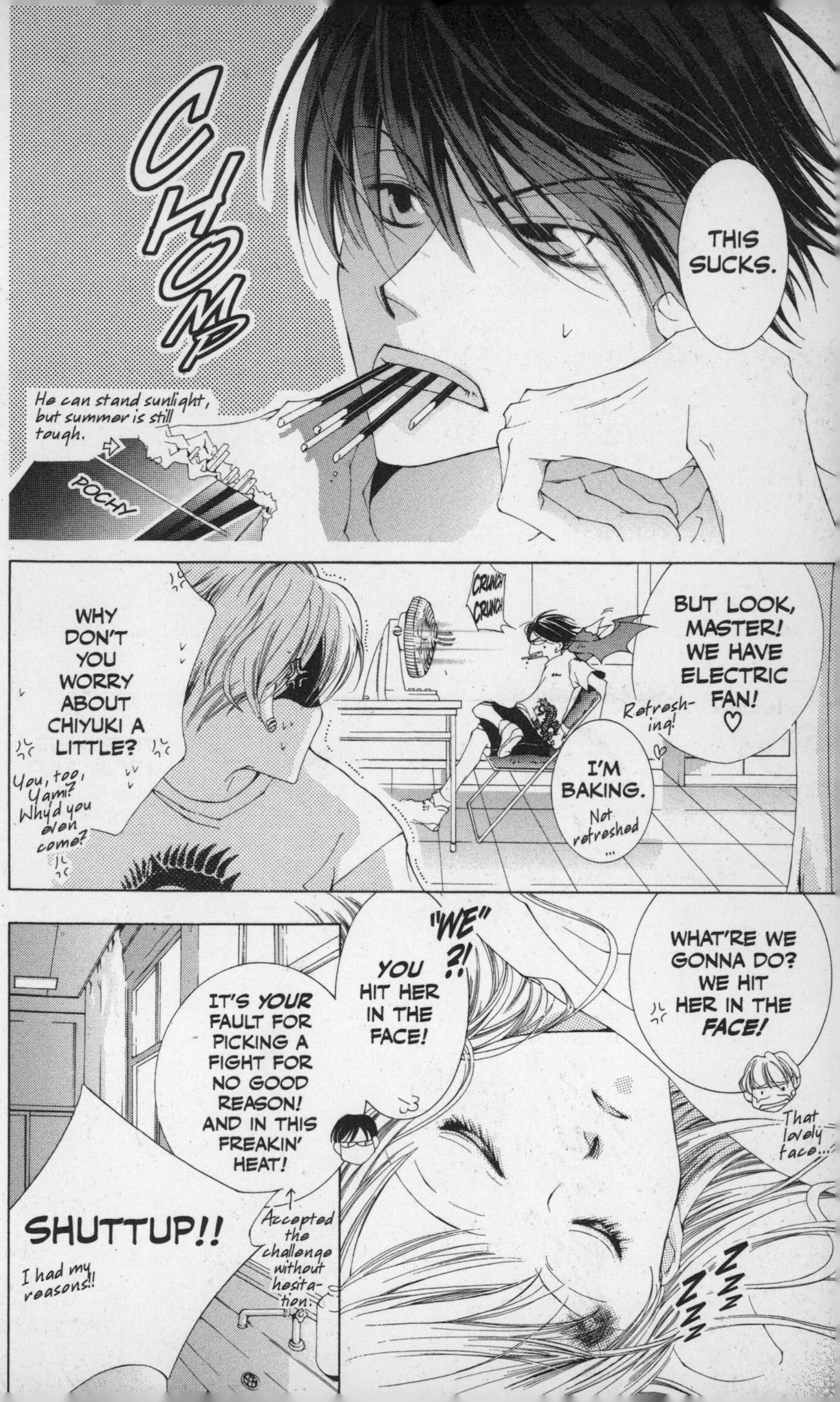
THIS SUCKS.
CHOMP
He can stand sunlight, but summer is still tough.
POCHY
BUT LOOK, MASTER! WE HAVE ELECTRIC FAN! ♡
Refresh-ing!
I'M BAKING.
Not refreshed ...
CRUNCH CRUNCH
WHY DON'T YOU WORRY ABOUT CHIYUKI A LITTLE?
You, too, Yami? Why'd you even come?
WHAT'RE WE GONNA DO? WE HIT HER IN THE FACE!
That lovely face...
"WE"?!
YOU HIT HER IN THE FACE!
IT'S YOUR FAULT FOR PICKING A FIGHT FOR NO GOOD REASON! AND IN THIS FREAKIN' HEAT!
Accepted the challenge without hesita-tion.
SHUTTUP!!
I had my reasons!!
ZZZ

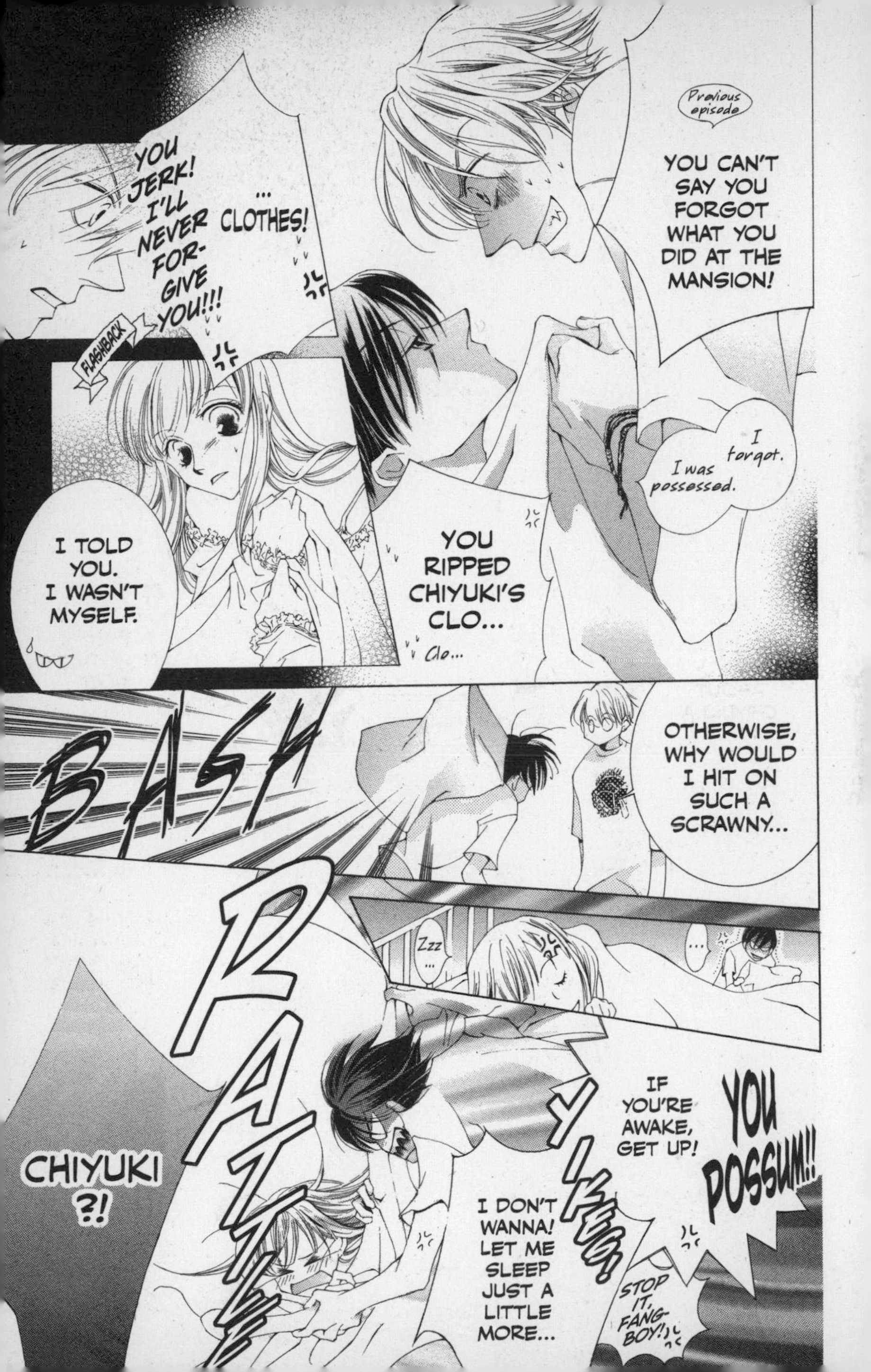
Previous episode
YOU CAN'T SAY YOU FORGOT WHAT YOU DID AT THE MANSION!
I forgot. I was possessed.
... CLOTHES!
YOU JERK! I'LL NEVER FOR-GIVE YOU!!!
FLASHBACK
YOU RIPPED CHIYUKI'S CLO...
Clo...
I TOLD YOU. I WASN'T MYSELF.
OTHERWISE, WHY WOULD I HIT ON SUCH A SCRAWNY...
BASH
...
Zzz ...
YOU POSSUM!!
IF YOU'RE AWAKE, GET UP!
STOP IT, FANG-BOY!
I DON'T WANNA! LET ME SLEEP JUST A LITTLE MORE...
CHIYUKI ?!

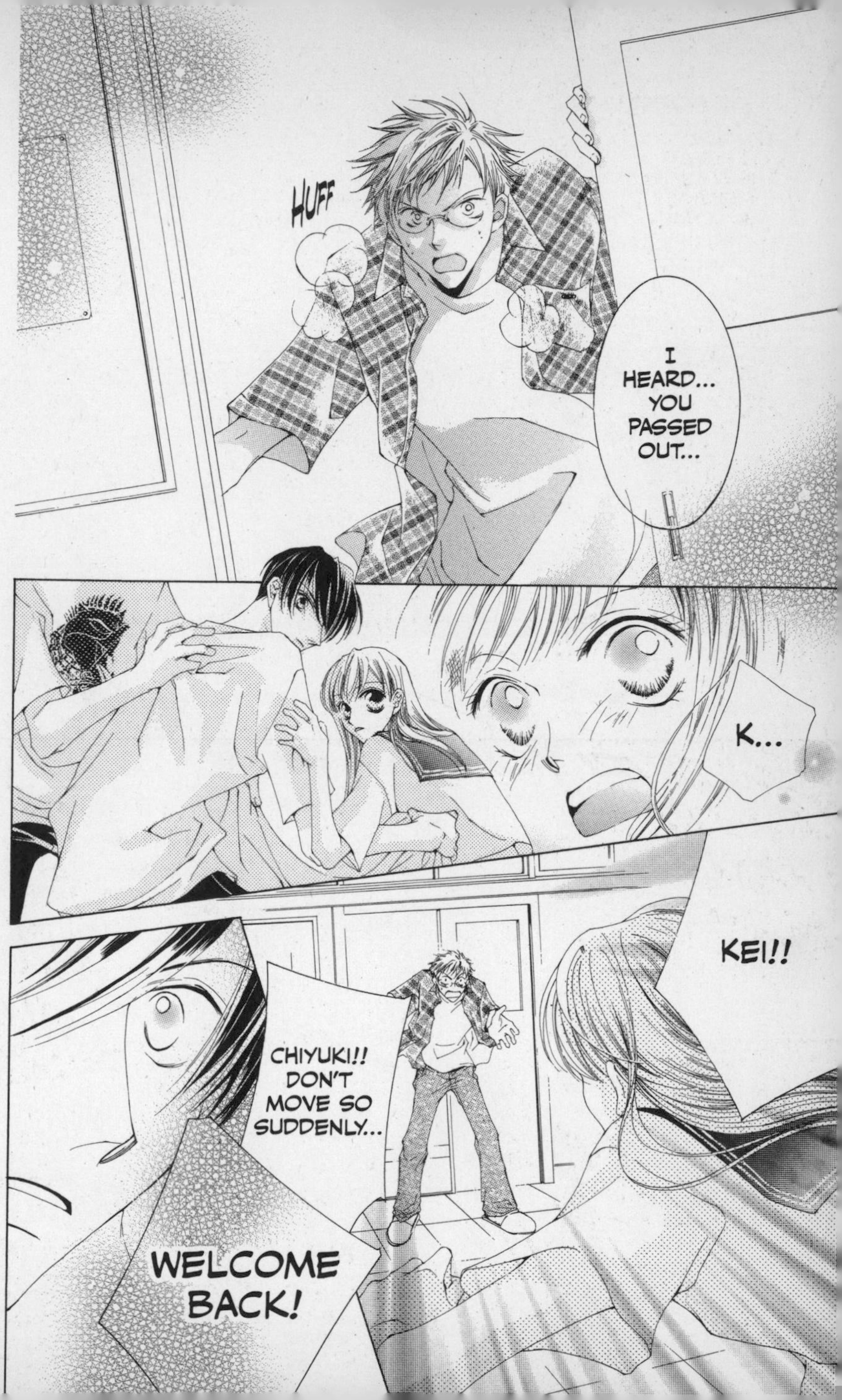
I HEARD... YOU PASSED OUT...
HUFF
K...
KEI!!
CHIYUKI!! DON'T MOVE SO SUDDENLY...
WELCOME BACK!

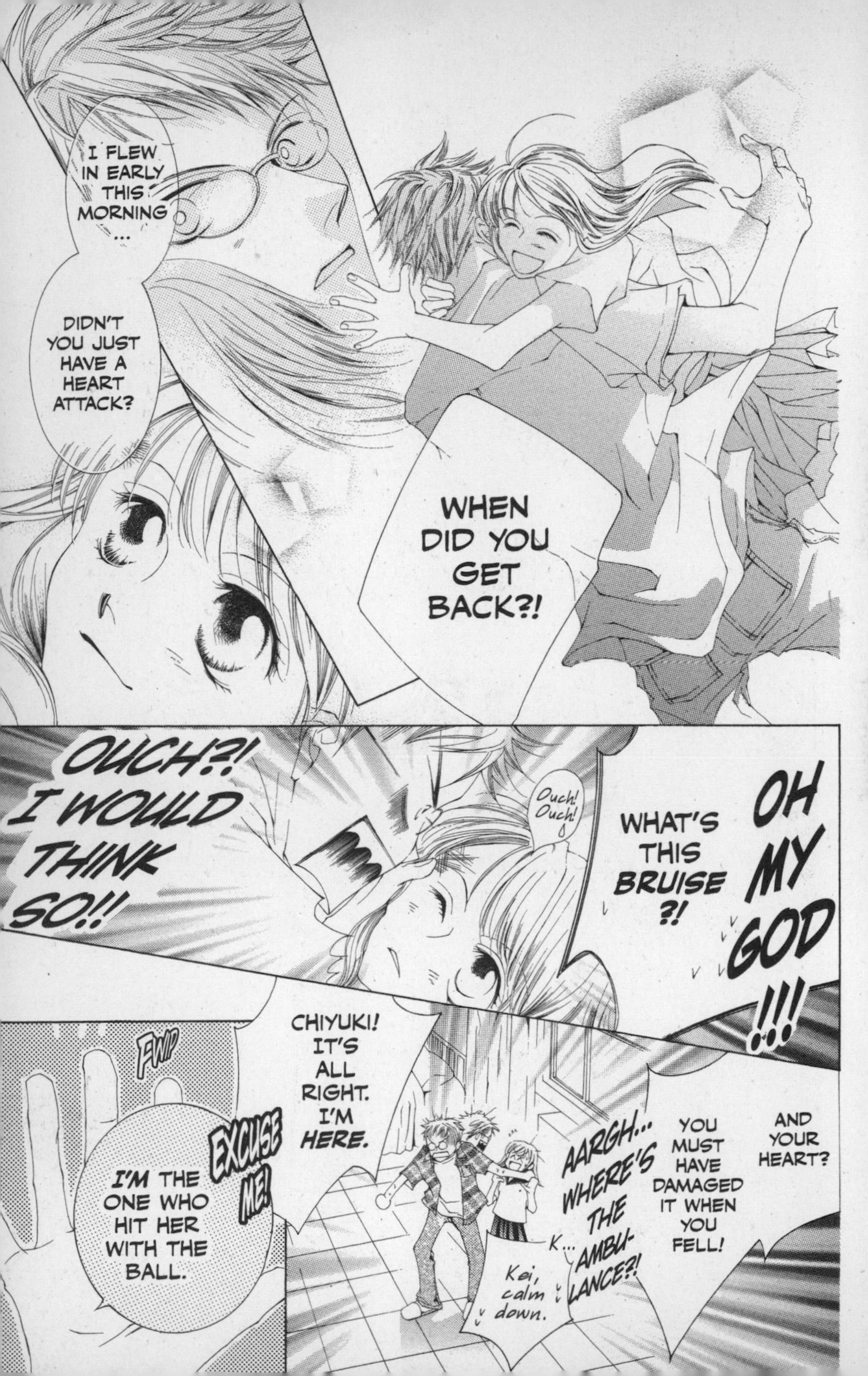
WHEN DID YOU GET BACK?!
I FLEW IN EARLY THIS MORNING...
DIDN'T YOU JUST HAVE A HEART ATTACK?
OH MY GOD!!!
WHAT'S THIS BRUISE?!
Ouch! Ouch!
OUCH?! I WOULD THINK SO!!
AND YOUR HEART?
YOU MUST HAVE DAMAGED IT WHEN YOU FELL!
AARGH... WHERE'S THE AMBULANCE?!
K...
Kei, calm down.
CHIYUKI! IT'S ALL RIGHT. I'M HERE.
FWIP
EXCUSE ME!
I'M THE ONE WHO HIT HER WITH THE BALL.

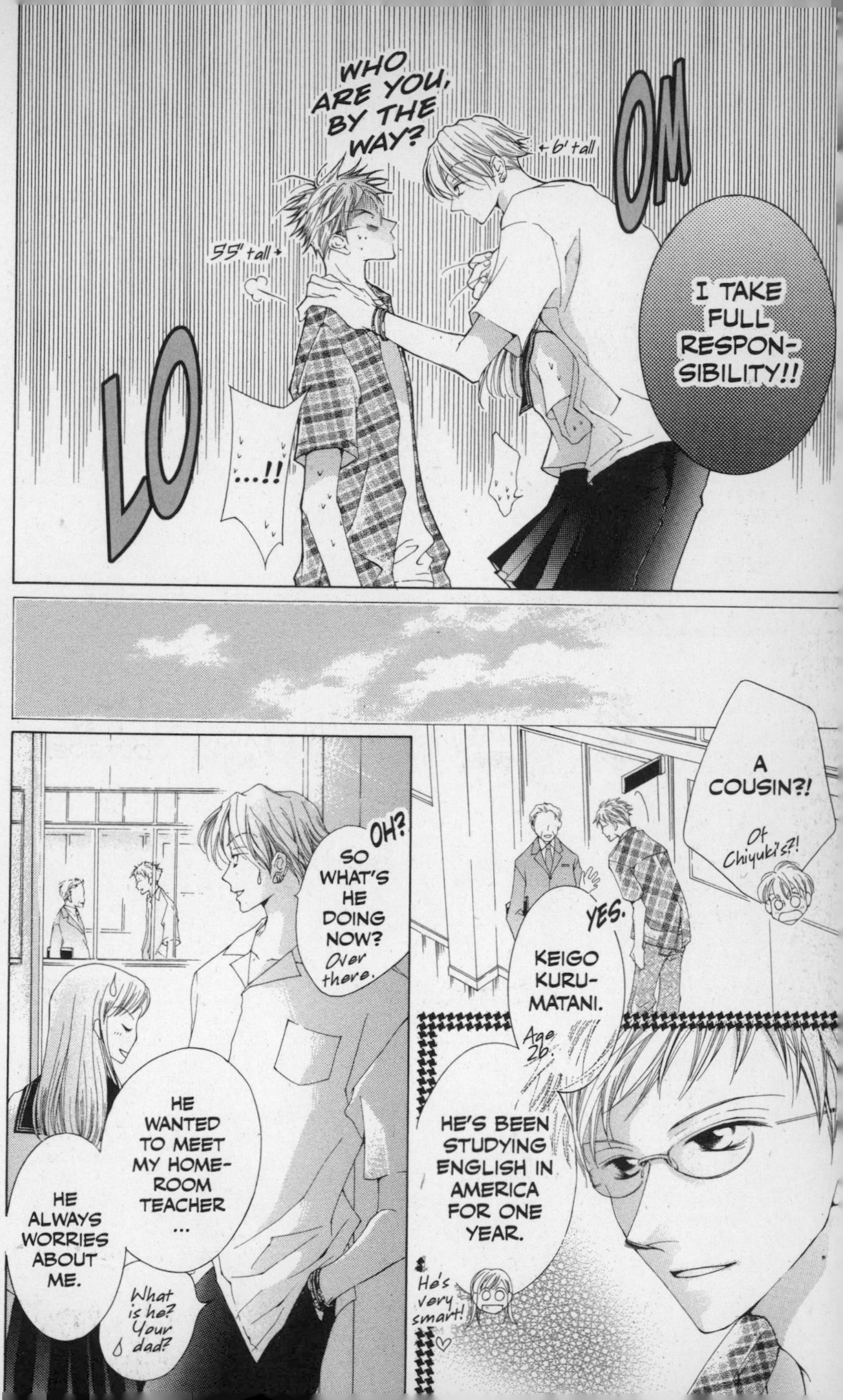
WHO ARE YOU, BY THE WAY?
← 6' tall
OM
I TAKE FULL RESPONSIBILITY!!
5'5" tall →
...!!
LO
A COUSIN?!
Of Chiyuki's?!
YES.
KEIGO KURU-MATANI.
Age 26.
HE'S BEEN STUDYING ENGLISH IN AMERICA FOR ONE YEAR.
He's very smart!
OH?
SO WHAT'S HE DOING NOW?
Over there.
HE WANTED TO MEET MY HOME-ROOM TEACHER ...
HE ALWAYS WORRIES ABOUT ME.
What is he? Your dad?

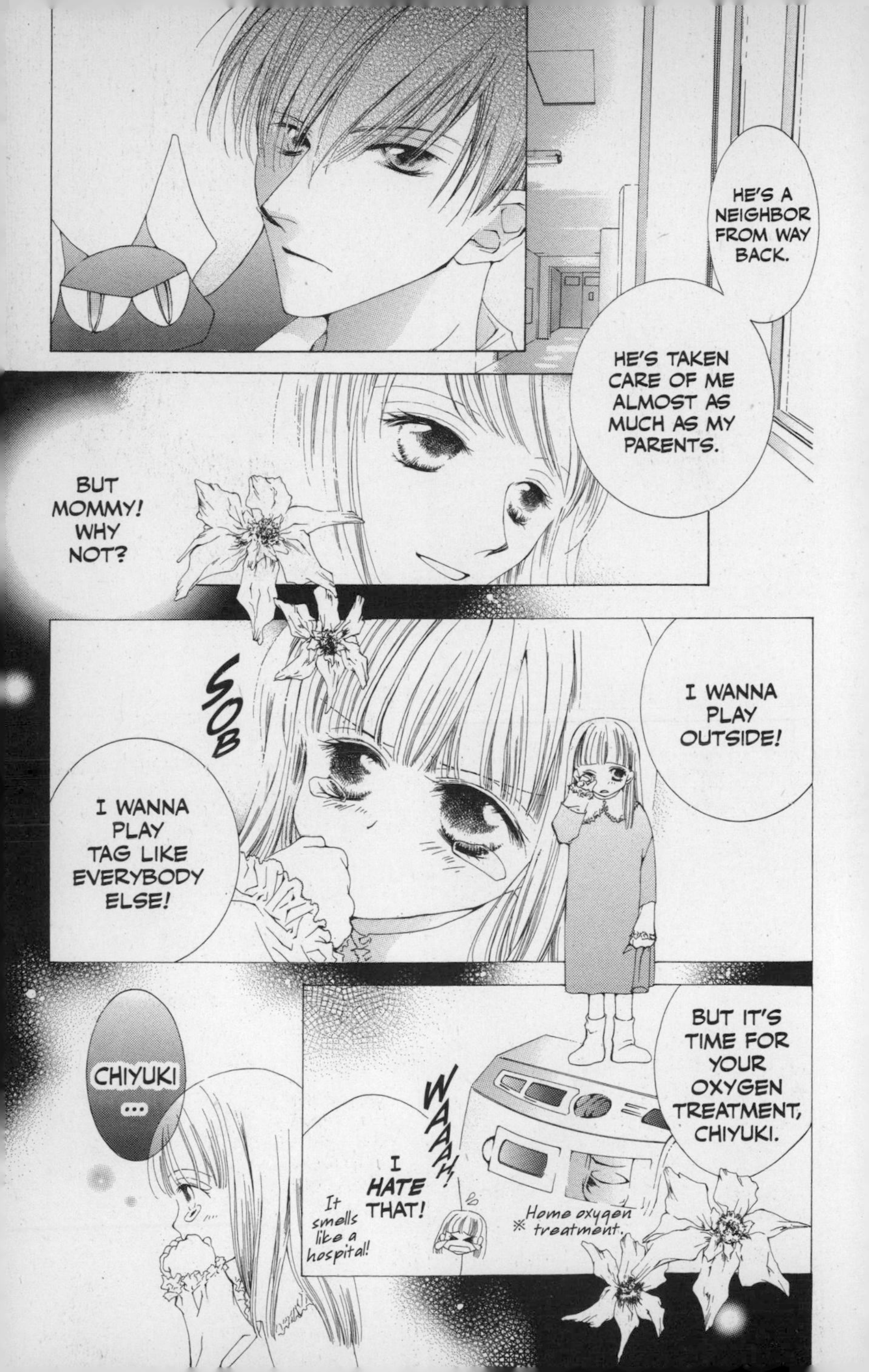
HE'S A NEIGHBOR FROM WAY BACK.
HE'S TAKEN CARE OF ME ALMOST AS MUCH AS MY PARENTS.
BUT MOMMY! WHY NOT?
I WANNA PLAY OUTSIDE!
SOB
I WANNA PLAY TAG LIKE EVERYBODY ELSE!
BUT IT'S TIME FOR YOUR OXYGEN TREATMENT, CHIYUKI.
※ Home oxygen treatment.
WAAAH!
I HATE THAT!
It smells like a hospital!
CHIYUKI ...

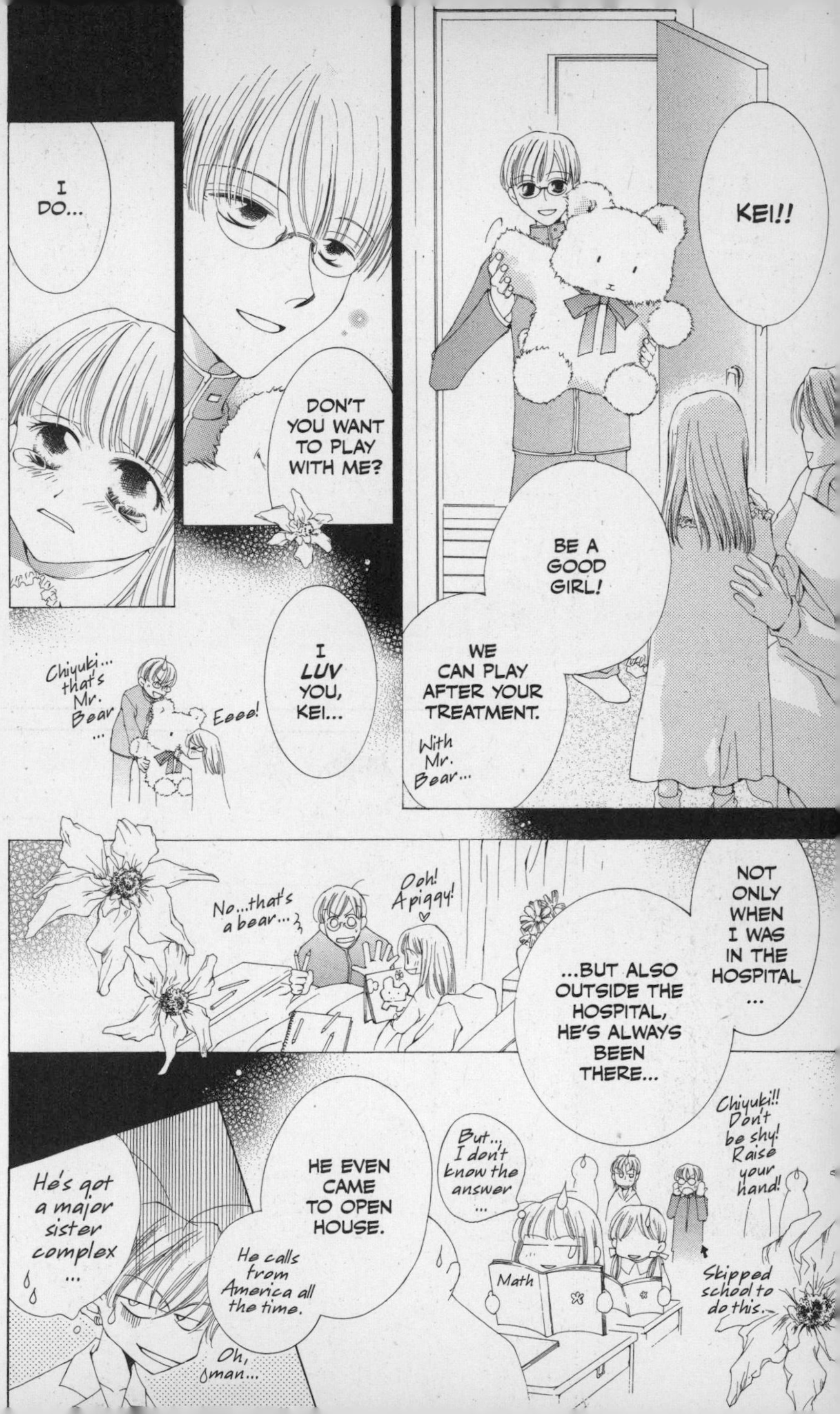
KEI!!
BE A GOOD GIRL!
WE CAN PLAY AFTER YOUR TREATMENT.
With Mr. Bear...
DON'T YOU WANT TO PLAY WITH ME?
I DO...
I LUV YOU, KEI...
Chiyuki... that's Mr. Bear...
Eeee!
NOT ONLY WHEN I WAS IN THE HOSPITAL...
...BUT ALSO OUTSIDE THE HOSPITAL, HE'S ALWAYS BEEN THERE...
Ooh! A piggy!
No...that's a bear...
Chiyuki!! Don't be shy! Raise your hand!
Skipped school to do this.
But... I don't know the answer...
Math
HE EVEN CAME TO OPEN HOUSE.
He calls from America all the time.
He's got a major sister complex...
Oh, man...

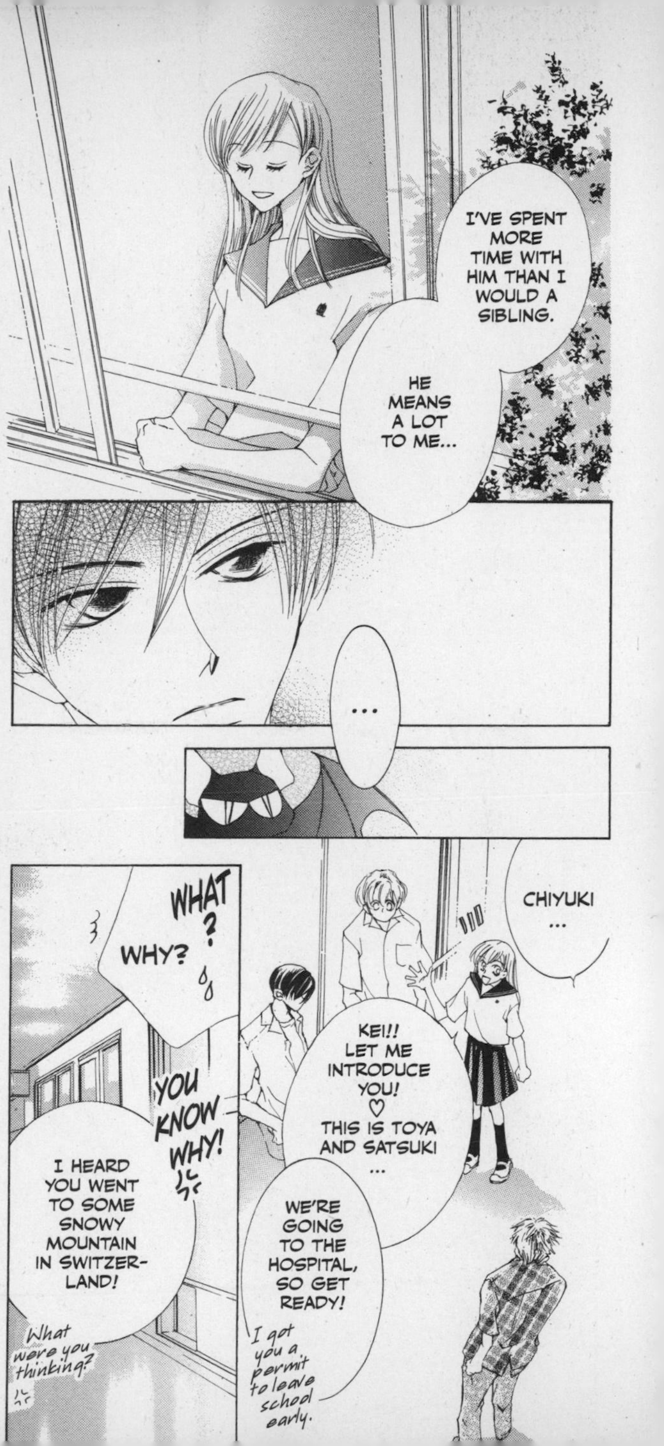
I'VE SPENT MORE TIME WITH HIM THAN I WOULD A SIBLING.
HE MEANS A LOT TO ME...
...
CHIYUKI...
KEI!! LET ME INTRODUCE YOU! ♡ THIS IS TOYA AND SATSUKI...
WE'RE GOING TO THE HOSPITAL, SO GET READY!
I got you a permit to leave school early.
WHAT?
WHY?
YOU KNOW WHY!
I HEARD YOU WENT TO SOME SNOWY MOUNTAIN IN SWITZER-LAND!
What were you thinking?

闇丸

YAMIMARU

"Yamimaru" is often written as "Ranmaru" in the letters I receive... Even my assistant, A-chan, calls him "Kuramaru." (lol) Out of all the characters of Millennium Snow, the little boy Yami is the easiest to draw. The hardest one is the grown-up Yami, so I guess everything balances out...? "Ranmaru" and "Kuramaru" each use a different first kanji for Yamimaru's name. "Ran" looks similar to Yamimaru's "Yami," which is why fans of Millennium Snow make this mistake. Incidentally, this "ran" is also the "ran" of "Ouran" of Ouran High School Host Club. It means "orchid." The "kura" of "Kuramaru" is similar in meaning to "yami." Thus, A-chan is calling him "Kuramaru" as a sort of pun.

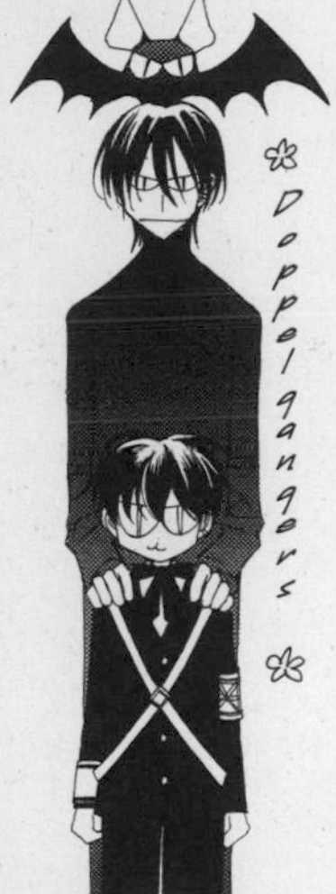
Doppelgangers

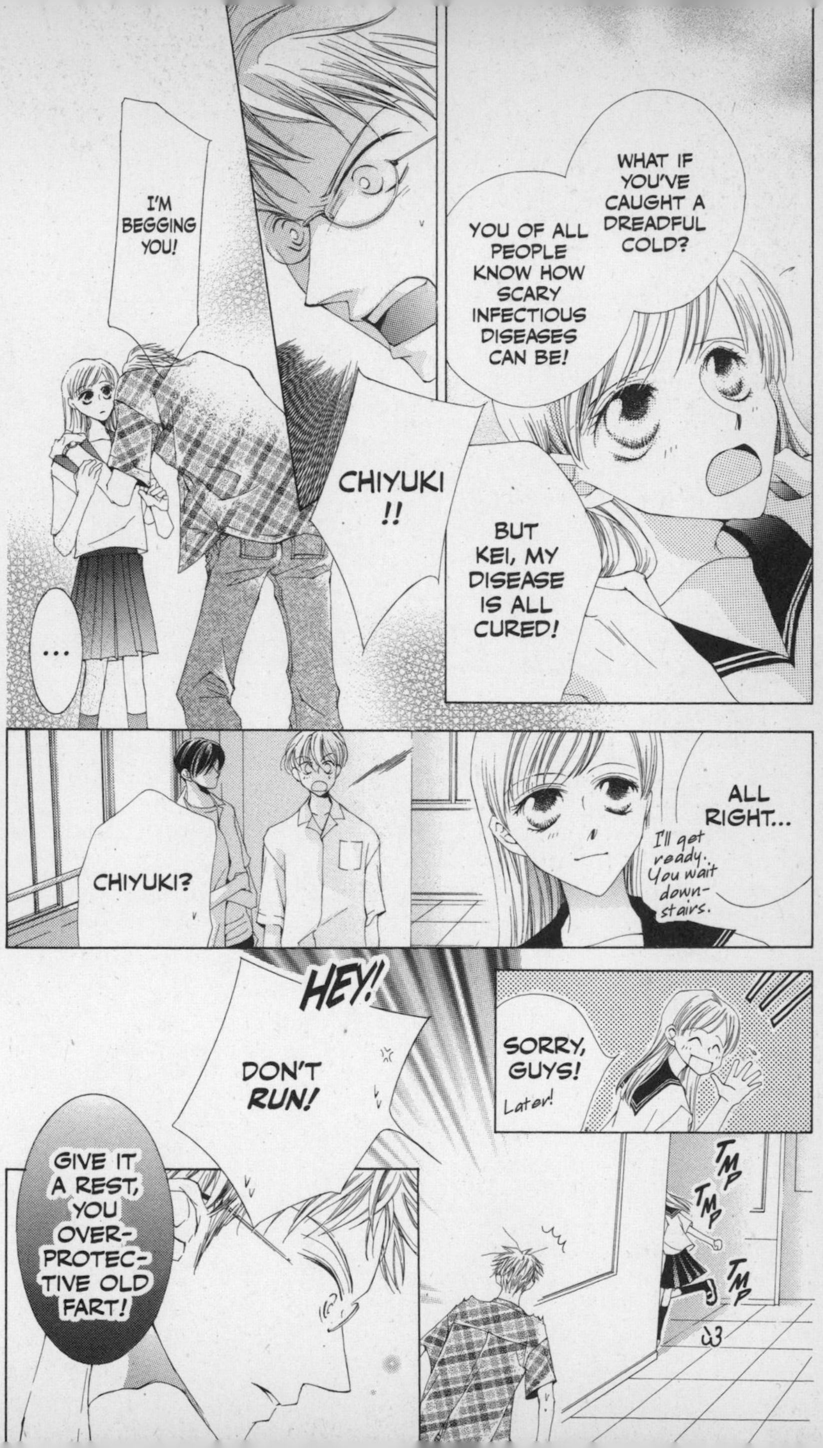
WHAT IF YOU'VE CAUGHT A DREADFUL COLD?
YOU OF ALL PEOPLE KNOW HOW SCARY INFECTIOUS DISEASES CAN BE!
BUT KEI, MY DISEASE IS ALL CURED!
CHIYUKI !!
I'M BEGGING YOU!
...
ALL RIGHT...
I'll get ready. You wait downstairs.
CHIYUKI?
SORRY, GUYS!
Later!
HEY!
DON'T *RUN!*
TMP TMP TMP
GIVE IT A REST, YOU OVERPROTECTIVE OLD FART!

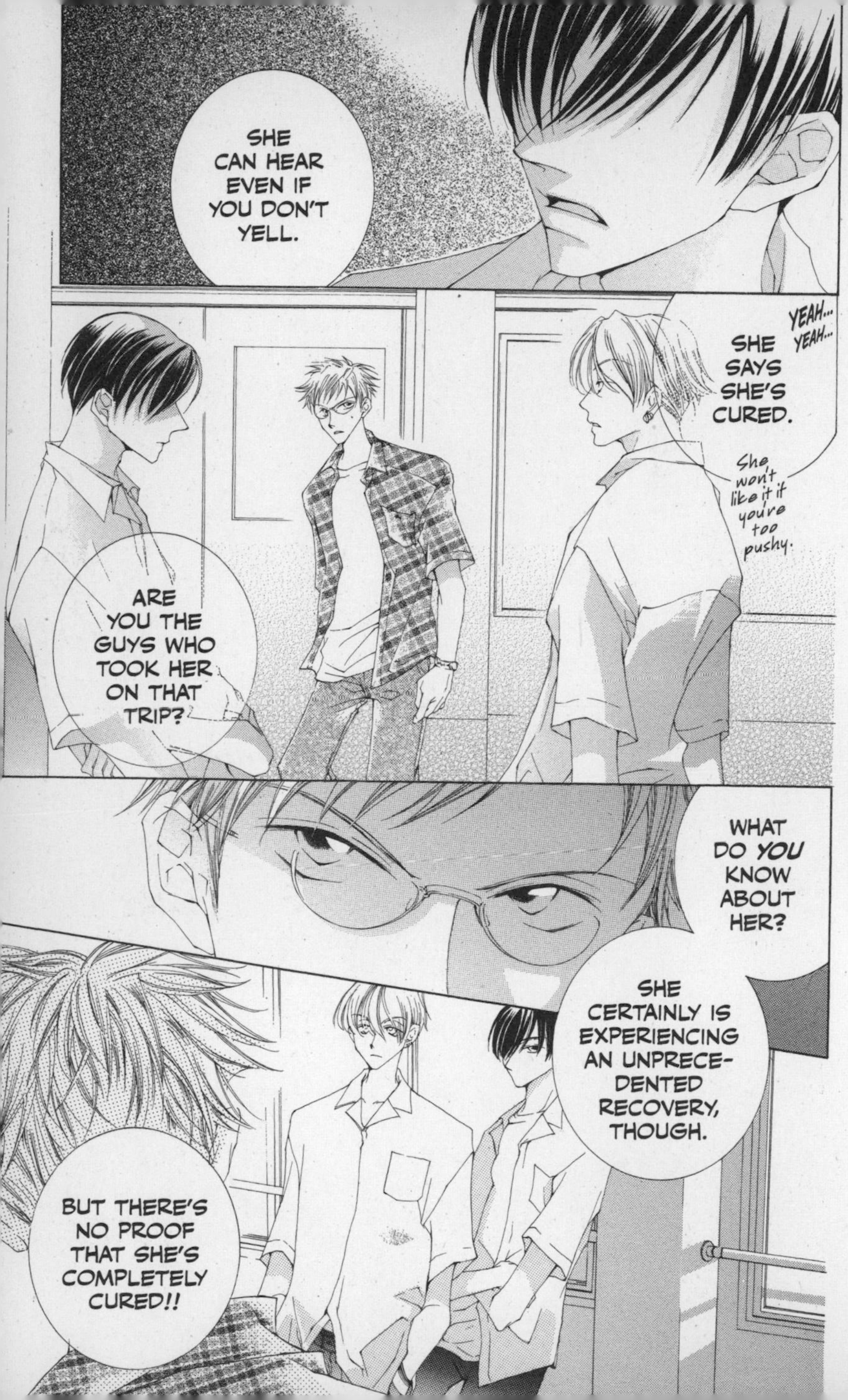
SHE CAN HEAR EVEN IF YOU DON'T YELL.
YEAH... YEAH...
SHE SAYS SHE'S CURED.
She won't like it if you're too pushy.
ARE YOU THE GUYS WHO TOOK HER ON THAT TRIP?
WHAT DO *YOU* KNOW ABOUT HER?
SHE CERTAINLY IS EXPERIENCING AN UNPRECE-DENTED RECOVERY, THOUGH.
BUT THERE'S NO PROOF THAT SHE'S COMPLETELY CURED!!

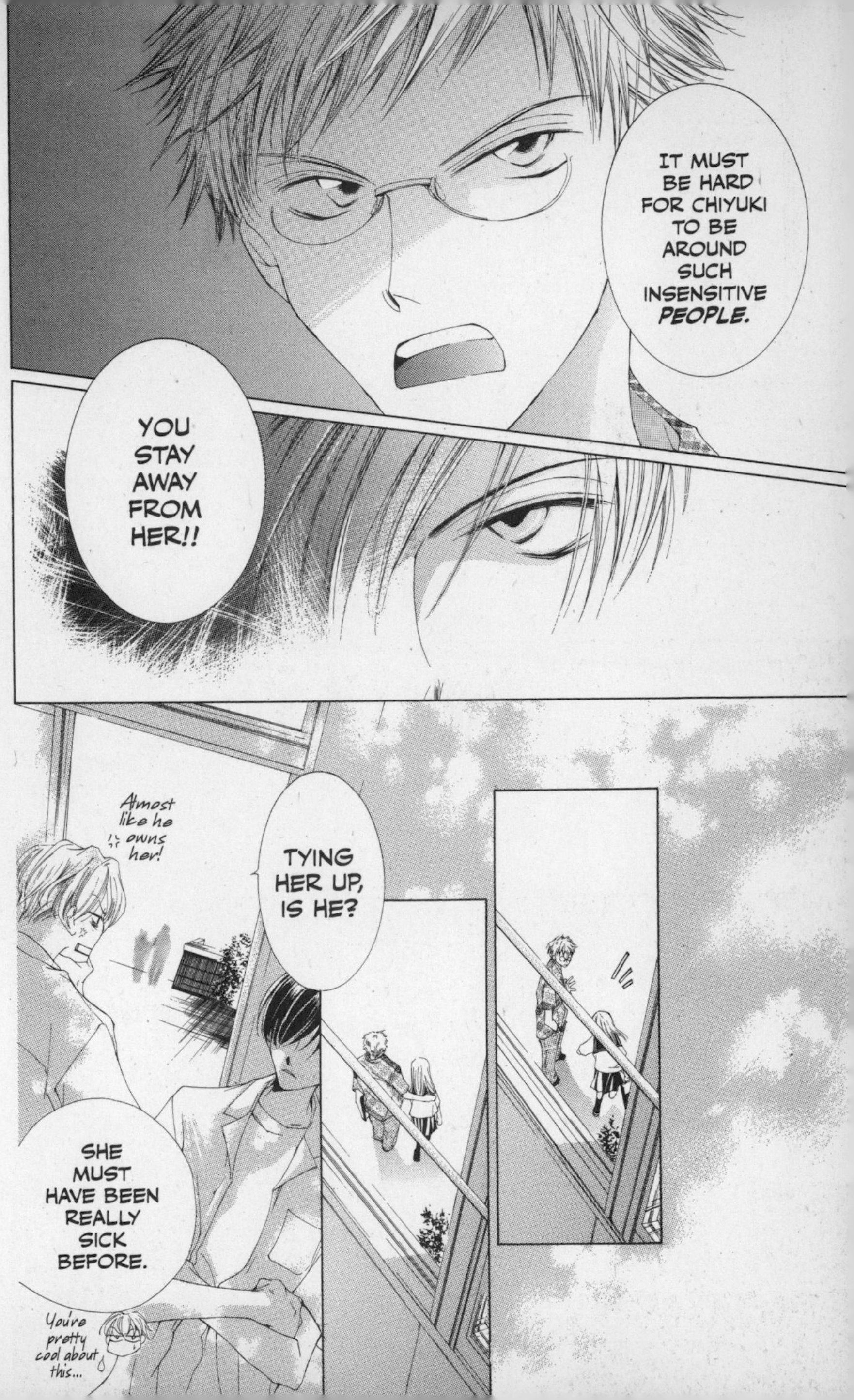
IT MUST BE HARD FOR CHIYUKI TO BE AROUND SUCH INSENSITIVE *PEOPLE.*
YOU STAY AWAY FROM HER!!
TYING HER UP, IS HE?
Almost like he owns her!
SHE MUST HAVE BEEN REALLY SICK BEFORE.
You're pretty cool about this...

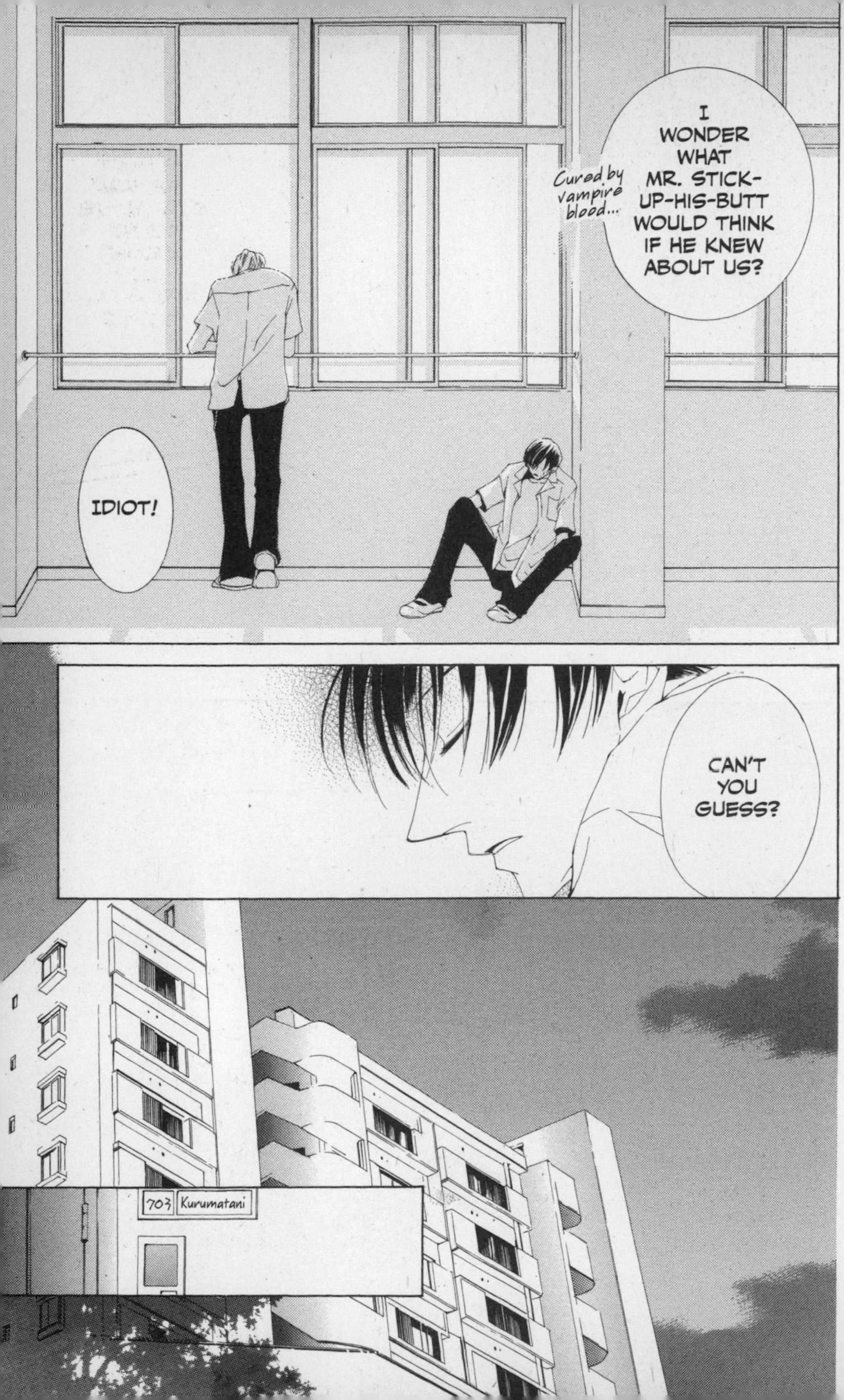
I WONDER WHAT MR. STICK-UP-HIS-BUTT WOULD THINK IF HE KNEW ABOUT US?
Cured by vampire blood...
IDIOT!
CAN'T YOU GUESS?
703 Kurumatani

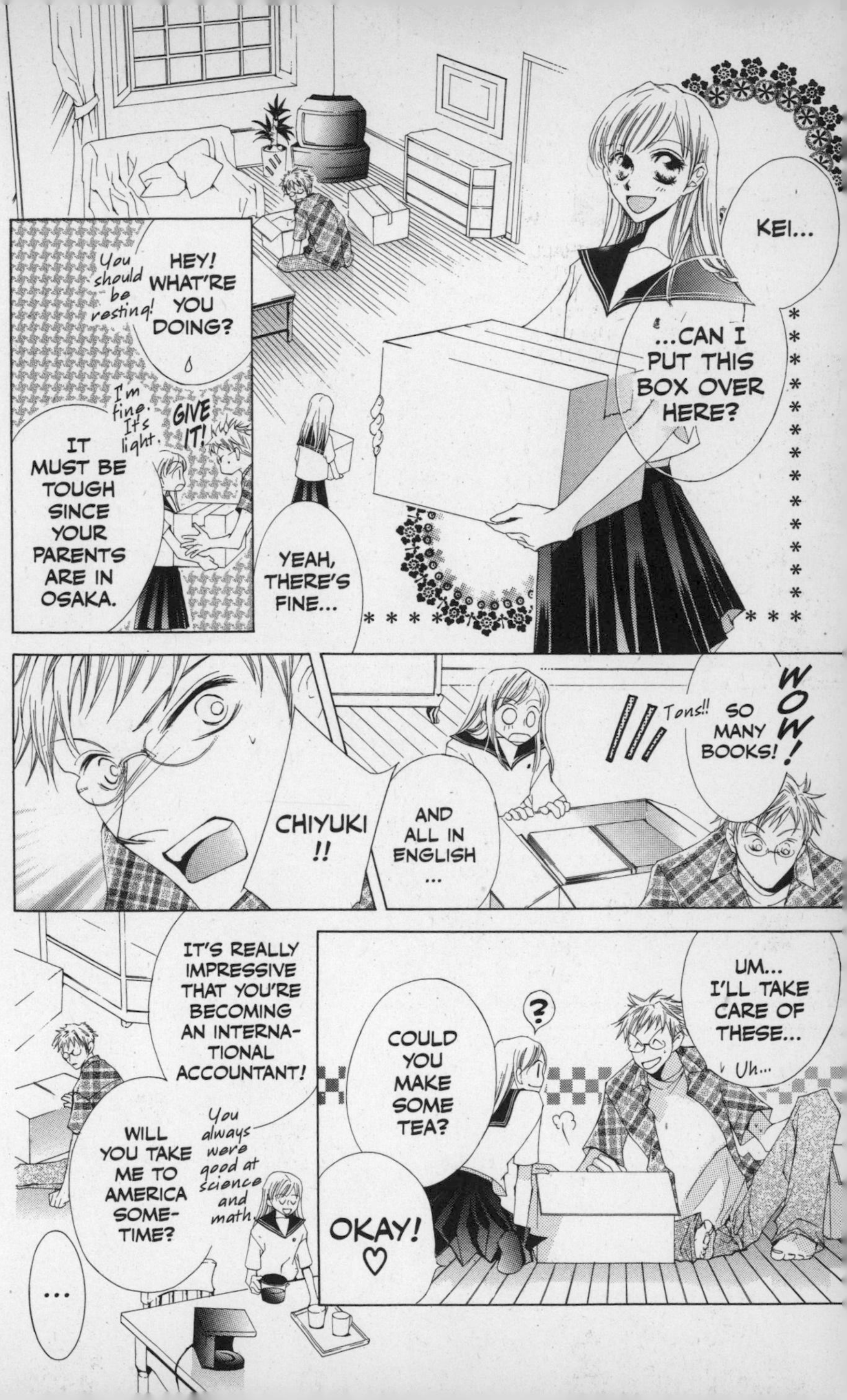
KEI...
...CAN I PUT THIS BOX OVER HERE?
YEAH, THERE'S FINE...
HEY! WHAT'RE YOU DOING?
You should be resting!
IT MUST BE TOUGH SINCE YOUR PARENTS ARE IN OSAKA.
GIVE IT!
I'm fine. It's light.
WOW!
SO MANY BOOKS!
Tons!!
AND ALL IN ENGLISH ...
CHIYUKI !!
UM... I'LL TAKE CARE OF THESE...
Uh...
?
COULD YOU MAKE SOME TEA?
OKAY! ♡
IT'S REALLY IMPRESSIVE THAT YOU'RE BECOMING AN INTERNATIONAL ACCOUNTANT!
You always were good at science and math
WILL YOU TAKE ME TO AMERICA SOMETIME?
...

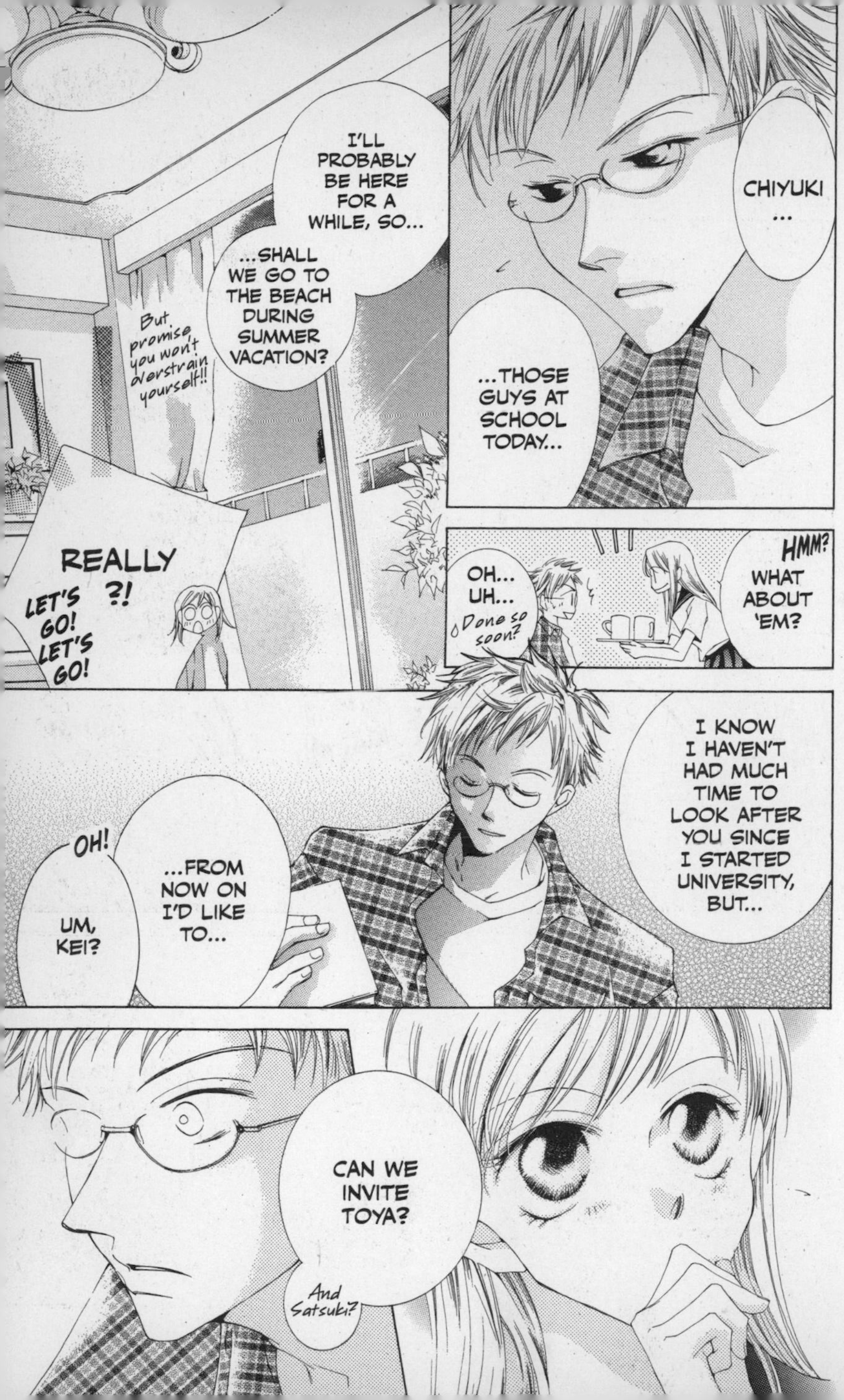
CHIYUKI ...
...THOSE GUYS AT SCHOOL TODAY...
HMM? WHAT ABOUT 'EM?
OH... UH...
Done so soon?
I'LL PROBABLY BE HERE FOR A WHILE, SO...
...SHALL WE GO TO THE BEACH DURING SUMMER VACATION?
But promise you won't overstrain yourself!!
REALLY ?!
LET'S GO! LET'S GO!
I KNOW I HAVEN'T HAD MUCH TIME TO LOOK AFTER YOU SINCE I STARTED UNIVERSITY, BUT...
...FROM NOW ON I'D LIKE TO...
OH!
UM, KEI?
CAN WE INVITE TOYA?
And Satsuki?

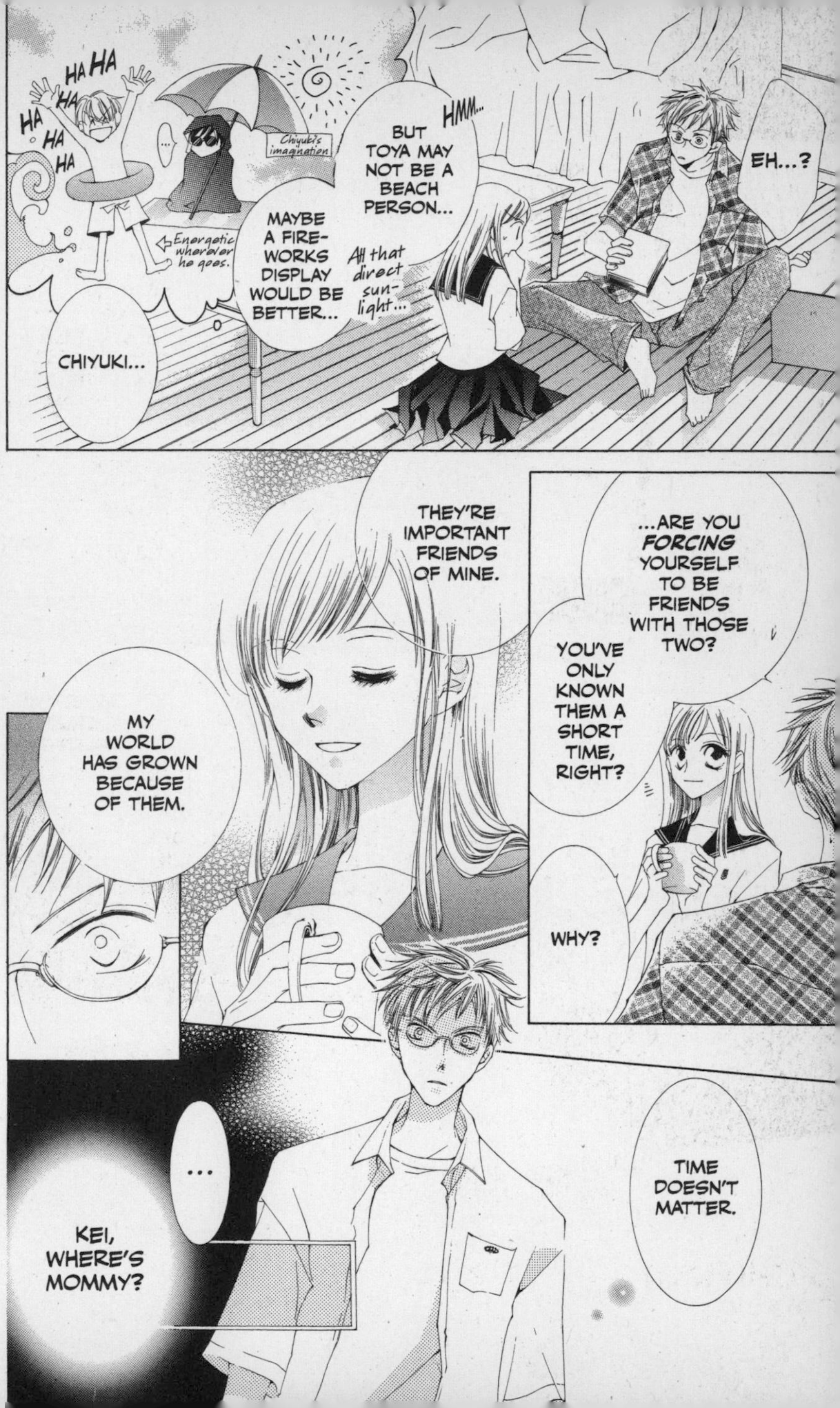
EH...?
HMM...
BUT TOYA MAY NOT BE A BEACH PERSON...
MAYBE A FIRE-WORKS DISPLAY WOULD BE BETTER...
All that direct sun-light...
Chiyuki's imagination
HA HA HA HA HA HA
...
Energetic wherever he goes.
CHIYUKI...
...ARE YOU FORCING YOURSELF TO BE FRIENDS WITH THOSE TWO?
YOU'VE ONLY KNOWN THEM A SHORT TIME, RIGHT?
WHY?
THEY'RE IMPORTANT FRIENDS OF MINE.
MY WORLD HAS GROWN BECAUSE OF THEM.
TIME DOESN'T MATTER.
...
KEI, WHERE'S MOMMY?

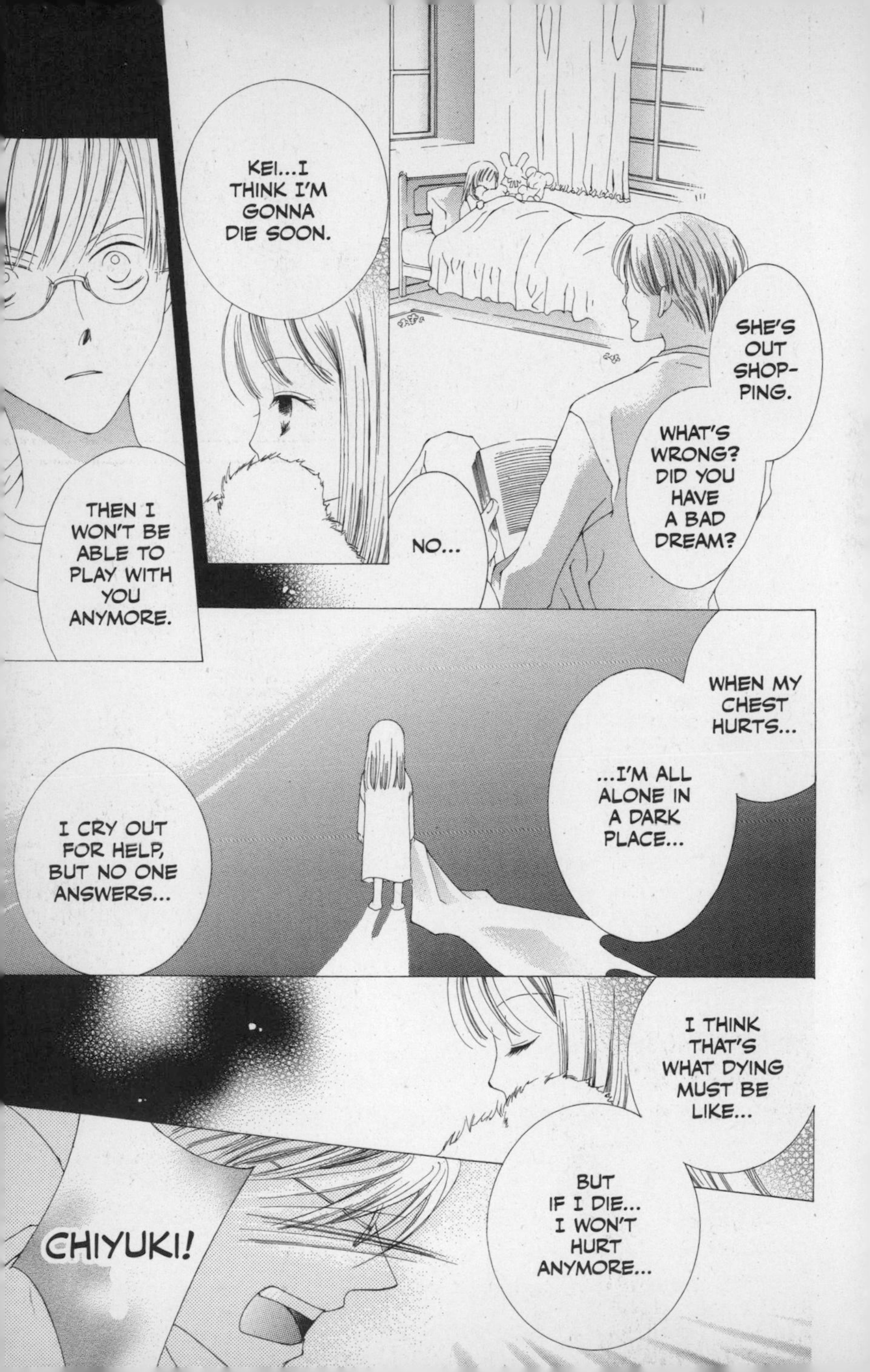
SHE'S OUT SHOP-PING.
WHAT'S WRONG? DID YOU HAVE A BAD DREAM?
NO...
KEI...I THINK I'M GONNA DIE SOON.
THEN I WON'T BE ABLE TO PLAY WITH YOU ANYMORE.
WHEN MY CHEST HURTS...
...I'M ALL ALONE IN A DARK PLACE...
I CRY OUT FOR HELP, BUT NO ONE ANSWERS...
I THINK THAT'S WHAT DYING MUST BE LIKE...
BUT IF I DIE... I WON'T HURT ANYMORE...
CHIYUKI!

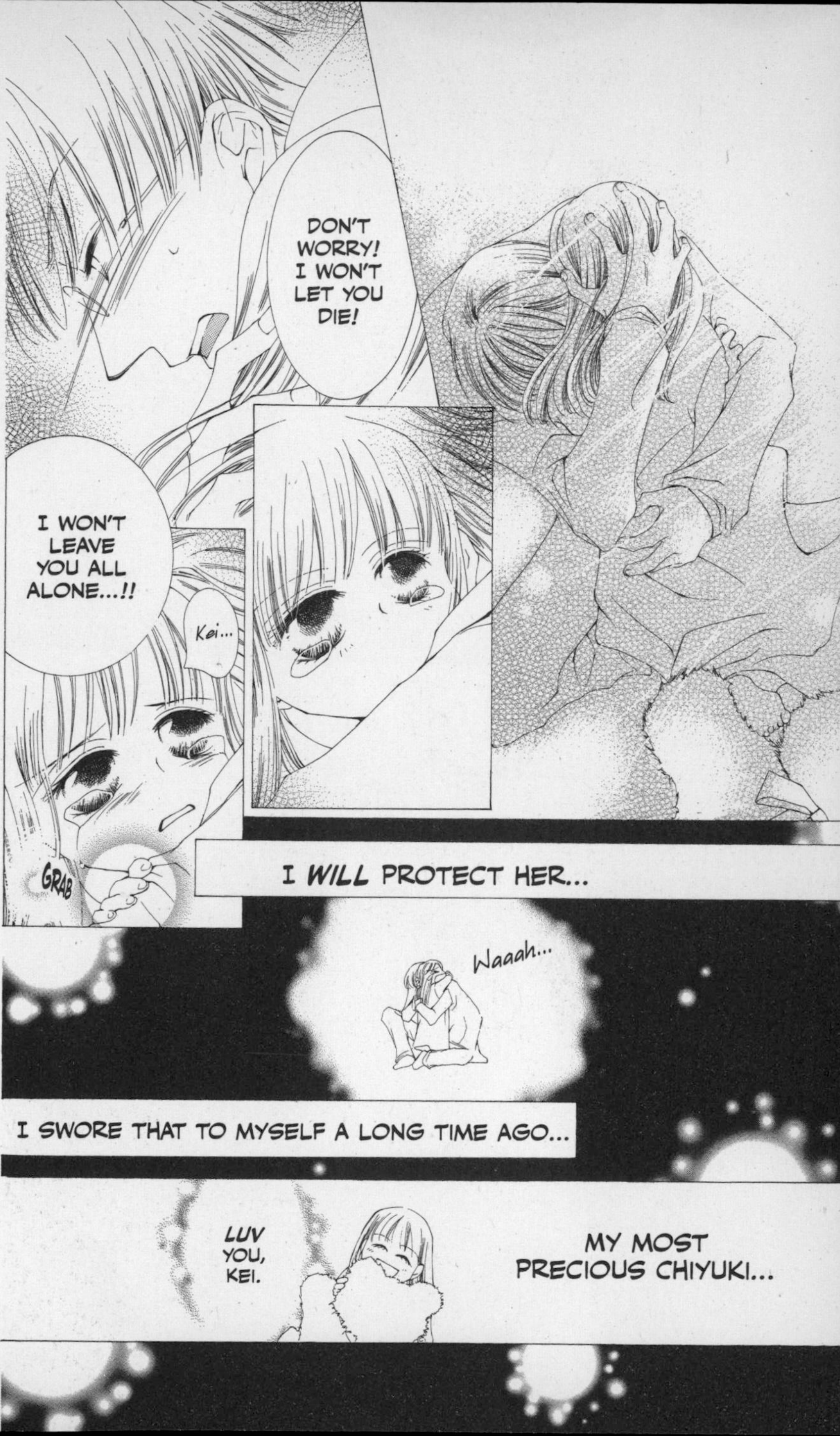
DON'T WORRY! I WON'T LET YOU DIE!
I WON'T LEAVE YOU ALL ALONE...!!
Kei...
GRAB
I *WILL* PROTECT HER...
Waaah...
I SWORE THAT TO MYSELF A LONG TIME AGO...
MY MOST PRECIOUS CHIYUKI...
*LUV* YOU, KEI.

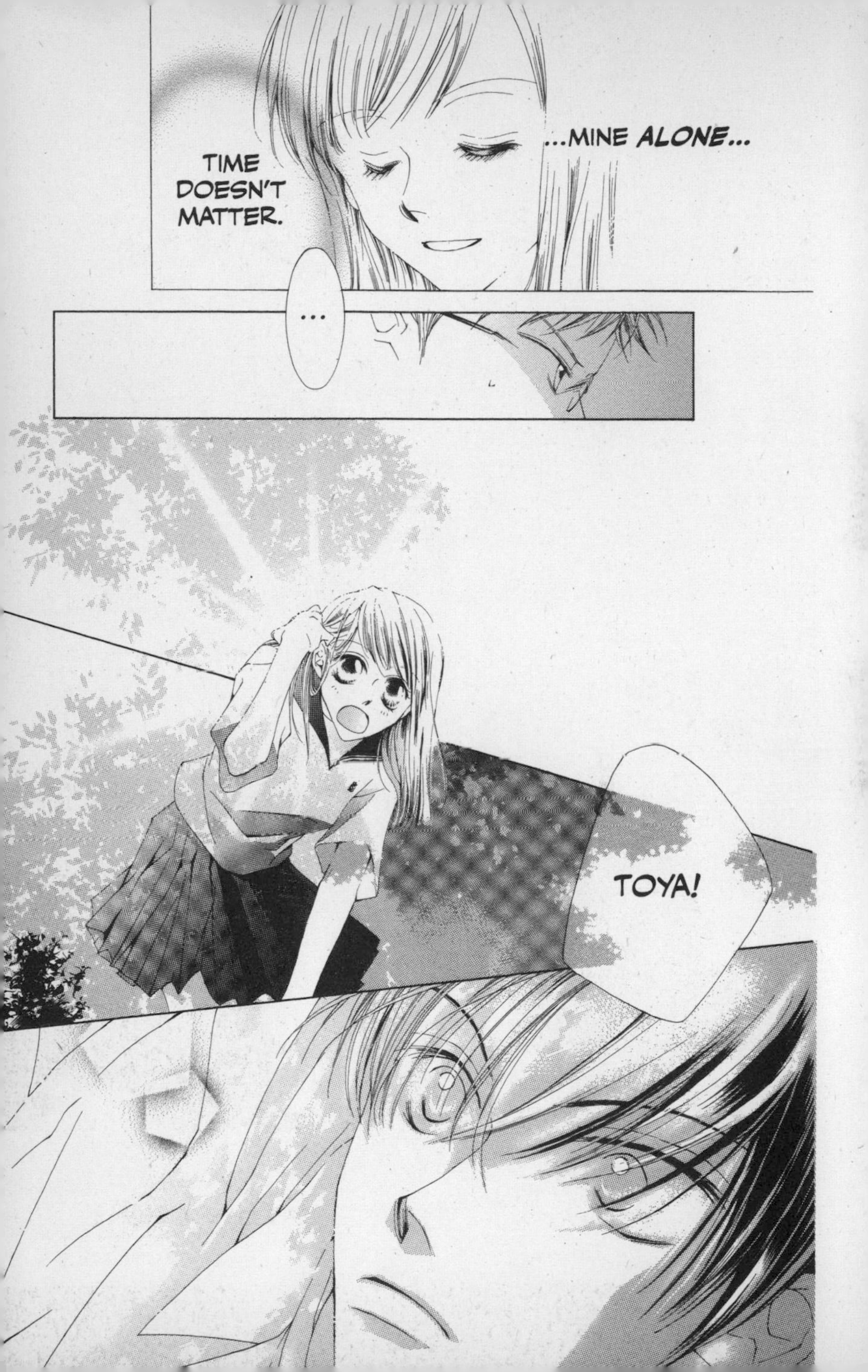
...MINE ALONE...
TIME DOESN'T MATTER.
...
TOYA!

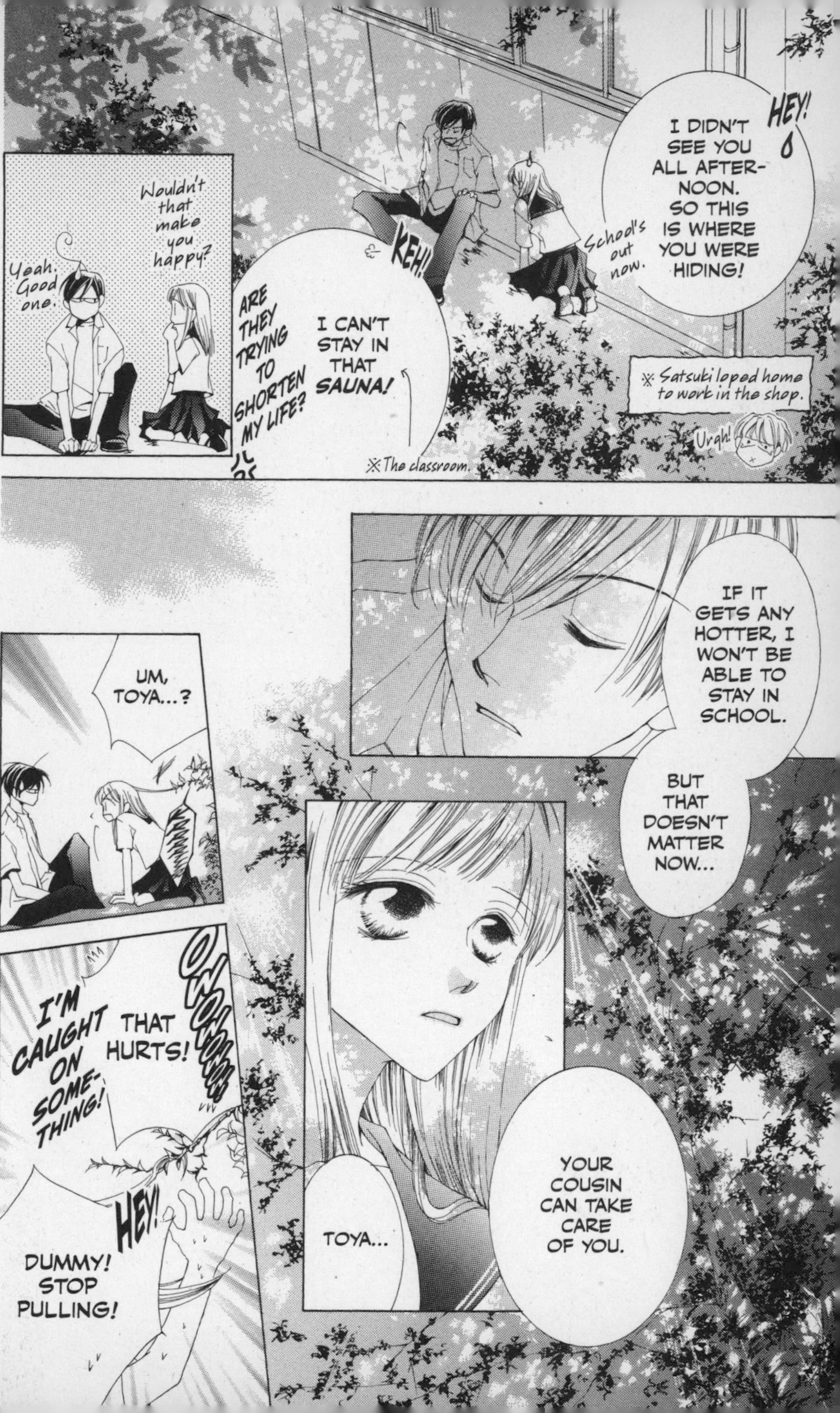
HEY!
I DIDN'T SEE YOU ALL AFTER-NOON. SO THIS IS WHERE YOU WERE HIDING!
School's out now.
KEH!
I CAN'T STAY IN THAT SAUNA!
ARE THEY TRYING TO SHORTEN MY LIFE?
※The classroom.
※Satsuki loped home to work in the shop.
Urgh!
Wouldn't that make you happy?
Yeah. Good one.
IF IT GETS ANY HOTTER, I WON'T BE ABLE TO STAY IN SCHOOL.
BUT THAT DOESN'T MATTER NOW...
YOUR COUSIN CAN TAKE CARE OF YOU.
TOYA...
UM, TOYA...?
THAT HURTS!
I'M CAUGHT ON SOME-THING!
HEY!
DUMMY! STOP PULLING!

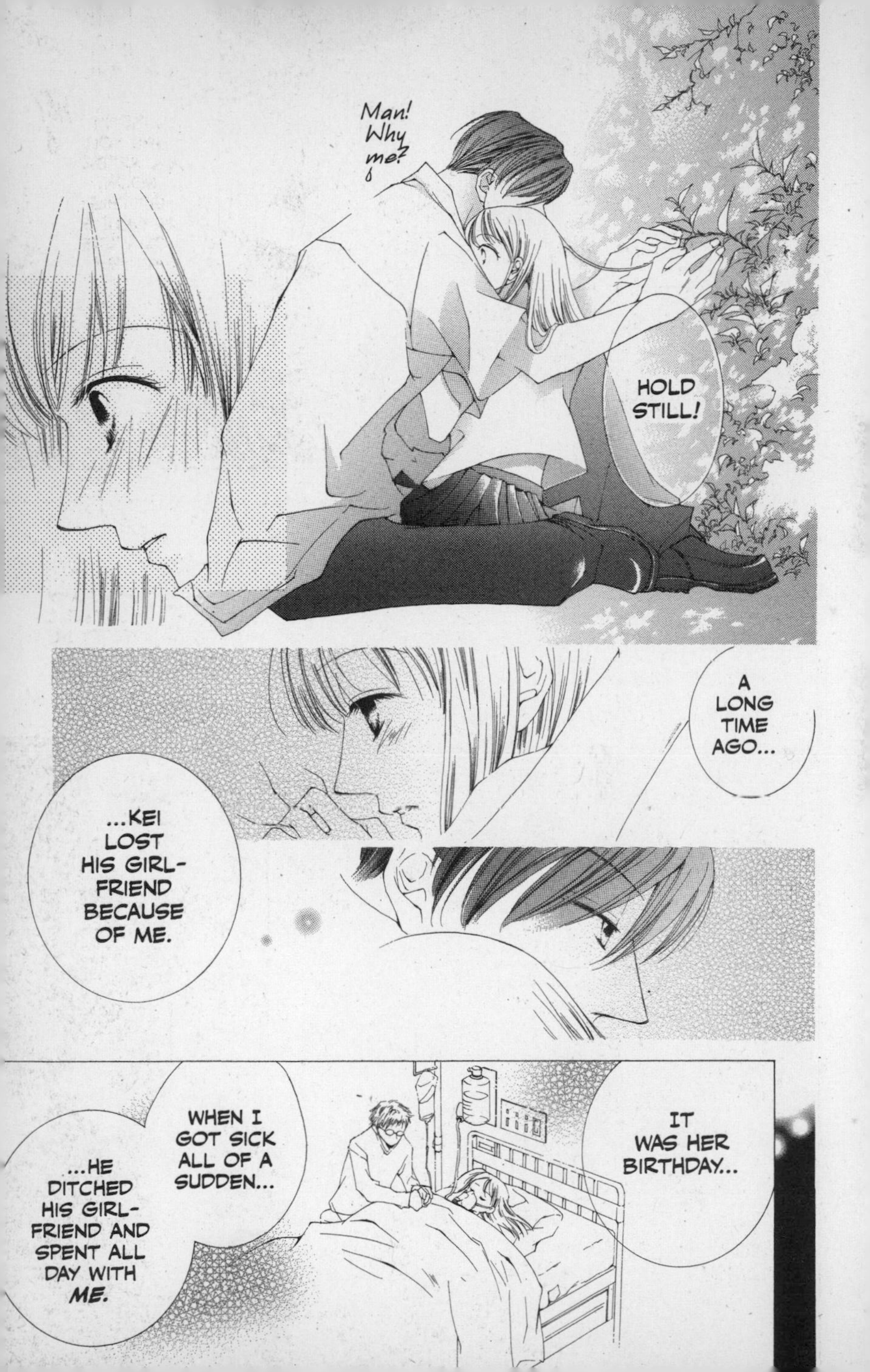
Man! Why me?
HOLD STILL!
A LONG TIME AGO...
...KEI LOST HIS GIRL-FRIEND BECAUSE OF ME.
IT WAS HER BIRTHDAY...
WHEN I GOT SICK ALL OF A SUDDEN...
...HE DITCHED HIS GIRL-FRIEND AND SPENT ALL DAY WITH *ME.*

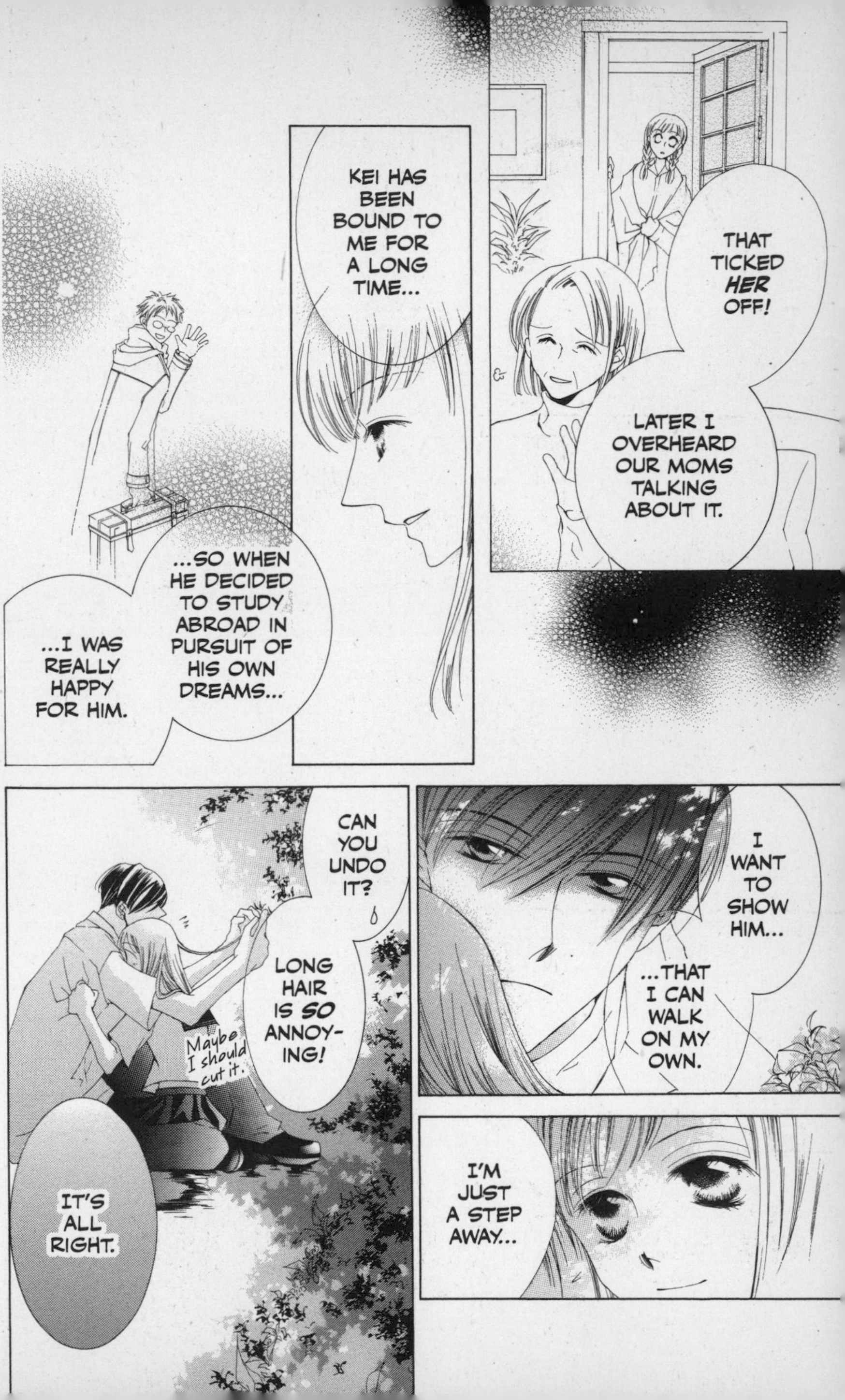
THAT TICKED *HER* OFF!
LATER I OVERHEARD OUR MOMS TALKING ABOUT IT.
KEI HAS BEEN BOUND TO ME FOR A LONG TIME...
...SO WHEN HE DECIDED TO STUDY ABROAD IN PURSUIT OF HIS OWN DREAMS...
...I WAS REALLY HAPPY FOR HIM.
I WANT TO SHOW HIM...
...THAT I CAN WALK ON MY OWN.
I'M JUST A STEP AWAY...
CAN YOU UNDO IT?
LONG HAIR IS *SO* ANNOYING!
Maybe I should cut it.
IT'S ALL RIGHT.

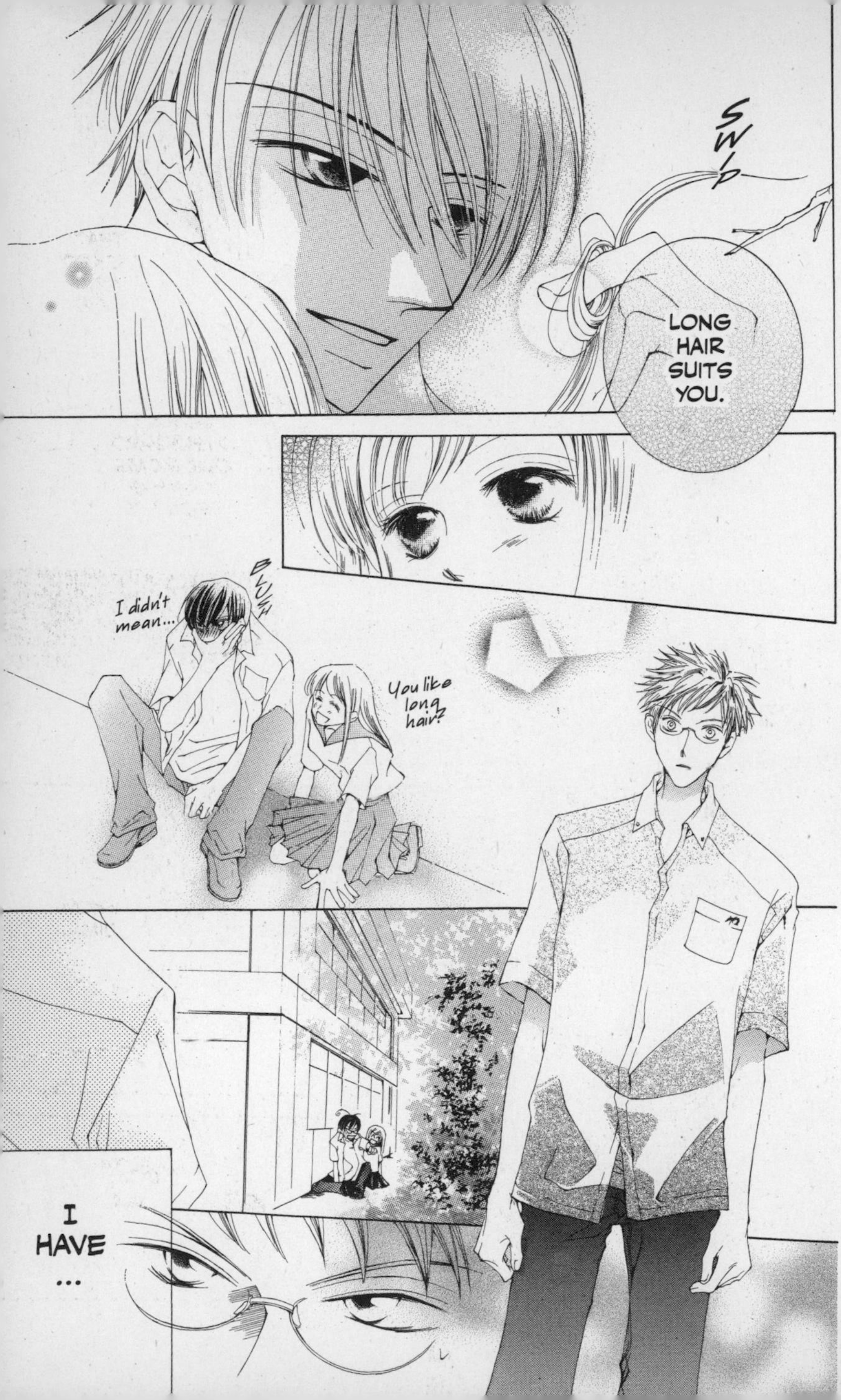
SWIP
LONG HAIR SUITS YOU.
You like long hair?
BLUSH
I didn't mean...
I HAVE ...

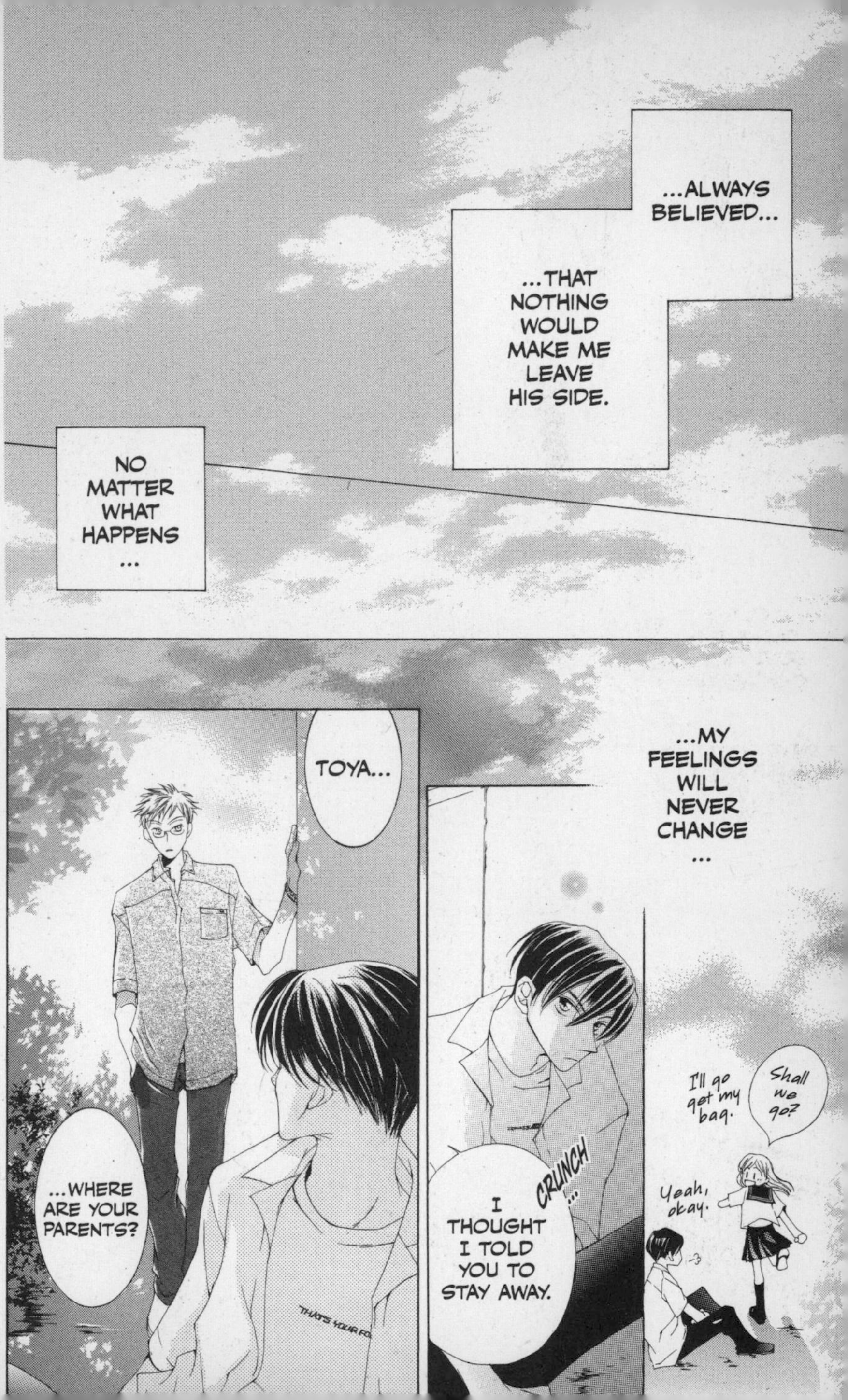
...ALWAYS BELIEVED...
...THAT NOTHING WOULD MAKE ME LEAVE HIS SIDE.
NO MATTER WHAT HAPPENS ...
...MY FEELINGS WILL NEVER CHANGE ...
Shall we go?
I'll go get my bag.
Yeah, okay.
CRUNCH...
I THOUGHT I TOLD YOU TO STAY AWAY.
TOYA...
...WHERE ARE YOUR PARENTS?

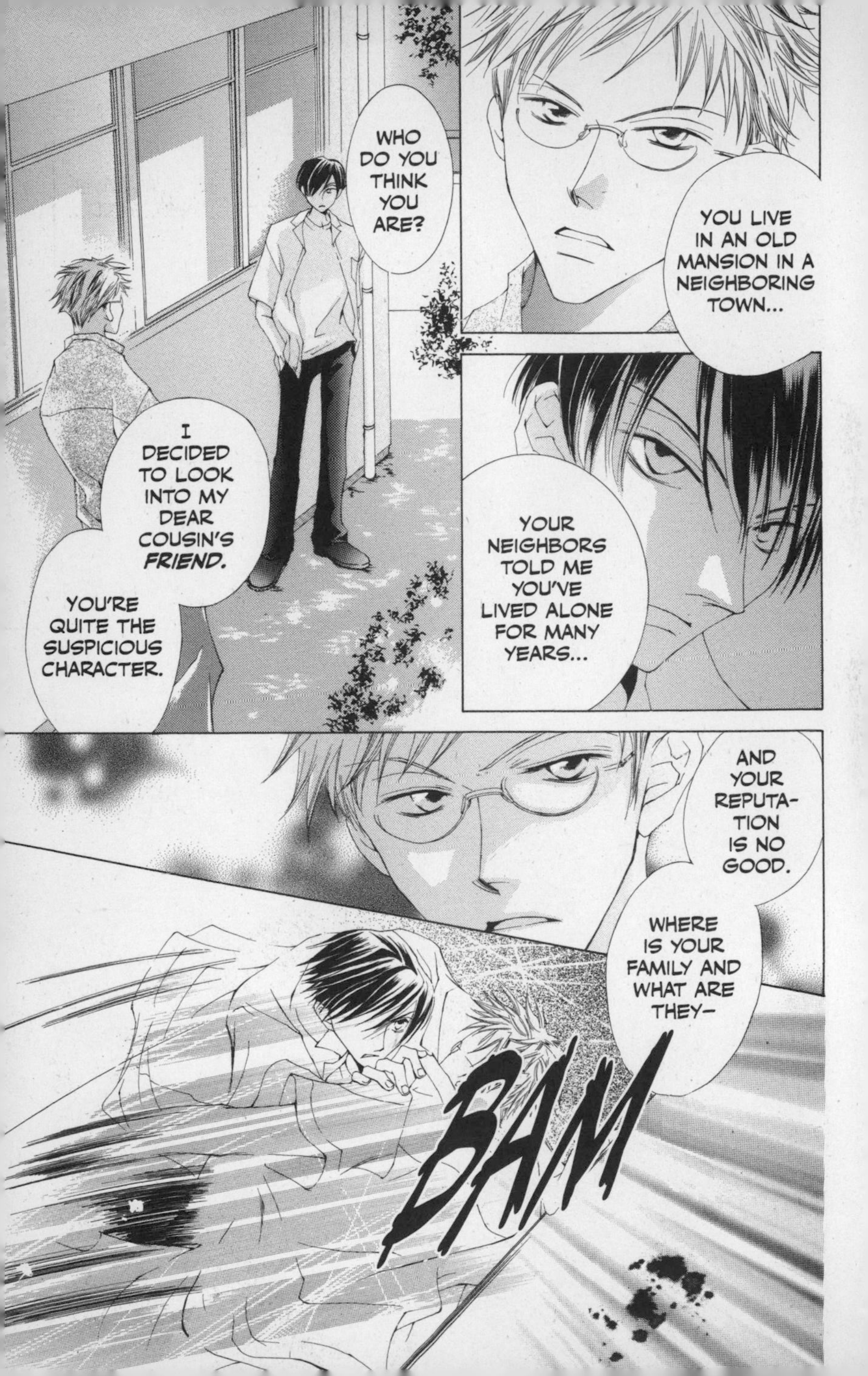
YOU LIVE IN AN OLD MANSION IN A NEIGHBORING TOWN...
YOUR NEIGHBORS TOLD ME YOU'VE LIVED ALONE FOR MANY YEARS...
WHO DO YOU THINK YOU ARE?
I DECIDED TO LOOK INTO MY DEAR COUSIN'S *FRIEND.*
YOU'RE QUITE THE SUSPICIOUS CHARACTER.
AND YOUR REPUTA-TION IS NO GOOD.
WHERE IS YOUR FAMILY AND WHAT ARE THEY—
BAM

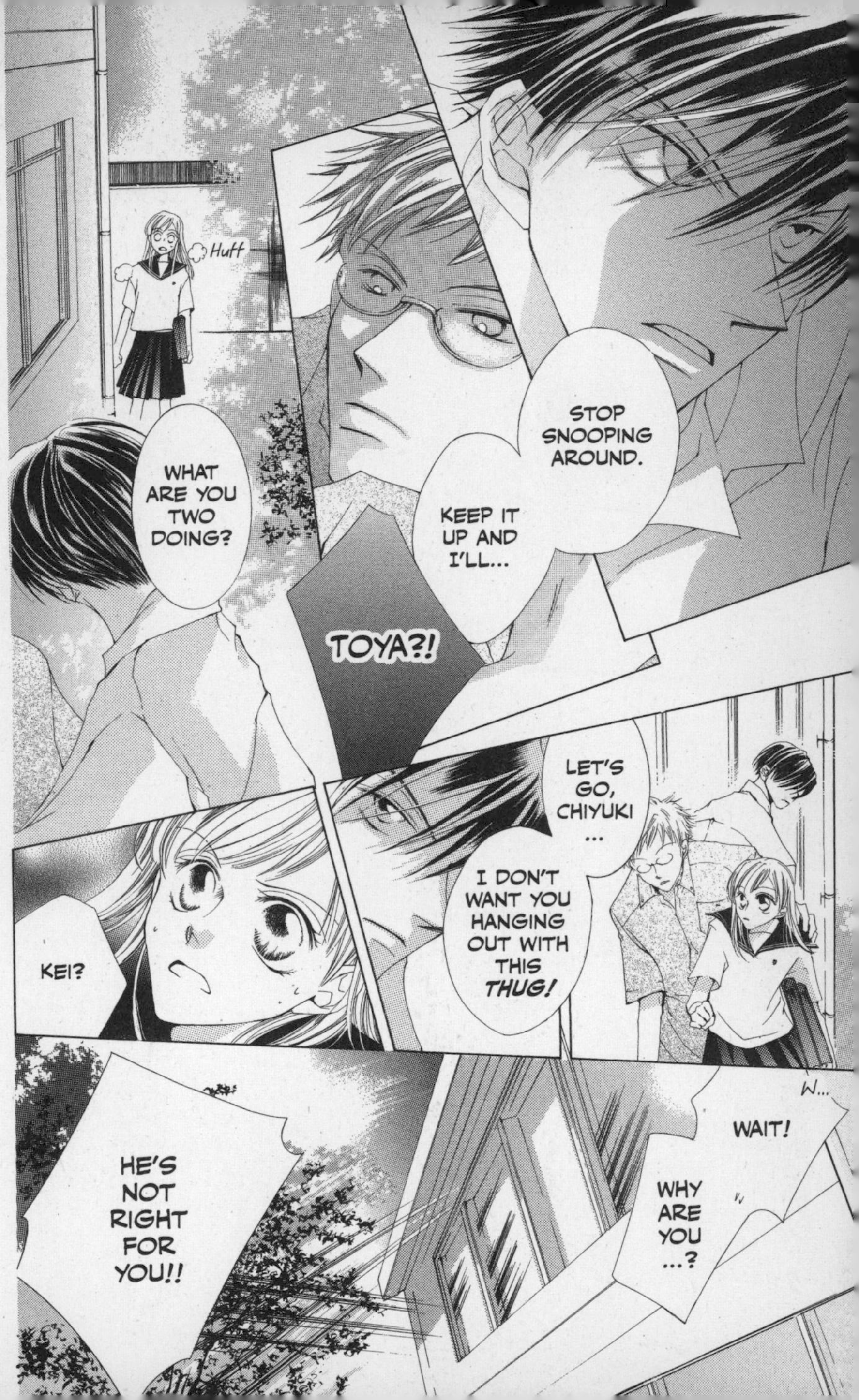
STOP SNOOPING AROUND.
KEEP IT UP AND I'LL...
TOYA?!
Huff
WHAT ARE YOU TWO DOING?
LET'S GO, CHIYUKI ...
I DON'T WANT YOU HANGING OUT WITH THIS *THUG!*
KEI?
W...
WAIT!
WHY ARE YOU ...?
HE'S NOT RIGHT FOR YOU!!

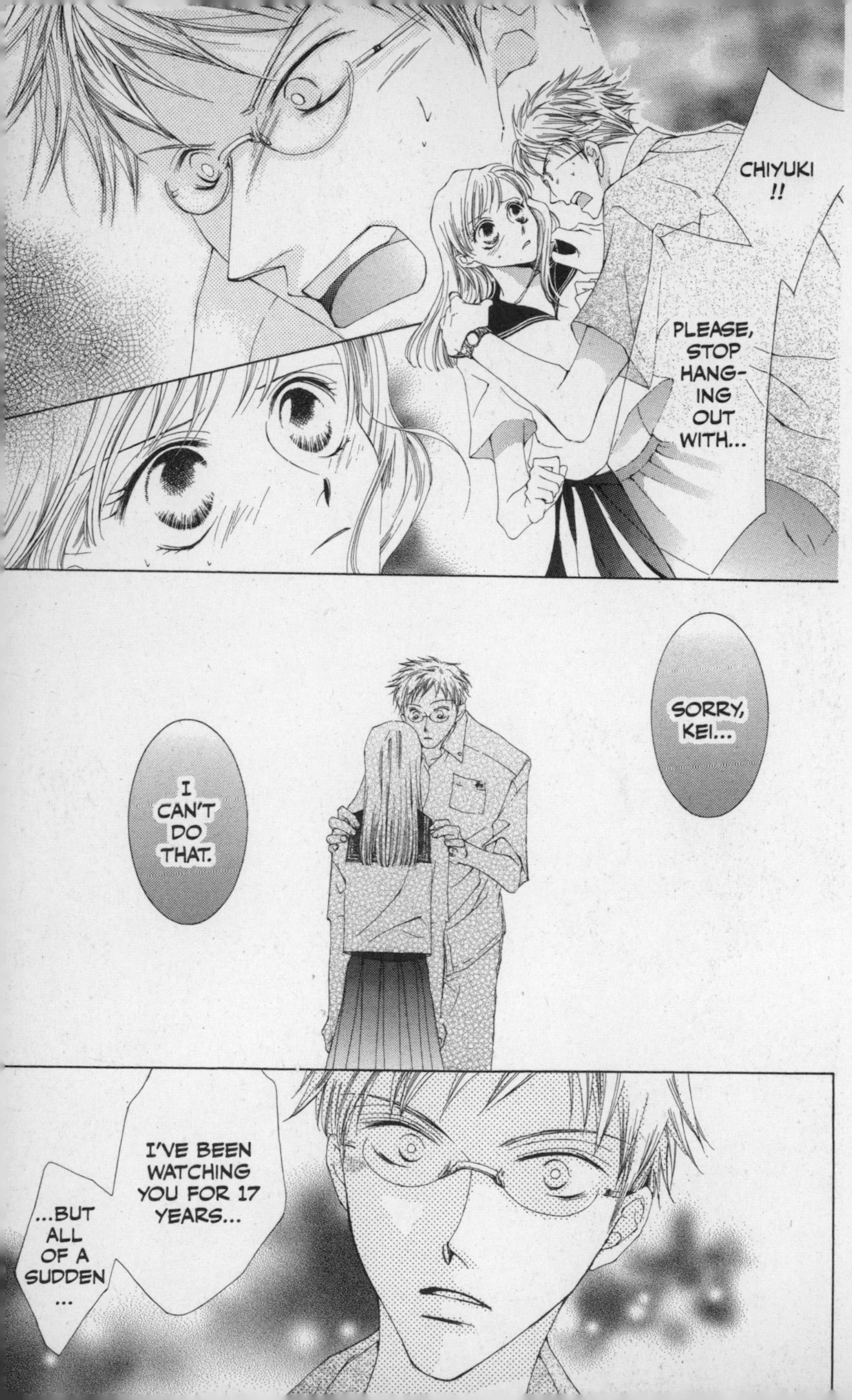
CHIYUKI !!
PLEASE, STOP HANGING-ING OUT WITH...
SORRY, KEI...
I CAN'T DO THAT.
I'VE BEEN WATCHING YOU FOR 17 YEARS...
...BUT ALL OF A SUDDEN ...

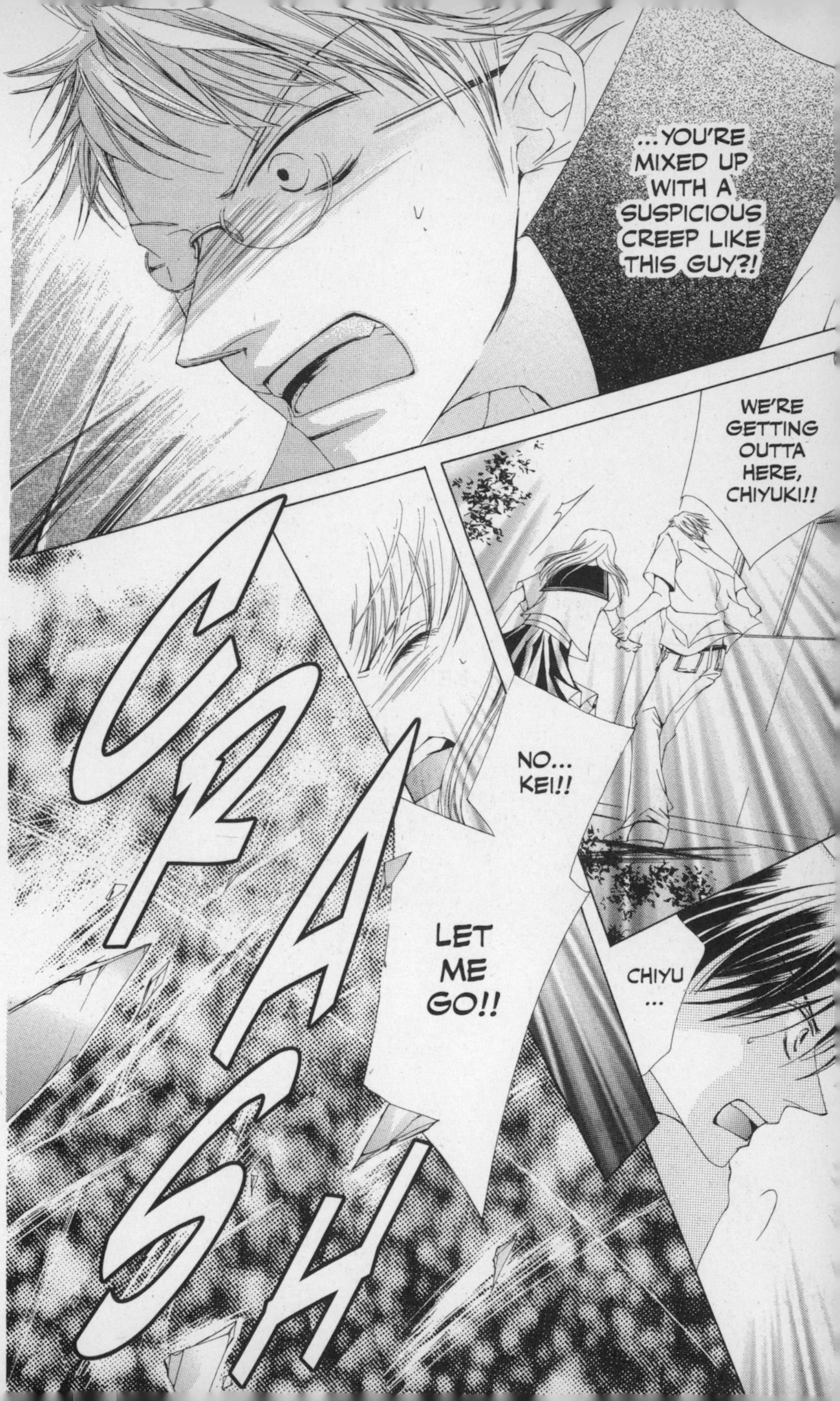
...YOU'RE MIXED UP WITH A SUSPICIOUS CREEP LIKE THIS GUY?!
WE'RE GETTING OUTTA HERE, CHIYUKI!!
NO... KEI!!
CHIYU...
LET ME GO!!
CRASH

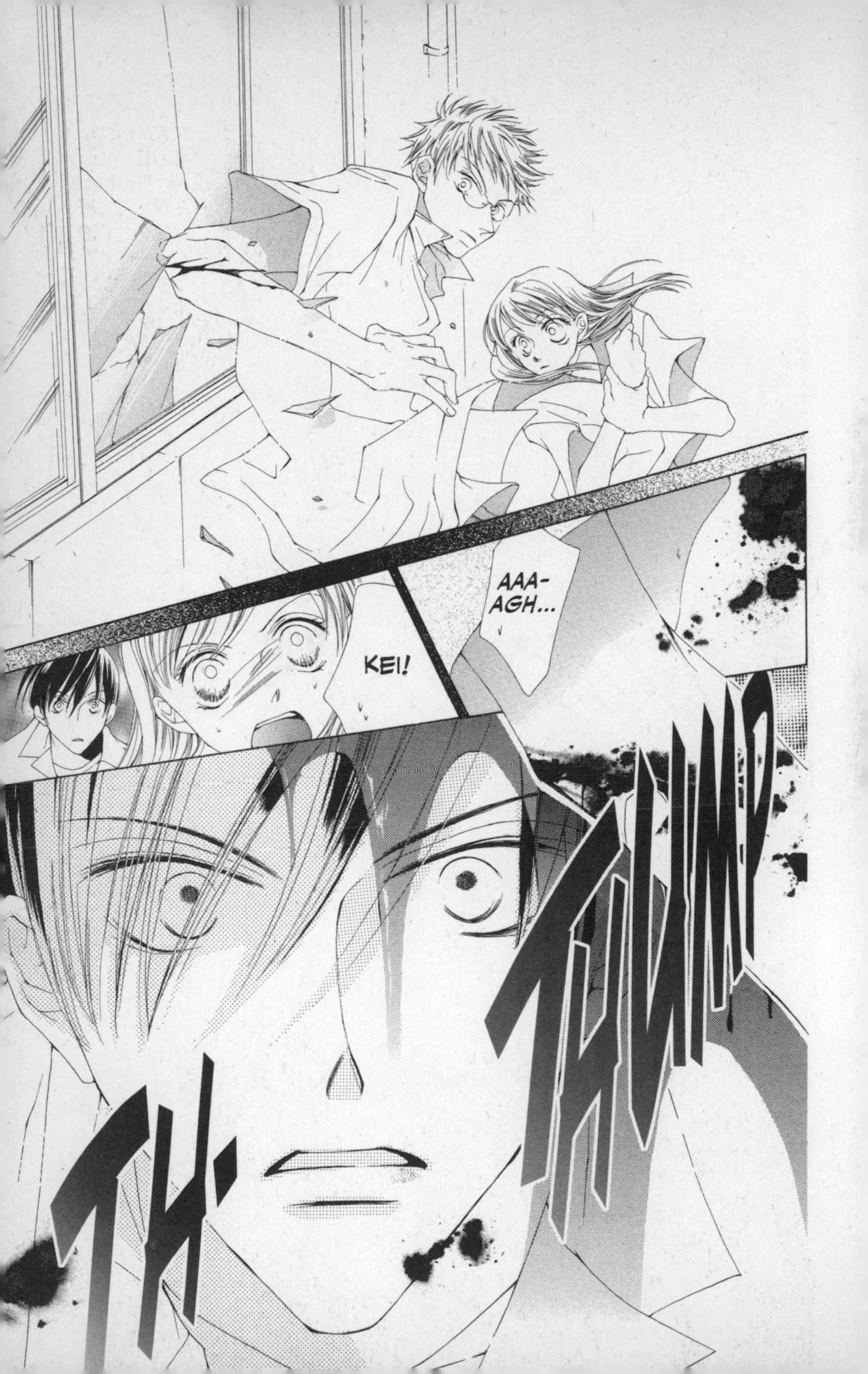
AAA-
AGH...
KEI!
THUMP
TH-

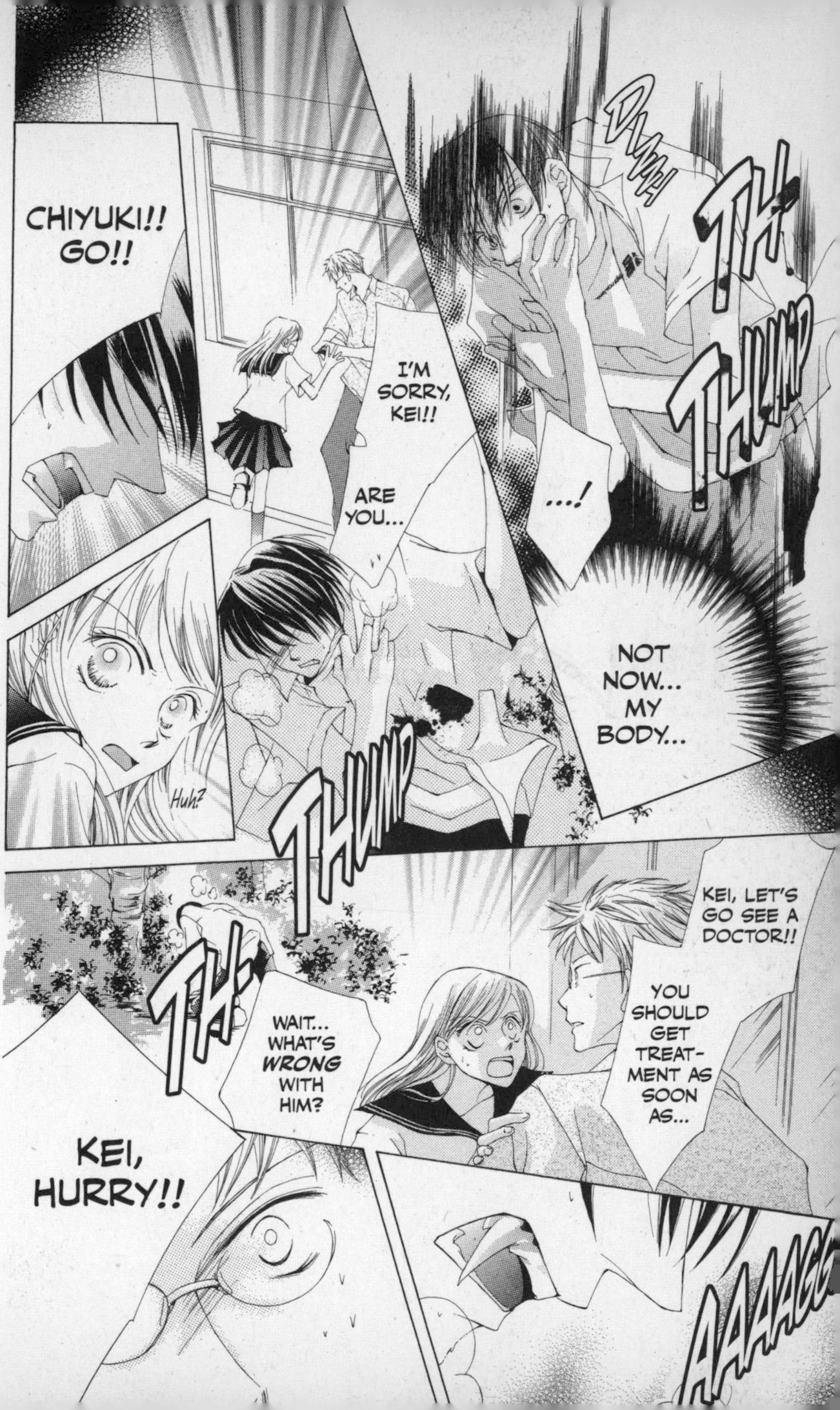
TH-THUMP
...!
NOT NOW... MY BODY...
I'M SORRY, KEI!!
ARE YOU...
THUMP
CHIYUKI!! GO!!
Huh?
KEI, LET'S GO SEE A DOCTOR!!
YOU SHOULD GET TREAT-MENT AS SOON AS...
WAIT... WHAT'S *WRONG* WITH HIM?
TH-
KEI, HURRY!!
AAAAG

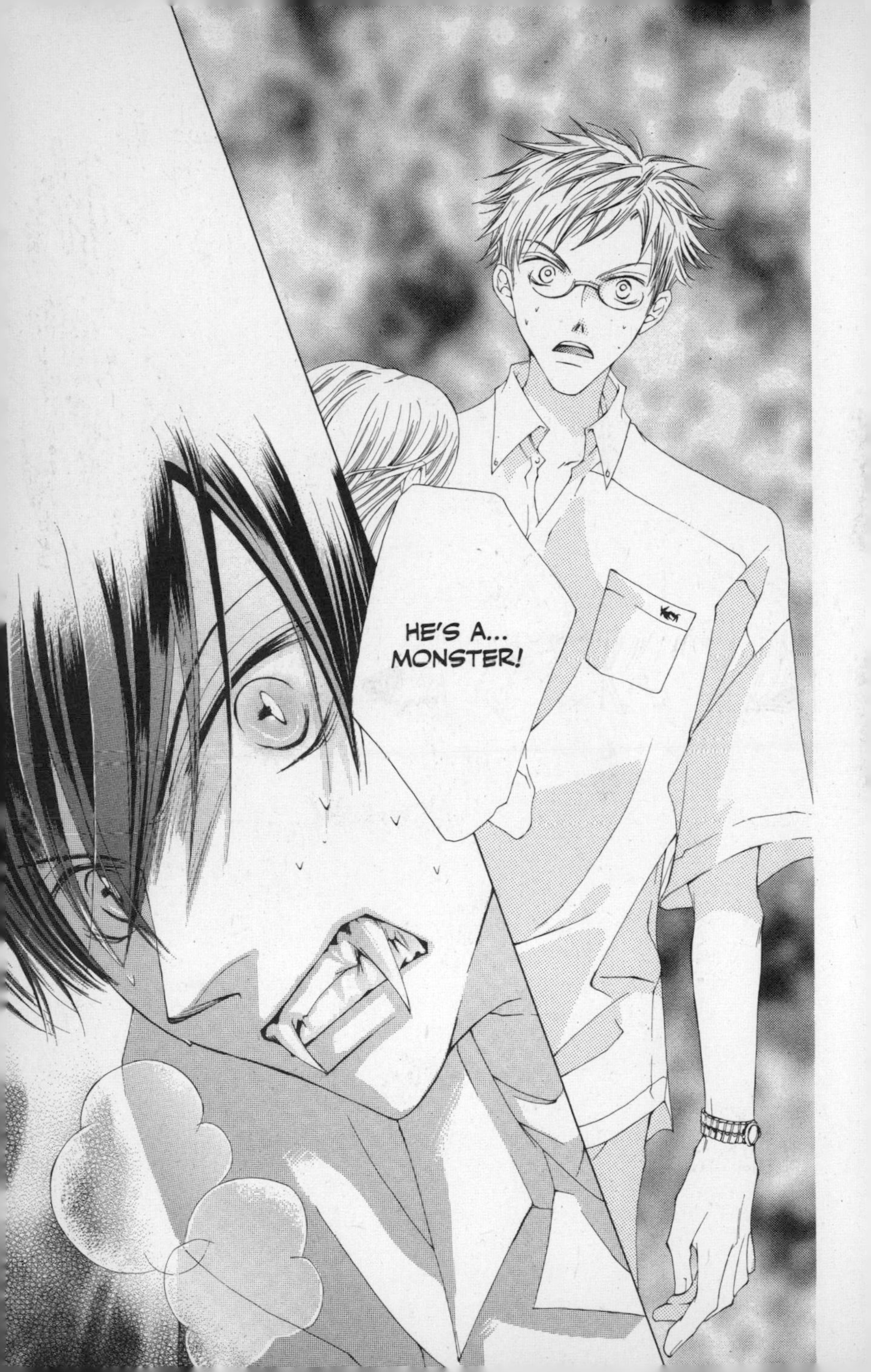
HE'S A... MONSTER!

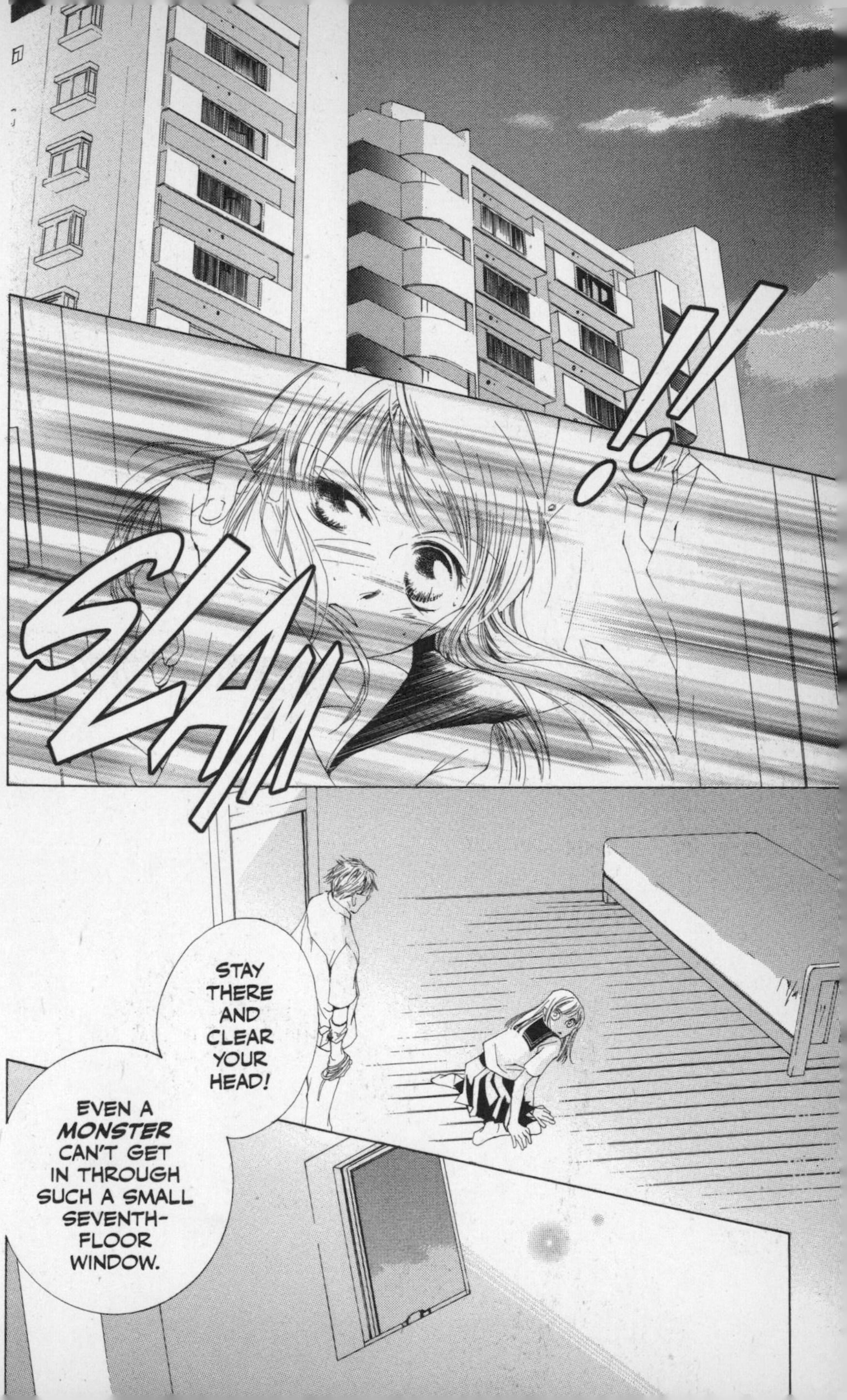
!!
SLAM
STAY THERE AND CLEAR YOUR HEAD!
EVEN A MONSTER CAN'T GET IN THROUGH SUCH A SMALL SEVENTH-FLOOR WINDOW.

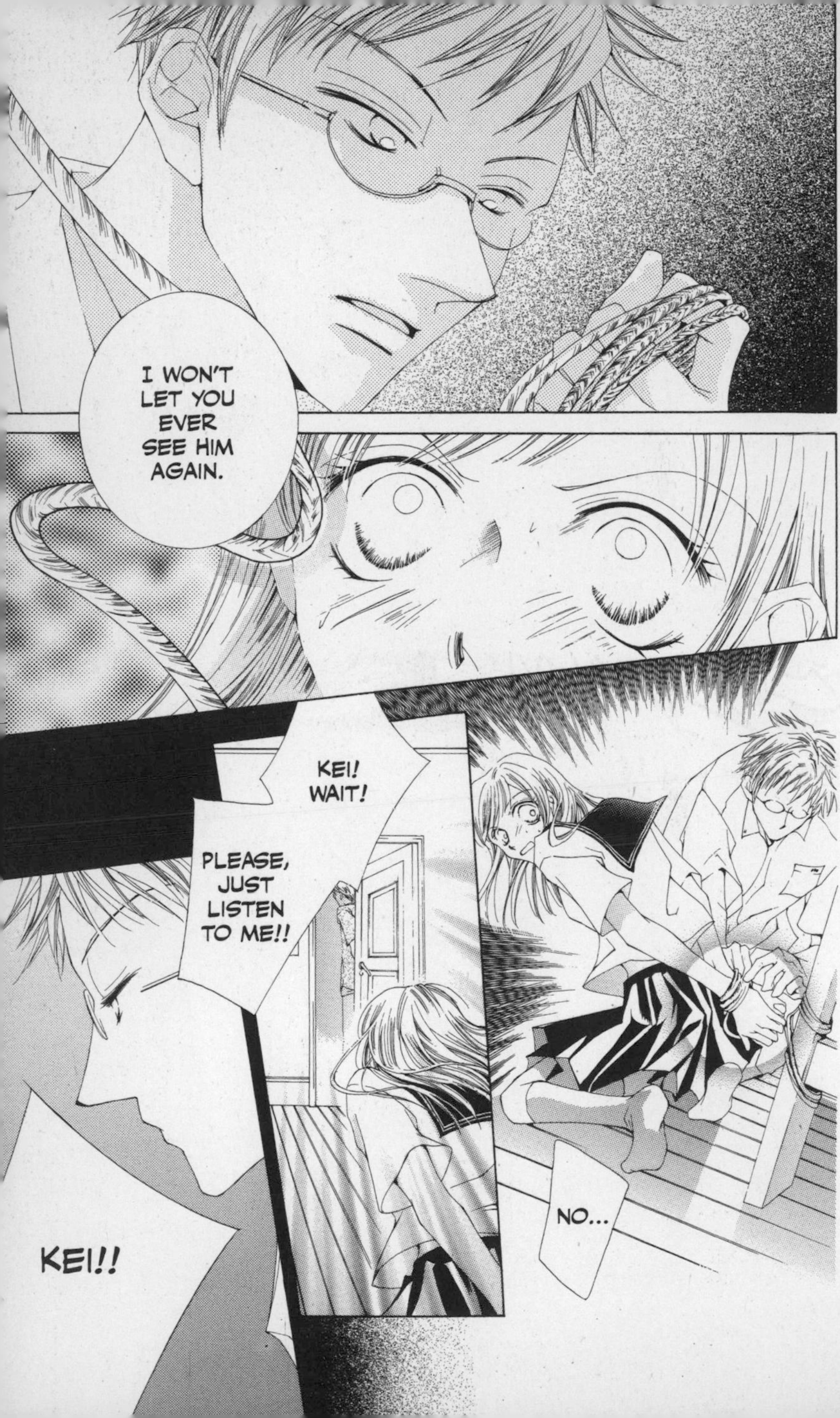
I WON'T LET YOU EVER SEE HIM AGAIN.
NO...
KEI! WAIT!
PLEASE, JUST LISTEN TO ME!!
KEI!!

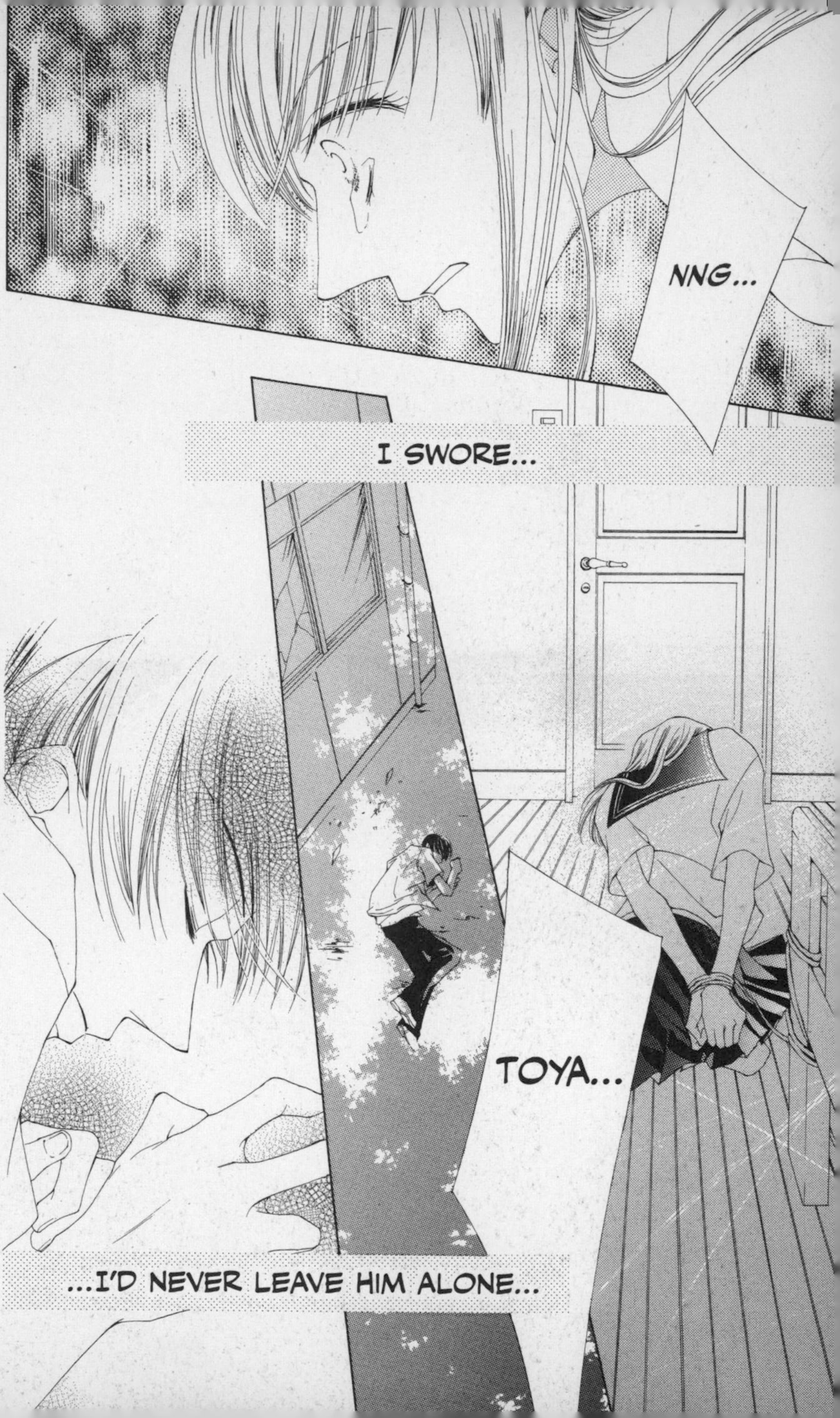
NNG...
I SWORE...
TOYA...
...I'D NEVER LEAVE HIM ALONE...

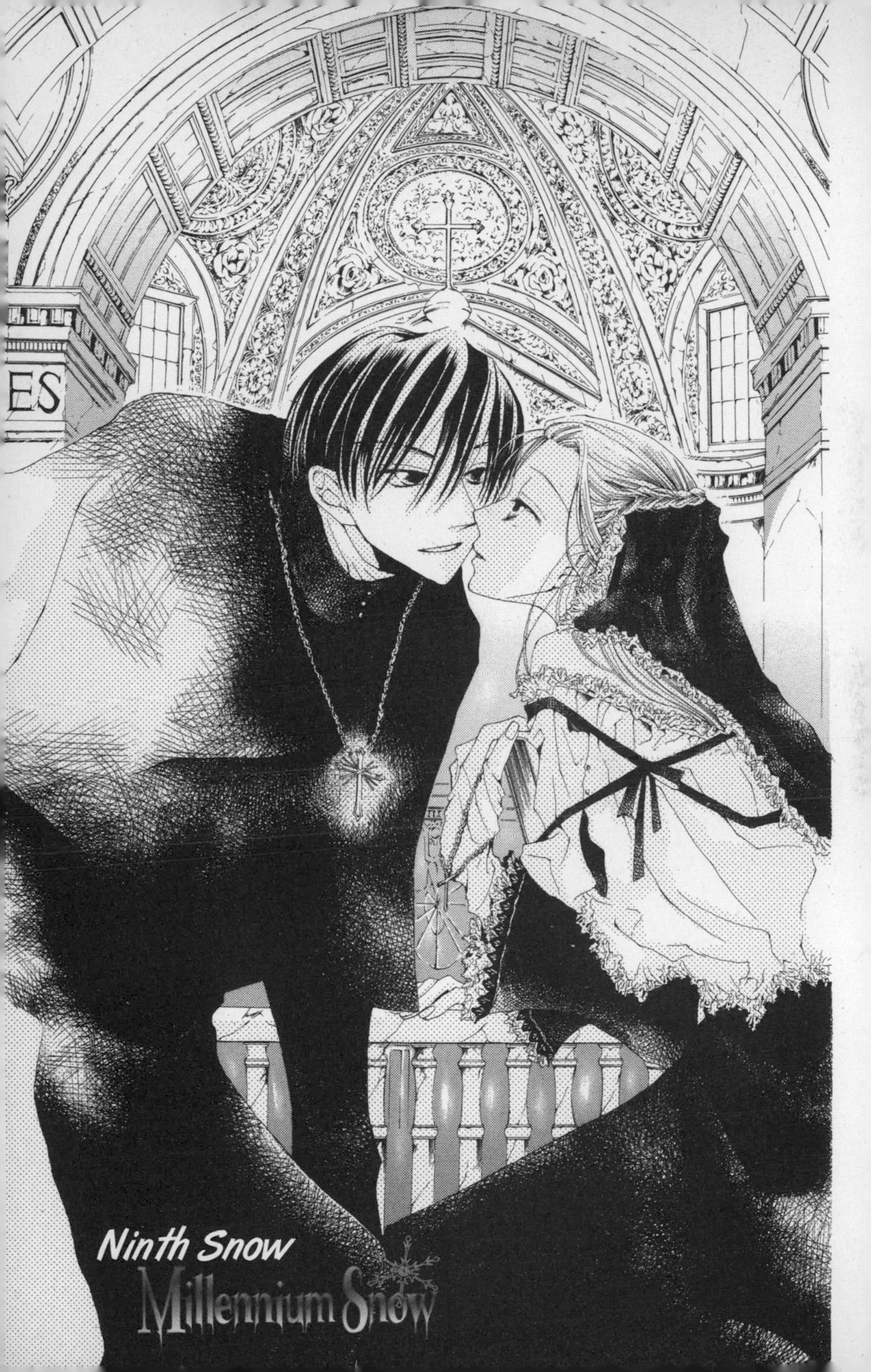
ES
Ninth Snow
Millennium Snow

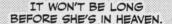
IT WON'T BE LONG
BEFORE SHE'S IN HEAVEN.

KEI,
LET'S
MAKE
A BET.

WHICH
CLOUD
DO YOU
THINK
WILL
SNOW
FIRST?

I KNOW THAT AS RAIN FALLS
AT LAST TO EARTH...

...SHE WISHES TO BECOME AS THE SNOW...

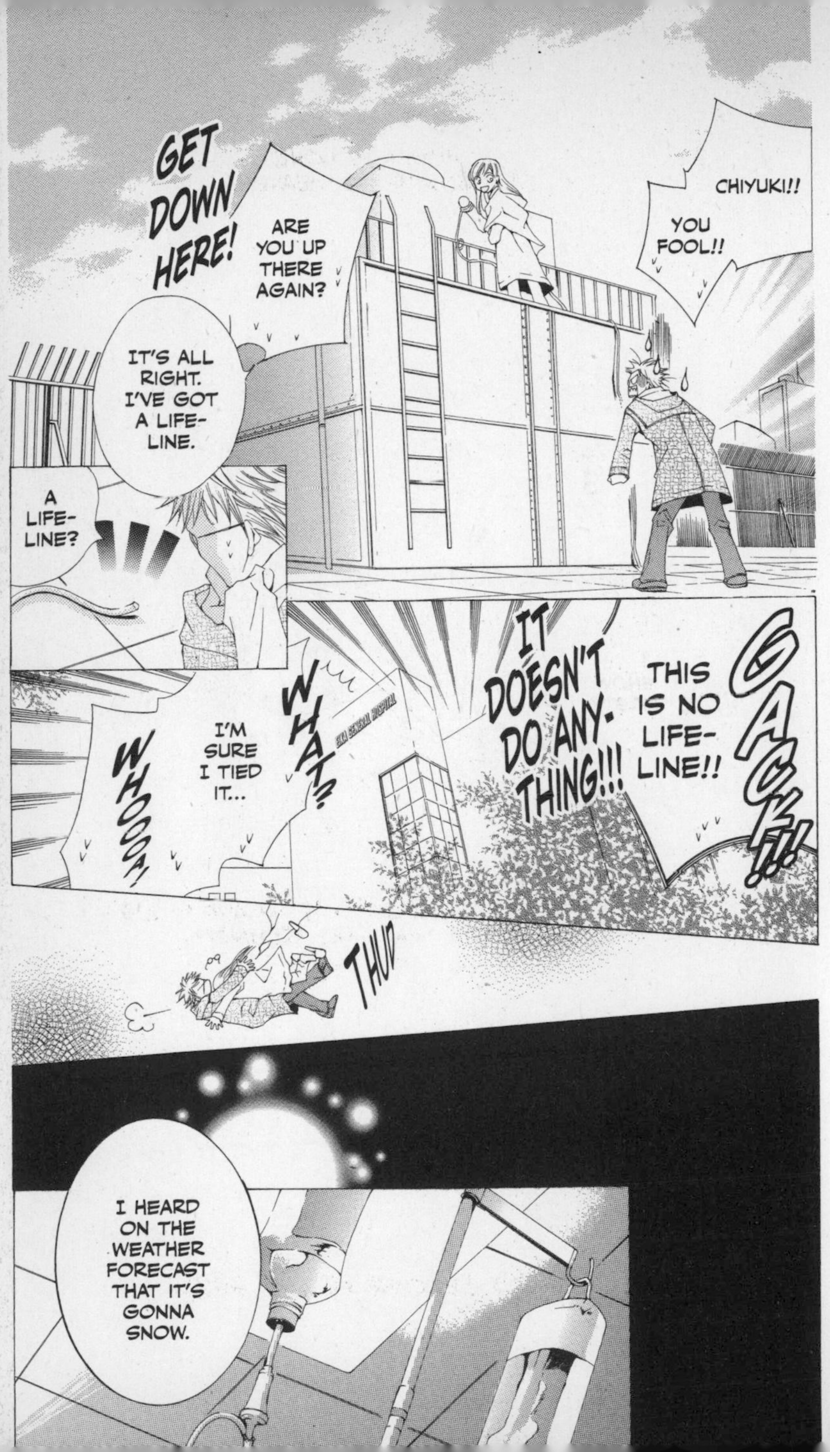
CHIYUKI!!
YOU FOOL!!
ARE YOU UP THERE AGAIN?
GET DOWN HERE!
IT'S ALL RIGHT. I'VE GOT A LIFE-LINE.
A LIFE-LINE?
GACK!!
THIS IS NO LIFE-LINE!!
IT DOESN'T DO ANYTHING!!!
WHAT?
I'M SURE I TIED IT...
WHOOOA!
THUD
I HEARD ON THE WEATHER FORECAST THAT IT'S GONNA SNOW.

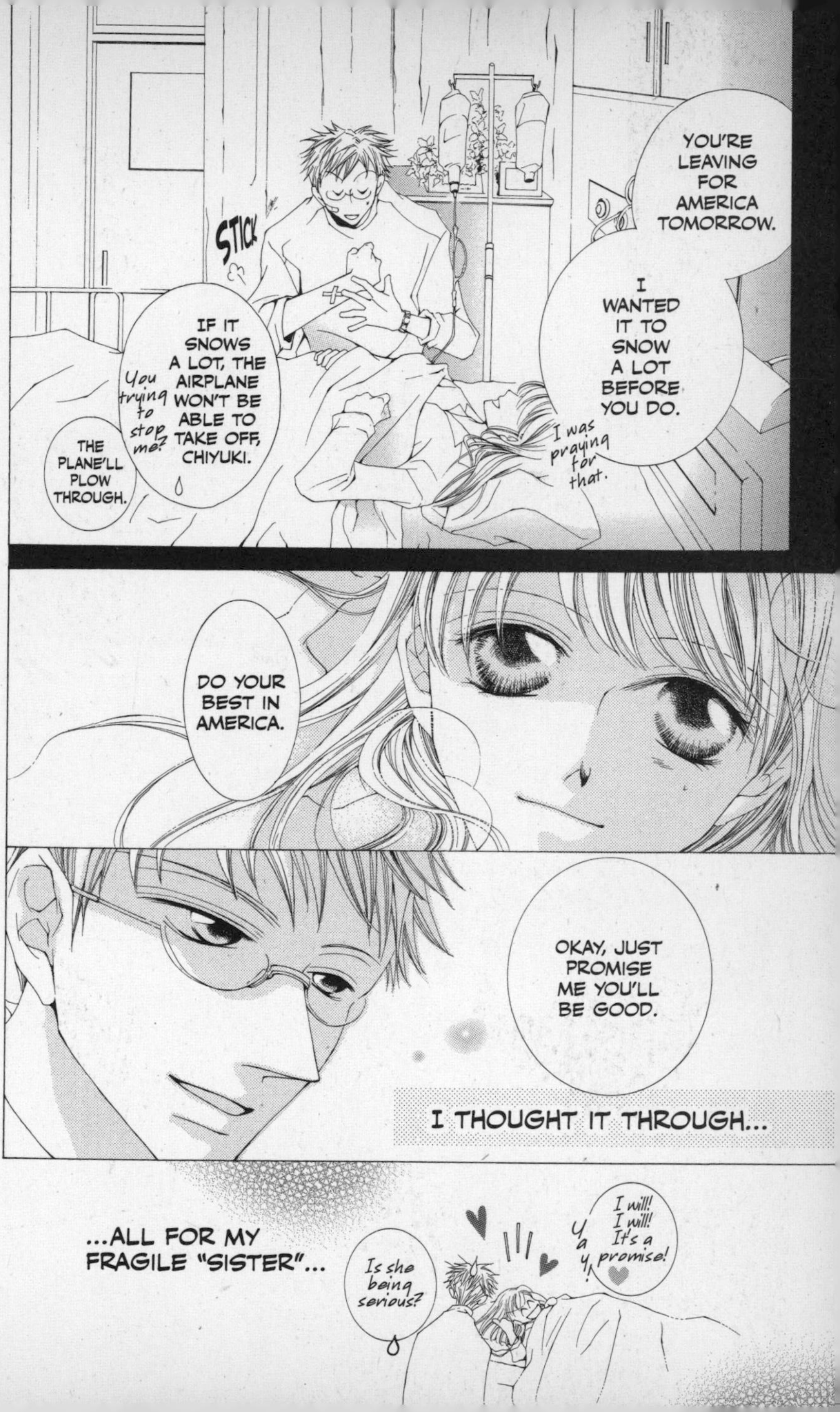
YOU'RE LEAVING FOR AMERICA TOMORROW.
I WANTED IT TO SNOW A LOT BEFORE YOU DO.
I was praying for that.
STICK
IF IT SNOWS A LOT, THE AIRPLANE WON'T BE ABLE TO TAKE OFF, CHIYUKI.
You trying to stop me?
THE PLANE'LL PLOW THROUGH.
DO YOUR BEST IN AMERICA.
OKAY, JUST PROMISE ME YOU'LL BE GOOD.
I THOUGHT IT THROUGH...
I will! I will! It's a promise!
Yay!
Is she being serious?
...ALL FOR MY FRAGILE "SISTER"...

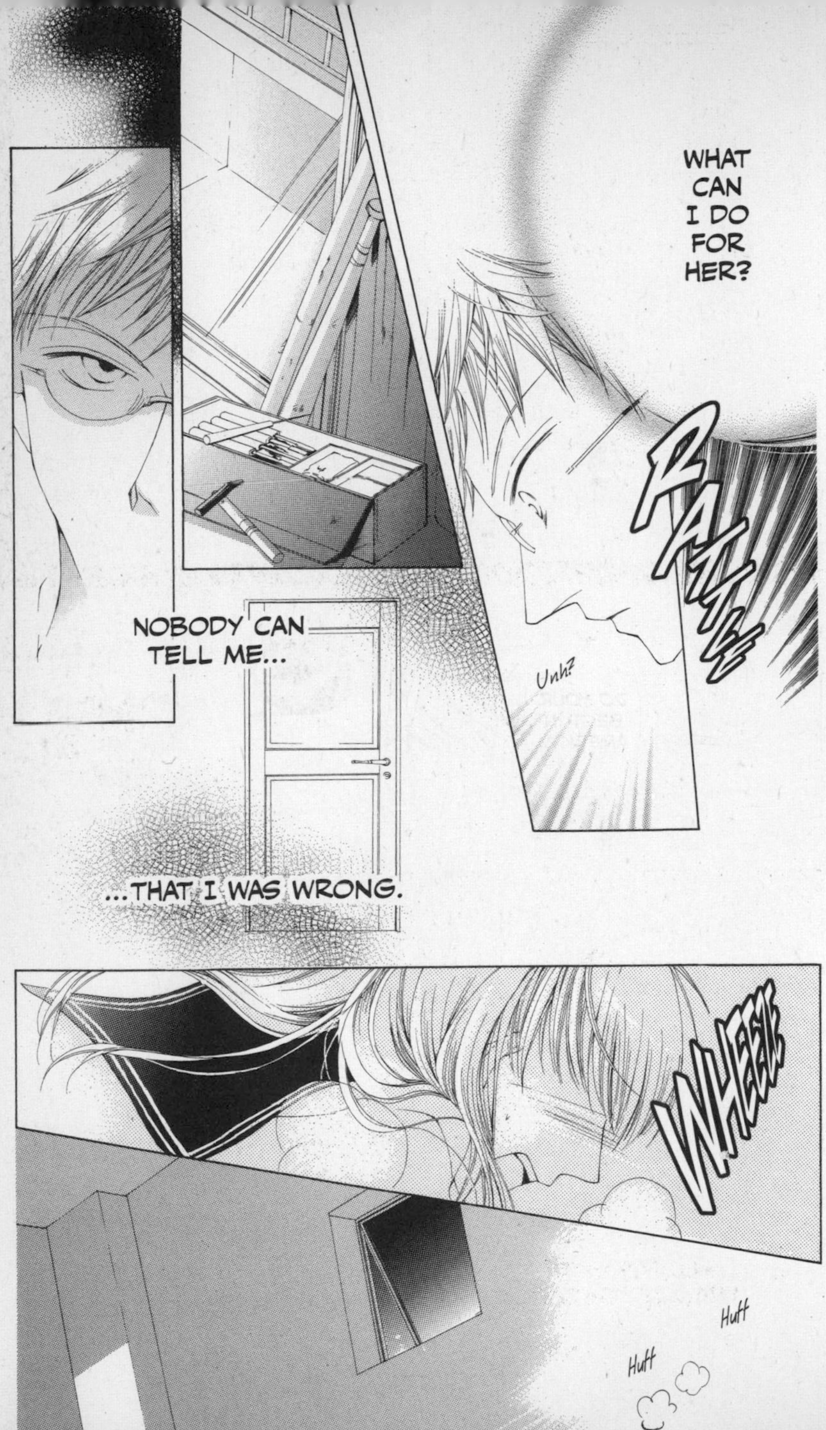
WHAT CAN I DO FOR HER?
RATTLE
Unh?
NOBODY CAN TELL ME...
...THAT I WAS WRONG.
WHEEZE
Huff
Huff

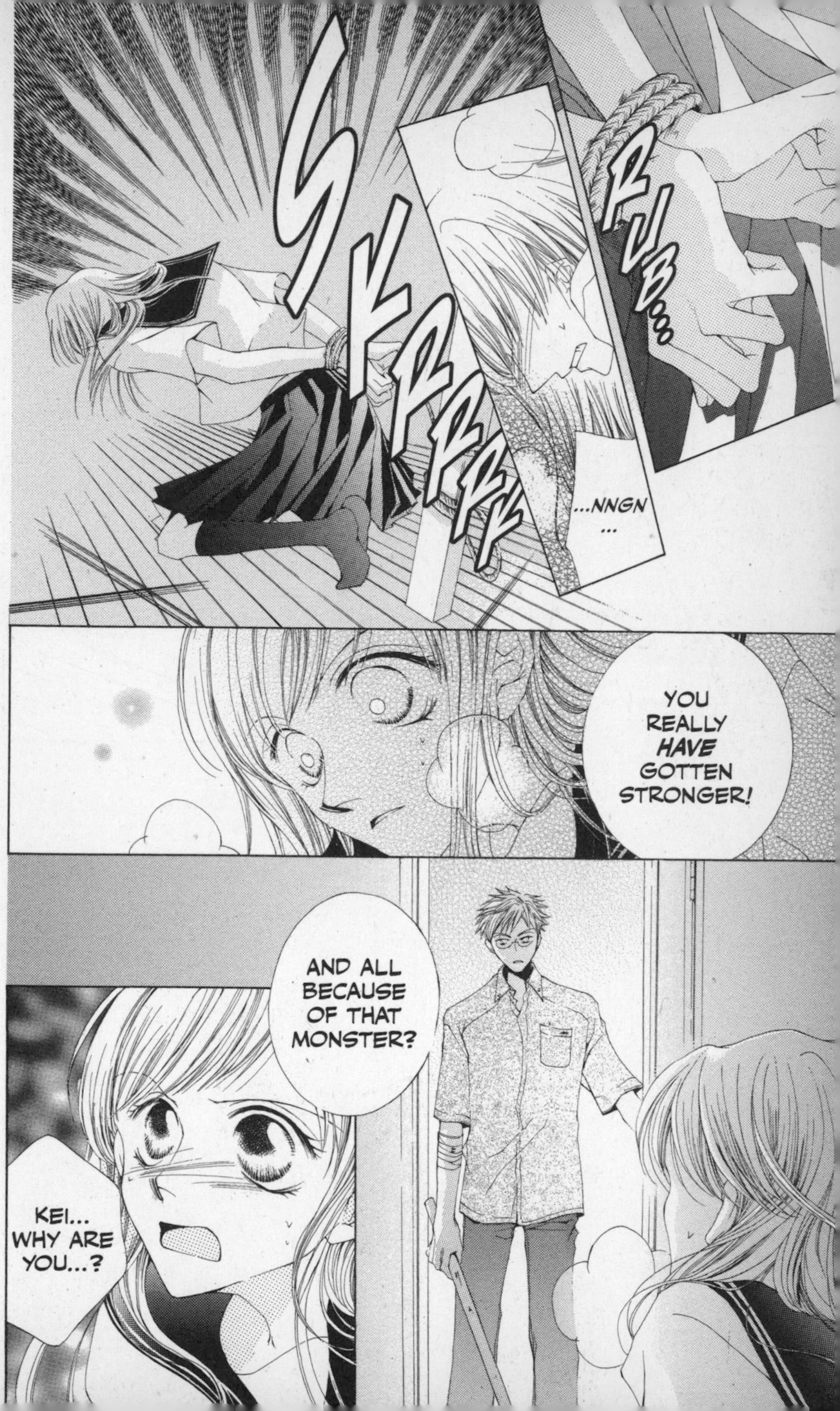
RUB...
...NNGN ...
SKRRRK
YOU REALLY *HAVE* GOTTEN STRONGER!
AND ALL BECAUSE OF THAT MONSTER?
KEI... WHY ARE YOU...?

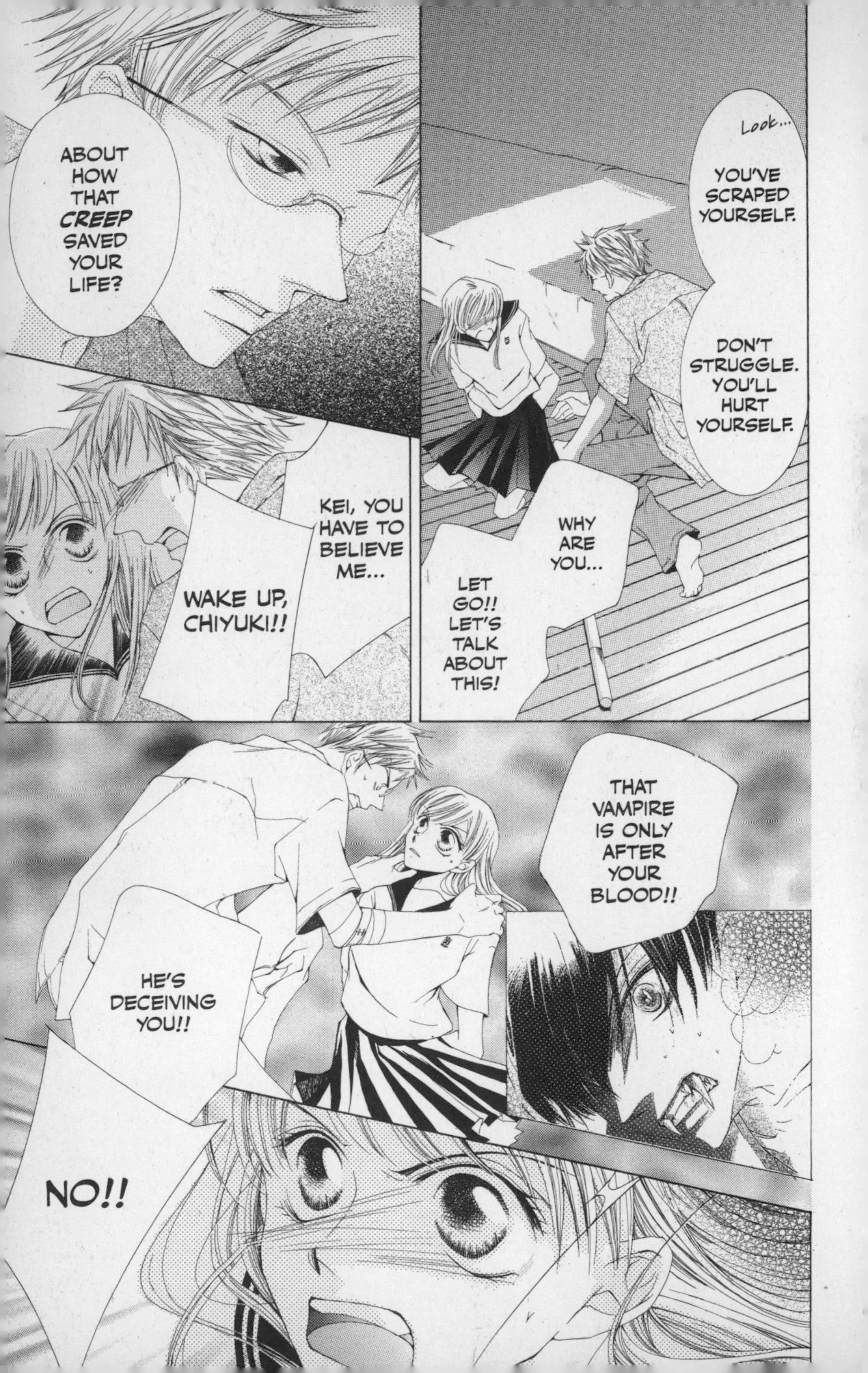

Look...
YOU'VE SCRAPED YOURSELF.
DON'T STRUGGLE. YOU'LL HURT YOURSELF.
WHY ARE YOU...
LET GO!! LET'S TALK ABOUT THIS!
ABOUT HOW THAT *CREEP* SAVED YOUR LIFE?
KEI, YOU HAVE TO BELIEVE ME...
WAKE UP, CHIYUKI!!
THAT VAMPIRE IS ONLY AFTER YOUR BLOOD!!
HE'S DECEIVING YOU!!
NO!!

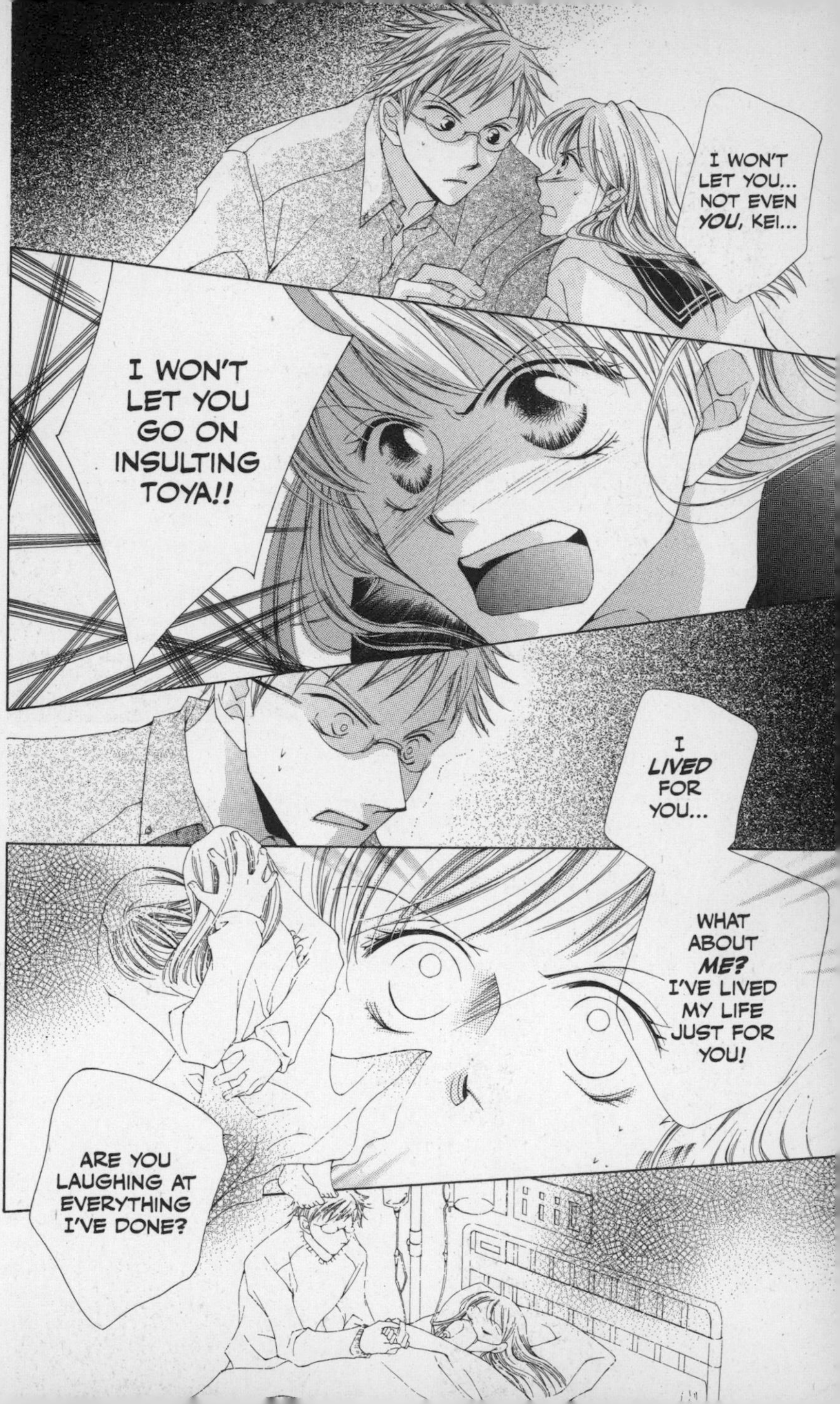
I WON'T LET YOU... NOT EVEN *YOU*, KEI...
I WON'T LET YOU GO ON INSULTING TOYA!!
I *LIVED* FOR YOU...
WHAT ABOUT *ME?* I'VE LIVED MY LIFE JUST FOR YOU!
ARE YOU LAUGHING AT EVERYTHING I'VE DONE?

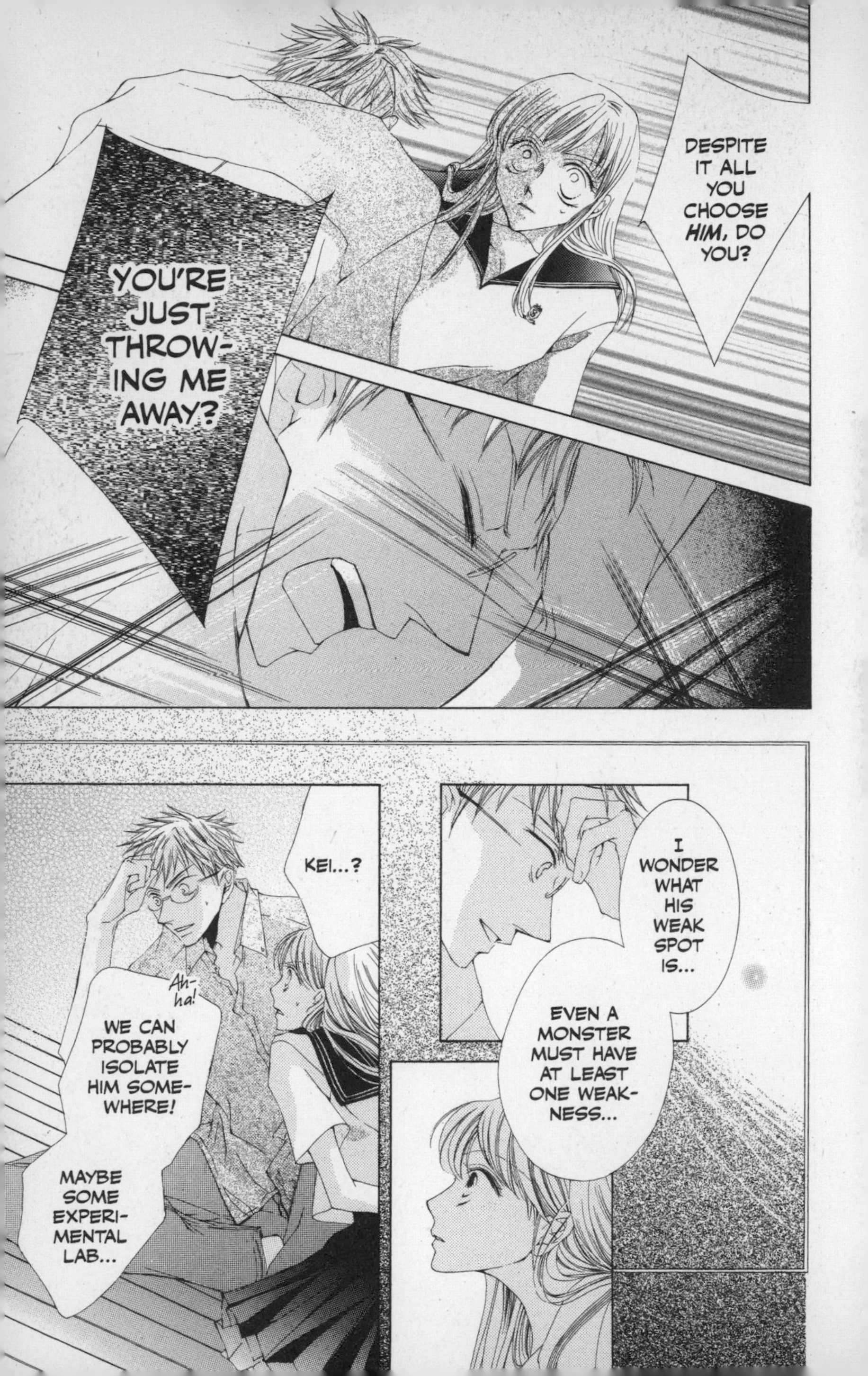
DESPITE IT ALL YOU CHOOSE *HIM*, DO YOU?
YOU'RE JUST THROWING ME AWAY?
I WONDER WHAT HIS WEAK SPOT IS...
EVEN A MONSTER MUST HAVE AT LEAST ONE WEAKNESS...
KEI...?
Ah-ha!
WE CAN PROBABLY ISOLATE HIM SOMEWHERE!
MAYBE SOME EXPERIMENTAL LAB...

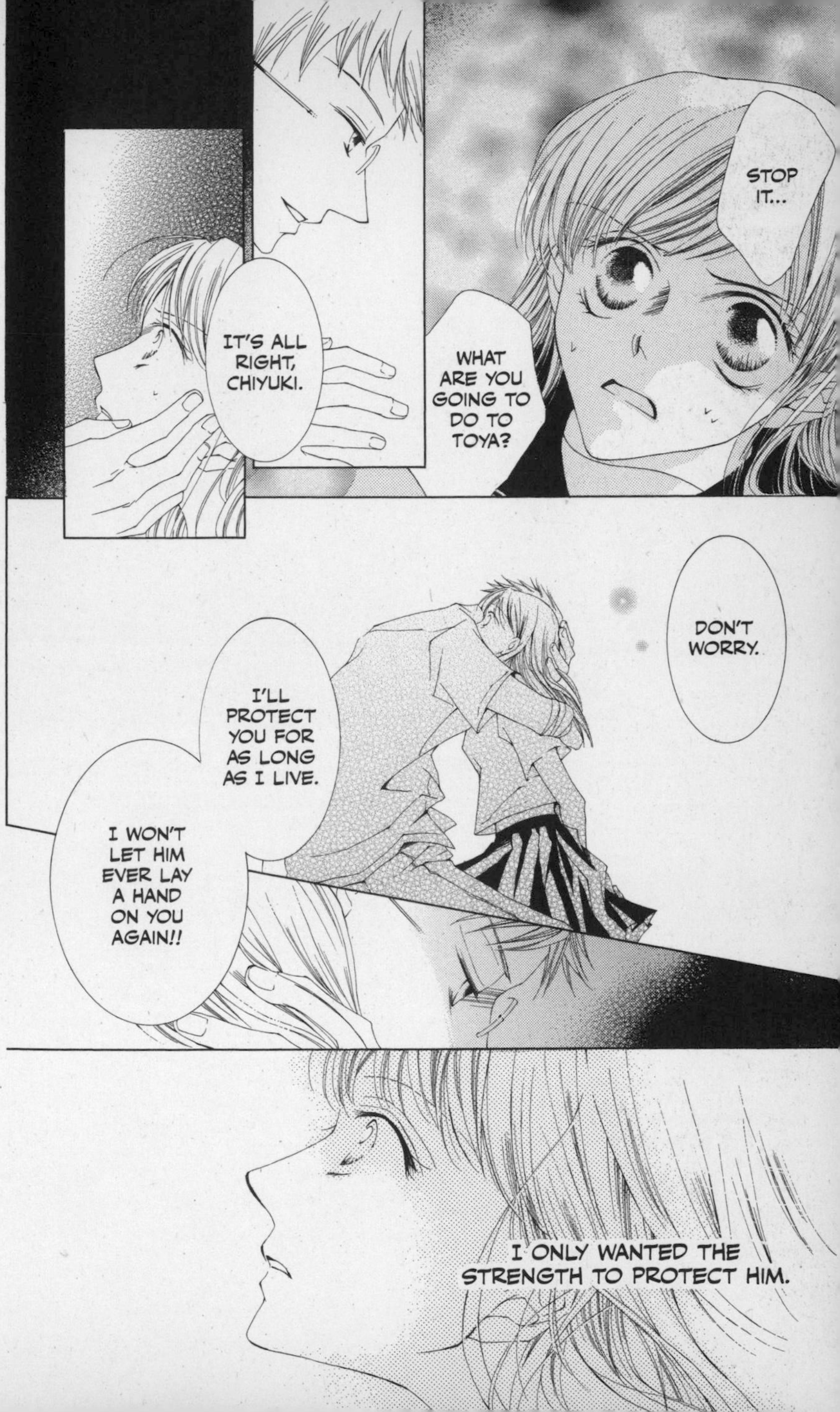
STOP IT...
WHAT ARE YOU GOING TO DO TO TOYA?
IT'S ALL RIGHT, CHIYUKI.
DON'T WORRY.
I'LL PROTECT YOU FOR AS LONG AS I LIVE.
I WON'T LET HIM EVER LAY A HAND ON YOU AGAIN!!
I ONLY WANTED THE STRENGTH TO PROTECT HIM.

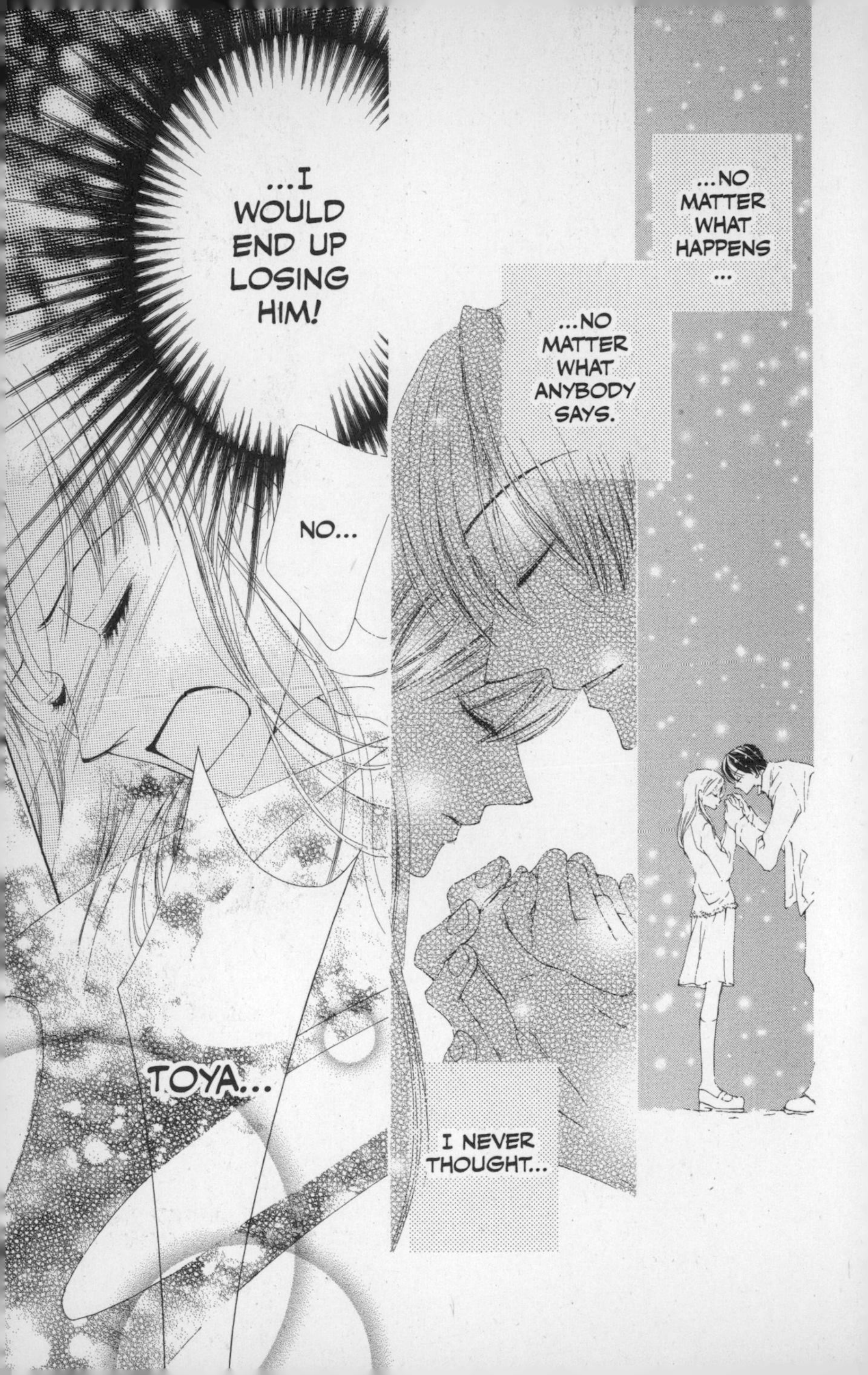
...NO MATTER WHAT HAPPENS...
...NO MATTER WHAT ANYBODY SAYS.
I NEVER THOUGHT...
...I WOULD END UP LOSING HIM!
NO...
TOYA...

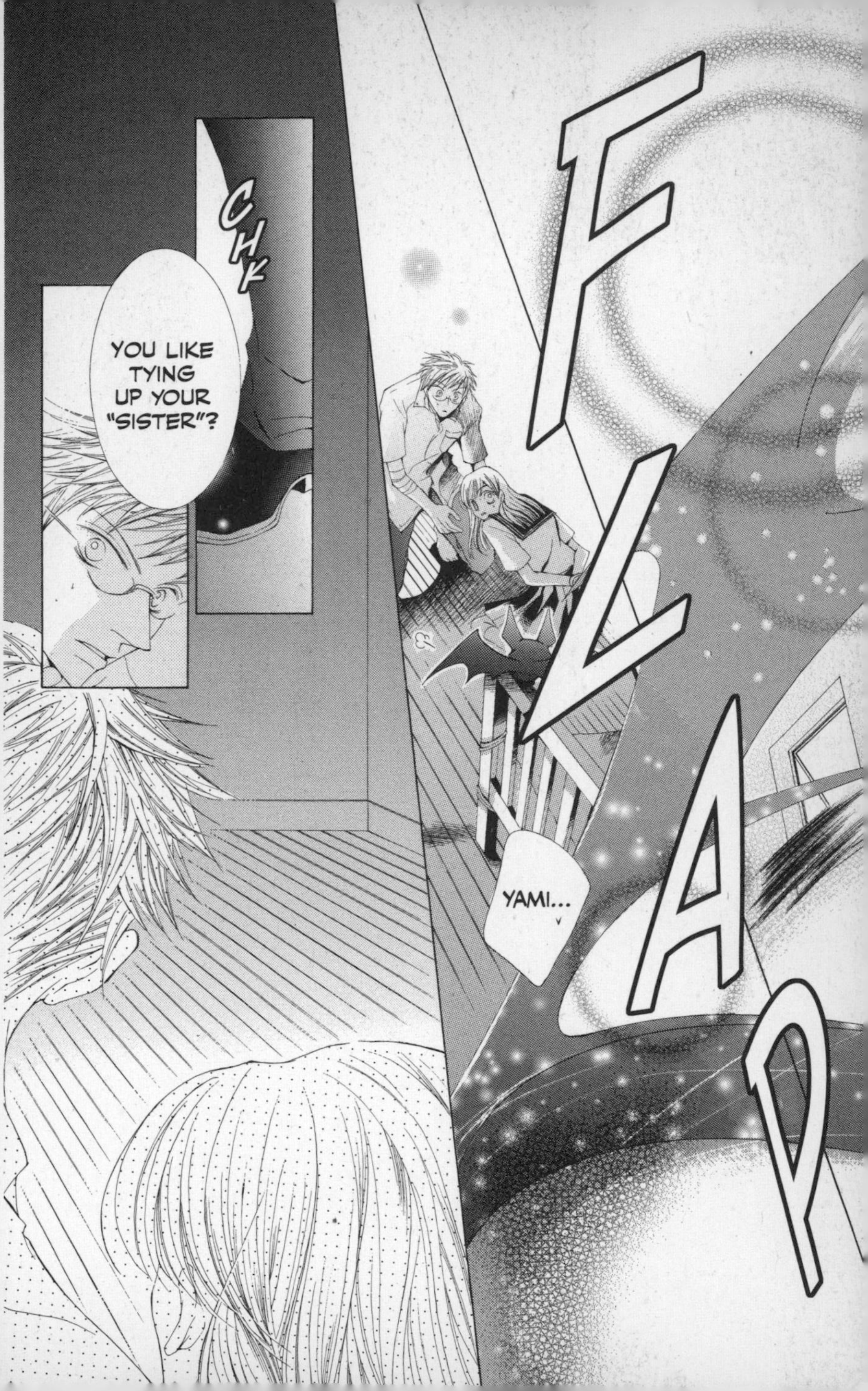
FLAP
YAMI...
CHK
YOU LIKE TYING UP YOUR "SISTER"?

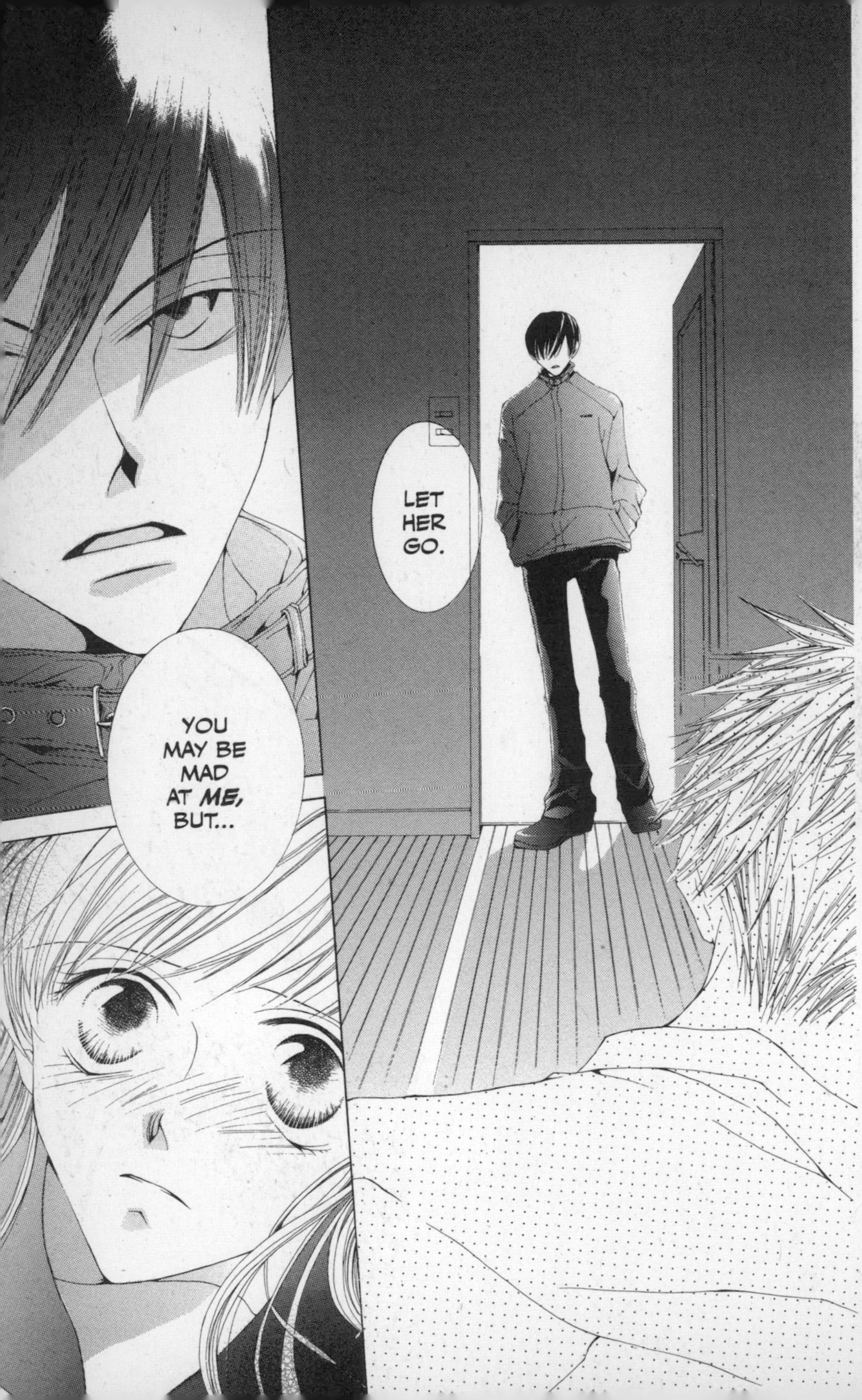
LET HER GO.
YOU MAY BE MAD AT *ME*, BUT...

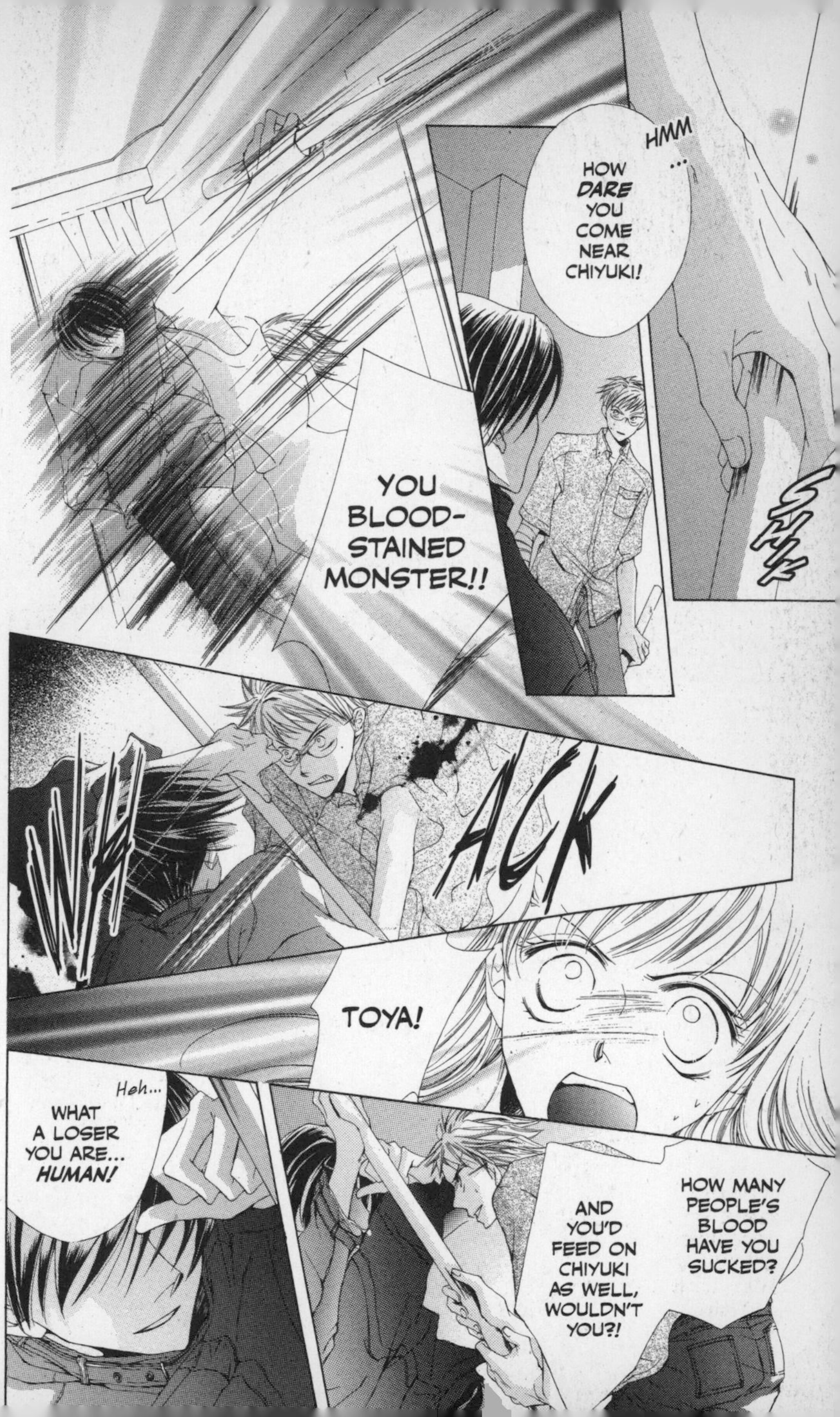
HMM ...
HOW DARE YOU COME NEAR CHIYUKI!
YOU BLOOD-STAINED MONSTER!!
ACK
TOYA!
HOW MANY PEOPLE'S BLOOD HAVE YOU SUCKED?
AND YOU'D FEED ON CHIYUKI AS WELL, WOULDN'T YOU?!
Heh...
WHAT A LOSER YOU ARE... HUMAN!

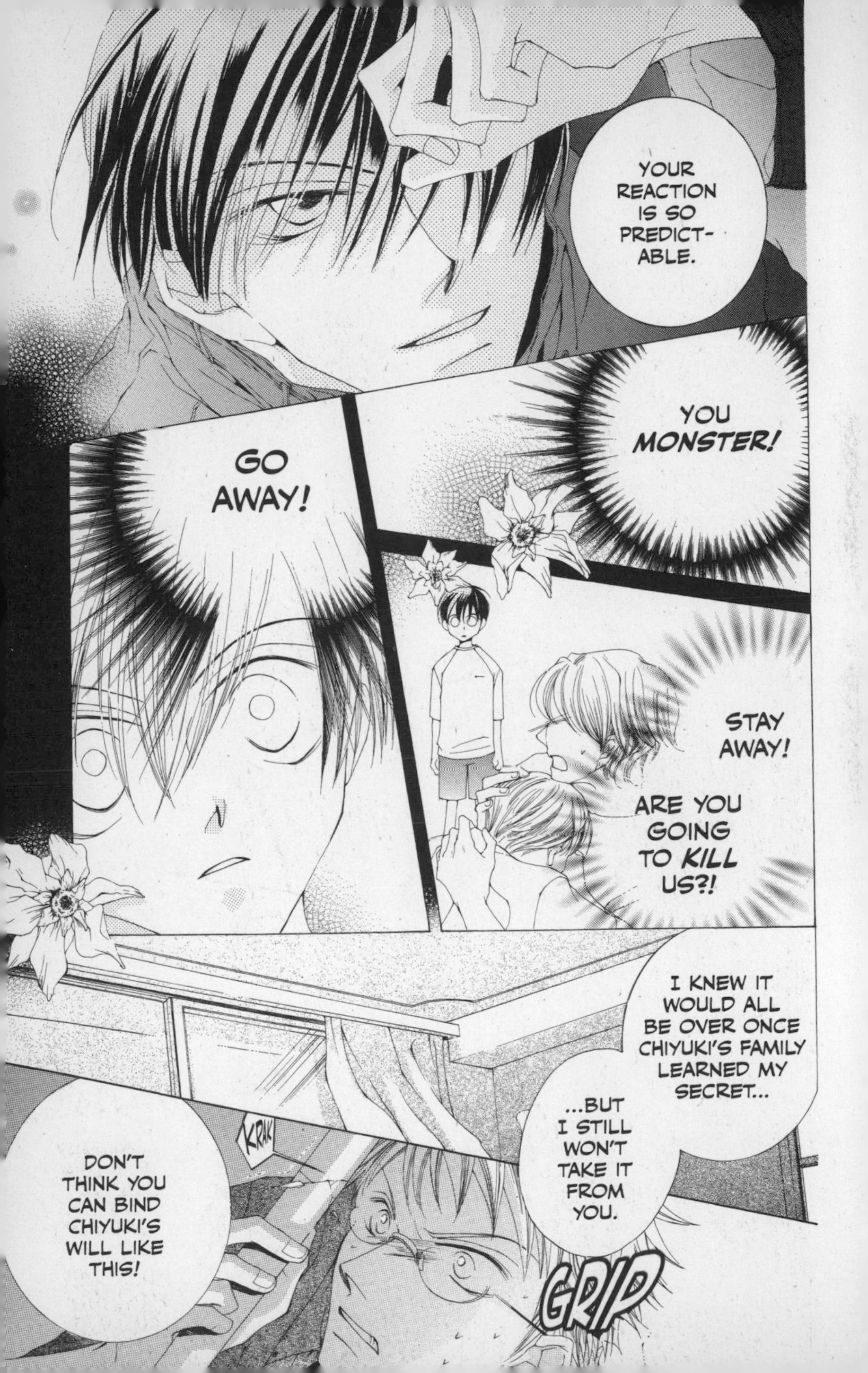
YOUR REACTION IS SO PREDICTABLE.
YOU MONSTER!
STAY AWAY!
ARE YOU GOING TO KILL US?!
GO AWAY!
I KNEW IT WOULD ALL BE OVER ONCE CHIYUKI'S FAMILY LEARNED MY SECRET...
...BUT I STILL WON'T TAKE IT FROM YOU.
KRAK
DON'T THINK YOU CAN BIND CHIYUKI'S WILL LIKE THIS!
GRIP

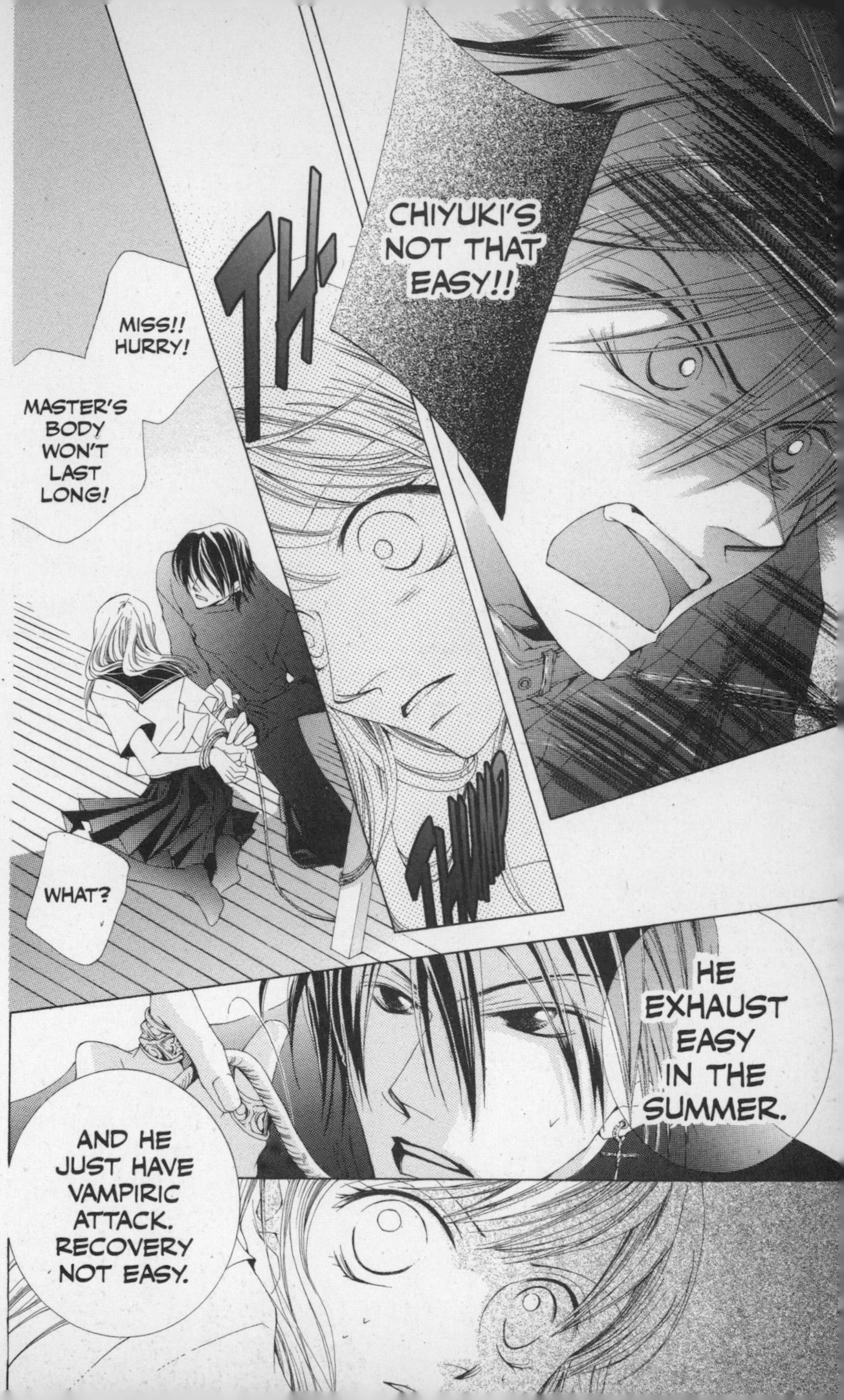
CHIYUKI'S NOT THAT EASY!!
MISS!! HURRY!
MASTER'S BODY WON'T LAST LONG!
WHAT?
HE EXHAUST EASY IN THE SUMMER.
AND HE JUST HAVE VAMPIRIC ATTACK. RECOVERY NOT EASY.

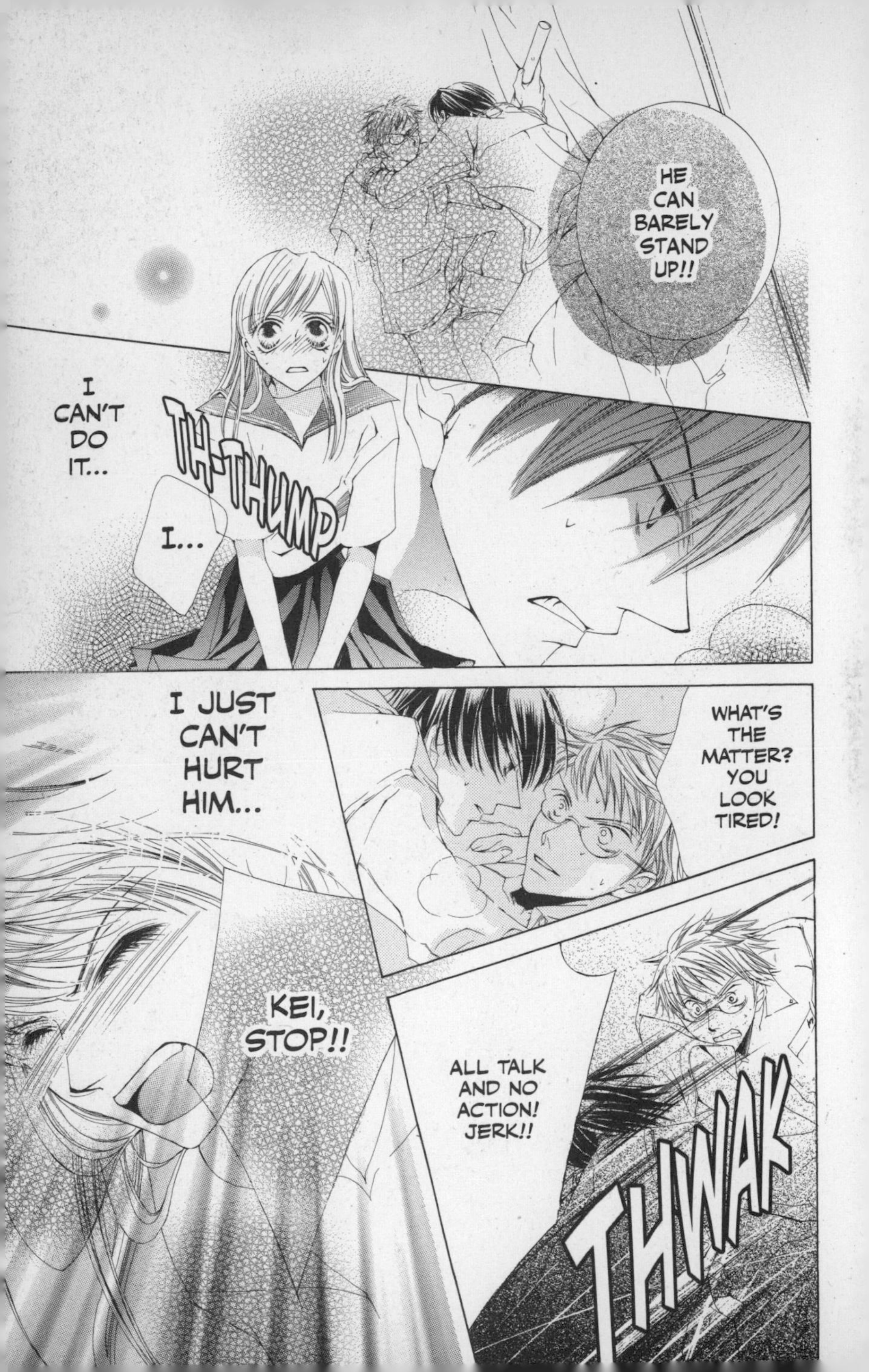
HE CAN BARELY STAND UP!!
I CAN'T DO IT...
TH-THUMP
I...
WHAT'S THE MATTER? YOU LOOK TIRED!
ALL TALK AND NO ACTION! JERK!!
THWAK
I JUST CAN'T HURT HIM...
KEI, STOP!!

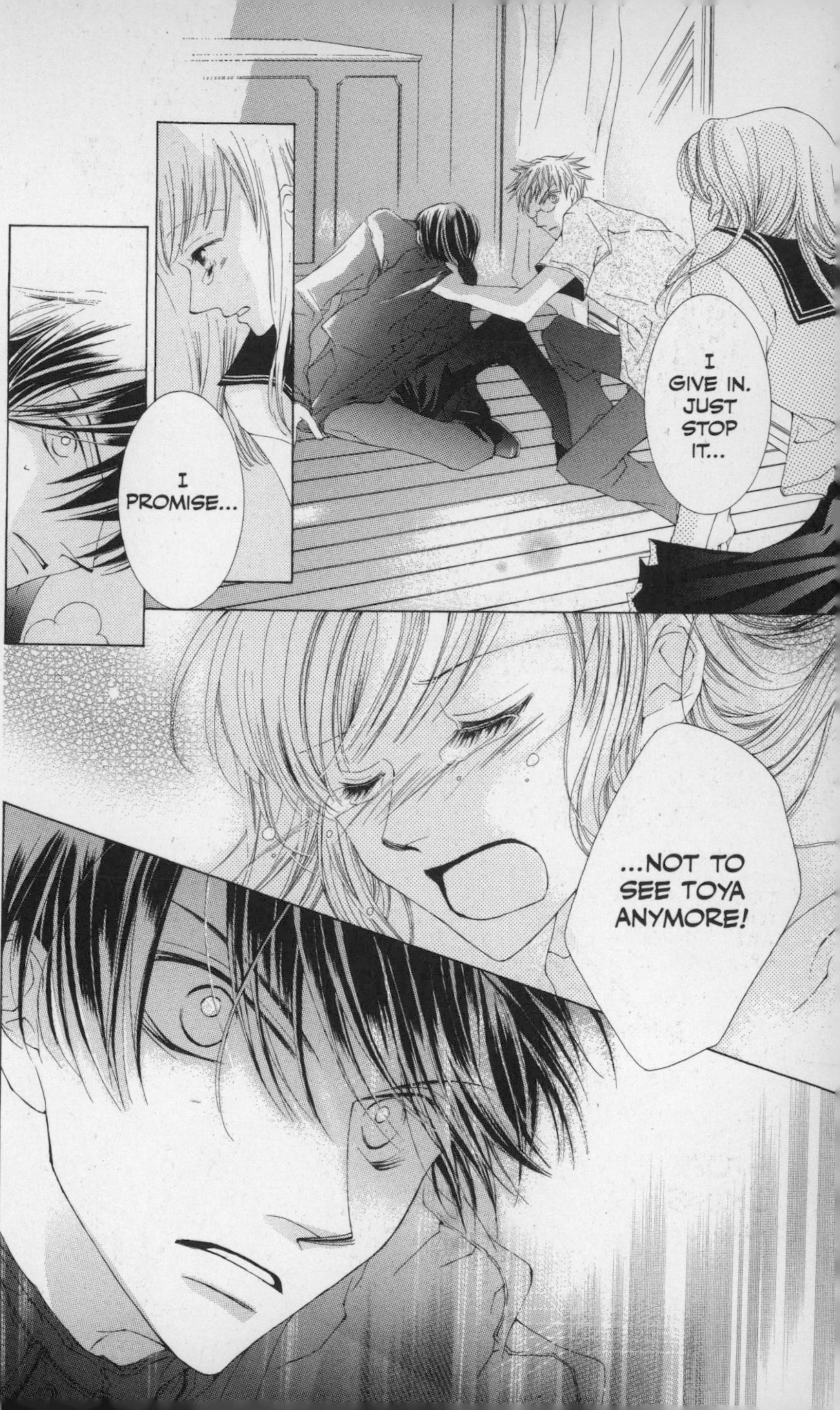
I GIVE IN. JUST STOP IT...
I PROMISE...
...NOT TO SEE TOYA ANYMORE!

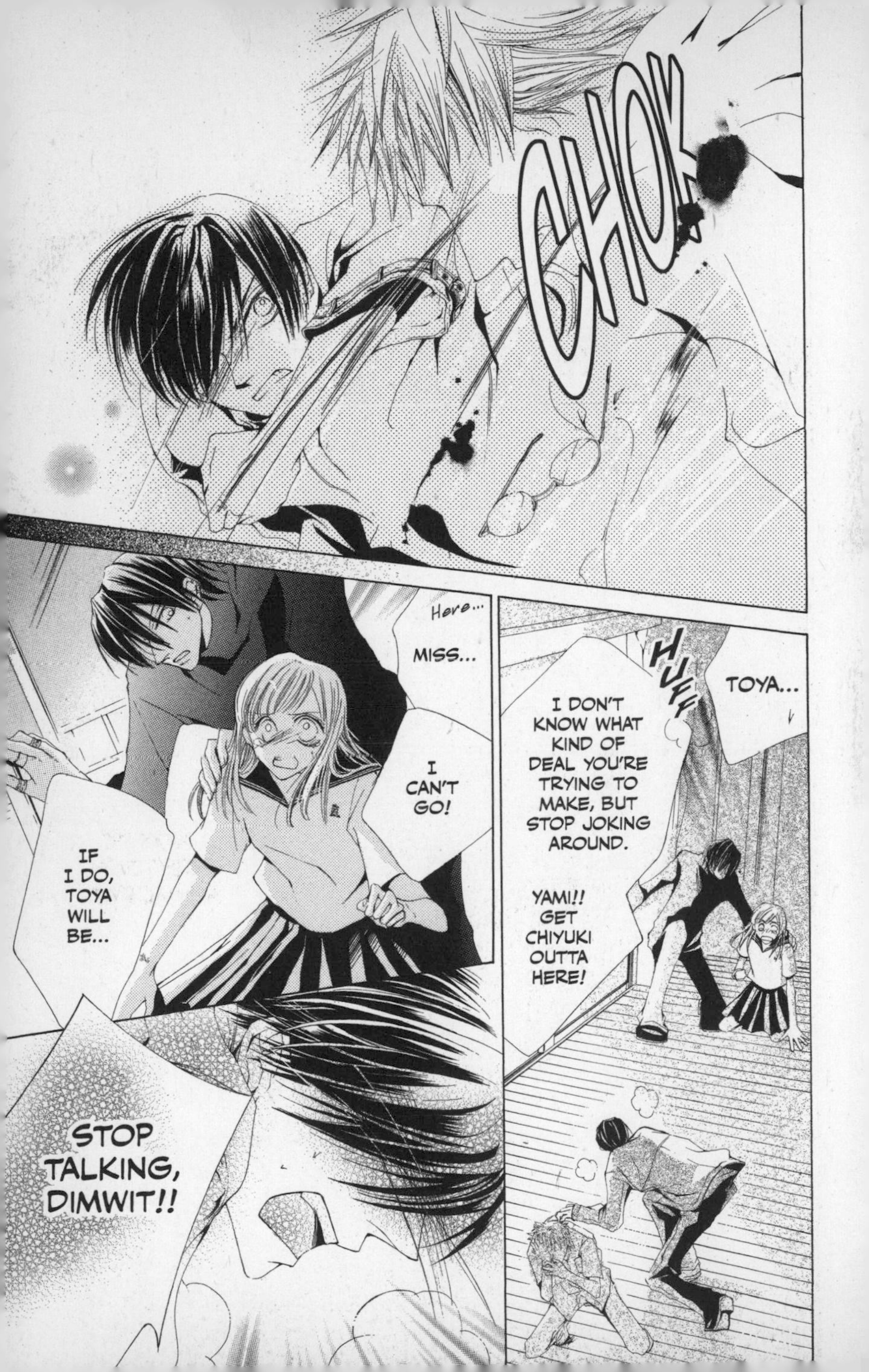
CHOK
TOYA...
HUFF
I DON'T KNOW WHAT KIND OF DEAL YOU'RE TRYING TO MAKE, BUT STOP JOKING AROUND.
YAMI!! GET CHIYUKI OUTTA HERE!
Here...
MISS...
I CAN'T GO!
IF I DO, TOYA WILL BE...
STOP TALKING, DIMWIT!!

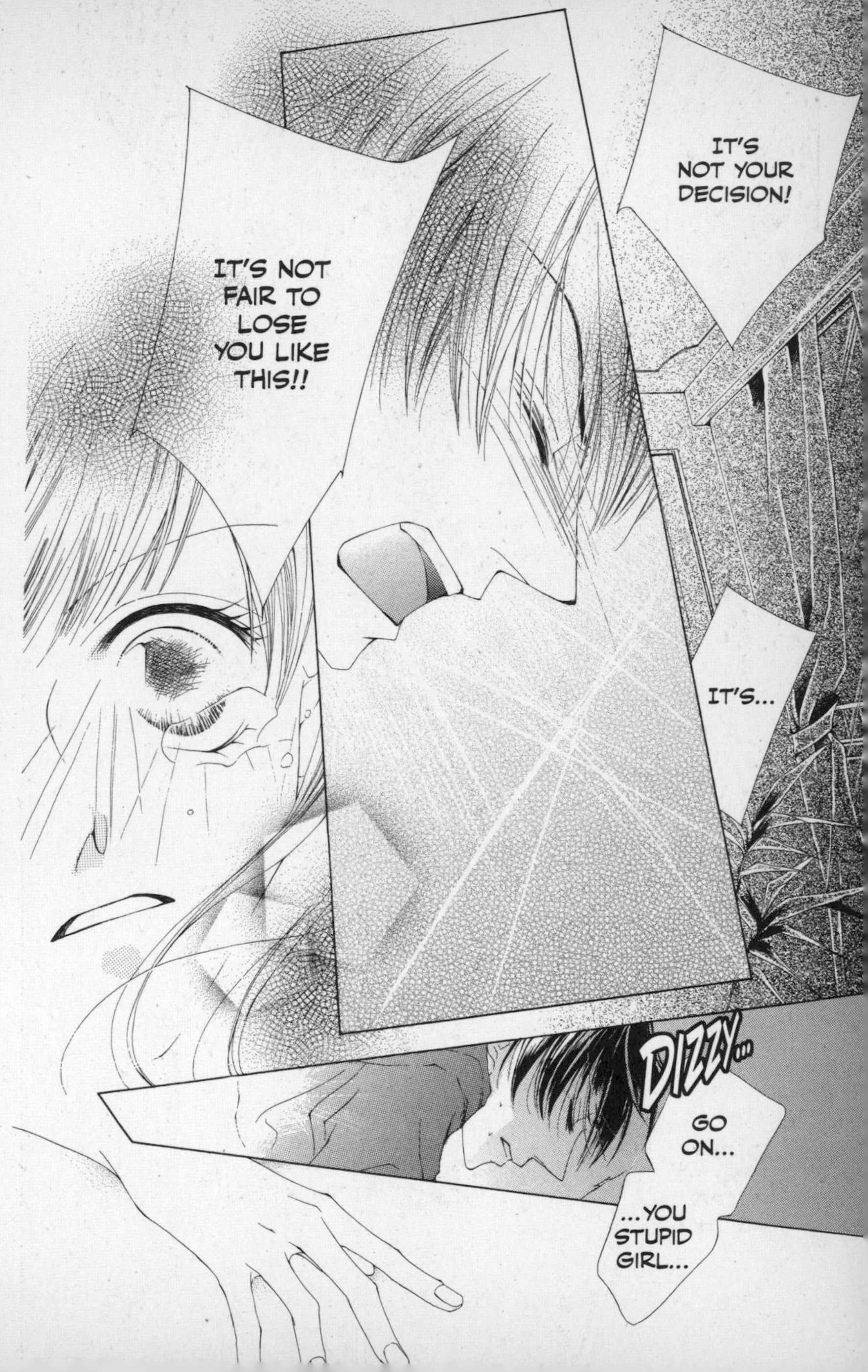
IT'S NOT YOUR DECISION!
IT'S NOT FAIR TO LOSE YOU LIKE THIS!!
IT'S...
DIZZY...
GO ON...
...YOU STUPID GIRL...

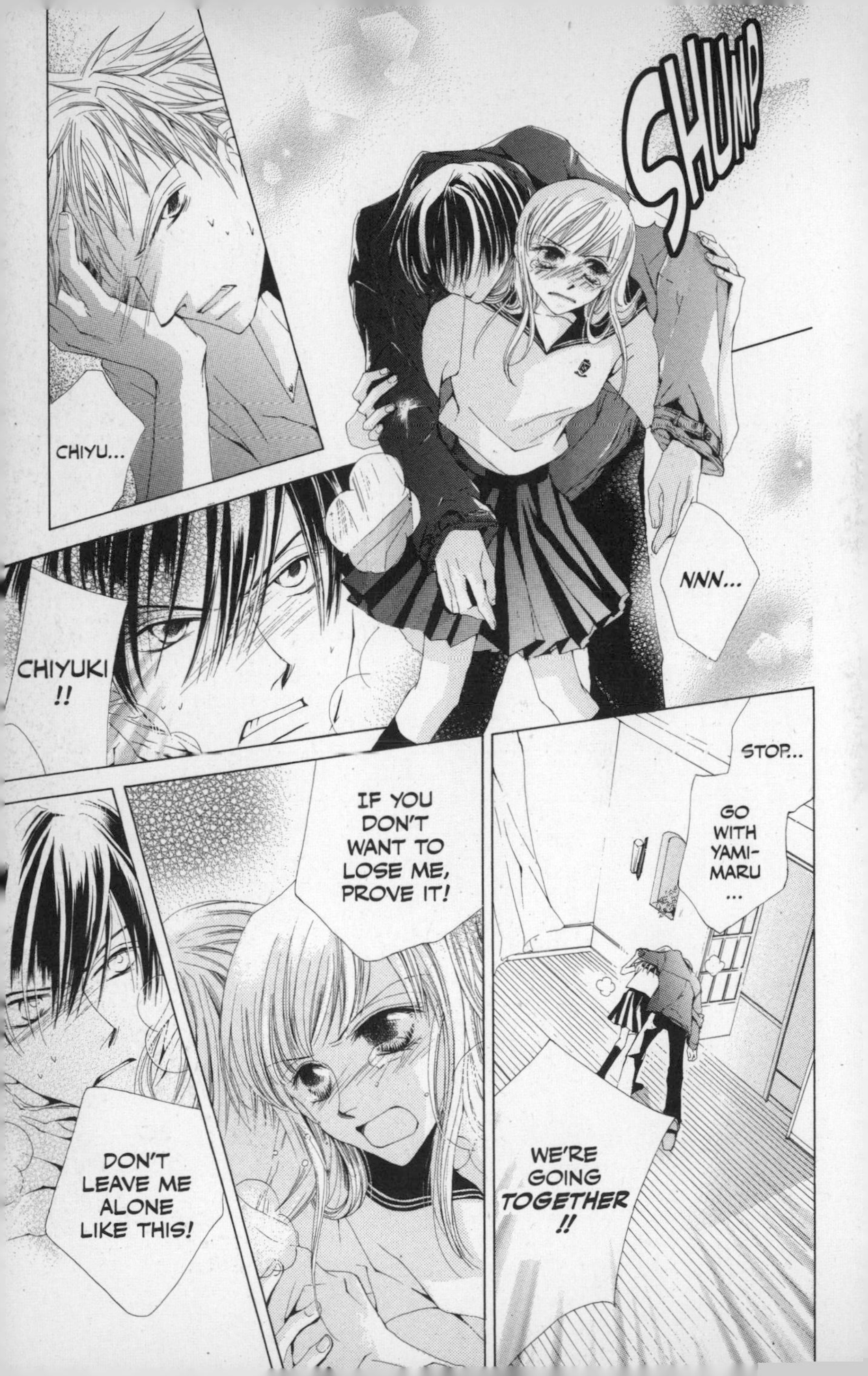
SHUMP
NNN...
CHIYU...
CHIYUKI !!
STOP...
GO WITH YAMI-MARU ...
WE'RE GOING TOGETHER !!
IF YOU DON'T WANT TO LOSE ME, PROVE IT!
DON'T LEAVE ME ALONE LIKE THIS!

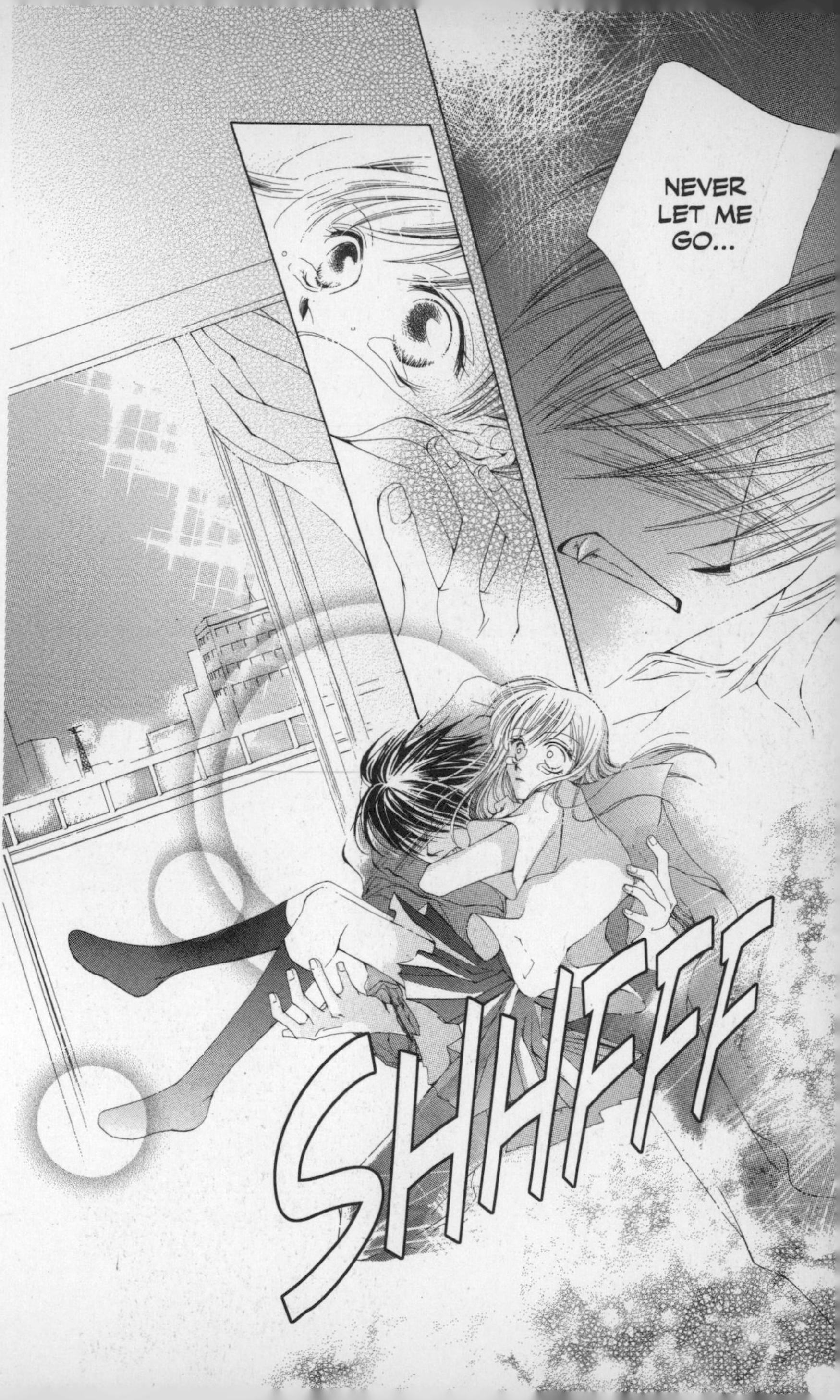
NEVER LET ME GO...
SHHFFF

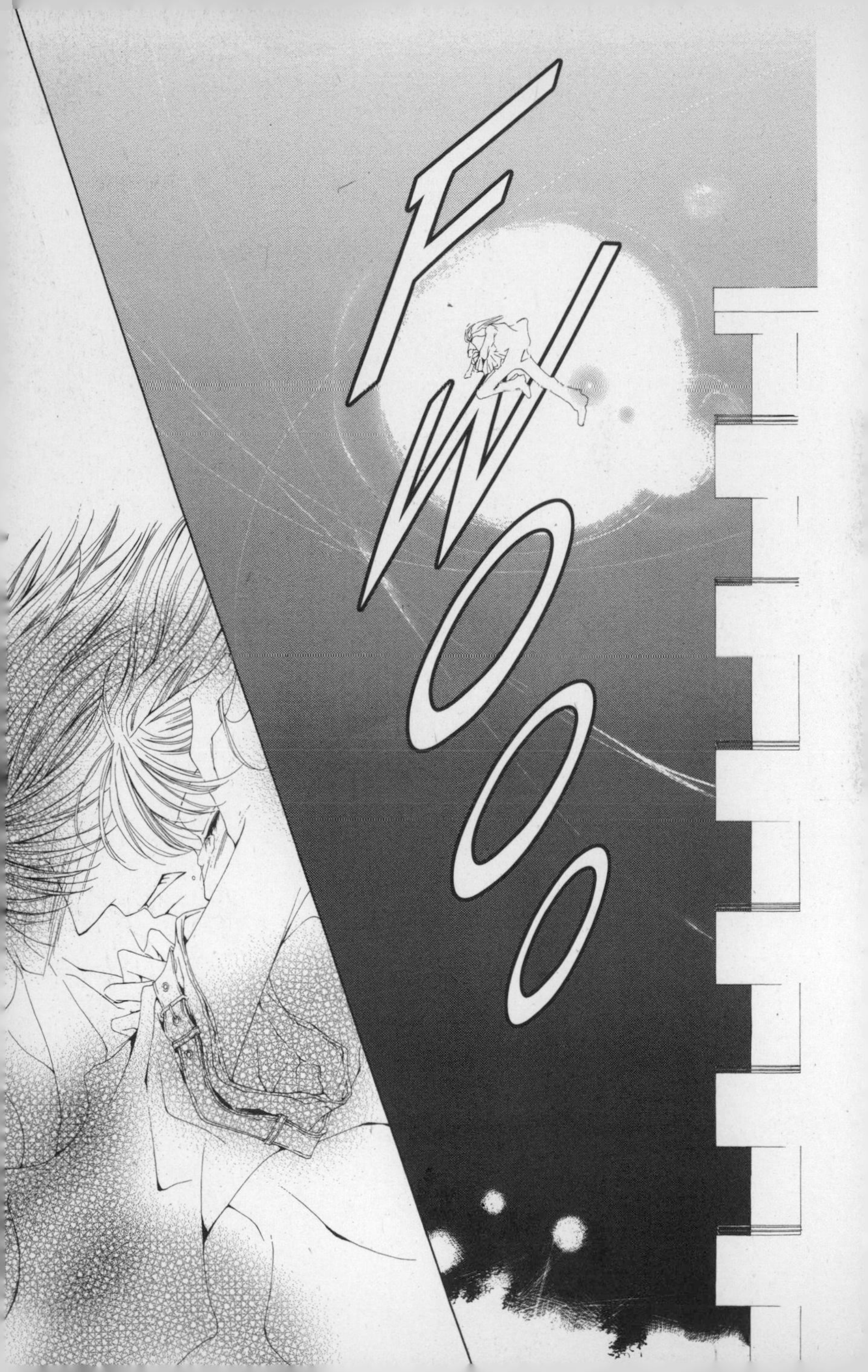
FWOOOO

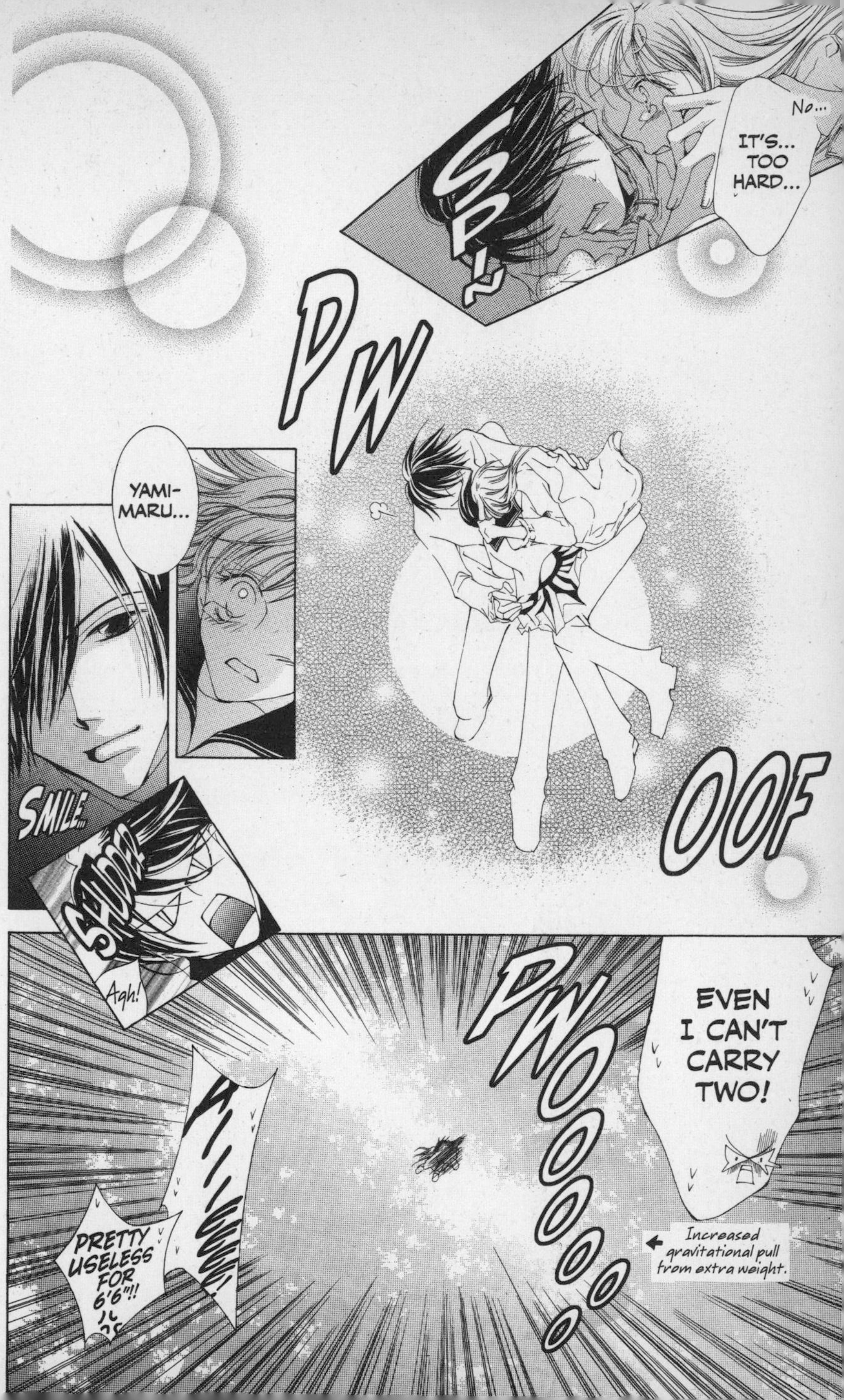
No...
IT'S... TOO HARD...
SPIN
PW
OOF
YAMI-MARU...
SMILE...
SHUDDER
Agh!
EVEN I CAN'T CARRY TWO!
PWOOOOOO
← Increased gravitational pull from extra weight.
AIIIEEEEE!
PRETTY USELESS FOR 6'6"!!

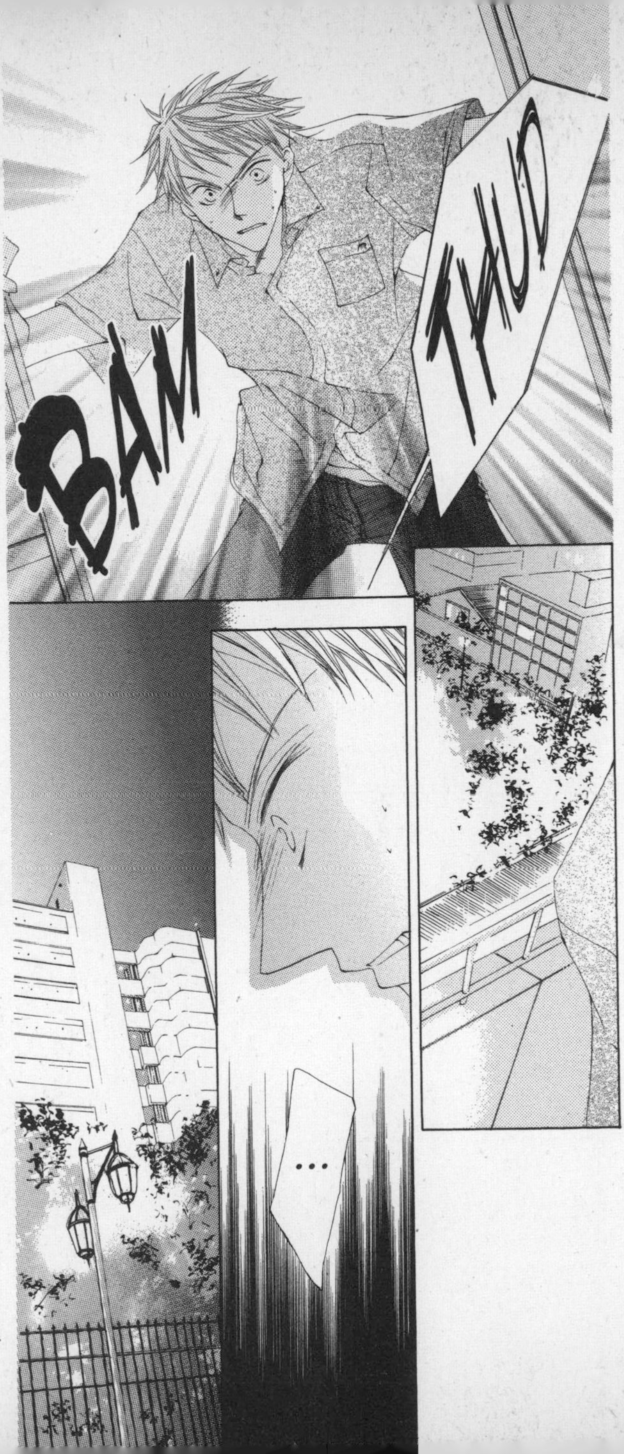
THUD
BAM
...

葉鳥 ビスコ
BISCO·HATORI

Lives in Tokyo
Virgo
Blood type: AB

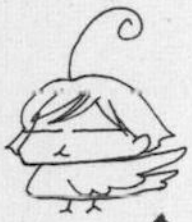

"Hatori-bird," thought up by Noriko Nagahama.

I love the images vampires conjure up, but I'm an extraordinarily faint-hearted person. I can't stand horror movies or even surgery scenes in television dramas. On top of hating bugs and dark places, I even hate bats. (They're too sinewy!)

I love anything written by Shuji Terayama and Ranpo Edogawa, but I can never watch them in visual form. Puppet animation, classic dolls, and deserted structures...the things I am attracted to and the things I am weak at are two sides of the same coin... That's Hatori. Cheers to a life of contradiction!

My latest crazes are Bump of Chicken and Ira Ishida's books. They're so great they make me cry!

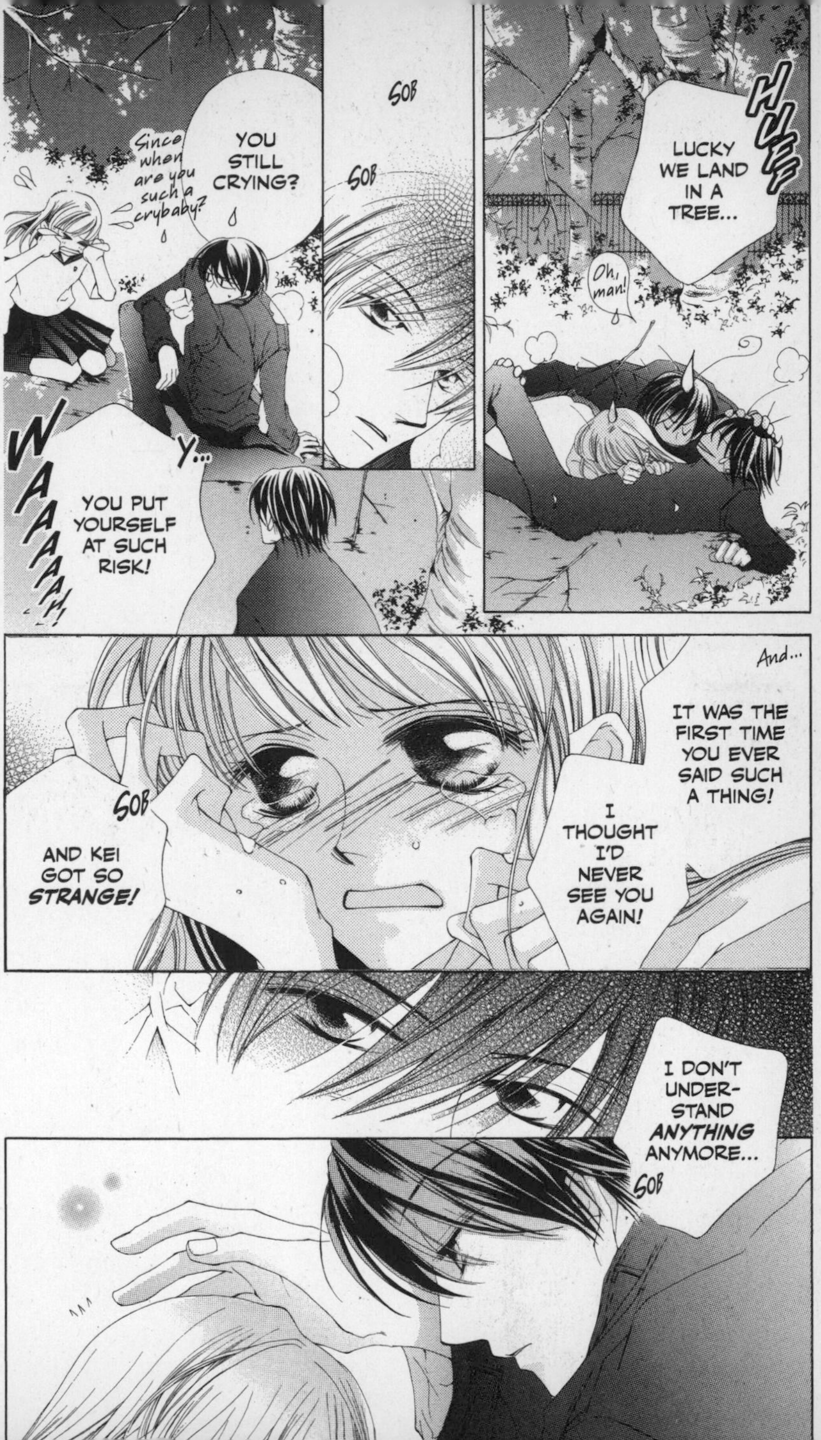
HUFF
LUCKY WE LAND IN A TREE...
Oh, man!
SOB
SOB
YOU STILL CRYING?
Since when are you such a crybaby?
Y...
WAAAAAAH!
YOU PUT YOURSELF AT SUCH RISK!
And...
IT WAS THE FIRST TIME YOU EVER SAID SUCH A THING!
I THOUGHT I'D NEVER SEE YOU AGAIN!
SOB
AND KEI GOT SO *STRANGE!*
I DON'T UNDER-STAND *ANYTHING* ANYMORE...
SOB

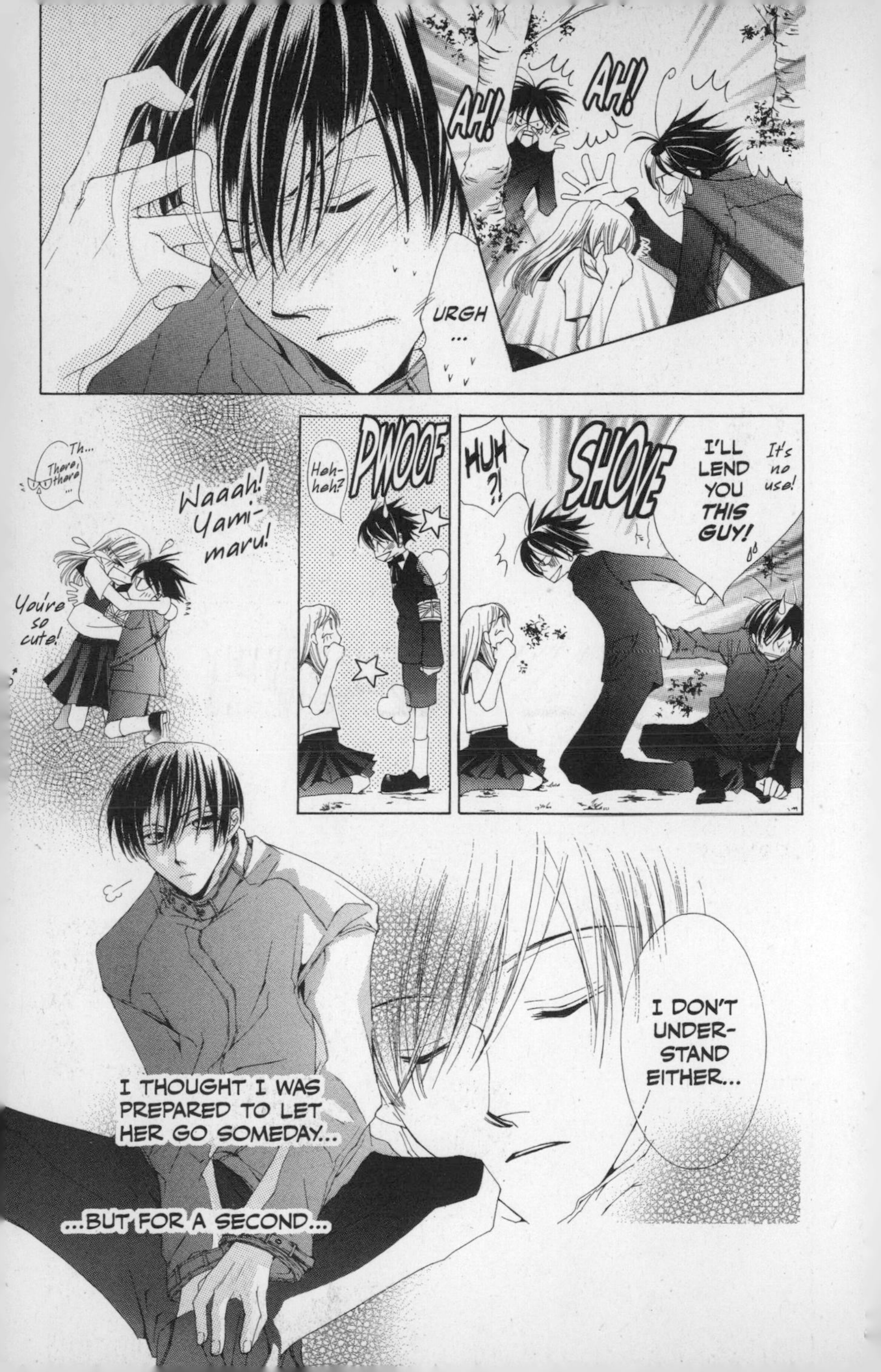
AH!
AH!
URGH ...
SHOVE
It's no use!
I'LL LEND YOU THIS GUY!
HUH ?!
PWOOF
Heh-heh?
Waaah! Yami-maru!
Th... There, there ...
You're so cute!
I DON'T UNDER-STAND EITHER...
I THOUGHT I WAS PREPARED TO LET HER GO SOMEDAY...
...BUT FOR A SECOND...

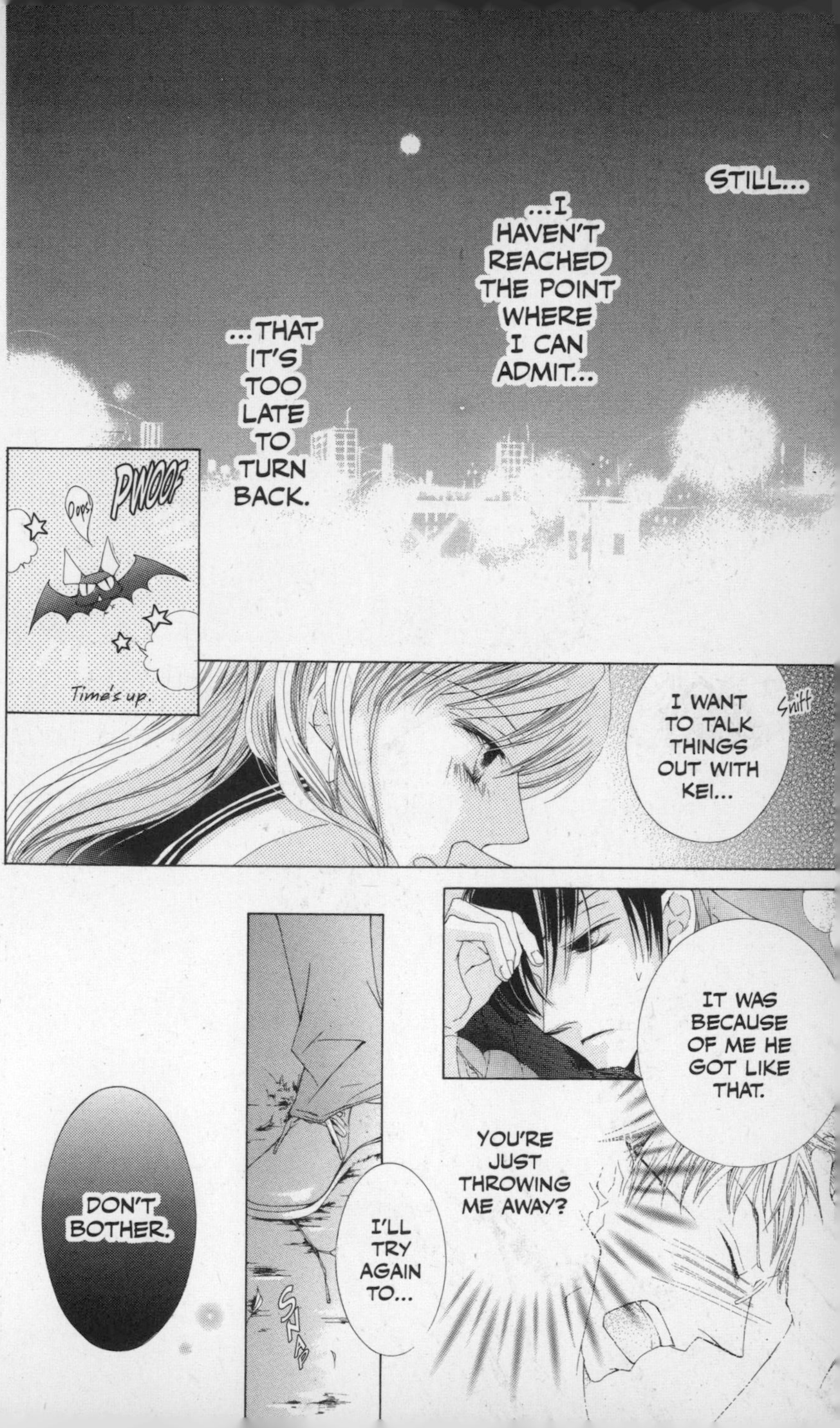
STILL...
...I HAVEN'T REACHED THE POINT WHERE I CAN ADMIT...
...THAT IT'S TOO LATE TO TURN BACK.
PWOOF
Oops!
Time's up.
I WANT TO TALK THINGS OUT WITH KEI...
Sniff
IT WAS BECAUSE OF ME HE GOT LIKE THAT.
YOU'RE JUST THROWING ME AWAY?
I'LL TRY AGAIN TO...
DON'T BOTHER.

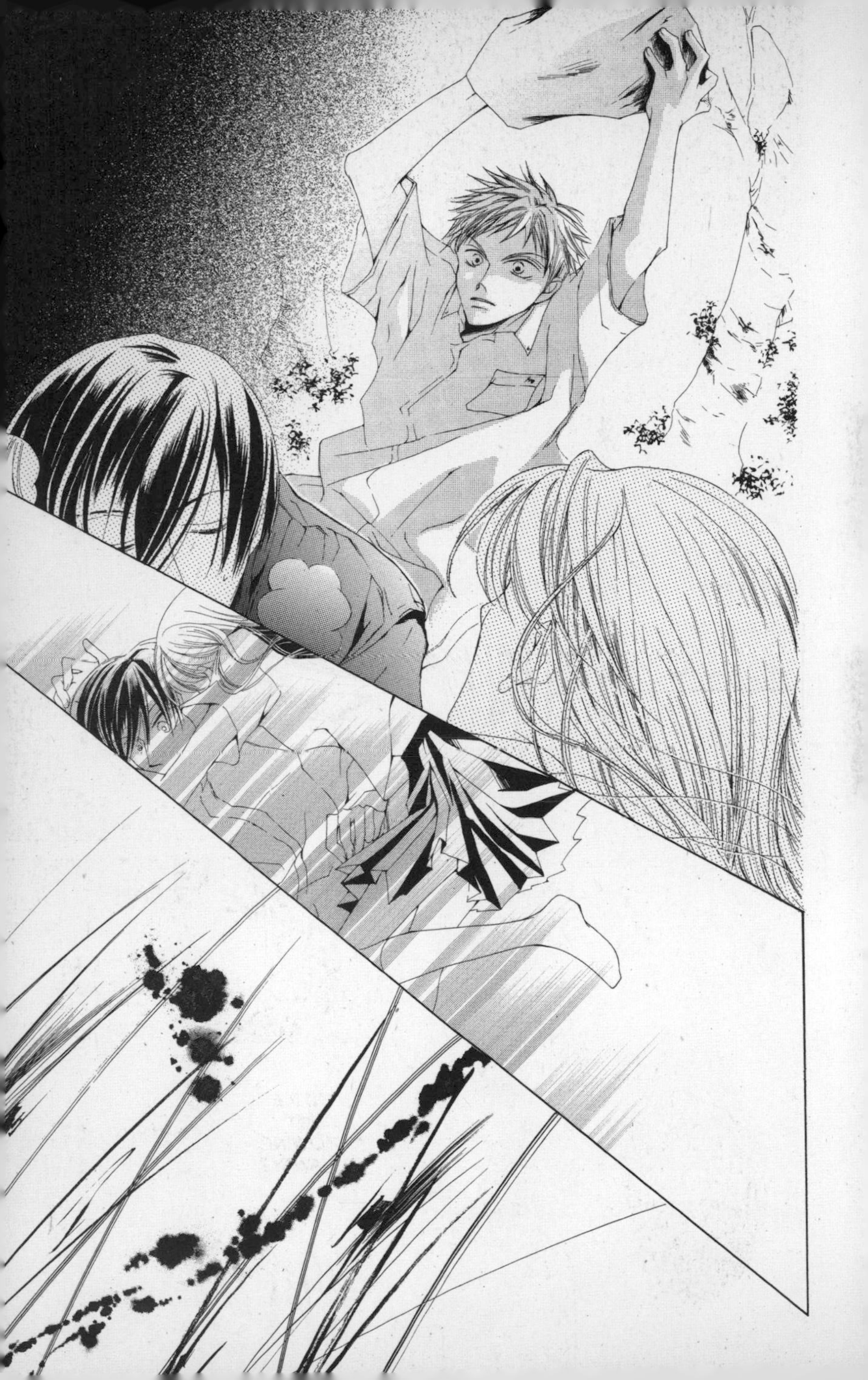

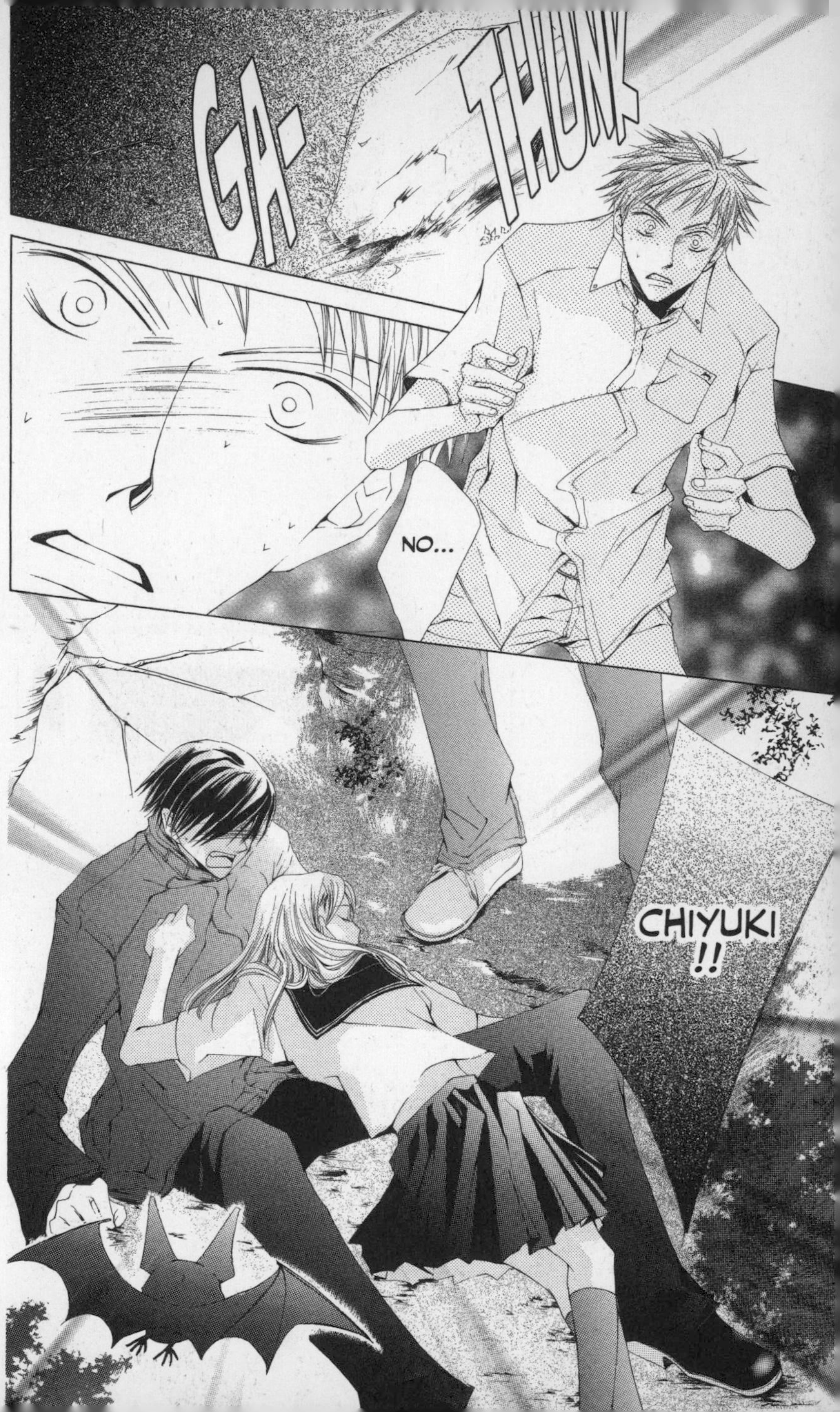
GA-THUNK
NO...
CHIYUKI!!

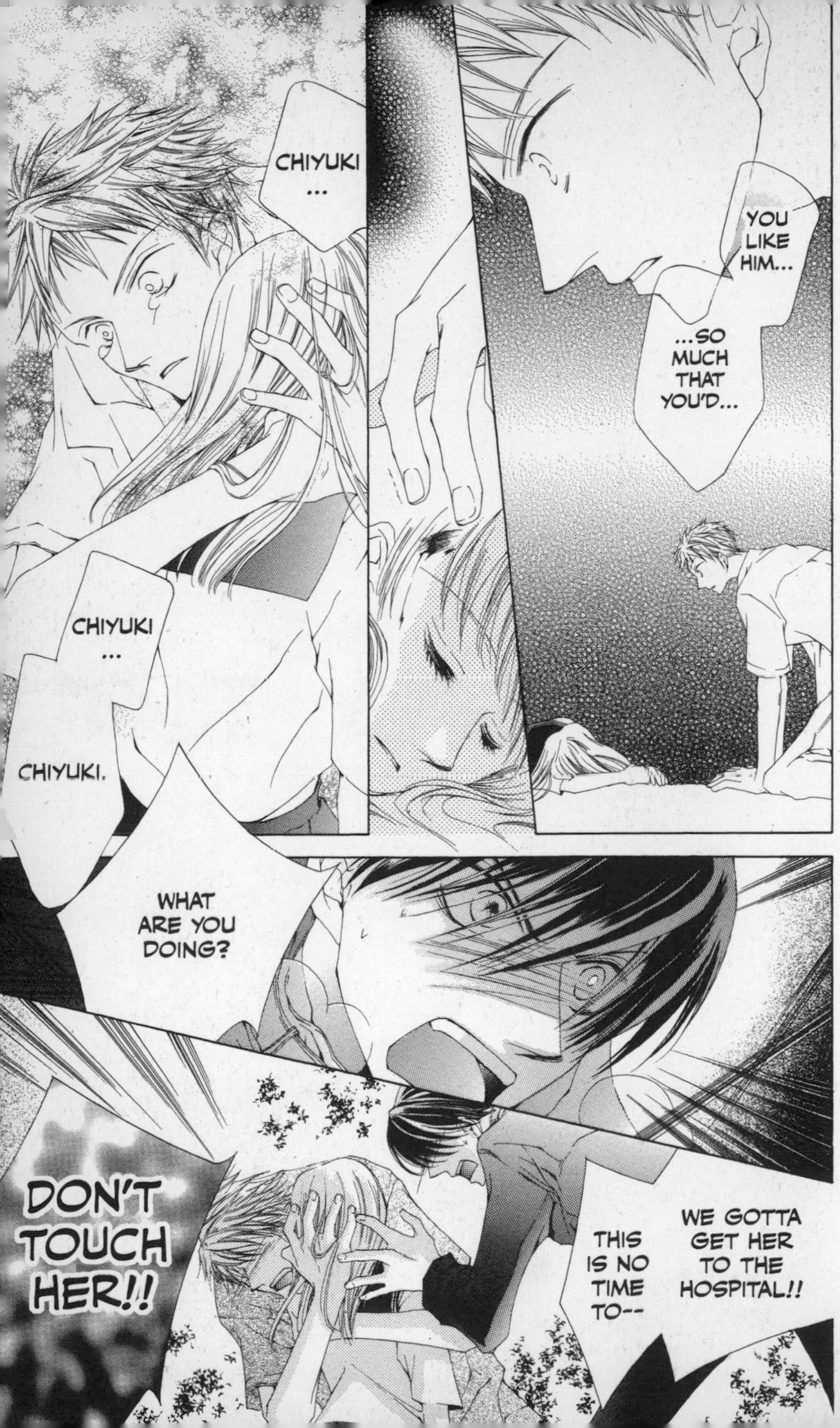
YOU LIKE HIM...
...SO MUCH THAT YOU'D...
CHIYUKI ...
CHIYUKI ...
CHIYUKI.
WHAT ARE YOU DOING?
WE GOTTA GET HER TO THE HOSPITAL!!
THIS IS NO TIME TO--
DON'T TOUCH HER!!

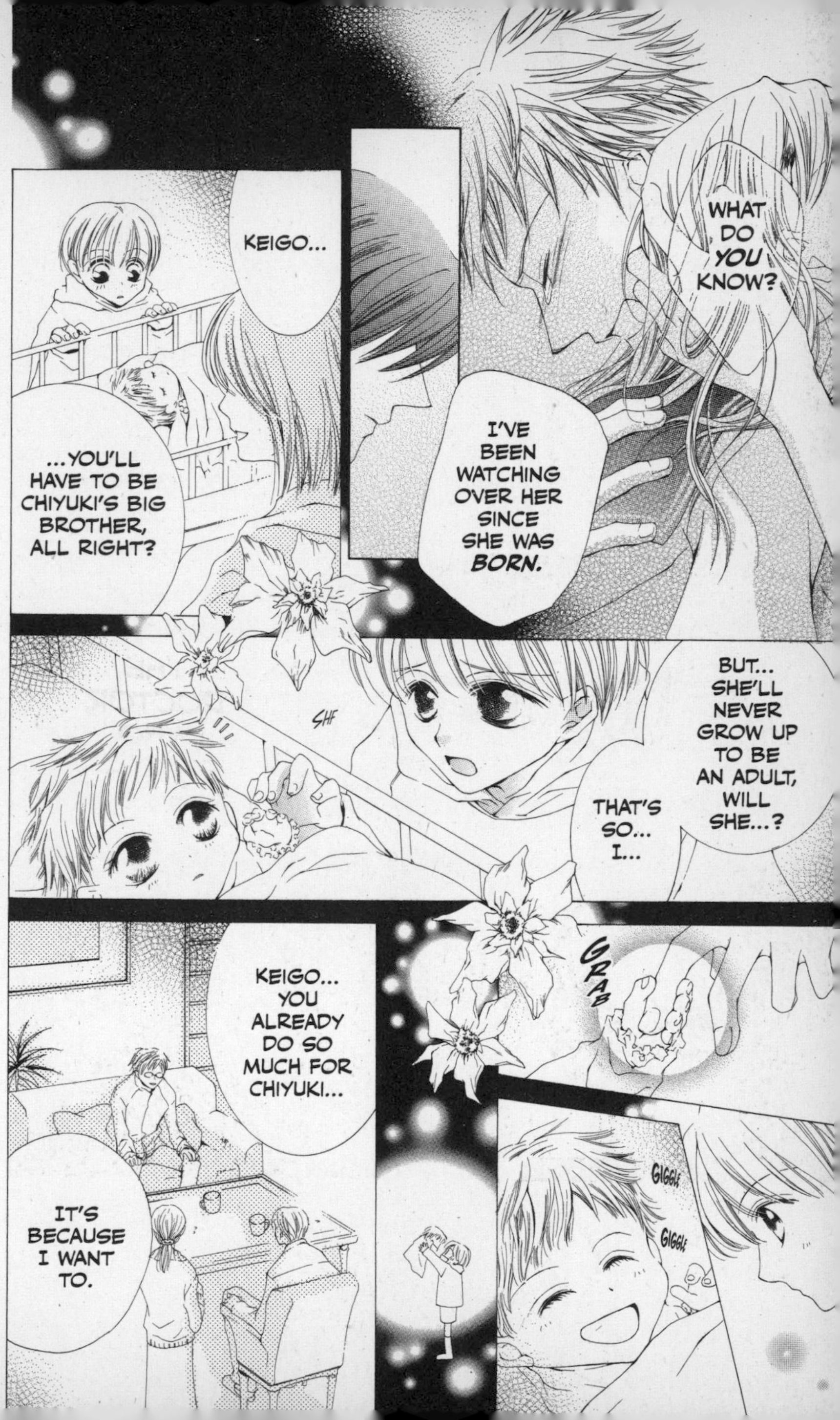
WHAT DO *YOU* KNOW?
I'VE BEEN WATCHING OVER HER SINCE SHE WAS *BORN.*
KEIGO...
...YOU'LL HAVE TO BE CHIYUKI'S BIG BROTHER, ALL RIGHT?
BUT... SHE'LL NEVER GROW UP TO BE AN ADULT, WILL SHE...?
THAT'S SO... I...
SHF
GRAB
GIGGLE
GIGGLE
KEIGO... YOU ALREADY DO SO MUCH FOR CHIYUKI...
IT'S BECAUSE I WANT TO.

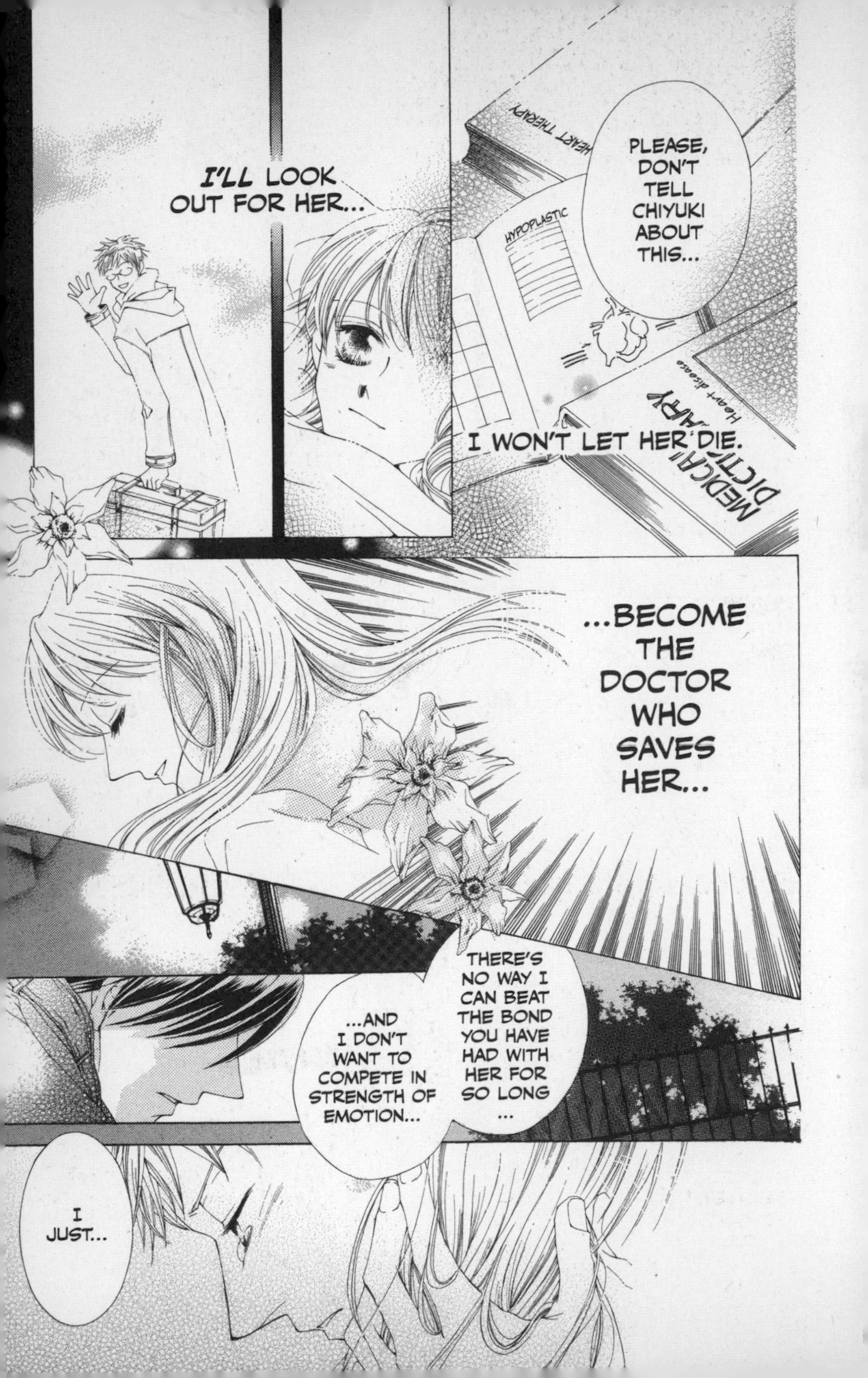
HEART THERAPY
HYPOPLASTIC
Heart disease
PLEASE, DON'T TELL CHIYUKI ABOUT THIS...
I WON'T LET HER DIE.
I'LL LOOK OUT FOR HER...
...BECOME THE DOCTOR WHO SAVES HER...
THERE'S NO WAY I CAN BEAT THE BOND YOU HAVE HAD WITH HER FOR SO LONG ...
...AND I DON'T WANT TO COMPETE IN STRENGTH OF EMOTION...
I JUST...

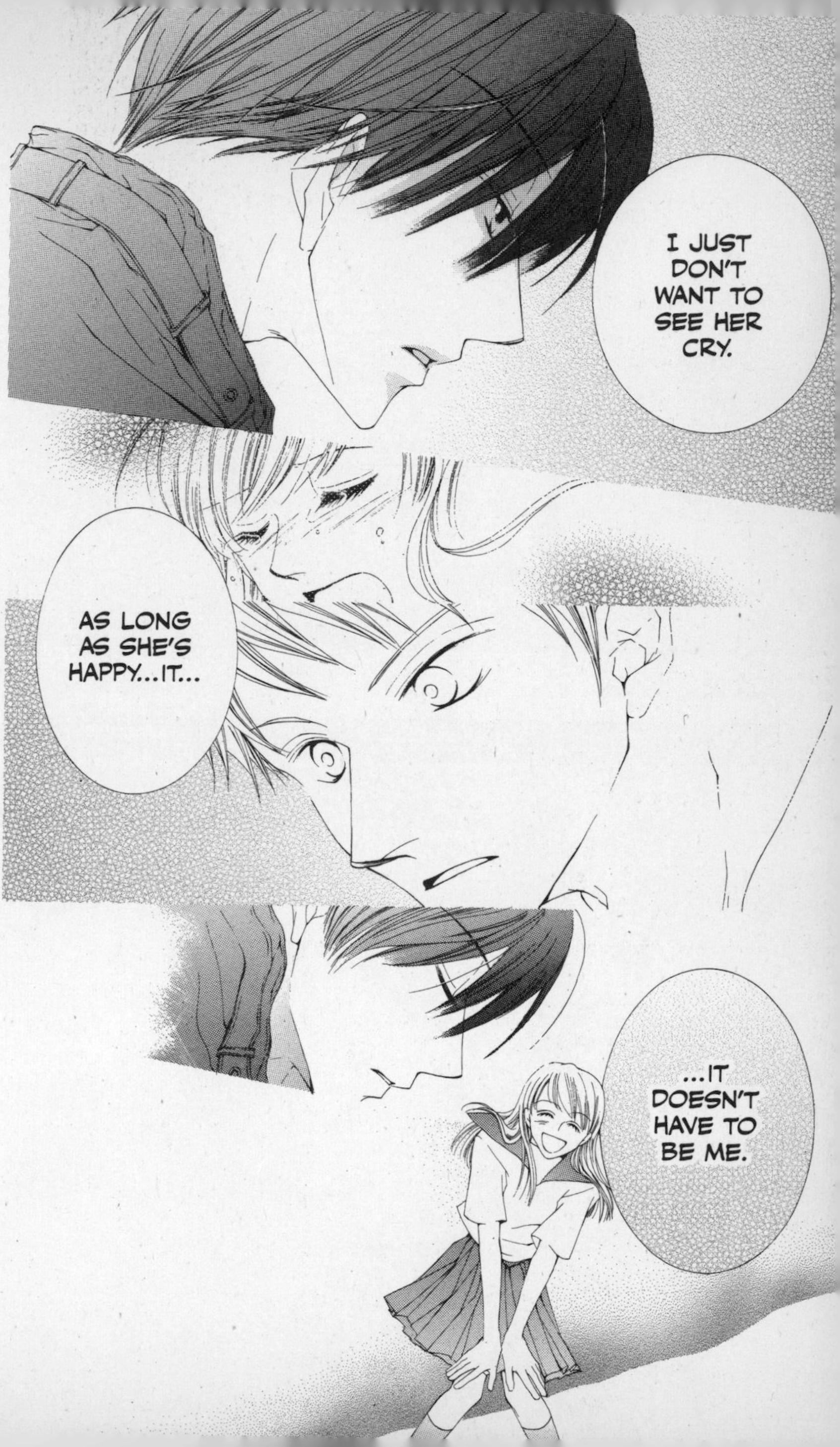
I JUST DON'T WANT TO SEE HER CRY.
AS LONG AS SHE'S HAPPY...IT...
...IT DOESN'T HAVE TO BE ME.

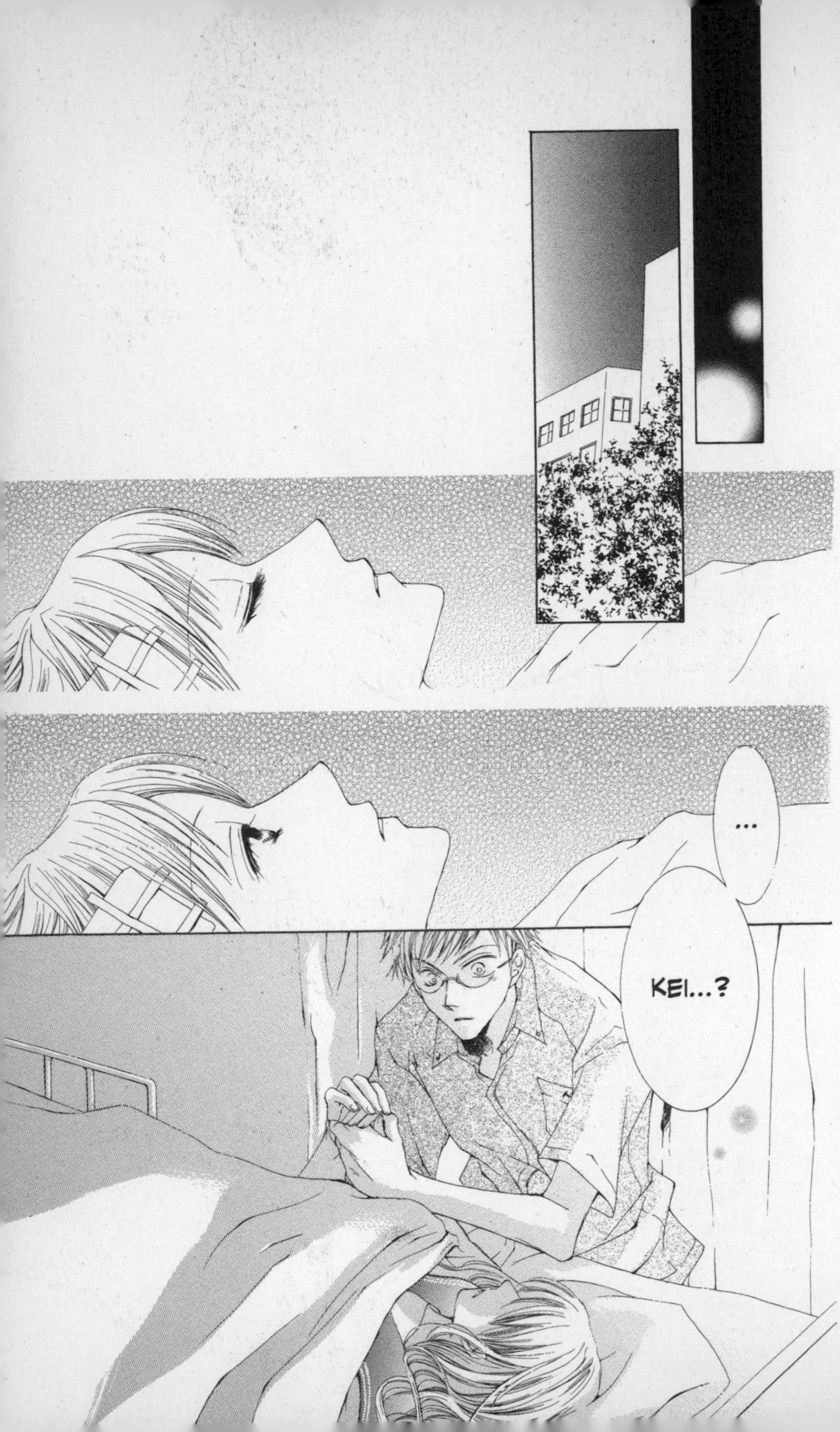
...
KEI...?

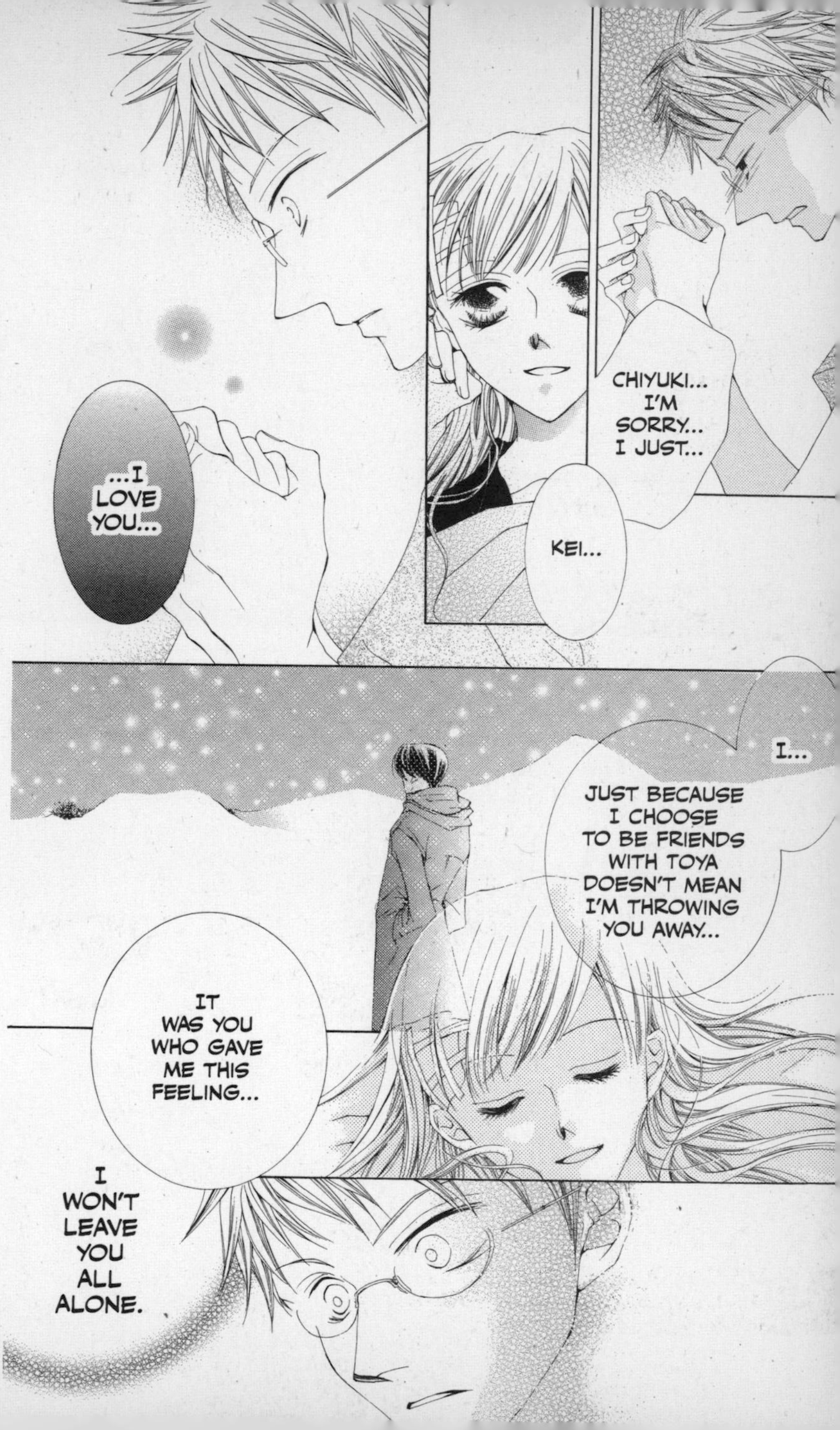
CHIYUKI... I'M SORRY... I JUST...
KEI...
...I LOVE YOU...
I...
JUST BECAUSE I CHOOSE TO BE FRIENDS WITH TOYA DOESN'T MEAN I'M THROWING YOU AWAY...
IT WAS YOU WHO GAVE ME THIS FEELING...
I WON'T LEAVE YOU ALL ALONE.

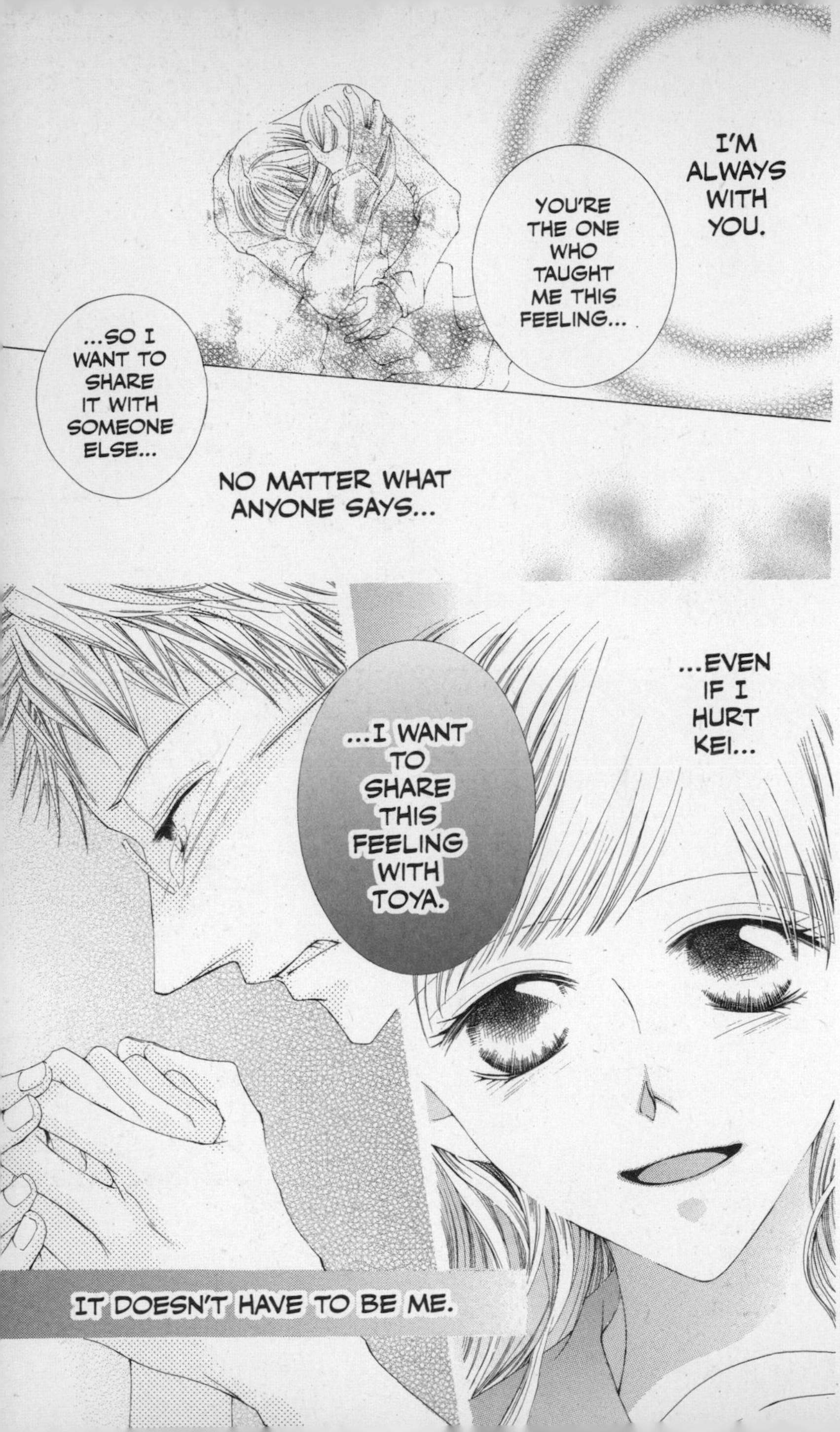
I'M ALWAYS WITH YOU.
YOU'RE THE ONE WHO TAUGHT ME THIS FEELING...
...SO I WANT TO SHARE IT WITH SOMEONE ELSE...
NO MATTER WHAT ANYONE SAYS...
...EVEN IF I HURT KEI...
...I WANT TO SHARE THIS FEELING WITH TOYA.
IT DOESN'T HAVE TO BE ME.

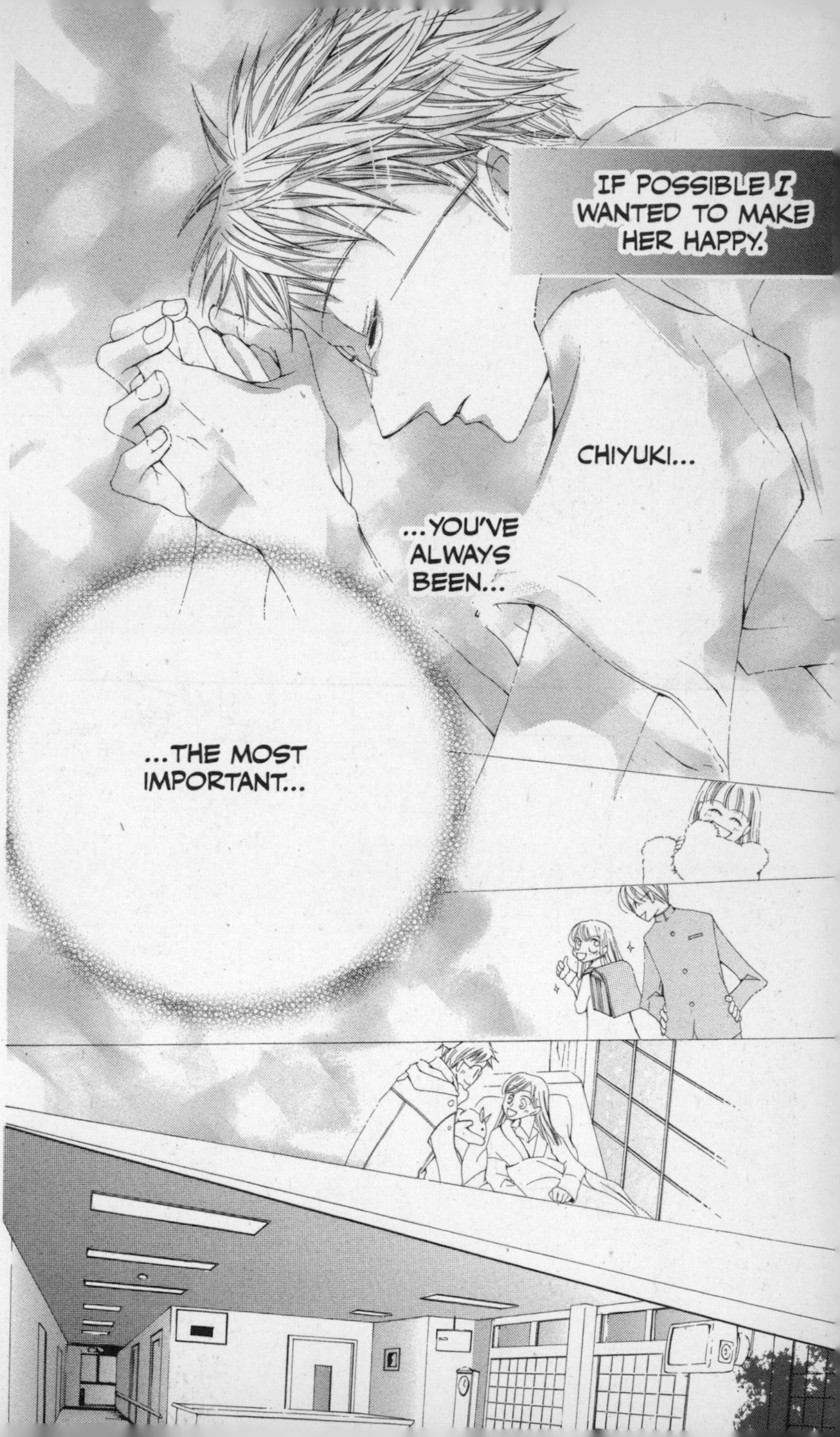
IF POSSIBLE I WANTED TO MAKE HER HAPPY.
CHIYUKI...
...YOU'VE ALWAYS BEEN...
...THE MOST IMPORTANT...

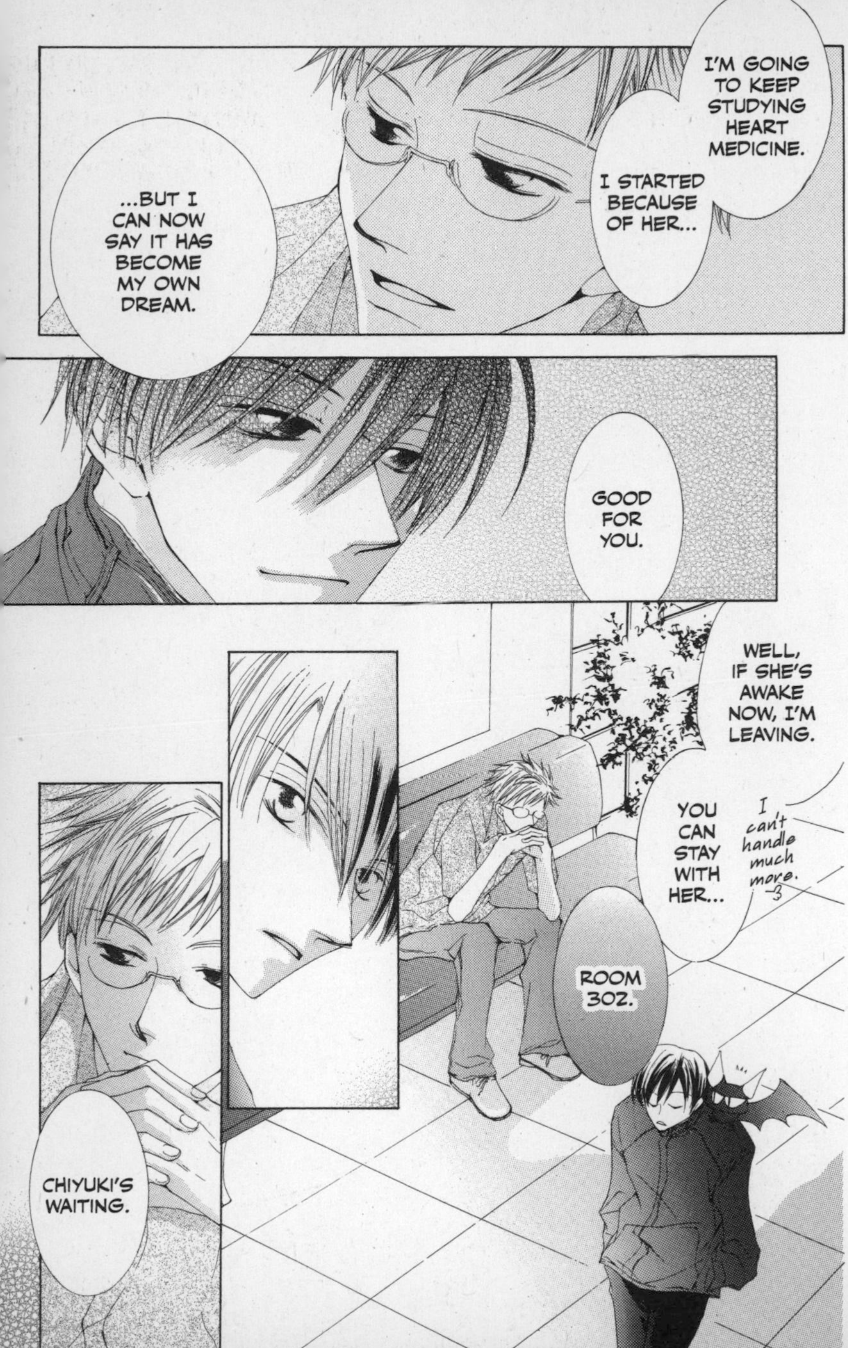
I'M GOING TO KEEP STUDYING HEART MEDICINE.
I STARTED BECAUSE OF HER...
...BUT I CAN NOW SAY IT HAS BECOME MY OWN DREAM.
GOOD FOR YOU.
WELL, IF SHE'S AWAKE NOW, I'M LEAVING.
YOU CAN STAY WITH HER...
I can't handle much more.
ROOM 302.
CHIYUKI'S WAITING.

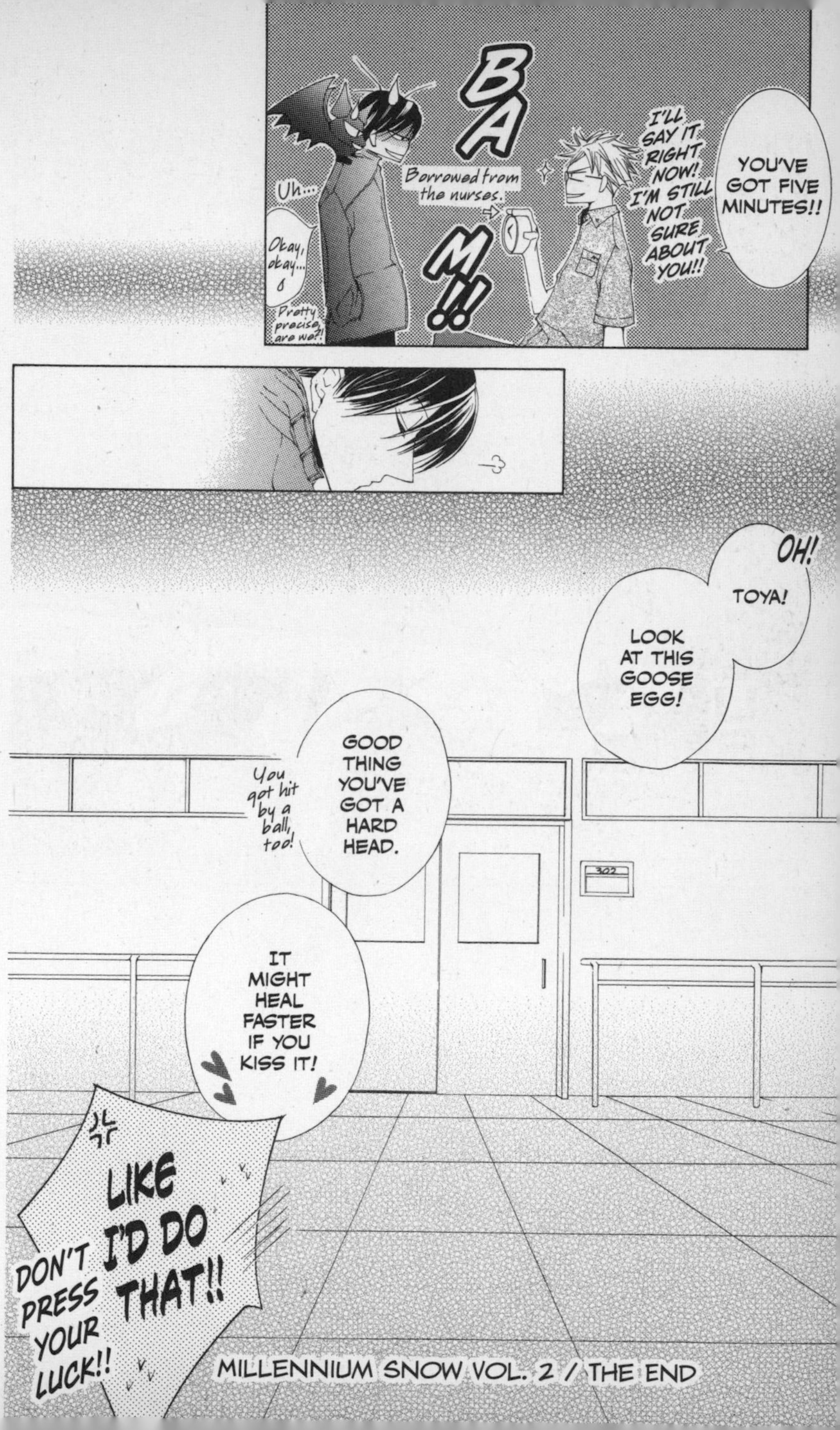
YOU'VE GOT FIVE MINUTES!!
I'LL SAY IT RIGHT NOW! I'M STILL NOT SURE ABOUT YOU!!
Borrowed from the nurses.
BAM!!
Uh...
Okay, okay...
Pretty precise, are we?!
OH!
TOYA!
LOOK AT THIS GOOSE EGG!
GOOD THING YOU'VE GOT A HARD HEAD.
You got hit by a ball, too!
IT MIGHT HEAL FASTER IF YOU KISS IT!
LIKE I'D DO THAT!!
DON'T PRESS YOUR LUCK!!
MILLENNIUM SNOW VOL. 2 / THE END

Dopplegangers ✿ Part 2

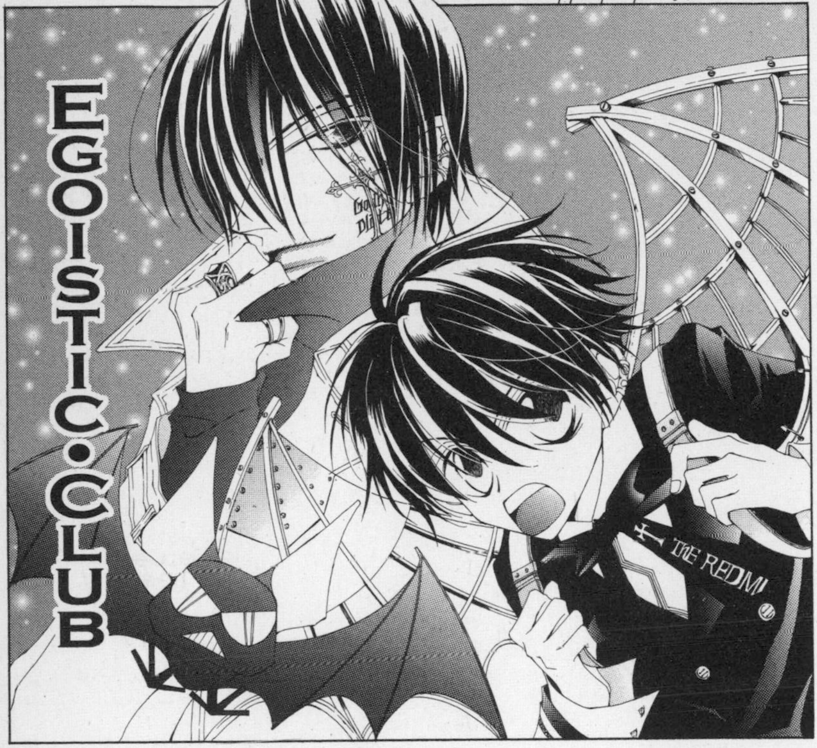
EGOISTIC•CLUB

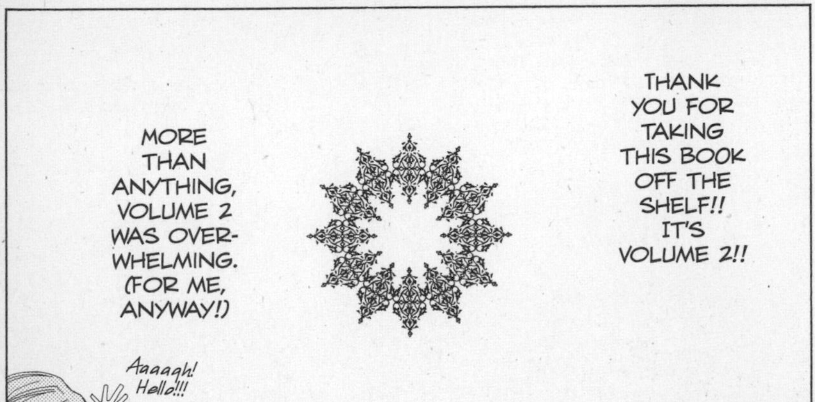
THANK YOU FOR TAKING THIS BOOK OFF THE SHELF!! IT'S VOLUME 2!!
MORE THAN ANYTHING, VOLUME 2 WAS OVER-WHELMING. (FOR ME, ANYWAY!)
Aaaagh! Hello!!!

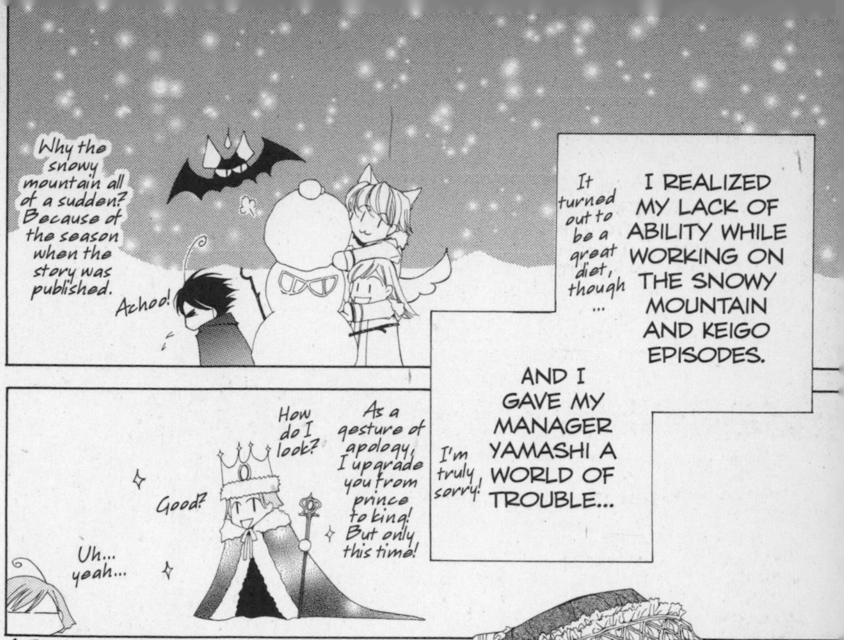
I REALIZED MY LACK OF ABILITY WHILE WORKING ON THE SNOWY MOUNTAIN AND KEIGO EPISODES.
It turned out to be a great diet, though...
Why the snowy mountain all of a sudden? Because of the season when the story was published.
Achoo!
AND I GAVE MY MANAGER YAMASHI A WORLD OF TROUBLE...
I'm truly sorry!
As a gesture of apology, I upgrade you from prince to king! But only this time!
How do I look?
Good?
Uh... yeah...

↑Bad attitude.

ISABEL'S NAME CAME FROM THE *TWINS AT ST. CLARE'S* CHILDREN'S NOVEL SERIES, WHICH I LOVED BACK WHEN I WAS IN ELEMENTARY SCHOOL. COME TO THINK OF IT, I HAD A WEAK SPOT FOR STUFF LIKE ENGLAND, BOARDING SCHOOLS AND TWINS AT THAT TIME. (THE MAIN CHARACTERS OF THE NOVEL ARE TWIN SISTERS.) I WAS ALSO INTO *CHARLIE & LOUISE* ABOUT THE SAME TIME. THEY'RE BOTH MASTERPIECES.

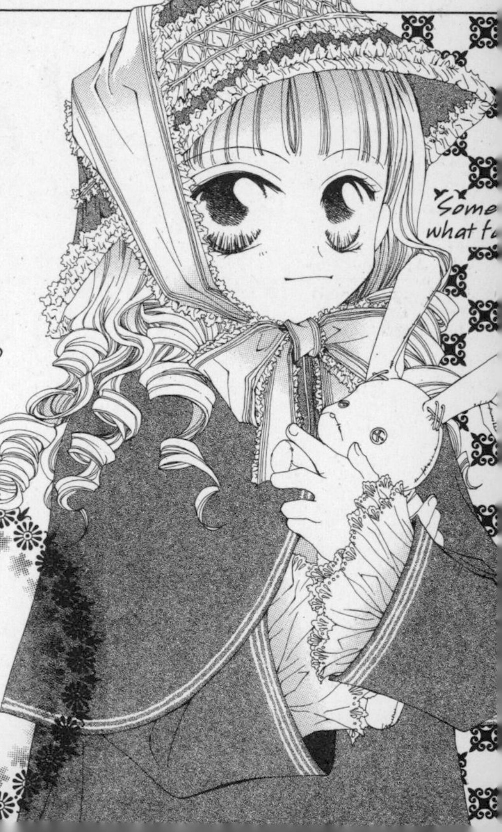

During the making of the snowy mountain episode, I realized I like drawing frilly dresses and ruins. I'm in seventh heaven when absorbed in detail.

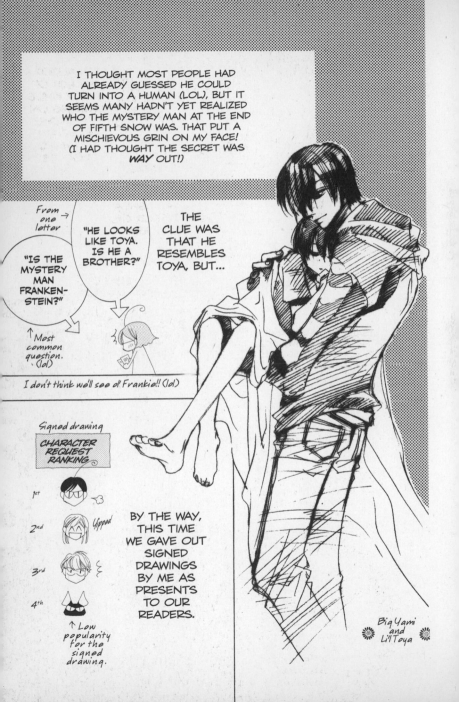

I THOUGHT MOST PEOPLE HAD ALREADY GUESSED HE COULD TURN INTO A HUMAN (LOL), BUT IT SEEMS MANY HADN'T YET REALIZED WHO THE MYSTERY MAN AT THE END OF FIFTH SNOW WAS. THAT PUT A MISCHIEVOUS GRIN ON MY FACE! (I HAD THOUGHT THE SECRET WAS ***WAY*** OUT!)

Big Yami and Li'l Toya

THE CLUE WAS THAT HE RESEMBLES TOYA, BUT...

From one letter →

"HE LOOKS LIKE TOYA. IS HE A BROTHER?"

"IS THE MYSTERY MAN FRANKENSTEIN?"

↑ Most common question. (lol)

I don't think we'll see ol' Frankie!! (lol)

BY THE WAY, THIS TIME WE GAVE OUT SIGNED DRAWINGS BY ME AS PRESENTS TO OUR READERS.

Signed drawing

**CHARACTER REQUEST RANKING**

1st

2nd Yipped

3rd

4th

↑ Low popularity for the signed drawing.

I was relieved when Toya won first place!

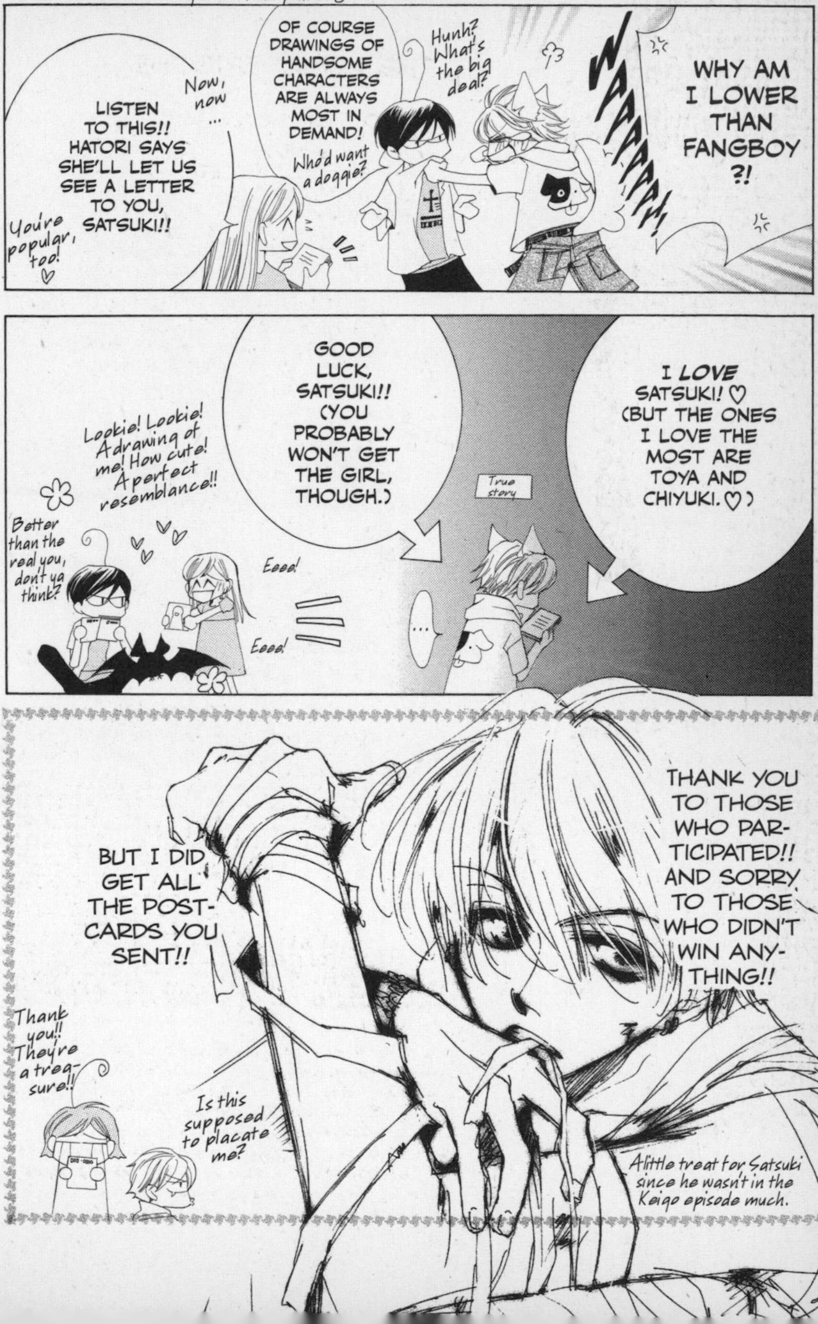
WHY AM I LOWER THAN FANGBOY?!
Hunh? What's the big deal?
OF COURSE DRAWINGS OF HANDSOME CHARACTERS ARE ALWAYS MOST IN DEMAND!
Who'd want a doggie?
Now, now ...
LISTEN TO THIS!! HATORI SAYS SHE'LL LET US SEE A LETTER TO YOU, SATSUKI!!
You're popular, too!
I *LOVE* SATSUKI! ♡ (BUT THE ONES I LOVE THE MOST ARE TOYA AND CHIYUKI. ♡)
GOOD LUCK, SATSUKI!! (YOU PROBABLY WON'T GET THE GIRL, THOUGH.)
True story
...
Eeee!
Eeee!
Lookie! Lookie! A drawing of me! How cute! A perfect resemblance!!
Better than the real you, don't ya think?
THANK YOU TO THOSE WHO PARTICIPATED!! AND SORRY TO THOSE WHO DIDN'T WIN ANYTHING!!
BUT I DID GET ALL THE POSTCARDS YOU SENT!!
A little treat for Satsuki since he wasn't in the Keigo episode much.
Is this supposed to placate me?
Thank you!! They're a treasure!!

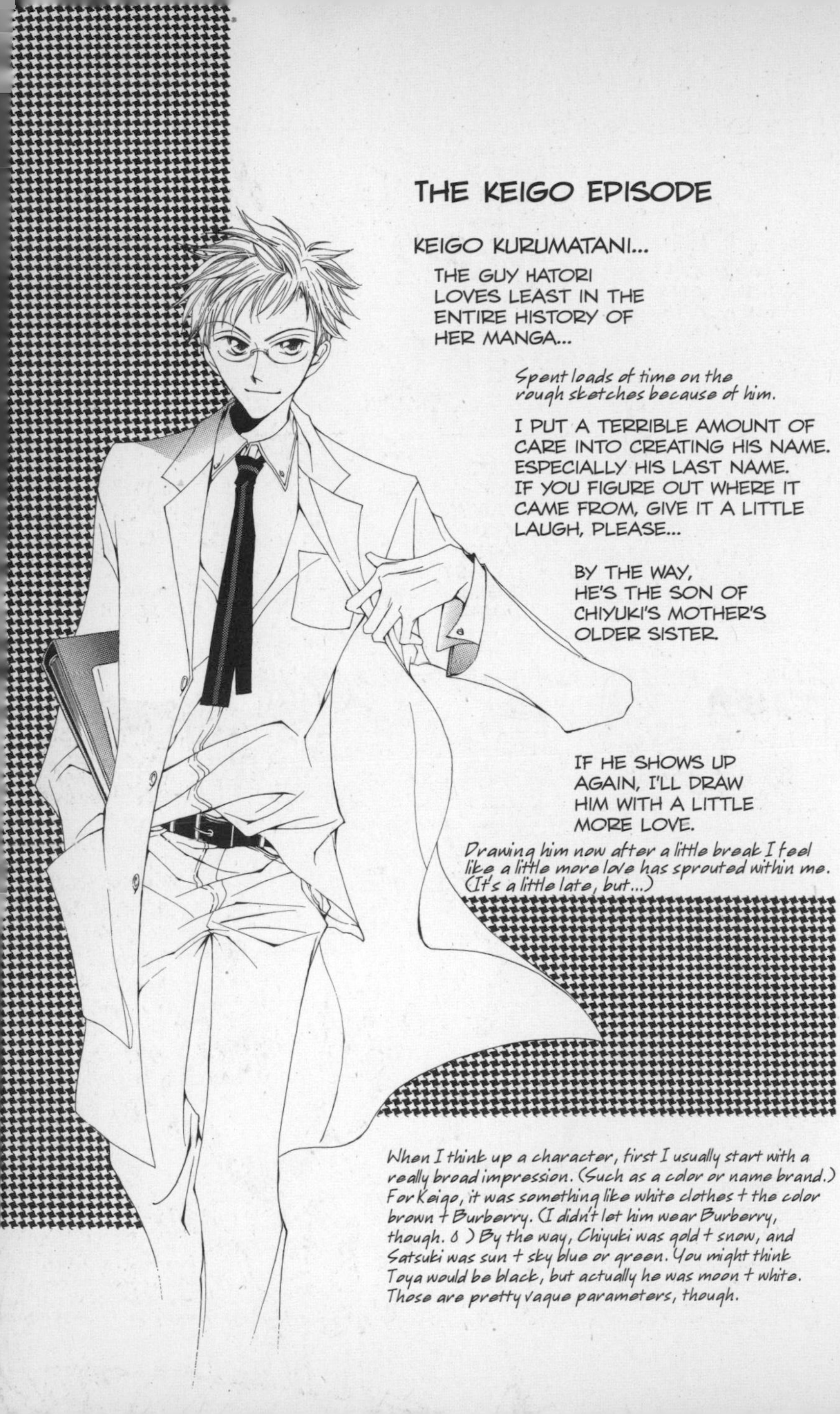

## THE KEIGO EPISODE

KEIGO KURUMATANI...

THE GUY HATORI LOVES LEAST IN THE ENTIRE HISTORY OF HER MANGA...

*Spent loads of time on the rough sketches because of him.*

I PUT A TERRIBLE AMOUNT OF CARE INTO CREATING HIS NAME. ESPECIALLY HIS LAST NAME. IF YOU FIGURE OUT WHERE IT CAME FROM, GIVE IT A LITTLE LAUGH, PLEASE...

BY THE WAY, HE'S THE SON OF CHIYUKI'S MOTHER'S OLDER SISTER.

IF HE SHOWS UP AGAIN, I'LL DRAW HIM WITH A LITTLE MORE LOVE.

*Drawing him now after a little break I feel like a little more love has sprouted within me. (It's a little late, but...)*

*When I think up a character, first I usually start with a really broad impression. (Such as a color or name brand.) For Keigo, it was something like white clothes + the color brown + Burberry. (I didn't let him wear Burberry, though. ◊ ) By the way, Chiyuki was gold + snow, and Satsuki was sun + sky blue or green. You might think Toya would be black, but actually he was moon + white. Those are pretty vague parameters, though.*

THANKS TO YOU THE READERS, I PLAN TO CONTINUE *MILLENNIUM SNOW* FOR A LITTLE WHILE MORE. I'M NOT SURE HOW FAR I'LL GET, BUT HOPEFULLY TO THE END...

PLEASE LET ME HEAR WHAT YOU THINK.

BISCO HATORI
C/O SHOJO BEAT
VIZ MEDIA
P.O. BOX 77010
SAN FRANCISCO, CA 94107

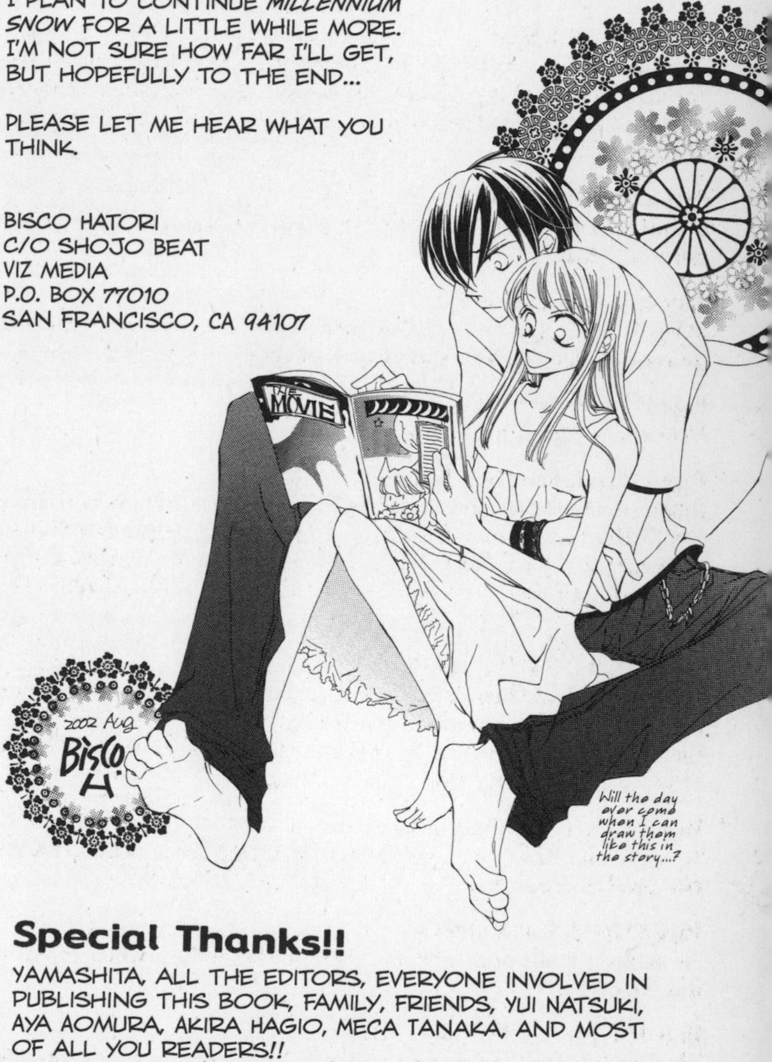
THE MOVIE
2002 Aug.
Bisco. H.
Will the day ever come when I can draw them like this in the story...?

## Special Thanks!!

YAMASHITA, ALL THE EDITORS, EVERYONE INVOLVED IN PUBLISHING THIS BOOK, FAMILY, FRIENDS, YUI NATSUKI, AYA AOMURA, AKIRA HAGIO, MECA TANAKA, AND MOST OF ALL YOU READERS!!

EGOISTIC CLUB / THE END

# Glossary

While the appeal of the vampire needs no help to cross the language barrier, here are a few terms that could use a little extra explaining.

**Page 22, panel 3: Miso**
Fermented soybean paste used to flavor many Japanese dishes, including soup. The nutritional value of miso has been widely touted; it has been considered efficacious against radiation sickness and was fed to patients in Nagasaki and Chernobyl.

**Page 23, panel 1: Boiled veggies**
In the original Japanese, it is *nimono*, or foods that have been simmered and seasoned simply.

**Page 121, panel 6: Possum**
In Japan, "playing possum" is called *tanukineiri*. It is named after the *tanuki* (raccoon dog), which is rumored to pass out or pretend to sleep when surprised.

**Page 177, side bar: Hatori-bird**
*Hato* means "pigeon" in Japanese.

**Page 177, side bar: Shuji Terayama**
Author, dramatist, and director who published almost 200 works and directed over 20 short and feature length films. Terayama was co-founder of the avant-garde theater Tenjo Sajiki and founder of the experimental cinema Universal Gravitation. He was born December 10, 1935 and died May 4, 1983 of cirrhosis of the liver.

**Page 177, side bar: Ranpo Edogawa**
Pen name of Taro Hirai, author and literary critic, he is most famous for his detective fiction featuring the character Kogoro Akechi. He derived his pen name from the Japanese spelling of Edgar Allan Poe. He was born October 21, 1894 and died July 28, 1965.

**Page 177, side bar: Bump of Chicken**
A J-rock band. The members are Motoo Fujiwara, Hiroaki Masukawa, Yoshifumi Naoi, and Hideo Masu.

**Page 177, side bar: Ira Ishida**
An author whose stories are published bi-weekly in the Japanese culture magazine *R25*.

**Page 194, panel 3: *Twins at St. Clare's***
The first of a series of six books written by Enid Blyton, set at the St. Clare's Boarding School. The eponymous twins are Patricia and Isabel O'Sullivan, who have myriad adventures.

Bisco Hatori made her manga debut with *Isshun Kan no Romance (A Moment of Romance)* in *LaLa DX* magazine. The comedy *Ouran High School Host Club* is her breakout hit. When she's stuck thinking up characters' names, she gets inspired by loud, upbeat music (her radio is set to NACK5 FM). She enjoys reading all kinds of manga, but she's especially fond of the sci-fi drama *Please Save My Earth* and *Slam Dunk*, a basketball classic...

# MILLENNIUM SNOW
## VOL. 2
### Shojo Beat Edition

## STORY & ART BY
## BISCO HATORI

Translation/RyoRca, Honyaku Center
English Adaptation/John Werry, Honyaku Center
Touch-up Art & Lettering/Gia Cam Luc
Design/Courtney Utt
Editor/Pancha Diaz

Sennen no Yuki by Bisco Hatori © Bisco Hatori 2001. All rights reserved.
First published in Japan in 2002 by HAKUSENSHA, Inc., Tokyo.
English language translation rights arranged with HAKUSENSHA, Inc., Tokyo.

New and adapted artwork and text © 2007 VIZ Media, LLC.

Printed in Canada

Published by VIZ Media, LLC
P.O. Box 77010
San Francisco, CA 94107

10 9 8 7 6 5
First printing, July 2007
Fifth printing, December 2012

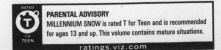

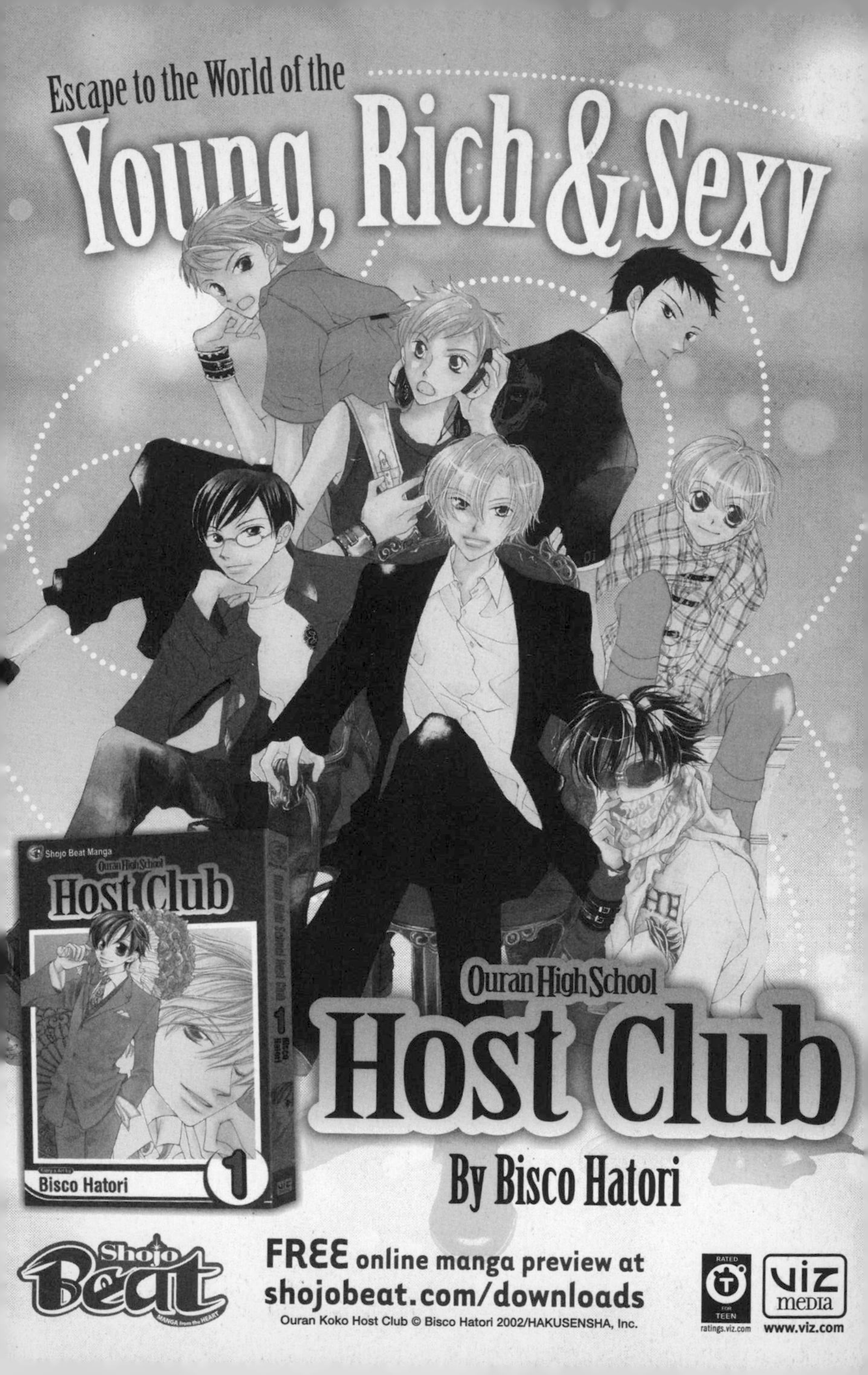
Escape to the World of the
Young, Rich & Sexy
Shojo Beat Manga
Ouran High School
Host Club
Bisco Hatori
1
Ouran High School
Host Club
By Bisco Hatori
Shojo Beat
FREE online manga preview at
shojobeat.com/downloads
Ouran Koko Host Club © Bisco Hatori 2002/HAKUSENSHA, Inc.
RATED T FOR TEEN
ratings.viz.com
VIZ media
www.viz.com

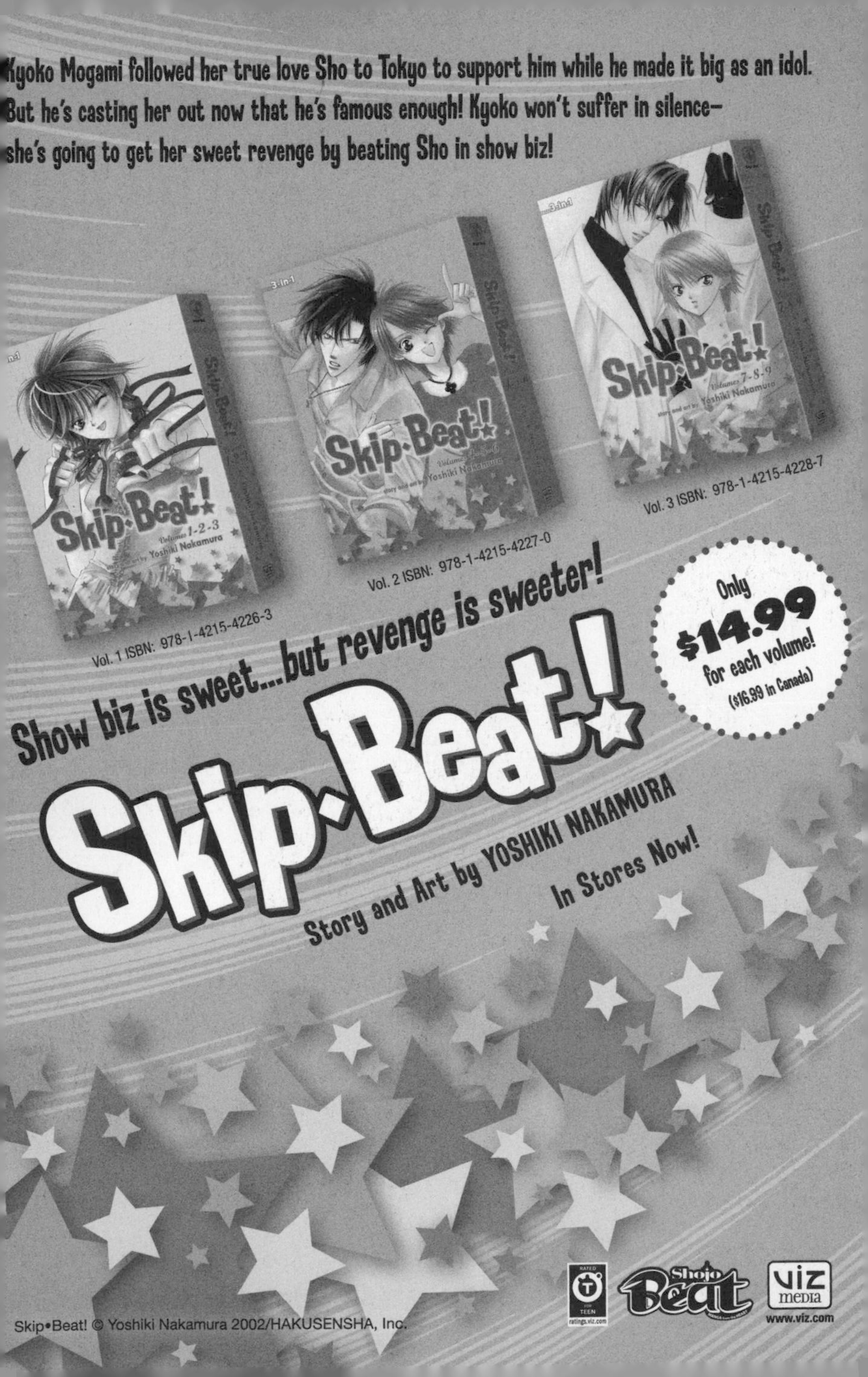
Kyoko Mogami followed her true love Sho to Tokyo to support him while he made it big as an idol. But he's casting her out now that he's famous enough! Kyoko won't suffer in silence–she's going to get her sweet revenge by beating Sho in show biz!
Vol. 1 ISBN: 978-1-4215-4226-3
Vol. 2 ISBN: 978-1-4215-4227-0
Vol. 3 ISBN: 978-1-4215-4228-7
Only $14.99 for each volume! ($16.99 in Canada)
Show biz is sweet...but revenge is sweeter!
Skip·Beat!
Story and Art by YOSHIKI NAKAMURA
In Stores Now!
Skip•Beat! © Yoshiki Nakamura 2002/HAKUSENSHA, Inc.
www.viz.com

# Natsume's BOOK of FRIENDS

STORY and ART by
### Yuki Midorikawa

## Make Some Unusual New Friends

The power to see hidden spirits has always felt like a curse to troubled high schooler Takashi Natsume. But he's about to discover he inherited a lot more than just the Sight from his mysterious grandmother!

$9.99 USA / $12.99 CAN *
ISBN: 978-1-4215-3243-1

On sale at **store.viz.com**
Also available at your local bookstore or comic store

# SURPRISE!

## You may be reading the wrong way!

It's true: In keeping with the original Japanese comic format, this book reads from right to left—so action, sound effects, and word balloons are completely reversed. This preserves the orientation of the original artwork—plus, it's fun! Check out the diagram shown here to get the hang of things, and then turn to the other side of the book to get started!

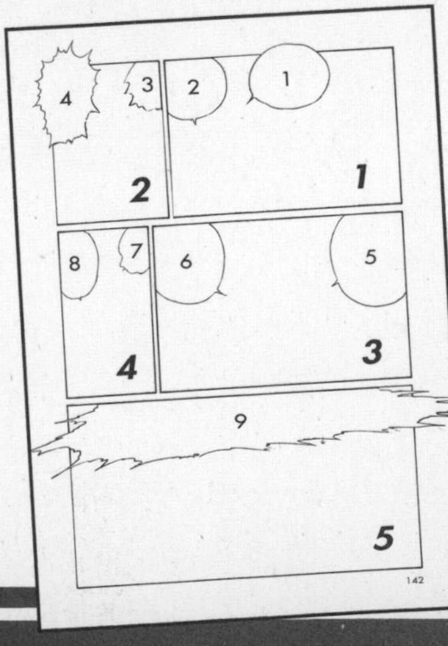
1
2
3
4
1
2
5
6
7
8
3
4
9
5
142

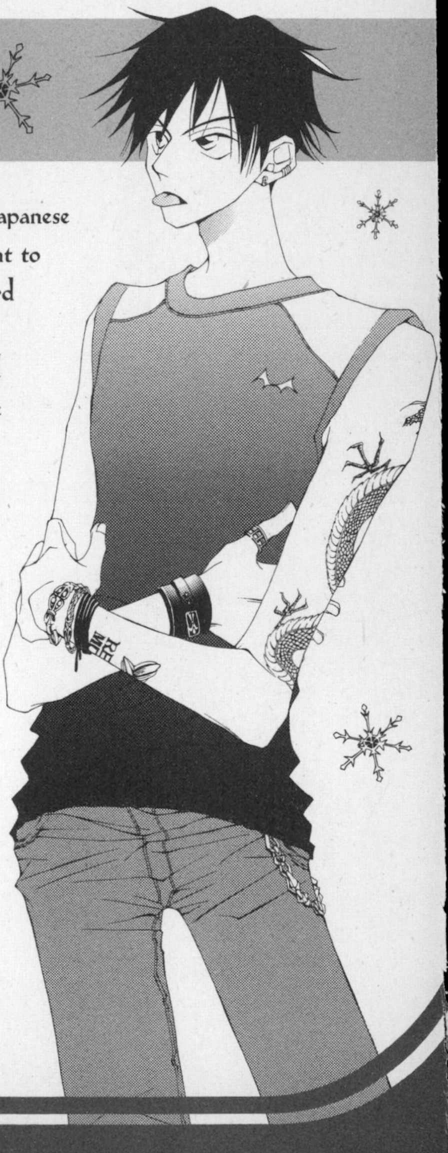